# Introduction to Political Ideologies

Visit the *Introduction to Political Ideologies* Companion Website at **www.pearsoned.co.uk/hoffman** to find valuable **student** learning material including:

- Original theory text extracts
- Case studies
- 'How to be a Theorist' guide
- Links to relevant sites on the web

# Introduction to Political Ideologies

**John Hoffman**
University of Leicester

**Paul Graham**
University of Glasgow

PEARSON
Longman

Harlow, England • London • New York • Boston • San Francisco • Toronto • Sydney • Singapore • Hong Kong
Tokyo • Seoul • Taipei • New Delhi • Cape Town • Madrid • Mexico City • Amsterdam • Munich • Paris • Milan

**Pearson Education Limited**
Edinburgh Gate
Harlow
Essex CM20 2JE
England

and Associated Companies throughout the world

*Visit us on the World Wide Web at:*
www.pearsoned.co.uk

First published in Great Britain in 2006

© Pearson Education Limited 2006

ISBN: 978-1-4058-2439-2

**British Library Cataloguing-in-Publication Data**
A catalogue record for this book is available from the British Library

**Library of Congress Cataloging-in-Publication Data**
Hoffman, John, 1944–
    Introduction to political ideologies / John Hoffman, Paul Graham.
      p.  cm.
    Includes bibliographical references and index.
    ISBN-13: 978-1-4058-2439-2 (alk. paper)
    ISBN-10: 1-4058-2439-5 (alk. paper)
    1. Political science—Philosophy.   I. Graham, Paul.   II. Title.

  JA71.H613 2006
  320.5—dc22

                                2005058690

10 9 8 7 6 5 4 3 2
10 09 08 07

Typeset in Sabon 10/12 by 59

Printed by Ashford Colour Press Ltd., Gosport

*The publisher's policy is to use paper manufactured from sustainable forests.*

# Brief Contents

# Contents

## Conclusion

## Glossary                                                                265

## Index                                                                   271

---

### Supporting resources

Visit **www.pearsoned.co.uk/hoffman** to find valuable password protected online resources

**Companion Website for students**
• Case studies
• Student guide to studying Political Theory
• Links to relevant sites on the web

**For instructors**
• Original theory text extracts
• Multiple choice questions for the original theory text extracts
• Instructor guide with teaching ideas for tutorials and case studies from the main book

**Also:** The Companion Website provides the following features:

• Search tool to help locate specific items of content
• E-mail results and profile tools to send results of quizzes to instructors
• Online help and support to assist with website usage and troubleshooting

For more information please contact your local Pearson Education sales representative or visit **www.pearsoned.co.uk/hoffman**

# Guide to Features

## How To Read Boxes

## Ideas and Perspectives Boxes

## Influences and Impact Box

# Guided Tour

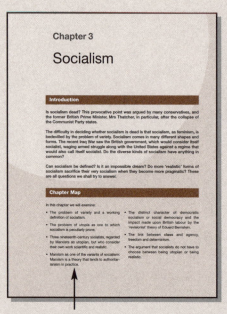

## Chapter 3

# Socialism

### Introduction

Is socialism dead? This provocative point was argued by many conservatives, and the former British Prime Minister, Mrs Thatcher, in particular, after the collapse of the Communist Party states.

The difficulty in deciding whether socialism is dead is that socialism, as feminism, is bedevilled by the problem of variety. Socialism comes in many different shapes and forms. The recent Iraq War saw the British government, which would consider itself socialist, waging armed struggle along with the United States against a regime that would also call itself socialist. Do the diverse kinds of socialism have anything in common?

Can socialism be defined? Is it an impossible dream? Do more 'realistic' forms of socialism sacrifice their very socialism when they become more pragmatic? These are all questions we shall try to answer.

### Chapter Map

In this chapter we will examine:

- The problem of variety and a working definition of socialism.
- The problem of utopia as one to which socialism is peculiarly prone.
- Three nineteenth-century socialists, regarded by Marxists as utopian, but who consider their own work scientific and realistic.
- Marxism as one of the variants of socialism: Marxism is a theory that tends to authoritarianism in practice.
- The distinct character of democratic socialism or social democracy and the impact made upon British labour by the 'revisionist' theory of Eduard Bernstein.
- The link between class and agency, freedom and determinism.
- The argument that socialists do not have to choose between being utopian or being realistic.

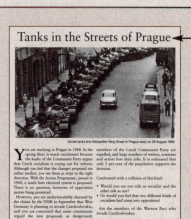

# Tanks in the Streets of Prague

Soviet tanks line Altstaedter-Ring Street in Prague early on 28 August 1968

You are studying in Prague in 1968. In the spring there is much excitement because that Czech socialism is crying out for reform. Although you feel that the changes proposed are rather modest, you see them as steps in the right direction. With the Action Programme, passed in 1968, a much freer electoral system is proposed. There is no question, however, of opposition parties being permitted.

However, you are understandably alarmed by the claims by the USSR in September that West Germany is planning to invade Czechoslovakia, and you are concerned that some communists regard the new proposals as dangerously 'revisionist'. In August of the same year, tanks roll into Prague from other countries in the Warsaw Pact (of which Czechoslovakia is a member), led by the USSR. Following the invasion Dubcek and the new president, Svoboda, are taken to Moscow and after 'free comradely discussion' they announce that Czechoslovakia will be abandoning its reform programme.

The claim is made that Dubcek intended to take his country out of the Warsaw Pact and reintroduce a capitalist society. Half a million

members of the Czech Communist Party are expelled, and large numbers of writers, scientists and artists lose their jobs. It is estimated that only 2 per cent of the population supports the invasion.

Confronted with a collision of this kind:

- Would you see one side as socialist and the other side as not?
- Or would you feel that two different kinds of socialism had come into opposition?

Are the members of the Warsaw Pact who invade Czechoslovakia:

- Betraying their commitment to socialism? or
- Is this the kind of action that flows from their commitment to Marxist principles?

Is Dubcek being naive to consider himself as a communist at all? Would the notion of change that he is proposing undermine not only Soviet control over Eastern Europe but lead to the development of market forces that would necessarily destroy socialism itself and lead to the introduction of capitalism?

**Test cases** focus on interesting and contentious real-life examples and are accompanied by questions to challenge your own views.

The **Introductions** concisely set the scene at the start of each chapter and **Chapter Maps** summarise the key points that will be covered.

The lives and achievements of the most important theorists are fully covered in **Biography** boxes throughout the text.

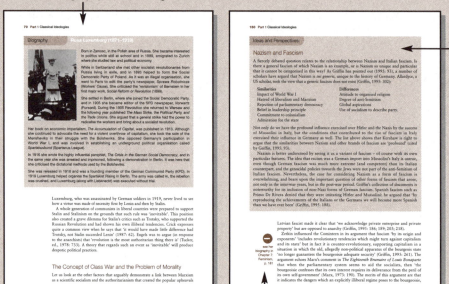

70 Part 1 Classical Ideologies

### Biography — Rosa Luxemburg (1871–1919)

Born in Zamosc, in the Polish area of Russia. She became interested in politics while still at school and in 1889, emigrated to Zurich where she studied law and political economy.

While in Switzerland she met other socialist revolutionaries from Russia living in exile, and in 1893 helped to form the Social Democratic Party of Poland. As it was an illegal organisation, she went to Paris to edit the party's newspaper, Sprawa Robotnicza (Workers' Cause). She criticised the 'revisionism' of Bernstein in her first major work, Social Reform or Revolution (1899).

She settled in Berlin, where she joined the Social Democratic Party, and in 1905 she became editor of the SPD newspaper, Vorwarts (Forward). During the 1905 Revolution she returned to Warsaw and the following year published The Mass Strike, the Political Party, and the Trade Unions. She argued that a general strike had the power to radicalise the workers and bring about a socialist revolution.

Her book on economic imperialism, The Accumulation of Capital, was published in 1913. Although she continued to advocate the need for a violent overthrow of capitalism, she took the side of the Mensheviks in their struggle with the Bolsheviks. She opposed Germany's participation in World War I, and was involved in establishing an underground political organisation called Spartakusbund (Spartacus League).

In 1916 she wrote the highly influential pamphlet, The Crisis in the German Social Democracy, and in the same year she was arrested and imprisoned, following a demonstration in Berlin. It was here that she criticised the dictatorial methods used by the Bolsheviks.

She was released in 1918 and was a founding member of the German Communist Party (KPD). In 1919 Luxemburg helped organise the Spartakist Rising in Berlin. The army was called in, the rebellion was crushed, and Luxemburg (along with Liebknecht) was executed without trial.

Luxemburg, who was assassinated by German soldiers in 1919, never lived to see how a virtue was made of necessity first by Lenin and then by Stalin.

A whole generation of communists in liberal countries were prepared to support Stalin and Stalinism on the grounds that such rule was 'inevitable'. This position also created a grave dilemma for Stalin's critics such as Trotsky, who supported the Russian Revolution and had shown his own illiberal tendencies. Crick expresses quite a common view when he says that 'it would have made little difference had Trotsky, not Stalin succeeded Lenin' (1987: 62). Engels was to argue (in response to the anarchists) that 'revolution is the most authoritarian thing there is' (Tucker, ed., 1978: 733). A theory that regards such an event as 'inevitable' will produce despotic political practices.

### The Concept of Class War and the Problem of Morality

Let us look at the other factors that arguably demonstrate a link between Marxism as a scientific socialism and the authoritarianism that created the popular upheavals

180 Part 1 Classical Ideologies

### Ideas and Perspectives:

#### Nazism and Fascism

A fiercely debated question relates to the relationship between Nazism and Italian fascism. Is there a general fascism of which Nazism is an example, or is Nazism so unique and particular that it cannot be categorised in this way? As Griffin has pointed out (1993: 93), a number of scholars have argued that Nazism is sui generis, unique to the history of Germany. Allardyce, a US scholar, took the view that a generic fascism does not exist (Griffin, 1993: 302):

| Similarities | Differences |
|---|---|
| Impact of World War I | Attitude to organised religion |
| Hatred of liberalism and Marxism | Degree of anti-Semitism |
| Rejection of parliamentary democracy | Global aspirations |
| Belief in leadership principle | Use of socialism to describe party. |
| Commitment to colonialism | |
| Admiration for the state | |

Not only do we have the profound influence exercised over Hitler and the Nazis by the success of Mussolini in Italy, but the conditions that contributed to the rise of Mussolini's Italy exercised their influence in Germany as well. The list above shows that Kershaw is right to argue that the similarities between Nazism and other brands of fascism are 'profound' (cited by Griffin, 1993: 93).

Nazism is better understood by seeing it as a variant of fascism – of course with its own particular features. The idea that racism was a German import into Mussolini's Italy is untrue, even though German fascism was much more extreme (and competent) than its Italian counterpart, and the genocidal policies towards the Jews were not part of the anti-Semitism of Italian fascism. Nevertheless, the case for considering Nazism as a form of fascism is overwhelming, and bears upon the important question of other forms of fascism that arose, not only in the inter-war years, but in the post-war period. Griffin's collection of documents is noteworthy for its inclusion of non-Nazi forms of German fascism. Spanish fascists such as Primo De Rivera denied that they were imitating Hitler and Mussolini; he argued that 'by reproducing the achievements of the Italians or the Germans we will become more Spanish than we have ever been' (Griffin, 1993: 188).

Latvian fascist made it clear that 'we acknowledge private enterprise and private property' but are opposed to anarchy (Griffin, 1995: 186; 189; 203; 218).

Zetkin influenced the Comintern in its argument that fascism 'by its origin and exponents' 'includes revolutionary tendencies which might turn against capitalism and its state' but in fact it is counter-revolutionary, supporting capitalism in a situation in which the old, allegedly non-political apparatus of the bourgeois state 'no longer guarantees the bourgeois adequate security' (Griffin, 1995: 261). The argument echoes Marx's comment in The Eighteenth Brumaire of Louis Bonaparte that when the parliamentary system seems to aid the socialists, then 'the bourgeoisie confesses that its own interest requires its deliverance from the peril of its own self-government' (Marx, 1973: 190). The merits of this argument are that it indicates the dangers which an explicitly illiberal regime poses to the bourgeoisie.

see her biography in Chapter 7: Feminism, p. 181

**Ideas and Perspectives** boxes focus on detailed issues.

Margin **cross references** emphasise the linkages between thinkers and ideas throughout the book.

**How To Read** boxes analyse key political texts and identify core points.

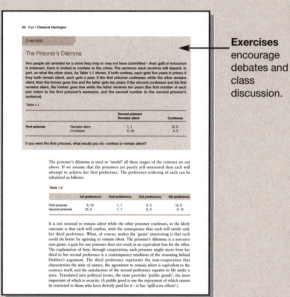

**Exercises** encourage debates and class discussion.

**Summaries** pull together the fundamental concepts presented in the chapter

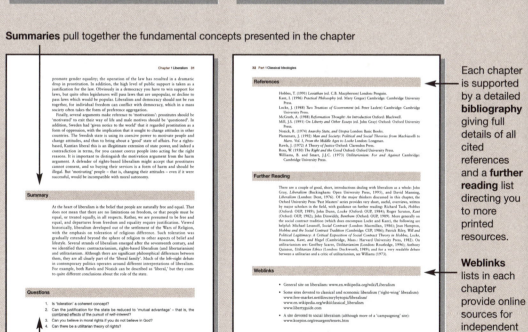

Each chapter is supported by a detailed **bibliography** giving full details of all cited references and a **further reading** list directing you to more printed resources.

**Weblinks** lists in each chapter provide online sources for independent study

Each chapter ends with **Questions** to test your understanding of the topics covered, reflect on the theories presented and to formulate your own opinions.

# Publisher's Acknowledgements

We are grateful to the following for their permission to reproduce copyright material:

Photographs: p11 (©Brooklyn Productions/CORBIS), p19 (©Getty/Hulton Archive), p24 (©Bettmann/CORBIS), p35 (©Jim Bourg/Reuters/CORBIS), p40 (©Christie's Images/CORBIS), p42 (©Bettmann/CORBIS), p46 (London School of Economics & Political Science), p50 (University of Chicago), p57 (©Bettmann/CORBIS), p61 (©Getty/Hulton Archive), p62 (Topfoto), p63 (©Getty/Hulton Archive), p65(©Michael Nicholson/CORBIS), p66 (©Getty/Hulton Archive), p70 (Topfoto), p71 (©Getty/Hulton Archive), p77 (Topfoto), p87 (©REUTERS/Dylan Martinez), p111 (©Getty/Peter Adams), p135 (Rex Features), p142 (©Bettmann/CORBIS), p147 (©Hulton-Deutsch Collection/CORBIS), p159 (Camera Press/Hutchinson/RBO), p173 (©Black Box RF/Alamy), p178 (©Lebrecht Music & Arts Photo Library/Alamy), p199 (Empics/EPA), p219 (©Getty/Peter Adams), p224 (©CORBIS), p227 (Vesa Lindqvist Matti Hurme/norden.org), p241 (©REUTERS/Mahfouz Abu Turk).

Glossary extracts reprinted by permission of Sage Publications Ltd from John Hoffman, *Citizen Beyond the State*, © John Hoffman, 2004.

In some instances we have been unable to trace the owners of copyright material, and we would appreciate any information that would enable us to do so.

# Authors' Acknowledgements

We are very grateful for the help received from Morten Fuglevand and David Cox of Pearson Education. David Cox read and commented on drafts with great enthusiasm and acumen and was an endless source of lively and interesting ideas. Morten and David's commitment to the book has been inspiring and sustaining. In addition, the anonymous referees made invaluable, if at times painful, observations and have played an important part in improving the quality of the book. We are also grateful to Julie Knight for all her help.

We found working together on this book a stimulating and enjoyable experience. Both of us are committed to making political theory more accessible and lively and have tried to write a book that is stimulating, provocative and interesting.

## John Hoffman

I would like to thank the publishers of the *Cambridge Dictionary of Sociology*, Cambridge University Press, for permission to draw upon entries submitted to this project. I am also very grateful to Edinburgh University Press for permission to use material that has also been submitted to a *Political Glossary* dealing with political theory, and to Sage Publications Ltd., who have kindly allowed me to draw upon my work *Citizenship Beyond the State* that appeared last year.

I have been supported by my partner, Rowan Roenisch, and my son, Fred and daughter, Frieda. All three have encouraged me in the project.

## Paul Graham

Edinburgh University Press kindly granted permission to draw upon an essay from *Political Concepts: a Reader and Guide* (edited by Iain Mackenzie), as did OneWorld Books for use of material from *Rawls* (forthcoming).

I would like to express my gratitude to my parents, Douglas and Heather Graham, for their support and encouragement, and to my colleagues in the Department of Politics at Glasgow University, for providing a stimulating intellectual environment in which to work.

# About the Authors

**John Hoffman** has taught in the Department of Politics, University of Leicester since 1970. He is currently Emeritus Professor of Political Theory, having retired at the end of September 2005. He has written widely on Marxism, feminism and Political Theory, with his most recent book being *Citizenship beyond the State*, published by Sage in 2004. He is currently working on John Gray and the problem of utopia.

**Paul Graham** is a Lecturer in Political Theory at Glasgow University. He teaches and researches in German and Anglo-American political thought, with a special focus on multiculturalism, human autonomy and rationality, freedom, and distributive justice.

# Introduction

Students of politics often believe that politics can be studied without theory. They take the view that we can focus upon the facts without worrying about general ideas. In everyday life, however, we are guided by notions of right and wrong, justice and injustice, so that everything we do is informed by concepts. Politicians are similarly guided. It is not a question of *whether* political animals follow theory, but a question of *which* theory or concept is supported when they present policies and undertake actions. We can argue as to whether the British prime minister or the US president acts according to the right political concepts, but it is undeniable that their actions are linked to theory. Humans in general cannot act without ideas: indeed it is a defining property of human activity that we can only act when we have ideas in our head as to what we should do.

In discussing ideas about the state or democracy or freedom in this book, we are talking about ideas or concepts or theories – we use the terms interchangeably – that guide and inform political action. The state is particularly important in Part 1 and readers should tackle this topic at an early stage. It is a great pity that theory is sometimes presented as though it inhabits a world of its own: as though it can be discussed and analysed in ways that are not explicitly linked to practical questions and political activity. This is, indeed, something this book seeks to address.

## Theory as Abstraction

We accept that all theory by definition involves abstraction. The very words we use involve a 'standing back' from specific things so that we can *abstract* from them something that they have in common. To identify a chair, to use a rather corny example, one needs to abstract the quality of 'chairness' from a whole range of objects, all of which differ in some detail from every other. Take another example. The word 'dog' refers both to particular dogs and dogs in general. If we define a dog as a mammal with four legs, it could be said that a dog is the same as an elephant. So our definition is too abstract. We need to make it more particularistic. A dog is a four-legged mammal with fur. But does this mean that all dogs are poodles? Such a view is too particularistic: we need to argue that 'dogness' is more abstract than just being a poodle.

The point is that we are abstracting all the time, whether we like it or not! This is the only way to understand. Thus, in an analysis of the recent war in Iraq, we might use a whole host of abstractions to make sense of what we see: 'war', 'violence', 'law', 'armies', the elusive 'weapons of mass destruction' etc. Particular things are injected with a conceptual dimension, so that references to 'democracy' or 'terrorism' (for example) reflect interpretations as well as physical events.

Political theory, however, seems rather more abstract than say an analysis of the Iraq war, because it considers the notion, for example, of 'violence' beyond any particular instance, asking what violence is in every circumstance that we can imagine. This apparent remoteness from specific instances creates a trap and gives rise to a pejorative use of the term 'abstract'. For thousands of years theorists have believed that the abstraction is somehow independent of reality, or even worse, that it creates reality. Because we cannot act without ideas, the illusion arises that ideas are more important than, and are even independent of, objects. We can, therefore, talk about democracy or the state, for example, without worrying about particular states or specific kinds of democracies. Understandably students may find it bewildering to be asked 'what is power?' or 'what is democracy?' without this being related to, for example, the power which Mao Zedong exerted over the Chinese people before he died in 1976 or the question of whether the inequalities of wealth in contemporary Britain have a negative impact upon the democratic quality of its political institutions.

We believe that this link between theory and recognisable political realities is essential to an understanding and appreciation of the subject. What gives concepts and theories a bad name is that they are all too often presented abstractly (in the pejorative sense). Thinkers may forget that our thoughts come from our experience with objects in the world around us, and they assume that political thought can be discussed as though it is independent of political realities. It is true that a person who is destitute and asking for money in the street is not necessarily conscious of whether he is acting with freedom and what this concept means; but it is equally true that a theorist talking about the question of freedom may not feel the need to relate the concept of freedom to the question of social destitution. It is this act of 'abstraction' that makes many students feel that theory is a waste of time and is unrelated to the world of realities. What we are trying to do in this book is to show that general ideas can help rather than hinder us in getting to grips with particular political events.

## The Distinction between Facts and Values

One of the common arguments that aggravates theory's abstractness (unless otherwise stated, we will use the term 'abstraction' in its pejorative sense), arises when people say that theory is *either* empirical *or* it is normative. In fact, it is always both. Facts and values interpenetrate, so that it is impossible to have one without the other.

Are facts the same as values? To answer this, we turn to a concrete example. It is a fact that in Western liberal societies fewer and fewer people are bothering to vote. George Bush was elected in 2000 in a situation in which only about half of the electorate turned out to vote. This fact has an implicit evaluative significance, because historically, democracy has implied participation, and this fact suggests either that Western liberal societies are minimally democratic, or that the notion of democracy has to be revised. The implicitly evaluative dimension of this fact is evidenced in the way it is challenged, or at least approached. It might be said that low voter participation is only true of *some* Western liberal societies (the United States in particular), and it might be said that voting is not the only form of political participation that counts – people can participate by joining single-issue organisations such as Greenpeace or Amnesty International.

The point about facts is that they are generally agreed upon, and can be verified in ways that are not particularly controversial. They are accepted much more widely than explicit value judgements. Evaluation, on the other hand, refers to the relationships that are only implicit in the fact. Thus the interpretation of the fact that fewer and fewer people in Western liberal societies vote raises the question of why. Does the reason for this arise from a relationship with poverty, lack of self-esteem, education, disillusionment, or is it the product of a relationship to satisfaction? The explanation embodies the evaluative content of the fact much more explicitly, since the explanation offered has obvious policy implications. If the reason for apathy is poverty, etc., then this has very different implications for action than an argument that people do not vote because they are basically satisfied with what politicians are doing in their name.

Therefore we would argue that although facts and values are not the same, they are inherently linked. In our view it is relationships which create values, so that the more explicit and far-reaching these relationships the more obviously evaluative is the factual judgement. The fact that the earth goes round the sun is not really controversial in today's world, but it was explosively controversial in the medieval world, because the notion that the earth was the centre of the universe was crucial to a statically hierarchical world outlook.

The idea that facts and even ideas can be value free ignores the linkage between the two. Not only is this empiricist view (as it is usually called) logically unsustainable, but it is another reason why students may find theory boring. The more you relate political ideas to political realities (in the sense of everyday controversies), the more lively and interesting they become. David Hume (1711–76) argued famously that it would be quite rational to prefer the destruction of the whole world to the scratching of my finger (1972: 157), but we would contest this scepticism. Reason implies the development of humans, and this is why political theory matters. Of course, what constitutes the well-being of people is complex and controversial, but a well-argued case for why the world should be preserved and its inhabitants flourish is crucial for raising the level of everyday politics.

## The Problem with the Contestability Thesis

As we see it, all theories and concepts are contestable, by which we merely mean that they are part of an ongoing controversy (Hoffman 1988). Thus, democracy is contestable because some identify democracy with liberal parliamentary systems that already exist such as the British or French or Indian systems, while others argue that democracy implies a high level of participation so that a society is not democratic if large numbers are not involved in the process of government.

But there is a more specialist use of the notion of 'contestability' associated in particular with a famous essay by Gallie (1955: 188–93). Gallie argued, first, that only some political concepts are contestable (democracy was his favoured example), and that when concepts are essentially contestable we have no way of resolving the respective methods of competing arguments. We can note the rival justifications offered (they are mere emotional outpourings), but we cannot evaluate them in terms of a principle that commands general agreement.

But this implies that evaluation is only possible on matters about which we all agree. Such an argument stems from a misunderstanding of the nature of politics. For politics arises from the fact that we all have different interests and ideas, and the more explicit the difference between us is, the more explicit the politics. It therefore follows that a political concept is always controversial and it cannot command general agreement. Where an issue ceases to be controversial, it is not political. In this case differences are so slight that conflict is not really generated. Let us assume that chattel slavery – the owning of people as property – is a state of affairs which is so widely deplored that no one will defend it. Slavery as such ceases to be a political issue, and what becomes controversial is whether patriarchal attitudes towards women involve a condoning of slavery, or the power of employers to hire and fire labour gives them powers akin to a slave-owner. We think that it is too optimistic to assume that outright slavery is a thing of the past, but it is used here merely as an example to make a point.

All political concepts are inherently contestable, since disagreement over the meaning of a concept is what makes it political. But does it follow that because there is disagreement we have no way of knowing what is true and what is false? It is crucial not to imagine that the truth has to be timeless and above historical circumstance. But this rejection of ahistorical, timeless truth does not mean that the truth is purely relative. A relativist, for example, might argue that one person's terrorist is another person's freedom fighter. But this would make an 'objective' definition of terrorism (to pursue our example) impossible.

To argue that something is true is not to banish all doubt. If something is true, this does not mean that it is not also false. It simply means that *on balance* one proposition is more true or less false than another. To argue otherwise is to assume that a phenomenon has to be one thing or another. Philosophers call this a 'dualistic' approach. By dualism is meant an unbridgeable chasm, so that in our example, a dualist would assume that unless a statement is timelessly true, it is absolutely false. In fact, to say that the statement 'George W. Bush is a good president' is *both* true and false. Even his most fervent admirers would admit (we hope!) that he is deficient in some regards, and even his fiercest critics ought to concede that he has some positive qualities.

Take the question of freedom, as another example. What is freedom for Plato (427–347BC) differs from what freedom is for Rousseau (1712–78), and freedom for Rousseau differs from what we in the twenty-first century normally mean by freedom. So there is an element of relativity: historical circumstances certainly affect the character of the argument. But we can only compare and contrast different concepts of freedom if we have an absolute idea as to what freedom is. The absolute notion of freedom refers to some kind of absence of constraint, but this absolute idea can only be expressed in one historical context rather than another, and it is this context that gives an absolute idea its relativity. As a consequence, there is *both* continuity (the absolute) *and* change (the relative).

There is a distinction between the absolute and the relative, but not a dualism, for we cannot have one without the other. The same is true of the distinction between the general and the particular, and the subjective and the objective. In our arguments in this book we strive to make our ideas as true as possible – i.e. we seek to make them objective, accurate reflections of the external world – but because they are moulded by *us,* and we live in a particular historical context, an element of subjectivity necessarily comes in.

What we think of freedom today will necessarily be refined by the events of tomorrow. We are only now becoming aware of how, for example, sexual orientation affects the question of freedom, and there is understandable concern about increasing freedom for people with disabilities. Health, physical and mental, also affects freedom, and all we can say is that our conception of freedom will inevitably alter in the future. But the change that will take place is not without its continuity with past concepts. Freedom is still an absolute concept, although it can only be identified in relative form.

The contestability thesis must, in our view, be able to address not merely the controversial character of political concepts, but how and why we can prefer some definitions in relation to others. Otherwise the thesis becomes bogged down in a relativism that merely notes disagreements, but has no way to defend preferences. A belief that the recent elections in Iraq will advance democracy is not an arbitrary assertion: it is the argument which can be defended (or challenged) with evidence and information to establish how much truth it contains.

## Structure of the Book

In our view, a work on political theory should address itself to the kind of issues that politicians and the media themselves raise, and which are part and parcel of public debate. In the first part of this work we seek to investigate the classical concepts. These are the ones that readers are likely to be more familiar with, if they have already read some political thought, and they represent the 'staple diet' of courses on political theory. This is our justification for dealing with these concepts first. We aim to explain even the older ideas as clearly as possible so that those who have had no contact with political theory at all will not feel disadvantaged.

Of course, the fact that these concepts are traditional does not mean that our treatment of them will be traditional. We seek to make them as interesting and contentious as possible, so that readers will be stimulated to think about the ideas in a new and more refreshing way. We aim to combine both exposition and argument to enable readers to get a reasonable idea of the terrain covered by the concept, and to develop a position on the concept, often in opposition to the one we adopt. The fact that this work is written by two people means that differences will manifest themselves in the way that ideas and ideologies are analysed.

The ideas that we deal with are interlinked so that, for example, the argument about the state (and its problematic character) has a direct bearing on democracy. It is impossible to discuss the issue of citizenship without, for instance, understanding the argument about justice. Of course, it is always possible to choose to present ideas differently. In some texts, for example, 'sovereignty' is dealt with as a separate topic. In making sense of ideas and ideologies, it is crucial to say something about the key thinkers and the key texts. Our biography boxes seek to show the background and wider interests of key thinkers, and the exercises will try to emphasise why the ideas in the chapter are so relevant to understanding significant events. We have tried to make political theory challenging and enjoyable, and to deal with more detailed issues in special sections entitled 'Ideas and Perspectives'. The use of arrows is intended to cross-reference both thinkers and ideas so as to emphasise linkages between them.

In Part 1 we look at the classical and more traditional ideologies such as nationalism, conservatism, fascism and liberalism first, before turning to more recent developments with ideologies such as feminism and multiculturalism. We have thought it appropriate to say something general about these new ideologies in terms of a discussion about new social movements. These contemporary ideologies naturally draw upon the more traditional ones, so that feminism, for example, builds upon liberalism and socialism, and fundamentalism has a particular relationship to conservatism.

Thus the outline of the book is as shown in the box.

**Part 1 – classical ideologies** (liberalism, conservatism, socialism, anarchism, nationalism, fascism)

**Part 2 – new ideologies** (feminism, multiculturalism, ecologism, fundamentalism)

It might be thought that the newer ideas and ideologies relate more specifically to political controversies, and of course it is true that recent debates have raised these questions acutely. But the classical ideologies and ideas have not lost their relevance. Think of the debate about smoking, for example. Arguments about whether to ban smoking in public places revolve around contradictory interpretations of freedom, and it is hard to make sense of US elections without a knowledge of liberalism and conservatism, and the different ways these ideologies are defined.

All the ideas and ideologies, whether contemporary or classical, are treated in ways that relate them to ongoing controversies, and show why an understanding of theory is crucial to an understanding of political issues.

# Questions

1. Is it possible to devise political concepts that have no normative implications, and are thus value free in character?
2. Can one make a statement about politics without theorising at the same time?
3. Should political theory embrace or seek to avoid controversy?
4. Do teachers of political theory make practical political judgements?
5. Is the use of logic and the resort to factual evidence ethically neutral?

# References

Gallie, W. (1955) 'Essentially Contested Concepts' *Proceedings of the Aristotelian Society,* 56, 167–98.

Hoffman, J. (1988) *State, Power and Democracy* Brighton: Wheatsheaf.

Hume, D. (1972) *A Treatise of Human Nature* Books 2 & 3 London: Fontana/Collins.

# Part 1

# Classical Ideologies

The term 'ideology' has acquired a fairly unsavoury meaning. Politicians regularly condemn policies they disagree with as 'ideological', meaning that such policies are dogmatic, prejudiced and blinkered. Ideologies are seen as closed systems, beliefs that are intolerant and exclusive, so that socialists, conservatives, liberals and anarchists are often anxious to deny the ideological character of their thought.

We are sceptical about this narrow use of the term ideology. An ideology is a system of ideas, organised around either an attempt to win state power or to maintain it. To call a set of beliefs ideological is merely to argue that ideas are organised for a particular statist purpose: they form the basis of a political movement (focused around the state) whether this is a movement we approve of or not. The term is generally used to denote a belief system: in our view, it is more than this. Ideologies are belief systems focused around the state. 'Moderate' movements are as ideological as extremist ones although some movements may embrace many ideologies, and in the case of nationalism, for example, ideologies that contradict one another. Tony Blair spoke of the 1997 election as the last election in Britain based on ideology, although he certainly identified New Labour as embracing a set of ideas.

The 'negative' connotation of the term can only be preserved by linking ideologies to the state; a post-ideological world is a world without the state.

## Origins and Development of the Term

The reality of ideology goes back to the birth of the state, so that it is impossible to agree with Habermas's argument that 'there are no pre-bourgeois ideologies' (McLellan, 1995: 2). We would see no problem in describing Aristotle's theory or St Thomas Aquinas's position as ideological since these were ideas that impacted upon society and moved people into action in relation to the state. However, the term itself was coined in the aftermath of the French Revolution by Antoine Destutt de Tracey, who used the idea positively to denote a science of ideas. The term denoted ideas that were progressive, rational, based upon sensation and free from metaphysical and overtly religious content. De Tracey was placed in charge of the *Institut de France* and regarded the spreading of ideology as the spreading of the ideas of the French and European Enlightenment.

However, the term soon became pejorative as Napoleon denounced ideology as an idea that was radical, sinister, doctrinaire and abstract – a 'cloudy metaphysics' that ignores history and reality (McLellan, 1995: 5). This seems to have been the view that Marx and Engels put forward in *The German Ideology* (1845, first published 1976), but they inject into the term two new connotations. First, ideologies are seen as infused with idealism – ideas held by individuals are substituted for reality: the belief that people drown because they subscribe to the notion that gravity exists is supremely ideological, as it blithely ignores the harsh facts of material reality. But second, ideologies appear to be ideas that mask material interests. Bourgeois 'ideologies' may support the proposition that it is natural for people to exchange products and for the thrifty to accumulate wealth, but these beliefs merely reflect the interests of the capitalist class. Unmasking such an ideology requires placing such ideas in their historical and social context.

Does this mean that Marxism itself cannot be ideological? Lenin and his Bolshevik supporters used the term ideology positively, so that Marxism was described as a scientific ideology that reflected the class interests of the proletariat. Because the proletariat was the class whose historical mission is to lead the struggle to convert capitalism into communism, its outlook (as interpreted by Marxists) is deemed scientific *and* ideological. Leninist Marxists would have no problem in describing their views as both ideological and true. Having nothing to fear from history and reality, the outlook of the proletariat is free from the 'cloudy metaphysics' that characterises the thought of classes that are in decline.

Is it possible to reconcile the views of Marx and Lenin on this matter? It could be argued that when Marx and Engels speak negatively of ideology they are referring to idealist ideology. There is an analogy here with their use of the term 'philosophy'. Marx refers dismissively to philosophers, not because he rejects philosophy, but because he challenges those who substituted philosophy for a study of historical realities. In other words, the term 'ideology' is used negatively when it refers to idealists such as the Young Hegelians but Marx and Engels's own theories are themselves ideological in the sense that they seek to transform society and the state through a political movement.

In the post-war world, many academic political theorists argued that ideology was 'dead' – by which they meant that ideas such as Marxism which sought to transform society from top to bottom were now archaic and dated. But this was itself the product of a political consensus, as Partridge (1967) pointed out at the time, and it was a view held not only by academics but by politicians as well. The argument was that all sensible people agreed on the foundations of society – liberal, welfare state capitalism – so that disagreements were over details and not the overall direction of society. Bernard Crick wrote a lively book, *In Defence of Politics,* in which he argues that politics is a flexible, adaptive and conciliatory activity. As such, it needs defending, he argues, against ideology. Ideological thinking is totalitarian in character: it reduces activity to a 'set of fixed goals'. It is rigid and extremist, and should be rejected by conservatives, liberals and socialists who believe in debate, toleration and the resolution of conflict through negotiation (Crick, 1982: 55). But Crick also identifies politics with the state, and, in our view, this makes his own definition of politics ideological.

## Isms as Ideologies

Liberals often argue that their values are too coherent and rational to be called 'ideological'. Here is a belief system (liberals contend) that has a plausible view of human nature, links this with a wide view of freedom and has become the dominant set of values in modern democratic societies: how can such views be called ideological? Certainly **liberalism** is a very successful ideology, and that has rendered acute the problem of the variety of liberalisms that confront the student of politics. This problem afflicts all ideologies, it is true, but liberalism seems particularly heterogeneous and divided. Old liberalism expresses the belief in a free market, limited state and an individual free from external interference. New liberalism, on the other hand, champions an interventionist state, a socialised and regulated market and social policies that are concerned with redistributing wealth and supporting collectivist institutions such as trade unions and cooperatives. Indeed, in the United States, old liberalism is confusingly called '**conservatism**' and new liberalism identified as a form of **socialism**. The 'L' word is highly pejorative, and it is a brave politician in the United States who calls herself a 'liberal'.

Nevertheless, two points can be made about liberalism that bear upon the question of ideology. The first is that all forms of liberalism have a belief in the priority of the individual even though old and new liberals differ significantly in how they interpret the freedom of this individual. Second, and perhaps more importantly, what makes liberalism an ideology is that it is a movement focused on the state. All liberals feel that the state is necessary to the well-being of society even though they differ in the kind of state they would support, and they may champion different movements to achieve their political ends. The fact that liberalism is a movement that has rationality, toleration and universality as its key virtues does not make it less ideological than movements that challenge these values. Liberalism is a belief system concerned with building a particular kind of society through a particular kind of state – that is enough to make it ideological.

For the same reason, conservatism is an ideology, although some conservatives strenuously deny this. Ideologies, they argue, ignore realities and existing institutions, and seek to impose abstract values upon historical facts. Ideologies seek to perfect the world whereas the truth is that humans are imperfect, and it cannot be said that people are rational beings who seek to govern their own lives. But the fact that conservatives may even disapprove of explicit political ideas on the grounds that it is an ill-governed country that resorts to political theory does not make their 'ism' non-ideological. Ideals might be identified as abstractions imposed upon a complex reality, and tradition exalted as a source of wisdom and stability. However, this does not make conservatism less of an ideology than, say, liberalism or socialism. The point about ideologies is they differ – not only from other ideologies – but internally as well. The relationship of the New Right and Thatcher's ideas and policies to conservatism (to take a British example) is quite complicated: there is a break from traditional conservatism in some areas that is sharp enough to allow her critics to accuse her of liberalism or, a peculiarly British term, Whiggism, i.e. seventeenth- and eighteenth-century liberalism. But conservatives see the state as essential even though they are more inclined (than old liberals) to view it as a 'natural' institution that is necessary to keep 'fallen' men and women in order. This makes conservatism ideological. It is true that where conservatism denotes an attitude, as in the argument, for example, that Stalinist communists are conservative in the sense that they idealise the past, it is not ideologically specific, but this is not a politically informed use of the term.

But what of socialism? Social democrats have long regarded themselves as pragmatic and flexible and regarded their opponents – whether on the left or the right – as being rigid and 'ideological'. Giddens has written a work entitled *Beyond Left and Right* (1994) in which he seeks to defend a non-ideological politics, and the New Labour hostility to ideology is linked to a belief in a 'third way' that tries to avoid the choice between traditional socialism and traditional capitalism. But whatever social democracy is (and it is a divided movement), it is certainly ideological in the sense that its policies and beliefs focus on the state. However, what are we to say of Marxism? This is a strand within socialism that explicitly rejects what it calls 'utopias' – beliefs that do not arise from the historical movement going on before our eyes – and sees its objective as the attainment of a society that is both classless and stateless in character. Marxism raises an important point about ideologies. Although it seeks to usher in a stateless society, it is ideological for two reasons. First, because it seeks to organise its supporters around a set of ideas that are concerned with the seizure of state power, and second, because although its long-term objective is the disappearance of the state, it could be argued that it makes assumptions which ensure that it will fail to achieve this end. It is therefore a statist doctrine, and that makes it as ideological as any other political movement.

see Chapter 3:
Socialism,
pp. 56–85,
particularly
p. 72

The one exception to this argument appears to be **anarchism**. After all, anarchists argue that political movements as they conventionally operate concentrate power in unaccountable leaderships, and seek either to control an old state or build a new one. Anarchism seeks to do neither. Surely, therefore, it is not an ideology. Here we must sharpen up a distinction that is implicit in our earlier analysis. Just as conservatives (or socialists and liberals) may *think* that they are not being ideological, but are, so is this true of anarchists as well. In practice, anarchists have to organise, and if they were ever successful they would, we think, have to establish a state in the short term, and what we will call government in the long term – contrary to their own principles. A state tackles conflicts of interest through force; government, as we define it, addresses conflicts through social pressures of a negotiating and arbitrational kind. Both ideas are rejected by anarchists, but it is impossible to envisage a society without conflicts of interest, and therefore it is impossible to envisage any society without a government to resolve these. Whether ideology will dissolve with the dissolution of the state is a matter we will tackle later, but it is clear that anarchism in practice would have to organise in relation to the state, and that makes it (in the particular view of ideology we have adopted here) ideological.

But what about **nationalism**? Nationalism has the opposite problem to anarchism. Nationalists are clearly ideological because they seek to organise 'their' people to win or to maintain the power of the state, but they attach themselves to different ideologies in doing so. Nationalists may be conservative or socialist, liberal and (in practice) anarchist, so that to call someone a nationalist is to leave open which particular social, economic and state policies they advocate. Nationalism, in our view, is ideological in a general sense: all nationalists use beliefs to galvanise their followers into action around a state. But the particular values that they adopt differ significantly, and invariably one finds one nationalism in collision with another. The African National Congress sees South Africa as a country that is mostly inhabited by blacks but in which there is a significant white minority: the old National Party (now dissolved) saw South Africa as a white country and sought through apartheid to give black Africans homelands in separate states. Both are or were nationalist: but their nationalism had a very different political content.

All political movements that seek to run the state are ideological in character, since we define ideologies as belief systems that focus on the state. Even movements that claim to reject ideology are ideological nevertheless, if this is what they do.

## Mannheim's Paradox: Are We Stuck?

Karl Mannheim wrote a classic book in 1929 entitled *Ideology and Utopia*, in which he raised an intriguing problem. Can we talk about ideology without being ideological ourselves? After all, if ideologies arise because of a person's social context, then is not the critique of ideology also situationally influenced, so that the critic of ideology is himself ideological? Mannheim was conscious that the term 'ideology' was often regarded as a pejorative one, so that he sometimes substituted the word 'perspective' when he talked about the way in which a person's social position influences the ideas they adopt (McLellan, 1995: 39).

Mannheim's argument raises very sharply the question as to whether we should define ideologies negatively or positively. If, as is common, we identify ideologies as negative bodies of thought, then we identify them as dogmas, authoritarian thought constructs that distort the real world, threats to the open-minded and tolerant approach that is crucial to democracy. But the negative definition seems naive, because it implies of course that while our opponents are ideological, we are not. The dogma expelled through the front door comes slithering in through the back, since the implication of a negative view of ideology might be that while ideologists distort reality, we have the truth. This seems not only naive, but also uncritical and absolutist.

On the other hand, a purely positive or non-judgemental view of ideology raises problems of its own. Supposing we insist that all ideas and movements are equally ideological, how do we avoid what philosophers call the problem of relativism? This is the idea that all ideas are of equal merit. There are a number of dictums – 'beauty lies in the eye of the beholder', 'one man's meat is another man's poison', etc. – which suggest that it is impossible to declare that one's own views are right and another's wrong. If all belief systems are ideological, does this imply that all are equally valid? After all, which of us can jump out of our skin, our time and place, and escape the social conditions that cause us to think one way rather than another? A relativist view of ideology has at least two problematic consequences.

The first is that it prevents us from 'taking sides'. Supposing we are confronted by a Nazi stormtrooper dragging a Jewish child to be gassed in a concentration camp. Each has their own set of values. A purely positive view of ideology might lead us to the position in which we note the ideology of the Nazi and the (rather different) ideology of his victim, and lamely conclude that each are valid for their respective holders. Mannheim sought to resist this argument by contending that his theory was one of 'relationism' and not relativism, and a relational position seeks to prefer a view that is more comprehensive and shows 'the greatest fruitfulness in dealing with empirical materials' (McLellan, 1995: 40). But are not 'comprehensiveness' and 'fruitfulness' other words for the truth? The question still remains: what enables some observers to find a true ideology, while others have ideologies that are false?

Mannheim's solution to the paradox was to focus on the particular social position of intellectuals, arguing that they constitute a relatively classless stratum that is 'not too firmly situated in the social order' (McLellan, 1995: 42). It is true that intellectuals do have positions that may allow for greater flexibility and a capacity to empathise with the views of others. Reading widely and travelling to other countries 'broadens the mind', but does it follow from this that intellectuals can cease to be ideological? John Gray cites the words of a Nazi intellectual who speaks of the need to exterminate gypsies and Jews, enthusing that 'we have embarked upon something – something grandiose and gigantic beyond imagination' (Gray, 2002: 93). Expansive ideas need not be progressive. It could be argued that intellectuals are particularly prone to impractical ideas which are especially ideological in the sense that they take seriously values and schemes that 'ordinary' people would reject. The attempt to transcend ideology by being a supposedly classless intellectual has been unkindly likened to Baron Munchausen in the German fairy story trying to get out of a bog by pulling on his own pigtail. It cannot be done!

We need a view of ideology that is both positive and negative. On the one hand, ideology is problematic and distorting, but it is inescapable in our current world. On the other hand, the notion of ideology as a belief system focused on the state does, we will argue, combine both the negative and the positive. While it is impossible not to be ideological in state-centred societies, in the struggle to move beyond the state itself we also move beyond ideas and values that are ideological in character.

## Facts, Values and the State

We have argued in the introduction to our book on political concepts that it is impossible to separate facts and values, since all statements imply that a relationship exists, and relationships suggest that values exist within facts. Thus, behaviouralists – a school of empiricial theorists who claim to be scientific and value free – argue that when people do not vote, this enables experts to make decisions for society. The link between apathy and democracy is deemed 'functional', but this contention necessarily implies that apathy is a good thing. When apparently value-free linguistic philosophers define the word democracy in parliamentary terms, they are taking a stand on the debate between representative and participatory democracy that is certainly evaluative or normative in character. One meaning of the term ideology is thought that is normative, but this, we would suggest, is unsatisfactory for at least two reasons. First, it naively assumes that ideas can be non-evaluative or purely factual in character. And second, it fails to see that ideology can be transcended, not by avoiding morality in politics, but by moving beyond the state.

But why should the state be linked to ideology? In our view, the state is best defined as an institution claiming a monopoly of legitimate force – a claim that is contradictory and implausible. In claiming a monopoly of legitimacy, supporters have to denigrate those who challenge this monopoly, presenting their own values as an exclusive system. Inevitably, a statist focus distorts realities. This problem is exacerbated by the fact that the state not only claims a monopoly of legitimacy, but a monopoly of force, and the use of force to tackle conflicts of interest acts to polarise society into friends and enemies, those who are respectable and those (an inexplicably violent minority) who are beyond the pale. This gives ideas an absolutist twist that is characteristic of ideologies, and explains why ideologies are problematic in character. This is unavoidable where the objective of a movement is win (or retain) state power. The Movement for Democratic Freedom seeks to unite conservatives, liberals and socialists against the tyrannical rule of Robert Mugabe and his ZANU (PF) party, and it cannot avoid an ideological character. In the same way, gay rights activists who organise to protect their interests and call upon the state to implement appropriate policies are acting ideologically.

But movements are not purely ideological, where they seek not only to transform the state but to move beyond it altogether. Take feminists, for example. Feminists do not normally believe that punishing aggressive men through the courts will solve the problem of male domination, although they may support it as a short-term expedient. In the longer term, they would argue that we need to change our culture so that force is seen as an unacceptable way of tackling conflicts of interest, and that we must resolve conflicts in what we have called a governmental way – i.e. through negotiation and arbitration and not through force. This longer-term aim is non-ideological because it rests upon trying to understand why **violence** arises and how we can move beyond it. It involves a politics beyond the state, and in seeking to face reality in all its complexities it is moving beyond ideology as well. The notion of 'monopoly' and the use of '**force**' that are inevitable when the state is involved limit the realism of ideas and make them ideological.

## References

Crick, B. (1982) *In Defence of Politics* 2nd edn Harmondsworth: Penguin.

Giddens, A. (1994) *Beyond Left and Right* Cambridge: Polity Press.

Gray, J. (2002) *Straw Dogs* London: Granta.

McLellan, D. (1995) *Ideology* 2nd edn Buckingham: Open University Press.

Mannheim, K. (1936) *Ideology and Utopia* London: Routledge & Kegan Paul.

Marx, K. and Engels, F. (1976) *Collected Works* vol. 5 London: Lawrence & Wishart.

Partridge, P. (1967) 'Politics, Philosophy and Ideology' in A. Quinton (ed.), *Political Philosophy* Oxford: Oxford University Press, 32–52.

# Chapter 1

# Liberalism

## Introduction

Liberalism has emerged as the world's dominant ideology, and much of the political debate of 'liberal democratic' societies takes place within liberalism. Because of its dominance liberalism can be a difficult ideology to pin down, and there are several quite distinct streams of thought within it. Liberals take individual freedom – or liberty – as a fundamental value, and although an individual's freedom can be limited – because it clashes with the freedom of others or with other values – what defines liberalism is the *presumption* that freedom is a good thing, meaning that limitations on freedom must be justified. A less obvious aspect of liberalism is its emphasis on equality, and again the presumption is that people are equal. Although this appears to generate a major contradiction at the heart of liberalism – after all, the exercise of freedom will often lead to inequality – the two can be reconciled if we assume people are *naturally* equal. Natural, or 'moral', equality may be compatible with material, or social, inequality. To say people are naturally equal amounts to the claim that political institutions must be justified to each individual, and each individual counts equally.

## Chapter Map

In this chapter we will:

- Explore the historical roots of liberalism.

- Identify the fundamental philosophical core of liberal thought.

- Recognise the distinct streams of liberal thought, and the tensions between them.

- Analyse political practice in liberal democracies and apply the insights gained to that practice.

# Prostitution Laws in Sweden

In 1998 the Swedish Parliament passed the Prohibition of the Purchase of Sexual Services Act. The Act does what its title suggests: it prohibits the sale of sexual services. Most countries have legal controls on prostitution, which often include banning brothels, pimping, kerb-crawling and advertising. The Swedish Act tightened up on these aspects, but it achieved international attention because it went much further than other European countries: it made it illegal to purchase or attempt to purchase 'casual sexual services'. The prohibition applied not only to street prostitution, brothels and massage parlours, but also escort services or 'any other circumstances' in which sexual services are sold. Obviously existing laws covered many of these cases, but the new law was a 'catch-all', and in that sense quite radical. One important point was that the buyer rather than the seller was criminalised.

It may seem odd to begin a chapter on liberalism with a discussion of prostitution laws in Sweden, but the reasons employed to justify the law reveal much about the nature of liberalism and, importantly, the tensions within it. And it is these reasons that are our focus. In a fact sheet produced by the Swedish government a number of arguments are advanced for this law and we outline these at the end of the chapter.

- List arguments for and against the criminalisation of the purchase of sexual services.
- Do you think the Swedish government was right to enact such a law?

## The Meaning of Liberalism

Liberalism has emerged as the world's dominant ideology. Europe provides a good example of the spread of liberal democratic values and institutions: the 1970s saw the transition from right-wing, military regimes in Greece, Spain and Portugal, and in 1989–91 the process of democratisation spread to Eastern Europe in the dramatic overthrow of state socialism from the Baltic states to Romania. While the depth of commitment at elite and popular levels to liberal democratic values in the 'emergent democracies' of Eastern Europe is a matter of much debate among political scientists, all these states subscribe to a liberal ideology. The accession in 2004 of nine Eastern European states, plus Malta, to the European Union, bringing the total from the original 6 in the 1950s to 25 today, is indicative of this commitment.

The very dominance of liberalism can make it a difficult ideology to grasp. In the history of political thought quite different bodies of thought are identified as 'liberal'. And in popular political discourse confusion can be caused when the term is applied to particular parties, movements or strands of thought *within* a liberal democracy. For example, many political parties have the word 'liberal' in their name; in Canada the Liberal Party is towards the left of the political spectrum, while in Australia the Liberal Party is to the right. In many European countries liberalism is associated with a strong commitment to the free **market,** whereas in the United States the term denotes a belief in central – that is, federal – state intervention in society and the economy, and so to be 'liberal' is to be on the left. Clarification is sometimes provided by a qualifying adjective: *economic* liberalism or *social* liberalism. Occasionally the term *classical* liberalism is employed to denote support for free trade and the free market.

Some distinctions will help to cut through the confusions of popular usage:

- **Justification** Political institutions can be described as 'liberal', but so can the method by which they are justified. Hobbes's defence of the state is a good example of this distinction. The institutions he defends appear highly illiberal but his method of justifying those institutions – **contractarianism** – is liberal. State authority is justified because we, as rational individuals, would calculate that it is in our interests to submit to it. Most of our attention in this chapter will be on the justification of institutions.

- **Constitution and policy** Turning to institutions, we can distinguish between the constitution and policy (or law making). The constitution determines the procedure by which laws are passed, while to a large extent leaving open the content of those laws. Although there may be debate about the constitution, most people are implicitly 'liberal' on the essentials of the constitution: the division of powers and the basic rights of individuals. They may not, however, support parties that describe themselves as liberal. The struggle between political parties normally operates *within* the constitution, rather than being a battle over the constitution. In short, at the constitutional level most of us are liberals, but at the policy level this may not be the case.

- **Attitudes** There is a distinction between how political theorists have defended – justified – liberal principles and institutions, and popular attitudes to those institutions. Understanding such attitudes is primarily the focus of empirical political science, using quantitative methods such as surveys. Although we do not discuss it here, the work of political scientists provides a useful perspective on liberalism – if people find it difficult to endorse liberal values then it should force liberals to reconsider how they defend liberal institutions.

Keeping these distinctions in mind, we can now attempt a rough definition of liberalism. As the etymology of the word implies, liberals emphasise liberty (freedom). As we will argue, a less obvious aspect of liberal thought is its emphasis on equality – not necessarily material equality, but a basic moral equality. A more precise definition of liberalism carries the risk of excluding from the liberal tradition important strands of thought. The best approach then is to look at a number of liberalisms. Although there may be more, four important ones can be identified: liberalism as **toleration** (or modus vivendi liberalism), contractarianism, **rights**-based liberalism (and, relatedly, **libertarianism**) and **utilitarianism**. If we look at ideas in their social context we will find these strands coexist. Much of the debate *within* liberalism is generated by the tensions between these different forms of liberalism, such that separating them out and clarifying each one is essential to understanding the values that underlie liberal democratic society.

## Liberalism as Toleration

### The Reformation and Wars of Religion

Many historians of political thought locate the origins of liberal discourse in the struggle for religious toleration generated by the Reformation and subsequent Wars of **Religion**. Although the term 'Wars of Religion' is sometimes reserved for a series of civil wars fought in France between 1562 and 1598, the term can be used more widely to include the struggle of the Protestant Netherlands (United Provinces) to free themselves from Catholic Spain, and the Thirty Years War (1618–48) in Germany. That the motivations of the protagonists was not necessarily theological in character does not detract from the fact that these wars produced a *philosophical discourse* in which toleration of difference became a central concern. It is this discourse, rather than the details of the wars, that concerns us.

Reformation box, p. 14

To understand the development of the concept of toleration we need a basic understanding of the theological core of the Reformation. The causes of the Reformation are many and varied, and as suggested a moment ago it is possible to explain it in social and economic, rather than theological, terms. However, we will take seriously the Reformation as a theological dispute. It is important to recognise that what is termed the Reformation had a number of distinct streams.

The two theological issues central to the Reformation were how doctrine is established and how human beings achieve salvation. Let us consider doctrine. Christianity is a bibliocentric religion – its teachings, or doctrine, are determined by a body of scripture. However, there has always been a debate over the correct

## The Reformation

We can identify two broad Reformation movements, which scholars term the Magisterial (or mainstream) Reformation, and the Radical Reformation (McGrath, 1988: 5–12):

- **Magisterial (or Mainstream) Reformation**: associated with Martin Luther (1483–1546), Huldrych Zwingli (1484–1531) and John Calvin (1509–64). There were some significant theological disputes between Lutherans and Calvinists, but they were agreed on many theological points and were committed to a strong church–state relationship.
- **Radical Reformation**: contained many different sects – and tended to be highly fractious. Radical reformers were 'theological individualists' – they rejected any role for a state-sponsored church.

Note: the term 'Protestant' as a synonym for the Reformation movement is misleading. Strictly speaking it denotes a particular protest at Speyer (1529) against the refusal of the Holy Roman Emperor to tolerate the religious conscience of a number of German princes and city-states.

There was also within the Church of Rome what came to be termed the **Counter-Reformation** – although many scholars reject that label on the grounds that it implies reaction to the 'Protestant' Reformation, and instead call it the **Catholic Reformation**. This reform movement can be traced back to the Council of Trent (1545–63).

interpretation of scripture and, relatedly, whether the Bible is a sufficient source of truth – the Catholic Church (Church of Rome) maintained not only that the priesthood played a special part in interpreting scripture, but that the Church, because it was founded by Christ, had the authority to augment Christian doctrine. Considering this question from the standpoint of the various movements outlined in the box above (and including the Catholic position) we can identify three opposing positions on the question of doctrine:

1. **Catholic – tradition 1 plus 2** Doctrine is determined by scripture as interpreted by the Church (tradition 1) and developed by the Church's leaders (tradition 2).
2. **Magisterial reformers – tradition 1** Human beings still require a body – the Church – which provides authoritative interpretation (tradition 1), but Christianity should rid itself of post-Biblical accretions, so no tradition 2. In addition, the Bible should be translated into vernacular languages so that believers – or at least the literate among them – can read it.
3. **Radical reformers – tradition 0** When you read the Bible you have direct experience of the word of God, unmediated by any tradition (McGrath, 1988: 144).

The second major theological issue was the nature of salvation. The common medieval view was that God had established a covenant with humanity, whereby he was obliged to justify – that is, allow into a **relationship** with himself, or 'save' – anybody who satisfied a minimum standard, which was defined as recognising one's sin. In practical terms, it meant remaining 'in communion' with the Church. Luther challenged this, arguing that human beings were so damaged by sin that there was nothing they could do by their own – or the Church's – efforts to save themselves. Rather, God freely gives – gratis, by grace – to those who have *faith* in him the means of salvation. The Catholic view came to be known, somewhat misleadingly, as salvation by works, in contrast to the Reformed position of salvation by faith alone.

Taken together these two theological disputes generated significantly different views of the role of the Church. For the mainstream reformers the Church's task is to teach doctrine rather than create it, and it has no direct role in human salvation – the Church cannot guarantee salvation. As the label suggests, the radical reformers went further: it was for individuals to determine correct doctrine. We can summarise the three positions on the nature of the Church:

1. **Catholic position** The Church was a visible, historical institution, grounded in the authority of Christ through his Apostles.

2. **Magisterial position** The visible Church is constituted by the preaching of the word of God – legitimacy is grounded in theological, not historical, continuity. The Church will contain both the saved and the unsaved.

3. **Radical position** The true Church was in heaven and no institution on earth can claim the right to be the community of Christ.

These two theological disputes, and the consequent re-evaluation of the role of the Church, had important immediate and long-term political implications. The immediate impact was on the relationship of the secular and spiritual powers. In the longer term the theological ideas generated by Reformed Christianity, and also, importantly, by Reformed Catholicism, gave rise to secular equivalents. For example, the theological individualism of Protestantism was 'translated' into a secular, philosophical individualism, which stressed individual responsibility. As we shall see, some theorists attribute the rise of national consciousness to the translation of the Bible into the vernacular languages of Europe. We shall focus here on the immediate political impact of the Reformation.

Ch 5:
Nationalism,
p. 118

Simplifying a great deal: political **power** in medieval Europe was characterised by a dual structure. On the one side there was the spiritual authority of the pontiff, and on the other his secular equivalent, the Holy Roman Emperor. The latter was relatively weak, and most secular power resided in the national and city-state powers. Nonetheless, the loyalties of individual citizens were split between pontiff and the national (or local) secular powers. Throughout the fourteenth century there were continual pressures on the Church to reform itself, and this was expressed as a demand for a general council (a council of lay people) to discuss reform. Although the Church of Rome was relatively tolerant of doctrinal difference – it only became 'authoritarian' after the Reformation – there was a refusal to call a council. Had such a council been called it is a matter of conjecture whether the schism between Rome and the various streams of the Reformation would have taken place; but the fact is that a council was not called, and an *institutional* break became inevitable.

The religious intolerance that eventually hardened into war cannot be attributed to the Church of Rome's attempt to suppress dissent. Rather, the institutional break created a legitimation crisis for the secular authorities. In states where the prince (or elector) had embraced Lutheranism or Calvinism, the continuing allegiance of some of their citizens to Rome was a threat to the prince's authority. Conversely, where the prince had remained loyal to Rome but some of his subjects had embraced Reformed religion there was a loss of spiritual authority – an authority that had underwritten secular authority in the pre-Reformation period.

## Reformation and Wars of Religion

**1517:** The first indication of the Reformation comes with Luther objecting to what he regarded as the Church's corrupt and theologically unsound practices

**1525:** The rise of Anabaptism – an important radical Reformation movement

**1529:** Diet of Speyer ends toleration of Lutheranism in Catholic districts – 6 princes and 14 cities 'protest', giving rise to the term Protestantism

**1545–63:** Council of Trent – beginnings of the Catholic (Counter-)Reformation

**1555:** Treaty of Augsburg

**1568:** Revolt of the (Protestant) United Provinces (Netherlands) – beginning of the 'Eighty Years War'

**1572:** St Bartholomew's Day Massacre of French Protestants (Huguenots) in Paris

**1598:** Edict of Nantes granted toleration of Protestants in France

**1618:** Beginning of the Thirty Years War

**1648:** Peace of Westphalia – regarded as the settlement of the major wars of religion

**1640–49:** English Civil War

In addition, the medieval division of spiritual and secular power had resulted in a dual structure of law, with much domestic law – for example, marriage – the responsibility of church courts rather than secular courts. In Reformed states, the legitimacy of that domestic law was now in question.

The first Europe-wide attempt to address, rather than simply suppress, this conflict of loyalties was the Treaty of Augsburg (1555), which produced the formula: *cujus regio, eius religio* – roughly translated as 'the ruler determines the religion'. Two points can be made about this formula. First, it tolerated rulers and not individual citizens. Second, it was a mere modus vivendi – that is, a way of living together, but without any underlying respect for the other person's beliefs or way of life. It was a recognition of the reality of power: neither could destroy the other, and it was in neither's interest for there to be continual war, so they 'agreed to disagree'. However, once the balance of power shifted, the newly dominant side had no reason not to suppress the other. Not surprisingly, the Augsburg settlement proved unstable, and it took a century more of conflict before the so-called Peace of Westphalia (1648) created a new, and relatively stable, European **order**. The Peace of Westphalia is the name given to a series of treaties that ended the last of the great wars of religion – the Thirty Years War (1618–48). It reaffirmed the formula of *cujus regio, eius religio*, but made some concession to toleration of individuals by respecting the beliefs of those resident in a particular territory prior to 1618. In addition, there was an implication that private belief and public practice should be separated – there were to be 'no windows into men's souls', to use Elizabeth I of England's expression. So long as there was outward conformity, there could be inner dissent.

## Toleration

The settlement of the Wars of Religion is credited with making toleration a central concept of political life, and in the process generating a body of political reflection and writing that can be described as 'liberal'. The term 'toleration' has, to twenty-first-century ears, a slightly negative connotation. It suggests grudging acceptance rather than respect. However, toleration remains a significant concept for liberals and it is important to be clear about its structure.

Toleration appears to require approving and disapproving of something at the same time. For example, person A:

1. Believes that the salvation is mediated by the Church (of Rome), so that outside the Church there can be no salvation;

2. Accepts that person B has the right to express her religious (or other) beliefs – person B is justified in not seeking salvation through the Church (of Rome).

The apparent tension between 1 and 2 is resolved if we recognise they refer to different actions: 2 is not direct approval of person B's choices, because that would contradict 1. The 'approval' in 2 might be of B's capacity to make a choice (we say 'might' because other reasons are possible). Nonetheless, there is still a tension between 1 and 2; what is required is a 'bridge' between them.

One bridge between them might be the acceptance of the sheer fact of religious **difference**. This is the Augsburg modus vivendi argument applied to toleration of individuals: terrible torture and other deprivations will not force (some) people to abandon their religious beliefs and practices, so it is both useless and politically destabilising to oppress them. Toleration grows out of recognition of this reality. But this is not really a justification for toleration – it does not provide reasons for toleration. To go beyond a modus vivendi person A would have to find something in his own religious beliefs that enables him to accept B's dissent from those beliefs. In the history of the development of religious toleration in the sixteenth and seventeenth centuries a range of such arguments were advanced. They included the following:

- *Latitudinarianism*: the belief in a minimal set of Christian doctrines, and the acceptance of dissent beyond that minimum.
- *Catholicism* (in the generic sense): the importance of Christian unity over uniformity.
- *Christian choice*: God gives us a choice, and so we are not entitled to deny people choice.

The list is far from exhaustive. What is striking, however, is that there is assumed an underlying commitment to Christianity, however Christianity might be understood. Insofar as there was toleration in the sixteenth and seventeenth centuries it tended to be limited to Catholicism and the two major branches of the magisterial Reformation – Lutheranism and Calvinism. It was rarely extended to radical Reformers, Jews and atheists. Only in the Netherlands and Poland did toleration go further. The explanation for this wider toleration in those two countries is complex, but in the Dutch case it is clearly connected to the early rise of **capitalism**, while in the Polish case it may have had its roots in a delicate religious balance.

In the eighteenth and nineteenth centuries the 'circle of toleration' is extended to include previously untolerated groups, and the justification of toleration shifts from religious to secular grounds. Here are a few secular arguments:

- *Scepticism*: it is impossible to prove the existence of God.
- *Progress*: humanity progresses if there is a competition of ideas.
- *Autonomy*: how we should behave can be determined rationally through the exercise of human reason.

Some contemporary theorists argue that these secular arguments are themselves intolerant and incompatible with a pluralistic society: scepticism is a rejection of religious belief, and autonomy, while not a rejection, cannot be endorsed by someone who believes revelation or natural law is the source for guidance on moral conduct. For this reason there has been a 'rediscovery' of modus vivendi toleration, and this is reflected to some extent in the **multiculturalism** debate. This rediscovery is also a reaction to the development of liberal thought in the following three centuries. In the rest of this chapter we consider that development, by focusing on three strands of theory: contractarianism, rights-based liberalism and utilitarianism.

Ch 8:
Multiculturalism,
pp. 210–11

## Contractarianism

Thomas Hobbes's *Leviathan* (1651) was published against the background of the English Civil War, which was, in part, a manifestation of the wider religious struggles in Europe. *Leviathan* is one of the great books of political theory, and arguably the first significant work of modern political thought. The conclusion Hobbes draws – that it is rational to submit to a powerful sovereign – may not appear liberal, but the way he reaches that conclusion draws on ideas which have become a major part of liberal reflection on the **state**. The method he uses for justifying obligation to the state is contractarian: we are to imagine a situation in which there is no state – the state of nature – and ask ourselves whether it is better we remain in the state of nature or agree to submit to a sovereign (or state).

It is important to understand the historical context of Hobbes's work. To a large degree Hobbes is concerned to provide an argument against rebellion. In mid-seventeenth-century England it was radical reformers – sects such as the Levellers and the Diggers – who were among the most likely rebels. A large part of *Leviathan* is concerned with blocking off theological arguments for rebellion. There is a tendency for contemporary readers to ignore this part of the book, regarding it as anachronistic, and concentrate on the apparently more 'secular' parts. But given that it is still the case that political order is challenged not just by competing interests, but also competing moral conceptions (some of which have a theological basis), the concerns which motivated the work cannot be dismissed as entirely irrelevant to the contemporary world.

Hobbes was the first of the classic contract theorists – later important contractarians are Locke, Rousseau and Kant. The contract tradition went into decline around the end of the eighteenth century. John Rawls is credited with reviving it in the second half of the twentieth century, with his influential book

## Biography — Thomas Hobbes (1588–1679)

Hobbes was born in 1588 in Malmesbury, Wiltshire. Allegedly his birth was brought on early as his mother heard of the approaching Spanish Armada – Hobbes was later to say 'fear and I were born twins'. His father was the local vicar, but after involvement in a brawl outside his own church fled to London, leaving his son to be brought up by a wealthy uncle.

Hobbes was educated at the local grammar school and at Oxford University. After graduation (1608) he became tutor to William Cavendish (later the 2nd Earl of Devonshire). A European tour with Cavendish (1610) reignited Hobbes's interest in scholarship; with relatively light duties to the Cavendish family Hobbes had time to read and write. William became the 2nd Earl in 1626, but died just two years later, and Hobbes lost a friend and employer.

For the next three years he was tutor to Sir Gervase Clinton, during which time he published a translation of Thucydides (1629). In the early 1630s Hobbes worked on the physical doctrine of motion; while not obviously political, his model of 'matter in motion' became a central premise of his later political theory. By the end of that decade England was experiencing considerable turbulence, culminating in the Civil War of 1642–9. It is, however, notable that his first important political work – *De corpore politico* (*The Elements of Law*) – although published in 1646, was written ten years earlier, and was not overly influenced by the political events of the time.

Hobbes, whose sympathies were with the soon-to-be-defeated Royalists, spent much of the late 1640s in, or near, Paris, working on his greatest work, *Leviathan* (full title: *Leviathan, or the Matter, Form and Power of a Commonwealth, Ecclesiastical and Civil*), which was published in 1651. The book had an impact: the secularism of the book alienated Royalists and Hobbes was forced to seek the protection of Oliver Cromwell's revolutionary government.

During the 1650s Hobbes was engaged in a controversy with Bishop John Bramhall over the possibility of free will and with John Wallis, Professor of Geometry, over the nature of mathematics.

After the restoration of the monarchy (1660), Hobbes was in favour with the new king, who awarded him a relatively generous pension and protected him from new laws intended to root out atheism. Nonetheless, out of fear of arrest Hobbes burnt many of his papers, and avoided writing on moral and political questions, preferring to translate the *Iliad* and *Odyssey*. He died in 1679.

*A Theory of Justice* (first published 1971). There are important differences between these thinkers, but there is a common, three-part structure to a contract theory:

1. a description of a situation in which there is no state;
2. an outline of the procedure for either submitting to a state or agreeing to a certain set of coercively enforced political principles – this is the 'contract';
3. a description of what is chosen – the state, or political institutions.

Since our concern is with contractarianism rather than the details of specific political theories, we will employ a modern treatment to explain the contract. In the following exercise, a situation is described in which you have a choice. The important feature of this exercise is that the outcome is partly determined by your choice, and partly determined by the other 'player'.

## The Prisoner's Dilemma

Two people are arrested for a crime they may or may not have committed – their guilt or innocence is irrelevant. Each is invited to confess to the crime. The sentence each receives will depend, in part, on what the other does. As Table 1.1 shows, if both confess, each gets five years in prison; if they both remain silent, each gets a year; if the first prisoner confesses while the other remains silent, then the former goes free and the latter gets ten years; if the second confesses and the first remains silent, the former goes free while the latter receives ten years (the first number of each pair refers to the first prisoner's sentence, and the second number to the second prisoner's sentence).

Table 1.1

|  |  | Second prisoner Remains silent | Confesses |
|---|---|---|---|
| **First prisoner** | Remains silent | 1, 1 | 10, 0 |
|  | Confesses | 0, 10 | 5, 5 |

If you were the first prisoner, what would you do: confess or remain silent?

The prisoner's dilemma is used to 'model' all three stages of the contract set out above. If we assume that the prisoners are purely self-interested then each will attempt to achieve her first preference. The preference-ordering of each can be tabulated as follows:

Table 1.2

|  | 1st preference | 2nd preference | 3rd preference | 4th preference |
|---|---|---|---|---|
| First prisoner | 0, 10 | 1, 1 | 5, 5 | 10, 0 |
| Second prisoner | 10, 0 | 1, 1 | 5, 5 | 0, 10 |

It is not rational to remain silent while the other prisoner confesses, so the likely outcome is that each will confess, with the consequence that each will satisfy only her third preference. What, of course, makes the 'game' interesting is that each could do better by agreeing to remain silent. The prisoner's dilemma is a non-zero sum game: a gain for one prisoner does not result in an equivalent loss for the other. The explanation of how, through cooperation, each prisoner might move from her third to her second preference is a contemporary rendition of the reasoning behind Hobbes's argument. The third preference represents the non-cooperation that characterises the state of nature, the agreement to remain silent is equivalent to the contract itself, and the satisfaction of the second preference equates to life under a state. Translated into political terms, the state provides 'public goods', the most important of which is security. (A public good is one the enjoyment of which cannot be restricted to those who have directly paid for it – it has 'spill-over effects'.)

Some commentators argue that the rational strategy for each prisoner is to forgo her first preference in order to achieve her second preference. This is incorrect: for each prisoner, achieving her first preference should remain her goal. What she wants is an agreement with the other prisoner that each will remain silent, but then to break the agreement in the hope that the other prisoner will honour it. Individual rationality dictates that she will aim to **free-ride** on the other's compliance; that is, gain the benefits of cooperation, which is the avoidance of five years in prison, without paying the cost of cooperation, which is one year in prison. Of course, as rational actors, each prisoner understands the motivations of the other, and so a 'voluntary' agreement is ineffective. What we need is a third-party enforcer of the agreement. The enforcer imposes sanctions on free-riders, such that there is an incentive to comply. In political terms, the enforcer is the state, an entity that, in the words of Max Weber, successfully commands a monopoly on the use of **coercion** in a particular territory.

There are three difficulties with the Hobbesian solution to the prisoner's dilemma:

1. The existence of an enforcer, or state, does not fundamentally alter the motivations of those subject to it: each still seeks to satisfy her own interests. This engenders a fundamental instability in the political order: we are always looking over our shoulder at other people, convinced that given the opportunity they will break the law. Such lawbreaking might, for example, take the form of evading payment of taxes necessary to maintain a police force.

2. The second objection to Hobbes can be broadened out into a critique of the aims of classical contract theory – as distinct from the aims of the contemporary contractarianism of Rawls. Hobbes, Locke, Rousseau and Kant were occupied above all with the question of an individual's obligation to obey the state and its laws. A law by its nature commands obedience, but what is termed '**political obligation**' is concerned with the existence of moral reasons for obeying the law: by asking whether a person has a political obligation we put into question the legitimacy of law. From the preceding discussion it is not difficult to see how a contractarian might argue for political obligation. We are all better off under a state than in a state of nature and therefore we are under an obligation to obey the state. But what if the benefits of cooperation are unequally distributed? Consider another version of the prisoner's dilemma:

**Table 1.3**

|  |  | Second prisoner<br>Remains silent | Confesses |
|---|---|---|---|
| **First prisoner** | Remains silent | 4, 1 | 10, 0 |
|  | Confesses | 0, 10 | 6, 5 |

The preference ordering of each prisoner is identical to the first version. The difference lies in the respective pay-offs from cooperation relative to non-cooperation: the first prisoner gains two years of freedom whereas the second prisoner gains four years. It might therefore be *rational* for each prisoner to submit to an enforced agreement, but it is not necessarily fair. Given the unfairness of the situation it is hard to argue that those who are disadvantaged relative to others have a *moral* obligation to obey the state. And this brings us to the third objection to Hobbes.

3. In both versions there was a unique solution to the dilemma – but what if instead of one set of pay-offs there were multiple sets? Let us imagine that the agreement is not about simply obeying or not obeying the state, but is concerned with the creation of a certain kind of state. We have to decide on the economic and political structure of society: should power be concentrated or dispersed? Should there be strong **private property** rights or, alternatively, collective ownership of economic resources? How much freedom should individuals have? Do we want an extensive welfare state or should individuals be required to buy health cover and education? Whatever is chosen, we are all better off under some kind of state than no state, but there is not a unique solution. The principles or institutions we choose will benefit people in different ways: if 'a' represents the state of nature, and 'b . . . z' a range of alternative political systems, then you might be better off under any of 'b . . . z' than under 'a', but your preferred system will not be shared by all other **citizens**. For twentieth-century contractarians the aim of the contract is to create a certain set of political institutions – or principles of **justice** – rather than simply contract into the state. For example, Rawls accepts the logic of the solution to the prisoner's dilemma, but that is merely the starting point for a theory of justice: it has to be both rational *and reasonable* to submit to the state.

The fundamental problem with Hobbes's argument is that he reduces the **legitimacy** of the state to self-interest. His starting point is a materialist conception of human nature: human beings are 'bodies in motion', continually desiring things, and never fully satisfied (Hobbes, 1991: 118–20). Because there is scarcity of desired objects, humans are brought into conflict with one another. Their greatest fear is death, and that fear is the key to understanding why the state of nature is a 'war of all against all' (Hobbes, 1991: 185–6). Although Hobbes outlines the 'laws of nature' that he claims exist in the state of nature, these are best interpreted as akin to scientific, rather than moral, laws. For example, we are required to seek peace, unless war is necessary for self-defence, but this can be understood as a prudential instruction rather than a moral requirement (Hobbes, 1991: 190).

A twentieth-century theorist, John Plamenatz, criticised Hobbes on grounds that if his description of the state of nature were accurate, then people would be too nasty to stick to any agreement, and if they stick to the agreement then the state of nature cannot be as Hobbes describes it (Plamenatz, 1992: 193–7). One of the insights of game theory, of which the prisoner's dilemma is an example, is to provide a solution to this apparent paradox: what we seek is an agreement, equivalent to the prisoners' agreement to remain silent, but what we fear is that other people will 'defect' from the agreement. It follows from this that prisoner's dilemma-type situations are 'assurance games'. In short, people are not nasty but fearful. Furthermore, the real challenge is not agreeing to create a state, but *maintaining* the state. Consequently the 'game' that models the problem is not a one-off prisoner's dilemma, but a repeated prisoner's dilemma. Using a real-world example: should you honour business contracts? If you acquire a reputation for breaking such contracts then people will not do business with you, so it pays to be trustworthy. Strictly speaking, this is not a prisoner's dilemma, for the incentive structure is changed; nonetheless, it supports Hobbes's argument without relaxing the derivation of political authority from self-interest.

Even if the need for a good reputation solves the first problem, it leaves unresolved the second and third problems. The second might simply be dismissed by Hobbes – after all, he makes no claim to the fairness of the state. All that is required is that each individual can ask himself or herself: am I better off under this state than in a state of nature? If the answer is 'yes' – and it almost certainly will be – then it is rational to submit to the state. The third problem is trickier. We said the context to Hobbes's political thought was the challenge to state authority generated by religious dissent. Given Hobbes's model of human nature, there seems no place for religious motivations. But if the Kingdom of God is not of this world, then contrary to what Hobbes claims, physical death is *not* the thing to be most feared. The worst thing is separation from God. Hobbes was certainly aware of the force of theologically grounded motivation, and argued that there should be a single state religion, with outward conformity, but no attempt to coerce a person's inner thoughts. What he did not reckon with was the challenge to the stability of the state – the agreement to submit – arising not from a clash of interests, but from differing moral judgements. When we contract into the state we do not simply give up our natural liberty to pursue our interests, we also give up the right to determine what is morally correct.

### Hobbes and Liberalism

The claim that Hobbes is a liberal rests on a number of characteristics of his thought:

(a) It implicitly entails a rejection of natural authority – the authority of the sovereign derives from a contract and not from inheritance or divine right.

(b) People are equal in the state of nature because, with stealth, the weakest can kill the strongest. Admittedly this is a claim about individuals' physical powers – and a questionable one at that – rather than a claim for moral equality.

(c) Later contract theorists fundamentally revised the nature of the contract, but the basic method remains, so Hobbes's argument has proved remarkably productive of liberal thought.

In the next section we turn to two other contract theorists – Locke and Kant – but we argue that their thought is sufficiently different to Hobbes's to warrant attributing a distinct stream of liberal argument to them.

## Rights-based Liberalism

## Locke

Most courses in the history of political thought yoke together Thomas Hobbes and John Locke, and compare and contrast their contract theories. A simplistic comparison would describe Locke's state of nature as a rather less unpleasant place to be than the Hobbesian equivalent, and that this affects their attitude to the contract, and to the rights individuals should enjoy under the state. For example, Locke thinks we have a right to rebel against the state, whereas Hobbes rejects such a right. But these superficial differences conceal more significant ones, such

## Biography          John Locke (1632–1704)

Born in 1632, and raised in a Puritan family, Locke was educated at Oxford University, graduating in 1656; he later earned a bachelor of medicine (1674).

In 1666 he met Anthony Ashley Cooper (1st Earl of Shaftesbury), who had come to Oxford to seek treatment for a liver infection, and Locke became Shaftesbury's physician, adviser and friend, moving into Shaftesbury's home in London in 1667, where he continued his medical training under the supervision of Thomas Sydenham. When Shaftesbury's condition worsened Locke oversaw the operation that removed the cyst. As Shaftesbury's power as Lord Chancellor grew, so did Locke's influence; however, in 1675 Shaftesbury fell from favour and Locke left England for France, where he continued his scholarly activities.

Shaftsbury's political fortunes underwent a brief revival in 1679, and Locke returned to England. However, under suspicion of involvement in the 1683 Rye House Plot – a plot to kill the king and ensure a Protestant succession – Locke fled to the Netherlands, where he remained until after the 'Glorious Revolution' and the accession of the Protestant William and Mary to the throne (1689). His major works were published between 1689 and his death in 1704: *A Letter Concerning Toleration* (1689), which argued for a 'broad' Anglican church; *An Essay Concerning Human Understanding*, and his most important political work, *Two Treatises of Civil Government*, both published in 1690.

that it is possible to say that Locke was not simply the next in line in the contract tradition, but articulated a distinct stream of liberal thought, one which emphasised moral rights. That tradition has had a huge impact not only on political thought in Locke's native England, but also, and perhaps especially, in the United States.

As we saw, Hobbes maintained that people were free and equal in the state of nature, and that there existed 'natural laws'. On the face of it, Locke offers a similar description of the state of nature, but his understanding of freedom, equality and natural law is quite different to that of Hobbes:

- Hobbes's liberty is simply the absence of restraint, whereas Locke's liberty takes the form of actionable rights.
- Hobbes understood equality in naturalistic rather than moral terms. For Locke, we are equal because no person has a natural right to subordinate another.
- Unlike Hobbes's laws of nature, Locke's laws have a theological basis – we have a natural duty to preserve ourselves, a duty owed to God, who created us.

For Locke, moral rights precede the contract to create a state, and the role of the state is to settle disputes over the interpretation of those rights, and ensure that violations of the rights are punished. The most important among the rights are rights to private property, which are grounded in rights in one's own body. Self-ownership is, however, derivative of God's right, as creator, in his creatures.

Contrary to Hobbes's assertions, economic and social life is possible in the state of nature. People can enter into contracts – that is, exercise their powers – and individuals have the right to enforce them. Furthermore, at an early stage in the economic development of society individuals are materially satisfied – they do not compete for scarce resources. Only later, with an increase in population, does the problem of scarcity arise (Locke, 1988: 297–8).

What makes the state of nature 'inconvenient' is the absence of a body that can *authoritatively* determine when rights have been violated and *effectively* enforce a remedy (329–30). Hobbes was obsessed with effectiveness, but because there was no pre-contractual law in Hobbes's state of nature there was nothing to adjudicate. Because individuals in Locke's state of nature have the capacity to recognise the moral law, and the state is created as a judge and an enforcer, it follows that should the state fail in these tasks individuals are justified in rebelling against it.

### Locke and Liberalism

There is much that is anachronistic in Locke. In particular, his claim that native Americans could not possess property because they could not recognise natural law, and thus the United States was 'unowned' (293), is an embarrassment to contemporary defenders of Locke. Also, the Christian basis of his thought is problematic in modern, pluralistic societies, although his appeal to natural law does provide a route to a secularised notion of human rights. However, overall, the key contributions that Locke made to the liberal tradition are:

(a) The idea that there are what Robert Nozick calls 'side constraints', which limit what the state, or society in general, can do to human beings (Nozick, 1974: ix).

(b) Natural (or moral) rights provide a standpoint from which we can judge the state. Unlike Hobbes, obligation to obey the state is not for Locke an 'all or nothing' matter. Although we give up a certain degree of moral judgement when we contract into the state, we do not 'hand over' all our autonomy.

(c) There is much more discussion of the institutions of liberal democracy in Locke than in Hobbes, and that discussion has been hugely influential. Locke is identified as a key influence on the formation of the American Constitution.

## Kant

From a different intellectual tradition Kant defends the idea of 'side constraints', and thus moral rights. More difficult to understand than Locke, he was, arguably, a more sophisticated philosopher. His moral theory is a standard part of the moral philosophy syllabus, whereas his political theory is less commonly found in a course on the history of political thought. However, one very powerful reason for studying Kant is that in the twentieth century there has been a huge revival of interest among political philosophers in his work, and he has been an important influence on such major thinkers as John Rawls and Jürgen Habermas.

We will briefly outline Kant's moral theory, and then explain how it underwrites his political theory. In *Groundwork of the Metaphysics of Morals* (Kant, 1996: 37–108) Kant outlines a method for determining how we should behave – the categorical imperative. He offers a number of formulations, the differences intended to capture different aspects of moral relationships. Simplifying a great deal, what is morally right is what would be chosen if we were to view a situation from the standpoint of autonomy, unaffected by emotional, and other, attachments. If we abstract from those attachments then we will necessarily see the world from a universal standpoint; moral reasoning entails *universalising* a 'maxim' (a maxim is a claim that we intend to form the basis of a moral law). If we cannot universalise that maxim then it cannot become a moral law.

Kant provides a simple example: a shopkeeper knows he can get away with over-charging a customer, but feels moved to inform the customer that she has been over-charged. So the 'maxim' is: 'I should always be honest' (53). This maxim can form the basis of a moral law only if it can be universalised, meaning that anybody in the shopkeeper's situation can make the same judgement, and the shopkeeper in a different situation can apply that maxim. Universalisation entails abstraction from people and situations. Perhaps the customer is a friend, and friendship moves the shopkeeper to be honest, or alternatively, the customer is a child, and the shopkeeper feels bad about cheating a child, or maybe the shopkeeper 'just knows' it is wrong to over-charge. These cannot justify the maxim because they depend on the particular identities of the agents, or on particular emotions.

The categorical imperative is not a tool for making everyday judgements. This becomes clear when Kant, in one of the formulations, maintains that you should will that your maxim becomes a 'universal law of *nature*' (73). This indicates that the task is not to make case-by-case judgements, but think 'holistically': we imagine a *society* governed by universal laws. Such a society Kant describes as a 'Kingdom of Ends', for if we universalise we must necessarily treat other human beings as ends and not means (80). In contrast to Locke, these laws are not given to us by God, or through our senses, but are 'constructed' by human beings exercising powers of reason. Through construction of moral laws we lift ourselves above our animal natures and prove our autonomy. There is a crucial political point here: we can be coerced into *conforming* with what morality requires, but we cannot be coerced into acting *for the right reasons*. The shopkeeper can be motivated to be 'honest' by threat of punishment, but he would not be acting morally because he is not being moved by reason.

Some contemporary political theorists draw an anarchist conclusion from Kant's argument. Robert Paul Wolff argues that we can never reconcile moral autonomy and political authority. But, in fact, in his political writings Kant does defend the state. He even maintains that a civilised state is possible among a 'nation of devils . . . just so long as they get the constitution right' (335). To understand the relationship between morality and politics we need to distinguish internal freedom and external freedom. The former – which can also be called autonomy – entails the ability to be motivated to act morally by the force of reason alone. The latter is the idea that the freedom of one person must coexist with the freedom of all others. This is expressed as a system of rights, coercively enforced by the state.

The state serves the end of morality by helping to realise the 'Kingdom of Ends'. The difficulty with this argument is that human agents must will the creation of that 'Kingdom', whereas in a political community – under the state – we are coerced into behaving in accordance with other people's rights. Attempting to resolve the conflict between autonomy and coercion has been central to the liberal project. One way of resolving it would be to posit two standpoints that a citizen can adopt: the standpoint of moral autonomy and the standpoint of a subject of law. As an autonomous agent you will the creation of a political community in which each person's rights are respected, but you also know enough about human nature to recognise that rights will have to be protected through coercion, such that you are at the same time willing the creation of a *coercive* political community. This would, of course, create a divide within human psychology between moral autonomy and political subjectivity.

### Kant and Liberalism

The rights-based tradition of liberalism has sometimes been characterised as entailing the priority of the right over the good. These terms are attributed to Kant, but the precise definition was given by moral philosopher David Ross. He defined the right as 'that which is obligatory' and the good as 'that which is worth pursuing' (Ross, 1930: 3). There are many different forms of **goodness**: aesthetic evaluation, friendship, the pursuit of truth are but a few. Kant's political theory can be categorised as 'right based' because the purpose of the state is not to realise goodness but to ensure that people respect each other's rights. The 'right' – note the singular – is the name Kant gives to the coexistence of individual rights. A political consequence of the priority of the right over the good is that the state's functions are limited.

Ch 2:
Conservatism,
pp. 45–9

If the state is only justified insofar as it protects individual rights it cannot have purposes of its own which are independent of that function. Michael Oakeshott, whose work draws on liberal and conservative thought, makes a useful distinction between the state, or political community, as an *enterprise association* and as a *civil association*. In an enterprise association people have a shared project, and the state acts as an agent to realise that project. Such a project might be theological in character, but it could also be secular. For example, the attempt to create an 'equal society', where equality is an end in itself, would constitute an enterprise. Oakeshott argues that a political community is a civil association of individuals with disparate aims, and the state works to permit the continuation of that association: the association has no ends of its own.

## Utilitarianism

Utilitarians hold that political institutions function to increase the overall level of welfare – or utility – of a society. At first sight this appears fundamentally opposed to rights-based liberalism, and indeed to contractarianism: utility maximisation implies that there is a thing called 'society' which has aims over and above those of individuals, or that the aims and interests of individuals are subsumed in 'society'. While there are tensions between utilitarianism and rights-based liberalism, and much of the debate within the liberal tradition is between these positions, there are shared historical roots, such that they are both clearly part of the liberal tradition. Furthermore, in the twentieth century revisions to utilitarian theory have had the consequence of closing the gap to some degree between utilitarianism and rights-based liberalism.

The claim that utilitarianism entails the maximisation of utility requires elaboration: what is utility? How do we maximise it? What does utilitarianism actually require of individuals? Different utilitarian thinkers have defined utility in different ways: Jeremy Bentham defined it as happiness, John Stuart Mill as pleasure, G.E. Moore as certain ideal states of mind. All of these definitions conceptualise utility as something 'mentalistic' – a feeling or state of mind. This raises an epistemological question: how do we know someone is happy, or feeling pleasure, or has the right state of mind? Contemporary utilitarians avoid the epistemological question by defining utility as preference satisfaction. This has the advantage that there are available real-world systems for ordering preferences: voting and markets. When we cast a vote or buy a pair of shoes we are expressing a preference.

To maximise utility we have to be able to measure it, and two options are available: either we add up instances of utility (cardinal measurement), or else we rank instances of utility (ordinal measurement). The definition of utility affects how we go about measuring it: mentalistic definitions lend themselves to cardinal measurement, while preference satisfaction fits best with ordinal measurement. In fact, it was the difficulty of measuring pleasure or happiness that led to a shift to defining utility as preference satisfaction.

We now come to the third – and most obviously political – question: if we are utilitarians, how should we behave? There are some standard criticisms of utilitarianism:

- What makes people happy, gives them pleasure, or what they prefer is completely open: if torturing another person gives you pleasure, then it must be counted into the 'maximand' (that which is to be maximised).
- We cannot respect the law if breaking it will increase utility.
- Utilitarians cannot respect individual rights because the demand to maximise utility may involve sacrificing an individual's rights, if respecting those rights would reduce utility.
- One person could be made to suffer excruciating pain in order to give a million people each a minuscule amount of pleasure. A less extravagant criticism is that utilitarians cannot be concerned about the distribution of welfare, but merely its overall level; imagine 100 units of utility distributed amongst five people – a distribution of 96 to one person and one unit to each of the other four is no worse than an equal distribution.
- You are as much responsible for what you allow to happen as what you do in a more direct sense of doing. For example, given the choice between (a) killing 1 person and 'allowing' 19 to live, or (b) 'standing by' while all 20 are killed, utilitarianism requires you to kill that 1 person (Williams, 1973: 98–9).

These criticisms are dismissed by utilitarians as unrealistic. The way to avoid them, it is claimed, is to distinguish between direct and indirect utilitarianism. Direct utilitarianism – or 'act utilitarianism' – requires that you seek to maximise utility on every occasion. Indirect utilitarianism, which includes 'rule utilitarianism' and 'institutional utilitarianism', separates action and justification: what we should do is follow rules, such as respecting individual rights, and the consequence of doing so is that utility will be maximised. Institutional utilitarianism is compatible with contractarianism: in the contract situation we agree to a set of institutions, the operation of which will maximise utility.

## Utilitarianism and Liberalism

There is no doubt that since the early nineteenth century, when some utilitarians advanced their – incoherent – requirement to seek the greatest happiness of the greatest number (incoherent, because you cannot simultaneously *maximise* two numbers), utilitarianism has developed in sophistication. However, our concern is with the relationship of utilitarianism to the other members of the 'liberal family'. What makes utilitarianism part of the family?

(a) Like Hobbes, Locke (despite his Christianity) and Kant, utilitarians reject 'natural authority'. Although it is possible to give utilitarianism a Christian cast, there is no doubt that it developed out of a secular, 'natural–scientific', world view. The calculability of pleasure or happiness fits neatly with the rise of science and the rejection of the idea that there are forces beyond human consciousness.

(b) Utilitarians still hold to the liberal 'presumption in favour of freedom' and the 'presumption of natural equality'. People are free to express their preferences, and coercion is only justified in order to bring about the greatest good. And people are equally 'generators' of utility – John Stuart Mill (a later utilitarian) attributed this formula to the earlier utilitarian thinker Jeremy Bentham: 'each to count for one and nobody for more than one' (Mill, 1991: 198–9).

(c) In concrete political terms, utilitarians have invariably been progressive or radical in their attitudes to social problems. In many ways they represent the 'left-wing' liberal alternative to the libertarianism of Locke and Kant, although you need not be a utilitarian to be on the left of the political spectrum.

(d) Most important of all, utilitarianism grew in parallel with the development of democracy. The high point of utilitarian thought was the nineteenth century, although it continued to be the dominant philosophical method for justifying political principles until the 1960s when there was a revival in contractarianism. The decline of contract thinking around 1800 went hand in hand with scepticism about using the contract – actual or hypothetical – to explain political obligation in a *mass* society. Utilitarianism seemed to provide a much more convincing method of justification in democratic societies: the calculation of utility dovetails with the counting of votes, although it was only in the twentieth century, with the development of preference satisfaction as the definition of utility, that a more direct link between utilitarianism and democracy was established.

## Conclusion: the Swedish Case Study

We began this chapter with a discussion of anti-prostitution laws in Sweden, and especially the prohibition on the purchase of sexual services. A number of arguments have been advanced by the Swedish government for that prohibition:

1. Prostitution is 'harmful not only to the individual prostituted woman or child, but also to society at large'.

2. Combating prostitution is central to Sweden's goal of achieving equality between men and women, at the national level as well as internationally. Prostitution is a gender-specific phenomenon: most prostitutes are female, and most buyers are male.

3. Women who suffer additional oppression, such as racism, are overrepresented in the global prostitution industry. In societies where the status of women has improved, prostitution has fallen.

4. The fact that an exchange relationship operates – sex for money – does not justify the relationship, because there is an immense imbalance in the power relation of buyer to seller.

5. It is important to 'motivate persons in prostitution to attempt to exit without risking punishment' (note: the seller of sexual services is not prosecuted).

6. Because it is assumed that men who buy sex are acting from a natural, male drive, their 'underlying motives have seldom been studied or even questioned'.

7. By adopting these measures Sweden has 'given notice to the world' that it regards prostitution as a serious form of oppression of women.

8. Since the Act came into force there has been a 'dramatic drop' in the number of women in street prostitution, and the number of men who buy sexual services has also fallen.

9. Public support for the law is 'widespread and growing': an opinion poll in 1999 revealed 76 per cent supported the law, and 15 per cent opposed it. In 2001 the figure in favour was 81 per cent, with 14 per cent against. (http://www.sweden. gov.se/content/1/c6/03/16/13/110ab985.pdf)

The first point to make is that critics of the law would argue for a distinction between public and private: it is possible to disapprove of prostitution but believe that consenting adults should have the right to make choices. This is a development of the argument for toleration, but here extended far beyond religious toleration. It may appear that the Swedish state has simply rejected toleration but, in fact, the language used to justify the law is an implicit acknowledgement that the limitation on the purchaser's freedom requires justification: 'in any other context, [prostitution] would be categorised as sexual abuse and rape' and 'the fact that these acts are committed in exchange for payment does not in any way diminish or mitigate the immense physical and mental damage inflicted on [prostitutes'] bodies and minds'. The power imbalance between prostitute and client is so great that the former cannot be deemed to be a consenting adult. Obviously one can disagree with this assessment, but the debate over the harm caused by prostitution, and whether prostitutes can really consent, is fought out on liberal terms.

Several of the arguments set out in the Swedish government's defence of the Sexual Services Act make reference to the good *consequences* of banning the sale of sexual services. It is often commented that Sweden has a particularly strong idea of the 'common good', and this has sometimes resulted in laws which seem to impinge on individual freedom. There are a number of reasons for this, one being the dominance of the centre-left Social Democrats in post-war Sweden. The general point is that utilitarian – or consequentialist – reasoning is clearly in evidence in the justification for the anti-prostitution law. The harm caused by prostitution is harm to 'society at large'; the law is part of a package aimed to promote gender equality; the operation of the law has resulted in a dramatic drop in prostitution. In addition, the high level of public support is taken as a justification for the law. Obviously in a democracy you have to win support for laws, but quite often legislatures will pass laws that are unpopular, or decline to pass laws which would be popular. Liberalism and democracy should not be run together, for individual freedom can conflict with democracy, which in a mass society often takes the form of preference aggregation.

Finally, several arguments make reference to 'motivations': prostitutes should be 'motivated' to exit their way of life and male motives should be 'questioned'. In addition, Sweden had 'given notice to the world' that it regarded prostitution as a form of oppression, with the implication that it sought to change attitudes in other countries. The Swedish state is using its coercive power to motivate people and change attitudes, and thus to bring about a 'good' state of affairs. For a rights-based, Kantian liberal this is an illegitimate extension of state power, and indeed a contradiction in terms, for you cannot coerce people into acting for the right reasons. It is important to distinguish the motivation argument from the harm argument. A defender of rights-based liberalism might accept that prostitutes cannot consent, and so buying their services is a form of harm and should be illegal. But 'motivating' people – that is, changing their attitudes – even if it were successful, would be incompatible with moral autonomy.

## Summary

At the heart of liberalism is the belief that people are naturally free and equal. That does not mean that there are no limitations on freedom, or that people must be equal, or treated equally, in all respects. Rather, we are presumed to be free and equal, and departures from freedom and equality require justification. Viewed historically, liberalism developed out of the settlement of the Wars of Religion, with the emphasis on toleration of religious difference. Such toleration was gradually extended beyond the sphere of religion to other aspects of belief and lifestyle. Several strands of liberalism emerged after the seventeenth century, and we identified three: contractarianism, rights-based liberalism (and libertarianism) and utilitarianism. Although there are significant philosophical differences between them, they are all clearly part of the 'liberal family'. Much of the left–right debate in contemporary politics operates around different interpretations of liberalism. For example, both Rawls and Nozick can be described as 'liberal,' but they come to quite different conclusions about the role of the state.

## Questions

1. Is 'toleration' a coherent concept?
2. Can the justification for the state be reduced to 'mutual advantage' – that is, the combined effects of the pursuit of self-interest?
3. Can you believe in moral rights if you do not believe in God?
4. Can there be a utilitarian theory of rights?

## References

Hobbes, T. (1991) *Leviathan* (ed. C.B. Macpherson) London: Penguin.

Kant, I. (1996) *Practical Philosophy* (ed. Mary Gregor) Cambridge: Cambridge University Press.

Locke, J. (1988) *Two Treatises of Government* (ed. Peter Laslett) Cambridge: Cambridge University Press.

McGrath, A. (1988) *Reformation Thought: An Introduction* Oxford: Blackwell.

Mill, J.S. (1991) *On Liberty and Other Essays* (ed. John Gray) Oxford: Oxford University Press.

Nozick, R. (1974) *Anarchy State, and Utopia* London: Basic Books.

Plamenatz, J. (1992) *Man and Society: Political and Social Theories from Machiavelli to Marx. Vol. 1, From the Middle Ages to Locke* London: Longman.

Rawls, J. (1972) *A Theory of Justice* Oxford: Clarendon Press.

Ross, W. (1930) *The Right and the Good* Oxford: Oxford University Press.

Williams, B. and Smart, J.J.C. (1973) *Utilitarianism: For and Against* Cambridge: Cambridge University Press.

## Further Reading

There are a couple of good, short, introductions dealing with liberalism as a whole: John Gray, *Liberalism* (Buckingham: Open University Press, 1995), and David Manning, *Liberalism* (London: Dent, 1976). Of the major thinkers discussed in this chapter, the Oxford University Press 'Past Masters' series provides very short, useful, overviews, written by major scholars in the field, with guidance on further reading: Richard Tuck, *Hobbes* (Oxford: OUP, 1989); John Dunn, *Locke* (Oxford: OUP, 1984); Roger Scruton, *Kant* (Oxford: OUP, 1982); John Dinwiddy, *Bentham* (Oxford: OUP, 1989). More generally on the social contract tradition (which does encompass Locke and Kant), the following are helpful: Michael Lessnoff, *Social Contract* (London: Macmillan, 1986); Jean Hampton, *Hobbes and the Social Contract Tradition* (Cambridge: CUP, 1986); Patrick Riley, *Will and Political Legitimacy: A Critical Exposition of Social Contract Theory in Hobbes, Locke, Rousseau, Kant, and Hegel* (Cambridge, Mass.: Harvard University Press, 1982). On utilitarianism see: Geoffrey Scarre, *Utilitarianism* (London: Routledge, 1996); Anthony Quinton, *Utilitarian Ethics* (London: Duckworth, 1989); and for a very readable debate between a utilitarian and a critic of utilitarianism, see Williams (1973).

## Weblinks

- General site on liberalism: www.en.wikipedia.org/wiki/Liberalism

- Some sites devoted to classical and economic liberalism ('right-wing' liberalism):
  www.free-market.net/directorybytopic/liberalism/
  www.en.wikipedia.org/wiki/classical_liberalism
  www.libertyguide.com

- A site devoted to social liberalism (although more of a 'campaigning' site):
  www.korpios.org/resurgent/tenets.htm

# Chapter 2

# Conservatism

## Introduction

Conservatism is an elusive ideology. Although there are conservative streams of thought in parties and movements calling themselves 'conservative', the main ideology of these movements is a combination of liberalism and nationalism, with the former particularly dominant. There are far fewer 'small c' than 'big c' conservatives. But despite its marginalisation, conservatism is a distinct ideology, and conservative thinkers present arguments of continuing relevance. Above all, conservatives challenge the idea that society can be planned in a rational way without regard to tradition and historical experience. This core idea leads them to support national institutions, but not radical nationalism; individual liberty against state power, but not the natural rights that many liberals defend; spontaneous order, but not anarchism; community, but not socialist collectivism.

## Chapter Map

In this chapter we will:

- Outline the main elements of conservatism.

- Discuss the work of four key conservative thinkers: David Hume, Edmund Burke, Michael Oakeshott and Leo Strauss.

- Draw out the practical implications of conservative thought.

- Distinguish conservatism from the other traditional ideologies.

# Reform or Revolution?

George W. Bush takes the Oath of Office on Capitol Hill in Washington, 20 January 2005

The election of George W Bush in 2000 was controversial. A protracted dispute in Florida was finally settled by a 5-4 vote in the Supreme Court in favour of suspending further recounts and certifying Bush's victory in Florida over Al Gore, thus giving Bush the state and, with it, the Presidency. Another aspect of the election which became the focus of attention, but not of legal dispute, was the fact that even after winning Florida Bush won fewer popular votes than Gore: 50.5 million (47.9 per cent) to Gore's 51 million (48.4 per cent). On paper, the 2004 election was more decisive, with Bush securing re-election with 62 million votes (50.7 per cent) to John Kerry's 59 million (48.2 per cent). But, had Kerry won the state of Ohio he, not Bush, would have taken the Presidency. Both the controversy in Florida and the fact (2000) and distinct possibility (2004) of 'minority' winners is due to the electoral college system. In all but two states, the candidate who takes most votes wins the entire slate of delegates: Bush's 537-vote victory (out of 6 million votes cast) in Florida gave him the entire 25-person Floridian delegation, and a national 271–266 (with one abstention) victory in the electoral college. After the 2000 election there was a clamour for a change in the way the President is elected, but defenders of the system argued that it was tried-and-tested – in essence, Americans should judge the system not by its apparent unfairness, but by its success over the last two centuries.

- Do you find this 'conservative' defence of the Electoral College convincing?

A useful web-based defence of the electoral college is provided by William Kimberling of the US Federal Election Commission: http://www.fec.gov/pdf/eleccoll.pdf

## Conservatism: an Elusive Ideology?

Anybody with a basic knowledge of party politics, but coming to political theory for the first time, may assume that 'conservatism' is simply the ideology of political parties calling themselves 'conservative', such as the Conservative Party in Britain, or the Conservatives in Canada (or one of its predecessor parties, the Progressive Conservatives). However, an analysis of the aims and policies of these parties would suggest that their ideological make-up is hybrid and changeable. Take the British Conservative Party, which was during the twentieth century the most electorally successful 'conservative' party in the world; its ideology shifted to such an extent that under Margaret Thatcher (British Prime Minister, 1979–90) it would be best described as 'national liberal'. The Thatcher government was economically liberal: it extended the use of market mechanisms in the domestic sphere, and pursued a pro-free trade policy in the international sphere, through, for example, the Single European Act (1986). But it was 'national' in that emphasis was placed on the restoration of national pride after what was perceived to be a policy of 'managed decline' in the period 1945–79. Although parties carrying the name 'liberal' tend to have a stronger social dimension, maintaining that welfare provision is necessary to enable people to live autonomous lives, social liberalism and economic liberalism are members of the same ideological family. They are not conservative.

If the Thatcher government was not really conservative, then what is conservatism? Etymology can mislead, but it is useful to start with the word 'conservative'. The idea of 'conservation' or 'preservation' suggests that conservatives stand opposed to progress. This is why the name of one of the predecessor parties to the Canadian Conservative Party – the Progressive Conservatives – seems like an oxymoron. In fact, as with compound names of many political parties, it was the result of a merger of two parties, rather than the 'progressive' being an adjectival qualification of 'conservative'. Nonetheless, even if it had been a deliberate ideological label, it is not an oxymoron: conservatives can be progressive. What is distinctive about conservatism is its attitude to progress – progress must be careful, tentative, respectful of past practices, pragmatic, and go with the grain of human nature. If conservatism has an enemy, it is 'rationalism' – an approach to political problems derived from the application of abstract concepts. Quite often conservative thinkers appear to reject abstract thought altogether, with the consequence that it is difficult to talk of a conservative political *theory*. However, it is still possible to identify features of conservative thought which allow us to describe conservatism as a distinct ideology.

## Basic Elements of Conservatism

As with all ideologies there are significant differences between different thinkers and streams of thought, but there are also some common elements, or themes, in conservatism. In this list of features we begin with the most 'philosophical' elements and gradually move to the more concrete, political ones:

1. **Rejection of 'rationalism'** Conservatives often use the metaphor of a ship at sea to explain their objections to what they call 'rationalism' (it should be noted that rationalism is a pejorative term and those identified as rationalists by conservatives would not use this label to describe themselves). You are at sea, and your ship develops a fault, which if not dealt with will result in the ship sinking. The 'ship' is the state, or the set of political institutions that make up the state, while the 'sea' is society or **culture** in the widest sense. The fault is analogous to those stresses and strains that political institutions frequently face, such as the crisis Americans faced after the 2000 Presidential Election. Rationalism would entail 'analysing' – or breaking down – the ship into its components in the hope of understanding the source of the fault and so rectifying it. The conservatives' point is not hard to discern: we cannot deconstruct the ship while at sea, but we must do something about the fault or we will drown.

2. **Experience matters** Continuing with the metaphor of the ship, our response to the fault must be based on past experience and, if necessary, a cautious process of trial and error. The 'conservatism' of conservatives rests not on an irrational veneration of the past but on a recognition of the limited nature of human reason, and for this reason conservatives can be progressive, and embrace change. What they fear are radical experiments: human beings cannot adequately predict the full consequences of their actions, and while some experiments may make the world a better place we cannot be sure that they will.

3. **Human nature** While there are some marked differences within conservative thought concerning human behaviour, capabilities and motivation, there is broad agreement that human beings are limited in their capacity to comprehend the society in which they live. This does not mean that humans are stupid, but rather that no individual mind can understand the complexity of social relations, and there is no 'super mind' which is capable of doing so. Here the conservative critique of socialism is most apparent: socialist planning presupposes a mind capable of making complex economic decisions. Socialism is doomed to failure because, first, it is inefficient, and, second (and perhaps more worryingly), it requires a concentration of power in the hands of the state. Conservatives tend to support the free market on the grounds that the distribution of goods depends on the decisions made by millions of individuals without the necessity for central control. This brings them close to the libertarian stream of liberalism but, importantly, conservative support for markets is not based on the individualist premise of moral rights to private property, but on a claim about the limits of human capabilities.

Ch 1: Liberalism, pp. 23–7

4. **Rejection of 'visionary politics'** Conservative thinker Edmund Burke famously observed that 'at the end of every vista, you see nothing but the gallows' (Burke, 1975: 344). He had in mind the visionary politics of the French Revolution (1789). Visionaries do not recognise the pluralism of everyday life – the fact that individuals have conflicting needs, desires and values. A vision implies a common project for society which overrides that pluralism. A later thinker, Michael Oakeshott, makes a distinction between society as a 'civic association' and an 'enterprise association': an enterprise implies a common purpose, whereas a civic association rests on certain rules of conduct that allow individuals to live together.

5. **Respect for institutions** An institution is a rule-governed activity. Conservatives maintain that institutions evolve, rather than being created at a determinate point in history. This may seem to misdescribe the history of many national institutions; for example, the United States and modern France had 'founding moments', and the process of decolonisation in the period after 1945 resulted in the creation of many new states. However, conservatives argue, first, that the instability of many newly created states is evidence of the importance of evolution, and, second, where institutions appear to be successful it is because they have adapted over time. The US political system is a good example – contemporary US institutions are radically different to those created by the founding fathers. The fact that many Americans do not recognise this fact, and hold that their institutions are continuous, actually reinforces the conservatives' argument: a belief in continuity, alongside adaptation, is a 'necessary fiction'. Institutions suppress the asocial tendencies of human nature, and they provide a focus for allegiance.

6. **Suspicion of authority** This feature of conservatism may seem to contradict the last one; however, to say that conservatives are suspicious of authority does not entail its rejection. What conservatives are wary of is the accumulation of state power, which for reasons discussed above is incompatible with a recognition of the limits of individuals to grasp complex social relations. Although politicians calling themselves 'conservatives' are not shy about using state power to suppress movements they consider to be a threat to social order, more reflective conservatives will argue that institutions are not abstract entities, but have to be run by human beings, who are always in danger either of abusing their position or, even if well meaning, of putting into practice policies that have unintended bad consequences. From this position conservatives can make some interesting alliances – while rejecting statements of universal **human rights** detached from a social or legal system, they nonetheless stress 'our ancient liberties' and will join forces with civil liberties groups against, for example, measures intended to combat **terrorism**.

These points are intended to provide an overview of conservatism. To get a better idea of conservative thought, and to understand its strengths and weaknesses, it is best to consider the work of particular thinkers. We focus on four: David Hume (1711–76), Edmund Burke (1729–97), Michael Oakeshott (1901–90), and Leo Strauss (1899–1973). Of the four, Leo Strauss's work least manifests the above elements of thought. However, he is an important influence on what is called 'neo-conservatism' – a term much used in current political debates in the United States – and the discussion of Strauss will allow us to assess the degree to which neo-conservatism is really conservative.

## Exercise

How valid is the metaphor of the ship to explain the nature of progress? Can you think of social and political problems that require *radical* solutions?

## Civil Liberties and Counter-terrorism Legislation

The challenge that terrorism poses to civil liberties provides an interesting example of how conservatives and liberals can join forces on a public policy issue but from subtly different perspectives. In the wake of the attack on the World Trade Center on 11 September 2001, many Western countries have introduced new counter-terrorism laws; in Britain, most controversially, this entailed internment of non-nationals on the authority of the Home Secretary (Interior Minister). That judgment was subject to a judicial review, but in secret, without all the evidence being available to an internee's lawyer, and internment ultimately being decided by the 'balance of probabilities' that the person is a threat rather than the belief that it is 'beyond reasonable doubt' that he or she is a threat. The highest legal authority (the Law Lords) determined that the law was unfair because it applied only to non-nationals, and was a 'disproportionate' response to the threat; in response the government offered 'control orders', such as restrictions on movement, instead of incarceration, and extended this to nationals as well as non-nationals. Liberals – in the wide, non-party, sense of that term – argued that the anti-terrorist laws in both original and revised versions were a violation of human rights, where rights are entitlements individuals have irrespective of their nationality. Conservatives – again, in the wide sense of the term – also attacked the legislation, but focused much more on the *erosion* of 'ancient liberties', such as habeas corpus – liberties achieved over centuries and contained in documents, such as Magna Carta (1215) and the Bill of Rights (1688).

## David Hume

Eighteenth-century Scottish philosopher David Hume is often described as the first conservative political theorist; certainly he is the first major thinker to offer a *philosophical* defence of conservatism. For that reason it is necessary to explain how Hume derives his political theory from his epistemology (what we can know) and practical philosophy (how we should behave, or what motivates us to act in certain ways).

Although their relevance to **politics** may not, at first sight, be obvious, it is necessary to set out a number of Hume's philosophical claims:

1. Human understanding must be drawn from experience. All the materials of thinking – perceptions – are derived either from sensations or from reflection. Although 'reflection' will generate complex ideas, which we do not directly experience, all such ideas are combinations of simple sensations. If philosophers use a term, such as 'cause' or **'freedom'**, then we can test whether it has any meaning by breaking the idea down to its simple sensations, or 'impressions'.

2. Simple impressions must be connected together, or 'associated'. At any moment there is a great deal going on in a person's mind, but we cannot reason if the contents of one's mind are arbitrary: we need to connect, or associate, ideas. There are three principles of association: resemblance, contiguity and causation. The last is problematic because it takes us beyond experience: Johnny throws a brick through the window and so 'causes' the window to break, but all we *see* are Johnny and his body movements, the trajectory of the brick, and the breaking window.

3. We attribute causes to events on the basis of experience and, more specifically, habit. For example, we grasp the 'causal properties' of gravity by observing falling

| Biography | **David Hume (1711–76)** |

Born into a relatively wealthy Scottish Borders family, Hume was educated by his widowed mother until, at the age of 11, he went to Edinburgh University. After leaving the university he was encouraged to pursue a career in law, but increasingly his interest turned to philosophy. As a consequence he engaged in private study, during which time he composed his three-volume *Treatise of Human Nature*, which was published in anonymous instalments (1739, 1740). That work is now regarded as a canonical text, but the lack of interest in it among his contemporaries led Hume to complain that it fell 'stillborn from the press'. The *Treatise* ranges over the central problems of philosophy, many of which have relevance to his political thought.

However, of more direct significance for politics was the two-volume *Essays, Moral and Political* (1741, 1742). In 1744–5 he was forced to withdraw as a candidate for the Professorship in Moral Philosophy at Edinburgh University in the face of opposition from the Church, which claimed – probably correctly – that Hume was an atheist.

Concerned that the *Treatise* had failed to attract attention because of its style rather than its content Hume published a single-volume 'popular' version entitled *Enquiry Concerning Human Understanding* (1748). It was based largely on Volume 1 of the *Treatise* but included direct attacks on religious belief; a rendition of Volume 3 was published as an *Enquiry Concerning the Principles of Morals* (1751), and is regarded as important in the development of utilitarianism.

Rejected by Glasgow University for a chair in philosophy, Hume used his position as librarian of the Advocate's Library in Edinburgh to pursue his interest in history; while there he wrote most of his six-volume *History of England* (1754–62).

Aged 50, in 1761, Hume was invited by the Earl of Hertford to accompany him as his secretary to Paris, where he received a warm reception. It was through French thinkers that Hume's thought percolated throughout Europe – French being the language of the educated. Returning to Edinburgh he spent his last years revising his works and eating, drinking and playing backgammon with friends.

objects. Beliefs are built on habits, but a belief is itself a sensation and not something external to experience. Although every occurrence is a simple, or unique, sensation, the observation of repetition creates an 'internal impression', or reflection.

In summary, we can say that what Hume rejects is the idea that 'reason' transcends, or goes beyond, what can be observed. To grasp the political significance of this rejection we need to consider Hume's moral philosophy. Morality is concerned with action, but not simply action, for a person's motives or 'reasons for action' are important in assessing whether an act is right or wrong, good or bad. In keeping with his emphasis on experience as the basis of knowledge, and applying it to action, Hume argues that any assessment of a person's actions, and that person's own assessment of what she should do, cannot be based on something which transcends experience. Indeed, reasoning about what should be done is itself severely limited: one can at best assess the most effective means to a given end, but the end itself is beyond assessment. If Jane wants to murder John, then reason can be used to determine the most effective means – shooting, poisoning, strangulation and so on – but it cannot be employed to assess the end itself, that is, whether Jane ought to kill John. Hume is not arguing that murder is acceptable, but rather that what stops Jane murdering John is *sentiment*: to twenty-first-century ears this word has slightly saccharine overtones, but in the eighteenth century it was an important philosophical concept. A sentiment is a pre-rational feeling towards somebody or something. Against Hobbes's theory, Hume does not believe that human beings are motivated purely by self-interest, but rather their sentiments are limited: they are concerned with their own interests, or those very close to them, such as family, but they are capable of 'sympathy', and so are moved to act in ways beneficial to other people.

Ch 1:
Liberalism,
pp. 18–23

Human beings' motives are mixed: although they are self-interested they are capable of limited sacrifices of their own self-interest for the benefit of others. And it is important that such 'beneficence' is based on a simple sympathy rather than being concealed self-interest. In Hobbes's political theory, although each person was better off under a – any – state than under no state, the absence of genuine moral sentiments made people distrustful of one another, and rendered society unstable. As does Hobbes, Hume argues that we are all better off under a state, especially a state that guarantees the protection of private property, but for Hume the very success of such mutual advantage depends on a suspension of self-interest. This observation leads to Hume's famous rejection of the social contract and, by extension, his rejection of the liberal tradition.

The social contract is a fiction: no political society was ever created by a contract. More important than Hume's historical observation is his discussion of the implications for political legitimacy of holding the view that society was the result of a contract. Political authority, or legitimacy, arises from the habit of obedience to a power that initially is recognised as neither legitimate nor illegitimate, but as simply 'given' – in legal language, such power would be termed de facto, as distinct from de jure (Hume, 1963: 462). The implication of Hobbes's argument was that any monopolistic political power was preferable to none at all, such that this distinction is invalid: whatever gets us out of the state of nature is 'legitimate'. Hume, in part, endorses Hobbes's argument for state over anarchy, but because Hume ties legitimacy to sentiment, and sentiment only develops gradually, the state acquires legitimacy after the fact of its existence (Hume, 1978: 538). And, crucially, the degree to which it is legitimate depends on how effective it is in protecting individuals' interests and engendering moral sentiments conducive to social order. While Hume rejects revolution as a leap into the unknown, the implication of his argument is that repressive, authoritarian states will have limited success in building their legitimacy.

Justice is a virtue operating in any society in which strangers come into contact with one another. The rules of justice are the product of 'artifice' and 'contrivance', and are intended to protect private property. Crucially, the rules evolve over time as people become habituated to them. We recognise that they serve our interests, but our allegiance to them cannot be reduced to self-interest, for we respect them even when it might be in our interest to break them. There develops an 'intercourse of sentiments' – a 'conversation' between citizens out of which emerges a 'limited benevolence' detached from narrow self-interest (602). Many critics suspect that moral sentiments, or sympathy, are still egoistic, for what human beings care about is that they will be held in esteem by others, and, therefore, doing the right thing is pleasurable. Hume himself seems to suggest this: 'every quality of the mind, which is *useful* or *agreeable* to the *person himself* or to *others*, communicates a pleasure to the spectator, engages his esteem, and is admitted under the honourable denomination of virtue or merit' (Hume, 1963: 277). However, pleasure is compatible with sociability in a way that self-interest is not.

## Edmund Burke

If Hume was the first great conservative thinker, then Burke must be the most famous. In part this is due to the fact that in the canon of *general* philosophers Hume is up there with Plato and Kant as one of the 'greats' but, because his contributions were primarily to the core areas of philosophy, Hume's political reflections are regarded as subsidiary. Burke, on the other hand, is not among the great general philosophers, and is regarded primarily as a political thinker (he did, nonetheless, make a notable contribution to aesthetics). Indeed, Burke was not only a political thinker, but that rarity among political philosophers – a politician.

As with Hume, the philosophical starting point for Burke's conservatism is his rejection of 'abstractions', such as the natural rights proclaimed by the French Revolutionaries in 1789. Abstractions become embodied in theories, and theories become dogma, and a dogmatic approach will not permit criticism. The political consequence of abstract thought, Burke argues, is terror. Against **abstraction**, theory and dogma, Burke defends habit, taste and **prejudice**. The concept of prejudice is the single most important concept in Burke's conservative political theory. Today, 'prejudice' is a pejorative term, so it is important to understand how

| Biography | Edmund Burke (1729–97) |
| --- | --- |

Born in Dublin to a Protestant father and Catholic mother, Burke was educated at a Quaker boarding school and Trinity College, Dublin (Dublin University).

Abandoning a legal career in favour of writing, in 1756 Burke published *Vindication of Natural Society* as well as his main contribution to aesthetics: *Philosophical Inquiry into the Origin of our Ideas of the Sublime and Beautiful*. In 1765 he entered the British Parliament; once there he made significant contributions to the debate over the Crown's powers, arguing for greater parliamentary control of royal patronage and spending. He was later to be instrumental in reforming the 'civil list', that was the money paid by parliament to the Crown. On colonial matters, Burke was progressive, arguing for recognition of indigenous cultures. Britain's taxation policies in the American colonies provoked a violent reaction, and Burke argued for more pragmatism.

His respect for India, and its Hindu society, led him to propose the East India Bill (1783), intended to control the activities of the East India Company. When that failed he sought the impeachment of the Governor-General of Bengal, Warren Hastings; the post of Governor was intended to act as a control on the East India Company, but Hastings had worked 16 years for the Company. There followed a seven-year trial (1788–95), which became a public spectacle as Burke argued his case against Hastings, and ultimately British policy in India. The culmination of the trial was Hastings' acquittal. However, it was not colonialism that was Burke's most famous target, but the 1789 Revolution in France, and it is his book, *Reflections on the Revolution in France* (1790), which is regarded as the classic statement of conservative thought. As Burke seems to have predicted the so-called Reign of Terror (1793–4), he became, unwittingly, the spokesman for counter-revolutionaries across Europe.

## How to read:

**Burke's *Reflections on the Revolution in France***

The full title of this work is *From Reflections on the Revolution in France, and on the Proceedings in Certain Societies in London relative to that Event: in a Letter intended to have been sent to a Gentleman in Paris.* The 'gentleman' in question was Charles-Jean-François Depont, a friend of Burke who sought his views on the 1789 Revolution in France. Once Burke had begun writing he realised that the topic required a literary form more extensive than a private letter, and, in fact, the real addressee of the 'letter' was an English radical Richard Price, who compared the French Revolution favourably with the English Glorious Revolution of 1688. Although the work is relatively brief there are no section breaks to help the reader. However, it can be divided into two parts. The first part, which takes up about two-thirds of the work, argues that the French enthusiasm for liberty has blinded them to the recognition that it is but one value, and indeed, crucially, only possible when balanced by other values, such as order. The second part focuses on equality, and maintains that the distribution of power between the three branches of state – executive, judiciary and legislature – had weakened political authority to the point where a military takeover was highly likely.

Burke uses it. A prejudice is a 'pre-judgement', or a judgement made without recourse to theoretical abstractions; in contemporary philosophical language we might use the term 'intuition' rather than prejudice. For Burke, the wisdom of other people, including previous generations, is a resource that must be respected if we are to avoid disastrous social consequences. The main thrust of Burke's *Reflections on the Revolution in France* is to contrast a society – France – which has abandoned prejudice in favour of 'theory', with a society – Britain – which has remained close to its traditions, to which it is prejudiced. Burke, claiming to speak on behalf of his fellow countrymen, observes:

> that we have made no discoveries, and we think that no discoveries are to be made, in morality; not many in the great principles of government, nor in the ideas of liberty, which were understood long before we were born, altogether as well as they will be after the grave has heaped its mould upon our presumption, and the silent tomb shall have imposed its law on our pert loquacity. (Burke, 1975: 84).

If Burke's view seems to us excessively deferential, it is worth considering a contemporary example of Burkean prejudice. Unless you have appropriate medical training, when you go into the operating theatre as a patient you permit people to do things to you that you do not fully understand, and to this extent you defer to the judgement of other people. But perhaps this example is a poor illustration of Burkean prejudice, because surgery is a technical skill, whereas we assume that any rational person can make a judgement, based on reason, regarding the organisation of society. Surgery is a specialism, politics is not. In the following section we discuss a more sophisticated version of this argument: Oakeshott's distinction between technical and practical knowledge.

To mid-twentieth-century conservatives, faced with what they termed 'totalitarian societies', Burke seemed ahead of his time, with the terror he predicted would follow the French Revolution being repeated in a more organised form in Stalin's Soviet Union and Hitler's Germany. However, it should be noted that Burke opposed the extension of democracy which would take place in the nineteenth century, and although there are, as John Stuart Mill observed, dangers in majoritarian democracy, the combination of civil liberties and participatory political structures – what later political scientists would term the 'civic culture' (Almond and Verba, 1963: 5–10) – has served as a bulwark against political authoritarianism. And, of course, while post-1789 French history has been complex, the Revolution did lay the groundwork for a strong liberal–democratic system.

Burke, as does Hume, rejects the liberal idea of a contract. Indeed, unlike Hume, he does not attempt to explain duty in any terms. To attempt an explanation of duty is futile, and liable to have deleterious political consequences. Furthermore, unlike liberals, Burke does not make a sharp distinction between state and society: the 'state' is the political organisation of society, and for that reason it emerges from society. Burke himself does not pursue this line, but a consequence of this argument is that the state has, for many conservatives, a role in shaping human behaviour, even in what liberals term the 'private' sphere. The irreducibility of duty to something else, and this organic state–society relationship give Burke's politics a religious cast. Although Burke was highly ecumenical in his religious beliefs – he admired Hinduism, and defended Irish Catholics – he does value religious belief and organisation, arguing that they are central to a prosperous, stable society.

Biography box, p. 42

Burke's conservatism is often misunderstood. He is sometimes assumed to be a straightforward reactionary. Yet his interventions on policy towards the American colonies, India and Ireland would suggest he was, in the context of his time, a progressive. In addition, he argued strongly for parliamentary control over the Crown. And, finally, he was not opposed to all revolutions, maintaining that the Glorious Revolution of 1688 in England was an historic achievement (although he denied the Glorious Revolution was, in fact, a revolution at all, but rather it was a reassertion and restoration of 'ancient liberties'). He also defended the American Revolution. While Burke is sometimes wrongly painted as a reactionary, there is another danger, and that is using Burke's arguments out of their historical context. Burke's famous 'Speech to the Electors of Bristol' has been quoted in subsequent centuries by elected representatives who vote in ways contrary to the wishes of their electors (as measured by such things as opinion polls). On his election as the representative for the English city of Bristol Burke addressed his 5,000 electors:

> Parliament is not a congress of ambassadors from different and hostile interests; which interests each must maintain, as an agent and advocate, against other agents and advocates; but parliament is a deliberative assembly of one nation, with one interest, that of the whole; where, not local purposes, not local prejudices, ought to guide, but the general good, resulting from the general reason of the whole. You choose a member indeed; but when you have chosen him, he is not member of Bristol, but he is a member of parliament. If the local constituents should have an interest, or should form an hasty opinion, evidently opposite to the real good of the rest of the community, the member for that place ought to be as far, as any other, from any endeavour to give it effect. (Burke, 1975: 158)

Burke's argument needs to be handled with care; he believes that parliament as an *institution* is what matters. Individuals do not have natural rights, the use of which transfers the individuals' authority on to the institution, but rather the institution has shaped individuals' rights, such as the right to vote. And this also explains why Burke was prepared to submit himself to the electors of Bristol and yet at the same time ignore their wishes if they conflicted with the collective judgement of parliament (in fact, faced with defeat at the subsequent election, in 1780, Burke decided against submitting himself once again to the electors of Bristol). When Burke is quoted today it is without adequate understanding of his conservatism; while a (philosophical, ideological) liberal may defend the idea that constituents' wishes on occasion be set aside, the reasons for doing so, and the mode in which it is done will be quite different to that of a (philosophical, ideological) conservative. For a liberal the strongest grounds for a representative to reject the majority preference of her constituents would be to defend minority rights; but, equally, a liberal would maintain that the representative should explain, or justify, her position to her constituents.

## Michael Oakeshott

Hume and Burke were, in approximate terms, contemporaries, writing as they were in the eighteenth century. We now, however, jump a century to consider the work of Michael Oakeshott. For Anglophone political theorists, Oakeshott is generally regarded as the key conservative thinker of the twentieth century. However, his philosophical position underwent a significant shift in the 40 years between his first major work, *Experience and its Modes* (published in 1933), and his last major work, *On Human Conduct* (1975). Our focus will be on one highly influential essay 'Rationalism in Politics' (1947), with a few comments on the latter book.

The 'rationalism' to which Oakeshott refers characterises Western culture as a whole, and not simply one particular ideology or party. Oakeshott's critique is not, therefore, directed solely at socialism, but at modern 'conservatives' who, in fact, are liberal rationalists. A rationalist 'stands (he always stands) for independence of mind on all occasions, for thought free from obligation to any authority save the authority of reason' (Oakeshott, 1962: 1). Oakeshott goes on to provide a detailed list of attributes of the rationalist in a florid style of writing that will attract some to Oakeshott's thought, but irritate those with a more analytical cast of mind. But then it is the analytical approach that, for Oakeshott, characterises rationalism.

The rationalist rejects (Burkean) prejudice, custom and habit, and believes in the 'open mind, the mind free from prejudice and its relic, habit' (3). The rationalist holds that it is possible to reason about political institutions, and the fact that something exists, and has existed for a long time, is no ground for respecting or retaining it. This lack of respect for the 'familiar' engenders a political attitude of radical change rather than gradual reform. Conservatives, who respect the familiar, will seek to 'patch up' existing institutions. The rationalist disrespect for institutions extends to the world of ideas; instead of a careful engagement with the complex intellectual traditions that have shaped Western societies, a rationalist engages in a simplification – an 'abridgement' – of those traditions in the form of an 'ideology' (7). The rationalist in politics is, in essence, an 'engineer', obsessed with the correct technique for solving the problem he perceives to be immediately at hand. Politics is a series of crises to be 'solved'. Because he rejects appeal to tradition, and tradition is specific to a particular culture, the rationalist assumes that there are universal solutions to problems, and that political institutions cannot

Born in Kent (England), Oakeshott was the second of three sons of Joseph Oakeshott, a civil servant and Fabian (Fabianism being a branch of, or movement within, English socialism).

He was educated at a progressive co-educational school (St George's, Harpenden), and at Cambridge University, graduating in history in 1923. He spent time at the German universities of Marburg and Tübingen.

Elected (appointed) a fellow of a Cambridge college in 1925, Oakeshott published his first major work, *Experience and its Modes*, in 1933. After serving in the British Army during World War II, Oakeshott returned to Cambridge in 1945, subsequently moving to Oxford as a fellow (1949–51), before taking up the chair (chief professorship) in political science at the LSE. He was there from 1951 to his retirement in 1969.

While at the LSE he published *Rationalism in Politics and Other Essays* (1962), as well as *The Voice of Poetry in the Conversation of Mankind* (1959). After his retirement he wrote *Hobbes on Civil Association* (1975) (he had previously written a book on Hobbes – *Hobbes's Leviathan* – in 1946), *On Human Conduct* (1975), and *On History* (1983). Many other essays and lectures have been published since Oakeshott's death in 1990. Described by one commentator, Noel Malcolm, as 'fey, almost Bohemian', with a 'complicated' love life, Oakeshott shunned the role of 'public intellectual', and turned down the offer of a knighthood.

be peculiar to this or that culture. Under the umbrella term of 'rationalism' Oakeshott places what appear to be diverse political positions, theories, projects and ideologies: the early nineteenth-century utopian socialism of Robert Owen; the League of Nations and the United Nations; all statements of universal human rights; the right to national or racial self-determination; the Christian ecumenical movement; a meritocratic Civil Service. He even goes on to list 'votes for women' as a rationalist project (6–7). We have not reproduced the entire list – it is long – but it is worth noting that it is so heterogeneous, and its items almost arbitrary, that one cannot help wondering whether Oakeshott himself is guilty of 'abridging' traditions of thought by subsuming diverse phenomena under the pejorative label of 'rationalism'. Aware of this charge, later on in the essay he maintains that rationalism, like an architectural style, 'emerges almost imperceptibly', and that it is a mistake to attempt to locate its origin (13).

In Part Two of his essay Oakeshott's argument becomes more interesting as he advances a theory of knowledge. Oakeshott distinguishes two kinds of knowledge: technical and practical (7–8). Technical knowledge is formulated into rules that are deliberately learnt, remembered, and put into practice. Whether or not such knowledge has *in fact* been formulated, its chief characteristic is that it *could* be. An example of technical knowledge is driving a car, the rules of which are, in many countries, set out in books, such as, in Britain, the *Highway Code*. Another example is cooking, where the rules can be found in cookery books. Practical knowledge, on the other hand, is acquired only in use; it is not reflective, and cannot be formulated as rules. Most activities involve the use of both types of knowledge, so a good cook will draw on both technical and practical knowledge. If you want to be a cook technical knowledge will be insufficient, for what you need is practice. The acquisition of practical knowledge requires an apprenticeship, but the key feature of an apprenticeship is not subordination to a 'master', but continuous contact with the object of the practice: it is the food that is important, not the master chef. This argument gives Oakeshott's observations a libertarian, even an anarchist, cast.

Rationalists reject practical knowledge, and recognise only technical knowledge. Because the latter can be contained between the covers of a book it seems to guarantee certainty, whereas practical knowledge is diffuse. An ideology, which is a form of technical knowledge, can be expressed in a set of propositions, whereas a tradition of thought – which is a kind of practical knowledge – cannot be. The list of features of conservatism provided in the first section of this chapter might be an example of 'rationalism', as it appears to reduce conservatism to a set of propositions, or elements (we would, however, argue that these elements were open, and fluid, and were only intended to orientate the thinker, rather than provide an exhaustive description). The certainty that the rationalist attributes to technical knowledge is, Oakeshott claims, an illusion, for technical knowledge is simply a reorganisation of existing knowledge, and only makes sense in the context of such pre-technical knowledge (Oakeshott, 1962: 12–13).

At the time of writing – 1947 – Britain, as with most other Western European democracies, was in the process of creating a relatively comprehensive welfare state, and developing more state interventionist economic policies, such as the nationalisation of key industries. The essay 'Rationalism in Politics' can be seen as part of a broader intellectual intervention. It is notable that a number of works that could be interpreted as critical of the extension of state planning, and state power, were published at this time, including Friedrich von Hayek's *Road to Serfdom* (1944) and Karl Popper's *The Open Society and its Enemies* (1945). But both of these works were clearly in the liberal (or libertarian) 'rationalist' tradition. Oakeshott observes that Hayek's book, although critical of state planning, exemplifies rationalism, for it develops one rationalist doctrine – free market **libertarianism** – in order to counter another – namely, state **socialism** (21–2). What this shows is that one can only participate in contemporary – that is, 1940s – politics by advancing a doctrine. This argument is lent retrospective force by the fact that Hayek became one of the major influences on the free market, or neo-liberal, reaction to the welfare state in both Britain, under Margaret Thatcher, and in the United States, under President Ronald Reagan. As we suggested at the beginning of this chapter, the Thatcher Government (1979–90) was really conservative, and despite the Republicans' use of the term 'conservative' the Reagan administration (1981–89) was likewise not, in Oakeshott's terms, conservative, but 'rationalist'.

Oakeshott is quite rude about politicians:

. . . book in hand (because, though a technique can be learned by rote, they have not always learned their lesson well), the politicians of Europe pore over the simmering banquet they are preparing for the future; but, like jumped-up kitchen-porters deputizing for an absent cook, their knowledge does not extend beyond the written word which they read mechanically – it generates ideas in their heads but no tastes in their mouths. (22)

Rationalism is the politics of the 'inexperienced'. Oakeshott uses the term 'experience' in a philosophical sense, meaning contact with tradition – certainly, politicians who have held office are experienced in the everyday sense of the word, but it is experience in problem solving rather than the recognition of the importance of tradition. Oakeshott argues that the history of Europe from the fifteenth century onwards has suffered from the incursion of three types of political inexperience: the new ruler, the new ruling class and the new political society. If a person does not belong to a family with a tradition of ruling then he requires a 'book' – a 'crib' – to tell him what to do. Machiavelli provided an early example, with *The Prince*. Later 'books' include Locke's *Second Treatise of Civil Government*, but in the history of rationalism nothing compares with the work of Marx and Engels, who wrote for a class 'less politically educated . . . than any other that has ever come to have the illusion of exercising political power' (26). This is a crude caricature of Marx and Engels, and indeed of their readership, although it does contain an element of truth: the recitation of doctrine can relieve people of the effort of thought.

Interesting in the light of Burke's support for American independence is Oakeshott's critique of the US political tradition. The newly independent United States had the advantage of a tradition of European thought to draw upon, but unfortunately the 'intellectual gifts' of Europe largely consisted of rationalist ideas. This, combined with the mentality of a 'pioneer people' creating political society from scratch, has given rise to a highly rationalist political system with, unsurprisingly, a powerful emphasis on legal documents, such as the Constitution. Somewhat ambivalently, Oakeshott suggests that this gave the United States an advantage; he does not develop this thought, but he might mean that the United States was eminently suited to the increasing rationalisation of domestic and world politics, and was 'on track' to become a superpower.

Oakeshott's critique is radical; indeed it is difficult from a reading of 'Rationalism in Politics' to see what political order would reconcile technical and practical knowledge. The attack on the 'new class' of politicians is so comprehensive as to imply that even Burke was insufficiently conservative. Oakeshott's argument would suggest a rejection of democracy. Since any return to a non-rationalist political project would itself be rationalist – for that non-rationalist order would have to be set out in a programme – Oakeshott's argument appears purely negative. And its negativity creates a contradiction: is not rationalism itself a tradition? This is a standard problem with conservative thought: if what matters is what exists, and if what exists is an apparently rationalist political order, then on what grounds can a conservative criticise it? The restoration of the 'old order' is not, and cannot be, a conservative project. Oakeshott's distinction between technical and practical knowledge, and the idea of an increasing predominance of the former over the latter, are interesting ideas, but they are not necessarily conservative ones.

In his book *On Human Conduct* Oakeshott presents a more 'positive' conception of politics. In that book he makes an important distinction between a civil association and an enterprise association. An enterprise association exists for, and justifies its existence in terms of, a particular end, or relatively coherent set of ends (Oakeshott, 1975: 108–18). These ends may be 'abstract', such as the maximisation of utility, or more concrete, such as the desire to maintain a particular cultural community. The enterprise association may not have a fully comprehensive set of aims – it might grant that individuals pursue different projects – but it will have some common aims.

The commonly expressed desire to 'make the world a better place' would imply an enterprise attitude, even if people disagree over the best means of achieving it. A civil association, on the other hand, is a situation of mutual freedom under the rule of law. It is more than a Hobbesian state, for it implies mutual respect, and as such is a moral conception, but it is less than an enterprise. The best way to think about a civil association is as a set of rules that command respect not simply because they serve each person's self-interest, but because they allow human beings to choose how to live their lives. Although Oakeshott appears reactionary with regard to democratic politics, his argument in *On Human Conduct* comes close to being a liberal one.

## Leo Strauss and American Neo-conservatism

An émigré from Nazi Germany to the United States, Strauss is regarded as an important influence on what is called neo-conservatism. Given the prominence of neo-conservative ideas in contemporary US political debate this makes Strauss a controversial figure and, as his ideas have become popularised, also a misunderstood one.

To understand Strauss's conservatism it is necessary to start with his approach to the history of ideas and the interpretation of texts. As we shall see, Strauss's conservatism is very different to that of Hume, Burke and Oakeshott, and it reflects the culture of both his adopted home of the United States and the history of his country of origin, Germany. After a brief discussion of Strauss's work we consider its influence on contemporary neo-conservative thought in the United States.

Strauss sought to revive both the reading of texts in the history of political thought and the natural right tradition. The relationship between *reading* and *natural right* may not, at first sight, be obvious, and even less their relationship to *conservatism*. But the three are closely entwined. Natural right stands opposed to cultural relativism. Modern thought, according to Strauss, is characterised by a rejection of objective validity in favour of relativism (Strauss, 1953: 9). The starting point for a defence of natural right is the claim that radical historicism – that is, the view that morality is the product of immediate historical circumstances – must hold at least one thing as given by nature, and that is experience. There are many definitions of nature, but Strauss identifies two relevant ones: nature as the beginning of all things and nature as the character of something. For human beings, recognition of the first must depend on authority. For example, in Judaism and Christianity, the book of Genesis provides an account of humankind's origins. A refusal to accept the authority of the Bible undermines the force of that account, and leads to disagreement about human origins. Recognition of the second – nature as the character of something – depends upon human experience. Hume exemplifies this approach: there must be a sensation in order to have confidence that a thing exists. Since moral ideas – right and wrong – cannot be observed, modern political thinkers deny their existence.

Natural right teaching, which can be traced back to the ancient Greeks, holds that the good life is that which perfects human nature – we become what, by nature, we should be ('nature' is here used in the second sense of 'character', rather than the first sense of 'origin'). The logic of natural right is that those

Biography | **Leo Strauss (1899–1973)**

Born in Kirchhain, Hessen (Germany), Strauss became a Zionist at the age of 17, and although his political and religious thought evolved his Judaism remained an important source of political and philosophical ideas throughout his life. He was educated at various German universities: Marburg, Freiburg and Hamburg.

In 1934, as a consequence of Hitler's rise to power, he moved to England, and between 1935 and 1937 held an academic position at Cambridge University. Moving to the United States in 1937, Strauss became research fellow in History at Columbia University (New York), and then lectured in political science at the New School for Social Research (1938–48). He became a US citizen in 1944. From 1949 to 1968 he was Professor at Chicago University.

Among political theorists, Strauss is regarded primarily as a historian of political thought. His peculiar method of reading historical texts has given rise to the label 'Straussian'. But among a wider audience in the United States he is seen as one of the 'fathers' of neo-conservatism. In fact, this situation has come about largely because of the influence of his protégé Alan Bloom (1930–92), whose book *The Closing of the American Mind* (1987), caused a significant impact. Strauss's best-known works are *Persecution and the Art of Writing* (1941), *Natural Right and History* (1953), *Thoughts on Machiavelli* (1958), and *Socrates and Aristophanes* (1966).

possessing the greatest wisdom should rule, and their power should be in proportion to their possession of the virtue of wisdom (102). This is incompatible with the modern – that is, post-Hobbesian – emphasis on consent: the rulers rule by the consent of the ruled and not by appeal to the rulers' superior wisdom. Strauss argues that under modern conditions the conflict can be reconciled by the rulers drawing up a code – or constitution – to which the people consent, and to which they can pledge allegiance. It is not difficult to see where this argument is heading: the recognition of the US Constitution as the expression of natural right. And that Constitution should not be interpreted simply as a framework through which conflicts are settled, but must be understood as embodying religious virtue. Commitment to a 'politics of virtue' requires the resistance of tyranny, and this has practical implications for foreign policy, which we discuss briefly at the end of this section.

Strauss links his defence of natural right with a particular interpretation of the history of political thought. Drawing on Judaic ideas, Strauss argues that when we read **pre-modern** – and some modern – political texts we must 'read between the lines' (Strauss, 1941: 490). The technical name for writing that requires this form of reading is esotericism. Esoteric writing has two levels: a popular or edifying teaching directed to a contemporary audience, and a 'hidden' or secret teaching that is only revealed on careful reading. The great political thinkers had a storehouse of literary devices that allowed them to obscure the meanings of their texts. The reason why they had to do this is made clear in the title of Strauss's

*Persecution and the Art of Writing*. Thought is the enemy of tyranny, but it can only fight tyranny in its own way, and on its own terms, and that is in a literary way. Esoteric writing survives tyranny and transmits its message between political thinkers, and to their intelligent readers, across the centuries. Quite clearly, a cultural relativist will reject this claim, and argue that the only audience capable of being moved by a writer is the contemporary, or near-contemporary, one.

Strauss died in 1973, but if you enter cyberspace and do a web search using the keywords 'Leo Strauss' you will encounter a heated debate over his influence. As with much internet debate, the subtleties of thought tend to be lost. However, it is interesting to explore the connections between Strauss and neo-conservatism. Although the term 'neo-conservative' – or 'neo-con' – is more often used as a pejorative term by its opponents than by those identified as neo-conservative it still has validity. The prefix neo- is intended to identify the movement as a distinct stream within US conservatism. It indicates that adherents are new to conservatism, but also that traditional conservatism is the subject of critique, and must be infused with new policy positions.

Many, but not all, leading neo-conservatives began their political life supporting what, in US terms, is the left: state intervention in the economy, policies to overcome poverty and the Civil Rights Movement. In demographic terms neo-conservatives are drawn disproportionately from the Jewish and the Catholic communities of mainland European origin. This is significant because traditional conservatism was perceived as dominated by the so-called WASPs (white Anglo-Saxon Protestants) and hostile to the waves of immigrants who came to the United States in the late nineteenth and early twentieth centuries. Those waves of immigrants were subjected to 'assimilationist' policies (the 'great melting pot') and neo-conservatives place great value on the idea of a common US culture against what they see as the separatist multiculturalist policies in operation since the 1960s. While many neo-conservatives strongly believe that the Civil Rights Movement was justified in its aims, they oppose affirmative action policies. Furthermore, neo-conservatives are much more prepared to support state spending if it will enable people to become responsible citizens, but this is combined with an emphasis on rewarding hard work through reductions in taxation. This twin-track approach is manifested in several key domestic policies of the Bush administration: the 'No Child Left Behind Act', which involves increased intervention by the centre (federal government) in the education system in order to improve educational standards among deprived groups; large tax cuts for the well off; and partial privatisation of the state pension system. There is a Straussian influence here: objective 'natural right' presupposes common standards and a common culture on which is based a political community that promotes virtue. The discrimination against black (and other) Americans is morally wrong, but so is what neo-conservatives believe to be the separatism inherent in **multiculturalism**. Individual initiative should be rewarded because it reflects a 'perfectionist' ideal: that is, we realise, or perfect, our nature through virtuous acts.

It is, however, in foreign policy that the influence of neo-conservatives is most keenly felt. As suggested above, Strauss argued that tyranny should be resisted, and that resistance must sometimes be in the face of widespread opposition. International institutions such as the United Nations simply reflect cultural

Ch 8:
Multiculturalism

relativism, such that a vote in the UN General Assembly or by the Security Council signifies nothing more than the balancing of interests, or cultural differences. A just **nation** must find the justification for its actions out of a reflection on natural right, and not through the support of international organisations, although it should attempt to persuade other nations to join it in a 'coalition of the willing'. What drove many thinkers and political activists from the Democratic Party to the Republicans was the perceived weakness of the left in confronting the Soviet Union in the 1970s – whereas the left sought containment of the USSR, the neo-conservatives argued for a 'roll-back' of Soviet power. In policy terms, the left supported Strategic Arms Limitation Treaties (SALT), whereas the neo-conservatives argued for an aggressive arms war so as to force the Soviet Union to spend beyond its means. Significantly, this critique of perceived weakness extended to traditional conservatives such as President Richard Nixon (US President, 1969–74) who initiated the SALT talks and also famously engaged with (Communist) China. At the beginning of the twenty-first century neo-conservatives see fundamentalist Islam as the main source of tyranny and liken the refusal of many European countries to engage with this perceived threat as a political manifestation of a deeper cultural **relativism**.

## Summary

The neo-conservatism inspired by Strauss seems a long way removed from the conservatism of Hume, Burke and Oakeshott. Given the historical distance from present events of Hume and Burke it is difficult, and perhaps intellectually suspect, to speculate on how they would respond to events in the twenty-first century, but certainly Oakeshott, who is not so distanced, would have rejected the foreign policy adventures of neo-conservatives. However, Oakeshott's work was aimed at a deeper level than policy, or even institutional design, for he saw rationalism in all spheres of social life, and in all political movements. Apart from a common emphasis on the interpenetration of state and society, and consequently the recognition that politics is concerned with the development of virtue and not simply the resolution of conflicting interests, there is little that holds the four thinkers together (and Oakeshott, in his later work, rejects the idea that politics should promote virtue). The contemporary relevance of traditional conservatism is seen less as an active ideology – party political conservatives are not really conservatives – but as an important source of ideas critical of the dominant liberal ideology. The core of conservatism is its critique of rationalism.

## Questions

1. If conservatives are sceptical about reason how can they criticise society?
2. What are the arguments for, and against, the monarchy, as it operates in the United Kingdom, the Netherlands, Spain and other countries? To what extent are arguments for the monarchy 'conservative'?

3. Under what circumstances should people attempt to overturn the existing political system?

4. 'Those who do not remember the past are condemned to repeat it' (George Santayana). Do you agree?

## References

Almond G. and Verba S. (1963) *The Civic Culture: Political Attitudes and Democracy in Five Nations* Princeton, New Jersey: Princeton University Press.

Burke, E. (1975) *On Government, Politics and Society* (ed. B.W. Hill) Hassocks: Fontana/The Harvester Press.

Hume, D. (1963) *Essays, Moral, Political and Literary* Oxford: Oxford University Press.

Hume, D. (1978) *A Treatise of Human Nature* (ed. A.L. Selby-Bigge) Oxford: Clarendon Press.

Kimberling, W. 'The Electoral College' – http://www.fec.gov/pdf/eleccoll.pdf

Oakeshott, M. (1962) *Rationalism in Politics and Other Essays* London: Methuen.

Oakeshott, M. (1975) *On Human Conduct* Oxford: Clarendon Press.

Strauss, L. (1941) 'Persecution and The Art of Writing' *Social Research* 8, 1: 4.

Strauss, L. (1953) *Natural Right and History* Chicago, Ill.: University of Chicago Press.

## Further Reading

General introductions to conservative thought and practice include: Noel O'Sullivan, *Conservatism* (London: Dent, 1976); Roger Scruton, *The Meaning of Conservatism* (Basingstoke: Palgrave, 2001); Ted Honderich, *Conservatism* (London: Penguin, 1991). Both Scruton and Honderich are quite polemical – Scruton from a 'right-wing' perspective sympathetic to conservatism, Honderich from a hostile 'left-wing' perspective. John Kekes, *A Case for Conservatism* (Ithaca, New York and London: Cornell University Press, 1998), is not an introduction but is interesting if you want a more involved defence of conservatism. There are various anthologies of conservative thought, the most useful being Roger Scruton (ed.), *Conservative Texts: An Anthology* (Basingstoke: Macmillan, 1991), and Jerry Muller (ed.), *Conservatism: An Anthology of Social and Political Thought from David Hume to the Present* (Princeton, New Jersey: Princeton University Press, 1997). In these books you will find extracts from the most important conservative thinkers, including the four discussed in this chapter. Scruton has also edited a series of essays on conservative thinkers, although, as with the anthologies, the definition of 'conservative' is stretched quite wide: Roger Scruton (ed.), *Conservative Thinkers: Essays from the Salisbury Review* (London: Claridge, 1988). Finally, a discussion of Strauss's influence on US conservatism can be found in Shadia Drury, *Leo Strauss and the American Right* (Basingstoke: Macmillan, 1997).

## Weblinks

Web searches using the key words 'conservative', 'conservatism' and even 'conservative thought' tend to throw up party political sites, or highly polemical sites. It is worth taking a look at these simply to get a flavour of how the term is used, and possibly abused, in cyberspace. However, for sites of greater relevance to this chapter we would recommend those dedicated to the conservative thinkers:

- David Hume: http://www.humesociety.org/; http://plato.stanford.edu/entries/hume/

- Edmund Burke: http://www.kirkcenter.org/burke/ebsa.html; http://plato.stanford.edu/entries/burke/

- Michael Oakeshott: http://www.michael-oakeshott-association.org/

- Leo Strauss: http://www.frontpagemag.com/Articles/ReadArticle.asp?ID=1233; http://www.straussian.net/

- Also useful is Roger Scruton's website: http://www.rogerscruton.com/ (as you will see from the Further Reading section Scruton is a prominent contemporary British conservative thinker).

# Chapter 3

# Socialism

## Introduction

Is socialism dead? This provocative point was argued by many conservatives, and the former British Prime Minister, Mrs Thatcher, in particular, after the collapse of the Communist Party states.

The difficulty in deciding whether socialism is dead is that socialism, as feminism, is bedevilled by the problem of variety. Socialism comes in many different shapes and forms. The recent Iraq War saw the British government, which would consider itself socialist, waging armed struggle along with the United States against a regime that would also call itself socialist. Do the diverse kinds of socialism have anything in common?

Can socialism be defined? Is it an impossible dream? Do more 'realistic' forms of socialism sacrifice their very socialism when they become more pragmatic? These are all questions we shall try to answer.

## Chapter Map

In this chapter we will examine:

- The problem of variety and a working definition of socialism.

- The problem of utopia as one to which socialism is peculiarly prone.

- Three nineteenth-century socialists, regarded by Marxists as utopian, but who consider their own work scientific and realistic.

- Marxism as one of the variants of socialism: Marxism is a theory that tends to authoritarianism in practice.

- The distinct character of democratic socialism or social democracy and the impact made upon British labour by the 'revisionist' theory of Eduard Bernstein.

- The link between **class** and agency, freedom and determinism.

- The argument that socialists do not have to choose between being utopian or being realistic.

# Tanks in the Streets of Prague

Soviet tanks line Atlstaedter-Ring Street in Prague early on 28 August 1968

You are studying in Prague in 1968. In the spring there is much excitement because the leader of the Communist Party argues that Czech socialism is crying out for reform. Although you feel that the changes proposed are rather modest, you see them as steps in the right direction. With the Action Programme, passed in 1968, a much freer electoral system is proposed. There is no question, however, of opposition parties being permitted.

However, you are understandably alarmed by the claims by the USSR in September that West Germany is planning to invade Czechoslovakia, and you are concerned that some communists regard the new proposals as dangerously 'revisionist'. In August of the same year, tanks roll into Prague from other countries in the Warsaw Pact (of which Czechoslovakia is a member), led by the USSR. Following the invasion Dubceck and the new president, Svoboda, are taken to Moscow and after 'free comradely discussion' they announce that Czechoslovakia will be abandoning its reform programme.

The claim is made that Dubeck intended to take his country out of the Warsaw Pact and reintroduce a capitalist society. Half a million members of the Czech Communist Party are expelled, and large numbers of writers, scientists and artists lose their jobs. It is estimated that only 2 per cent of the population supports the invasion.

Confronted with a collision of this kind:

- Would you see one side as socialist and the other side as not?
- Or would you feel that two different kinds of socialism had come into opposition?

Are the members of the Warsaw Pact who invade Czechoslovakia:

- Betraying their commitment to socialism?
- Or is this the kind of action that flows from their commitment to Marxist principles?

Is Dubcek being naive to consider himself as a communist at all? Would the notion of change that he is proposing undermine not only Soviet control over Eastern Europe but lead to the development of market forces that would necessarily destroy socialism itself and lead to the introduction of capitalism?

## The Problem of Variety

Tony Wright calls his book *Socialisms* (1996) in order to emphasise the plurality of approaches and doctrines that make up the socialist movement. The term is certainly elastic and covers a wide range of contradictory movements.

Some socialists are religious, others doggedly atheistic in character. Some advocate revolution, others reform. Nor are the alignments simple. Authoritarian socialisms may be atheistic (as in the communist tradition) but they need not be (think of Saddam Hussein's regime, which claimed adherence to some kind of Islamic tradition). Some socialists such as Tony Benn may be radical and admire the role of parliament, other socialists may stress the importance of parliament as a bulwark against **radicalism**. Still others invert this view and see parliamentary democracy as an obstacle to socialist advance.

The distinction between **Marxism** and social democracy is the major fault line among socialisms. We will use the term social democracy interchangeably with democratic socialism. The history of socialist thought is thick with accusations of betrayal. Lenin believed that social democrats were traitors to socialism because they supported World War I and opposed the Russian Revolution; socialists influenced by libertarian or anarchist ideas felt that Lenin and the Bolsheviks had betrayed the Soviet experiment by crushing the rebellion of Bolshevik sailors that took place in Kronstadt in 1921; Trotsky and his supporters felt that Stalin had reneged on the revolutionary traditions of Lenin by seeking to build socialism in one country; Mao and many Chinese communists believed that the Russians had surrendered to capitalism and the market after 1956.

see Case
Study, p. 57

These differences have deeply divided socialists. The British Labour Party repeatedly refused the request for affiliation from the Communist Party of Great Britain (CPGB) on the grounds that the latter supported dictatorship and not democracy, while communists have been deeply divided among themselves. This could come to armed conflict – as between the Soviet Union and the People's Republic of China in the 1960s, or the intervention of Vietnam into Cambodia or Kampuchea in 1978. The Warsaw Pact's interventions into Hungary in 1956 or Czechoslovakia in 1968 were intended to snuff out reform communists, and Western communists influenced by social democratic and liberal ideas called themselves 'Eurocommunists' so as to distance themselves from the Soviet system.

| Social Democracy/Democratic Socialism | Marxism/Scientific Socialism |
| --- | --- |
| Moderate classes | Eliminate classes |
| Utilise the state | Go beyond the state |
| Parliament | Workers' councils |
| Ethically desirable | Historically inevitable |
| Nation as a whole | Workers and their allies |

## Defining Socialism

It is interesting that Bernard Crick in his book *In Defence of Politics,* which originally appeared in 1963, saw conservatives, social democrats and liberals as exponents of politics – which Crick defined as an activity that seeks to conciliate and compromise. He contrasted them with nationalists, communists and extremists of various kinds. Nevertheless, despite their differences, we shall locate the common features of *all* socialists in terms of the following:

(a) **an optimistic view of human nature** – a view that human nature is either changeable or does not constitute a barrier to social regulation or ownership. The notion that humans are too selfish to cooperate and have common interests contradicts socialist doctrine.

(b) **a stress on cooperation** – all socialists hold that people can and should work together so that the market and capitalism need at the very least some adjustment in order to facilitate cooperation. Competition may be seen as an aid to, or wholly incompatible with, cooperation, but the latter is the guiding principle.

(c) **a positive view of freedom** – a notion that the question of freedom must be examined in a social context and therefore in the context of resources of a material kind. The right to read and write, for example, requires the provision of schooling if such a right is to be meaningful.

(d) **support for equality** – socialists define equality in dramatically different ways, but all, it seems to us, must subscribe to equality in some form or other. This, Crick argues, is 'the basic value in any imaginable or feasible socialist society' (1987: 88).

These characteristics explain why socialism, though a broad church, is not infinitely elastic. Dr Verwoerd, the architect of apartheid, was sometimes accused by his free market critics of being a socialist, and the Nazi Party described itself as a 'national socialist' organisation. We want to argue that although socialism stretches from Pol Pot to Tony Blair it cannot incorporate those who specifically and deliberately reject the notion of equality.

There is a further characteristic of socialism that is more contentious.

## The Problem of Utopia

All socialists are vulnerable to the charge of utopianism – of trying to realise a society that is contrary to human experience and historical development. Socialists disagree as to whether utopianism is a good thing or a bad thing. In his famous book on the subject, More in *Utopia* created the notion of a good society (eutopia) that is nowhere (utopia = no place) (Geoghegan, 1987: 1). Karl Mannheim (an inter-war German sociologist) in *Ideology and Utopia* (1936) defined utopia as an idea that was 'situation transcending' or 'incongruent with reality': it 'breaks the bonds of the existing order' (Mannheim, 1960: 173).

While some socialists have seen utopia as a good thing, liberals and conservatives regard the notion of utopia as negative – an irresponsible idealism that rides roughshod over the hard facts of reality that can at worst lead to nightmarish regimes of a highly oppressive and totalitarian kind. Heywood argues that all socialists are utopians since they develop 'better visions of a better society in which human beings can achieve genuine emancipation and fulfilment as members of a community' (1992: 96). He even extends this to Marxism where he describes communism as 'a utopian vision of a future society envisaged and described by Marx and Engels'. On the other hand, he acknowledges that the issue is controversial, since he also notes that Marx and Engels supported 'scientific socialism' and rejected what they called the 'utopian socialism' (1992: 115; 127).

Geoghegan declares himself 'in praise of utopianism' despite the fact that utopianism is characterised as a defence of an activity that is 'unrealistic', 'irrational', 'naive', 'self-indulgent', 'unscientific', 'escapist' and 'elitist'. He premises his praise on support for an 'ought' that is in opposition to an 'is' (Geoghegan, 1987: 1–2). But does this mean that socialism can never be realised? It is not clear from Geoghegan's argument whether socialist utopianism is an 'ought' permanently at war with an 'is', or whether the problem lies with the critics of utopianism who are guilty of a 'sad **dualism**': unreality, error and subjectivity on the one side; realism, truth and objectivity on the other (1987: 22). Can socialism overcome this dualism – so that it is both realist and utopian at the same time?

Bauman argues that we should view utopias positively – as a necessary condition of historical change (1976: 13). But is it possible for a utopia to avoid the charge that it is inherently unrealistic? Bauman insists that a utopia 'sets the stage for a genuinely realistic politics'. It extends the meaning of realism to encompass the full range of possible options (1976: 13). Utopias make conscious the major divisions of interest within society: the future is portrayed as a set of competing projects (1976: 15). Bauman draws a distinction between perfection as a stable and immutable state, and perfectibility that paves the way for utopia (1976: 19).

But it is still unclear whether we can ever have a society that is socialist. Bauman appears to argue that socialism is the counter-culture of capitalist society (1976: 36), and it cannot be empirical reality, a society in its own right.

Oscar Wilde commented:

> A map of the world which does not include Utopia is not worth glancing at, for it leaves out the one country at which Humanity is always landing. And when Humanity lands there, it looks out and, seeing a better country, sets sail. Progress is the realisation of Utopias.
>
> ('*The Soul of Man Under Socialism*', Complete Works of Oscar Wilde, *p. 1184, Glasgow: HarperCollins, 1996*).

## Science and the 'Utopian Socialists'

Three socialists were singled out by Engels as being utopian:

- Henri Saint-Simon (1760–1825)
- Charles Fourier (1772–1837)
- Robert Owen (1771–1858)

In fact, each of them considered their own work to be scientific and practical.

Saint-Simon took the view that the French Revolution had neglected class structure in the name of human rights. He included industrialists and bankers in the 'producing' class, believing that workers and capitalists have a unity of

Biography                    **Claude-Henri de Rouvroy Saint-Simon (1760–1825)**

The son of a minor noble, Saint-Simon was born in Paris. Privately educated, he served in the French Army during the American War of Independence. Afterwards he travelled to Mexico and Spain trying in vain to persuade the Viceroy of Mexico to finance a canal linking the Atlantic and Pacific through Lake Nicaragua.

A supporter of the French Revolution in 1789, he immediately renounced his title. He made a fortune buying and selling the houses abandoned by exiled or executed noblemen. He was imprisoned during the Terror but was released after spending nine months in captivity. He became convinced that a programme of social reorganisation was needed and moved from liberalism to a doctrine containing socialist elements.

His first book on political theory, *Letters of a Genevan to his Contemporaries,* was published in 1802. This was followed by his *Work of Science in the 19th Century* (1807), *Memoir on the Science of Man* (1813), *On the Reorganisation of European Society* (1814) and *The New Christianity* (1825). In this final work he argued that a new religion led by the most able thinkers in society (scientists and artists) would express dominant beliefs for a new industrial order.

Saint-Simon argued that Europe was in 'critical disequilibrium' and would soon undergo reconstruction. He argued strongly for a planned economy. He suggested a framework of three chambers: one body made up of engineers and artists to propose plans, a second of scientists responsible for assessing the plans, and a third group of industrialists whose task would be implementing the schemes according to the interests of the whole community.

After his death in 1825 Saint-Simon's ideas were developed by a group of loyal followers such as Olindes Rodriguez, Armand Bazard and Barthelemy-Prosper Enfantin. In 1830 the group published *An Explanation of the Doctrine of Saint-Simon*. They interpreted Saint-Simon as a socialist and argued for the redistribution of wealth for the benefit of society. Saint-Simon's theories also influenced figures such as Alexander Herzen, Thomas Carlyle and J.S. Mill.

interests, sustained by what Saint-Simon believed would be a spread of wealth and ownership across society as a whole.

Is it right to call this argument 'utopian'? Saint-Simon believed that the old order had unwittingly produced the basis for a new order, and indeed he sounds like a Marxist steeped in Hegelian dialectics when he argues that 'everything is relative – that is the only absolute' (Geoghegan, 1987: 11). His celebrated argument that the state gives way to administration (so central to Marxist theory) was based upon a belief that the modern credit and banking system had already demonstrated its attachment to scientific principles, and that these could exert a discipline that would make the **state** redundant. Why did Engels call this system 'utopian' when it so manifestly stresses the importance of science and historical necessity? Saint-Simon clearly does not fit into Engels's view that modern socialism is based upon the class antagonism between capitalist and wage worker (Marx and Engels, 1968: 399). But it does seem unfair to ascribe to Saint-Simon (as Engels does to the

Biography

## Charles Fourier (1772–1837)

Born in Besancon. The son of a cloth merchant, he was educated at the local Jesuit college. During the French Revolution he witnessed the hoarding of the merchants, and lost his patrimony. After serving in the French Army he worked as a clerk in Lyon.

In 1808 he published his first book, *The Social Destiny of Man*, where he criticised the immorality of the business world, arguing that 'truth and commerce are as incompatible as Jesus and Satan'. In the book Fourier advocated a new socialist system of cooperation, urging that 'phalansteries' should be established. These would be scientifically planned to offer a maximum of both cooperation and self-fulfilment to their members. Fourier suggested that these communes should contain about 1,600 people and should attempt to be compatible with each member's 'natural talents, passions, and inclinations'.

One of Fourier's supporters, Victor Considerant, established a newspaper in order to promote the cause. Others attempted to establish their own phalanstery. This included one at Rambouillet in France that was under-capitalised and eventually went bankrupt (1834–6). Another more successful attempt was made by George Ripley at Brook Farm in Massachusetts (1841–6).

Although no long-term phalansteries were established, Fourier's ideas influenced a generation of socialists, anarchists, feminists, pacifists, internationalists and others questioning the morality of the capitalist system. Marx and Engels used Fourier's ideas to develop their theory of alienation.

Fourier also published *The New World of Communal Activity* (1829) and *The False Division of Labour* (1835). However, his attempts to find a rich benefactor to fund a phalanstery ended in failure.

utopians in general) the view that socialism is not an 'inevitable event' but a happy accident, when Saint-Simon had laid so much emphasis on science and historical development.

Fourier, on the other hand, did consider the worker and capitalists to have conflicting interests. He was particularly concerned at the way in which the Industrial Revolution stripped work of its pleasure. His solution was to establish 'phalanteres' – cooperative communities of some 1,600 people working in areas of around 5,000 acres in the countryside or small towns. Fourier was adamant that his was not a utopian socialism. He described utopias as 'dreams', schemes without an effective method that have 'led people to the very opposite of the state of well being they promised them' (Geoghegan, 1987: 17). He believed that his socialism was based on a scientific project for **reconstruction**. Indeed, so precise a science was socialism that Fourier took the view that civilised society has 144 evils; humans have 12 basic passions; they do 12 different jobs; and need nine meals to sustain them.

As for Robert Owen: he saw himself as a practical, hard-headed person of business, and he owned cotton mills in New Lanark in Scotland. He was struck as to how under rational socialist management they could still be profitable, and he decided to advocate village cooperatives between 300 and 2,000 people working land between 600 and 1,800 acres. It is true that his schemes were dogged by

## Biography                 Robert Owen (1771–1858)

The son of a saddler and ironmonger from Newtown in Wales, Owen did well at his local school, and at the age of 10 he was sent to work in a large drapers in Stamford, Lincolnshire. In 1787 Owen found employment at a large wholesale and retail drapery business in Manchester.

With the financial support of several businessmen from Manchester, Owen purchased Dale's four textile factories in New Lanark. However, he was not only concerned with making money, but interested in creating a new type of community at New Lanark. Owen believed that a person's character is formed by the effects of their environment. He was a strong opponent of physical punishment in schools and factories and immediately banned its use in New Lanark.

One of the first decisions taken when he became owner of New Lanark was to order the building of a school, and he stopped employing children under 10 and reduced child labour to ten hours a day. The young children went to the nursery and infant schools that Owen had built. Older children had to attend his secondary school for part of the day.

In 1813 he wrote *The Formation of Character* and the following year *A New View of Society*, where he argued that religion, marriage and private property were barriers to progress. In 1815 Owen sent detailed proposals to parliament about his ideas on factory reform, and appeared before Peel and his Commons Committee in April 1816.

Owen toured the country making speeches on his experiments at New Lanark. He was, he argued, creating a 'new moral world, a world from which the bitterness of divisive sectarian religion would be banished'. Disappointed with the response he received in Britain, Owen decided in 1825 to establish a new community in the United States based on his socialist ideas. He purchased an area of Indiana for £30,000 and called the community he established there New Harmony.

By 1827 Owen had sold his New Lanark textile mills and while his family moved to New Harmony he stayed in England supporting organisations attempting to obtain factory reform, adult suffrage and the development of successful trade unions. In *The New Moral World*, published in 1834, he presented socialism in the manner of an inspirational gospel.

Owen also played an important role in establishing the Grand National Consolidated Trade Union in 1834 and the Association of All Classes and All Nations in 1835. He also attempted to form a new community at East Tytherly in Hampshire. However, like New Harmony in America, this experiment came to an end as a result of disputes between members of the community. Although disillusioned with the failure of these communities and most of his political campaigns, Robert Owen continued to work for his 'new moral order' until his death.

failure. The community that he established at New Harmony in the United States collapsed after three years in 1827, and his labour bazaars at which goods were to be exchanged according to the amount of labour embodied in them did not survive the economic crisis of 1834. His national trade union was called a 'grand national moral union for the productive classes', but his dictatorial leadership demonstrated the problem with his theory of character. Character was, as Geoghegan (1987: 14) points out, externally determined, so that only an exceptional person (such as Owen!) could initiate reform for a relatively passive population.

He had, however, a lasting effect on the British labour movement as a practical reformer, and the consumer cooperatives that he advocated – the Co-op stores – still exist on almost every high street in British cities today. Although Owen's notion of science stems from an uncritical reading of the Enlightenment, he certainly regarded himself as a person of scientific, secular and empirical values. Indeed, a youthful Engels was to describe Owen's views as 'the most practical and fully worked out' of all the socialists (Geoghegan, 1987: 23).

## Introducing Marxism

The belief that socialism should be scientific and not utopian is highly contentious. There is a terminological point that we need to tackle right away. In the *Communist Manifesto* of 1848, Engels was to explain that the term 'communism' was preferred because it was seen as a working-class movement from below. Socialism, he argued, was a respectable movement initiated from above (Marx and Engels, 1967: 62). Later Marxists called themselves socialists and social democrats. It was only after 1917 when Lenin and the Bolsheviks wanted to distance themselves from other socialists (who had supported World War I and opposed the Russian Revolution) that the term 'communist' was resurrected.

Berki has argued that Marx transformed socialism from underdog to a 'fully grown part of the modern landscape' (1974: 56). Both Marx and Engels prized scholarship and learning highly. Marx was a philosopher, who devoted most of his life to studying political economy, and in 1863 published *Das Kapital*, or *Capital*, a work that Engels was to describe as the bible of the working class. Engels, for his part, read and wrote widely about natural science, anthropology, history, politics and economics, and both regarded science not as the pursuit of facts rather than values, but simply as coherent and systematic thought.

Why did Engels in particular see Saint-Simon, Fourier and Owen as utopians? In the *Communist Manifesto* Marx and Engels praised the 'utopians' for producing 'the most valuable materials for the enlightenment of the working class'. Measures such as the abolition of the distinction between town and country; the disappearance of the family; the wages system; the private ownership of industry; the dying out of the state; and a positive relationship between the individual and society were suggested by the 'utopians' and became part of Marx and Engels's own arguments. Nevertheless, the label is contentious, for Marx and Engels clearly regarded the 'utopians' as painting 'fantastic pictures of a future society', a fantasy that reflected the historically undeveloped state of the working class itself (1967: 116).

Why then was Marxism seen as scientific? Marxism, Marx and Engels argued, is a scientific socialism, because it is:

- **a theory of class conflict** It holds that in class-divided societies there are incompatible social interests that lead to exploitation. This is why class is both an economic and a political reality, since between the classes there is war. In contrast, the utopians seek change through general principles of 'reason' and 'justice'.

Biography  **Karl Marx (1818–83)**

Born in Trier, Germany and, as a child, became a Protestant. After schooling in Trier (1830–5), Marx entered Bonn University to study law. At university he spent much of his time socialising and running up large debts. His father insisted that he move to the more sedate Berlin University.

Here he came under the influence of one of his lecturers, Bruno Bauer, whose atheism and radical political opinions got him into trouble with the authorities. Bauer introduced Marx to the writings of Hegel, who had been the Professor of Philosophy at Berlin until his death in 1831.

In 1838 Marx decided to become a university lecturer. After completing his doctoral thesis at the University of Jena, Marx hoped that his mentor, Bruno Bauer, would help find him a teaching post. However, in 1842 Bauer was dismissed as a result of his outspoken atheism and was unable to help.

Marx moved to Cologne, where the liberal opposition movement was fairly strong. *The Rhenish Gazette* published Marx's defence of the freedom of the press. In 1842 Marx was appointed editor of the newspaper, but in 1843 it was banned by the Prussian authorities.

Warned that he might be arrested, Marx moved to Paris, where he became the editor of the *Franco-German Yearbook*. Mixing with members of the working class for the first time, he now described himself as a communist. In 1844 Marx wrote *Economic and Philosophic Manuscripts*, where he developed his ideas on the concept of alienation. While in Paris he became a close friend of Engels, and they decided to work together. In 1845 Marx was deported from France and went to Brussels, where he wrote *The German Ideology*, a work not published in his lifetime.

In 1847 Marx attended a meeting of the Communist League's Central Committee in London, and this was the organisation that commissioned the *Communist Manifesto*. Marx moved to Cologne, where he founded the *New Rhenish Gazette*, which published reports of revolutionary activity all over Europe. The revolutions were defeated, the *New Rhenish Gazette* closed down, and Marx settled in Britain. With only the money that Engels could raise, the Marx family lived in extreme poverty.

Between 1852 and 1862 Marx wrote for the *New York Daily Tribune*, and in 1859 he published *A Contribution to the Critique of Political Economy*. In 1867 the first volume of *Das Kapital* appeared. Marx began work on the second volume of *Das Kapital*, but died in 1883. Volumes 2 and 3 appeared after his death, as did the *Theories of Surplus Value*.

- **a theory of revolution** Such is the incompatibility of class interests that change can only come through **revolution**. Although the *Communist Manifesto* describes revolution in violent terms, Marx's later position was that revolutions can be peaceful, even constitutional, but they will be violent if necessary. Because classes are political as well as economic entities, they seek to control the state in their own interest, so that the state has a class character. Utopians, by contrast, seek peaceful and sometimes piecemeal change, appealing to all classes in society for support, and invariably seeing the state as part of the solution rather than part of the problem.

## Biography — Friedrich Engels (1820–95)

Born in Barmen, Germany, the eldest son of a successful industrialist. Engels was sent to Britain to manage the factory in Manchester, and in 1844 he published his *Condition of the Working Classes in England*.

In the same year he began contributing to the *Franco-German Yearbook,* edited by Marx. During a six-week spell in Britain Engels introduced Marx to several of the Chartist leaders – radicals who were campaigning for universal suffrage.

Engels took part in developing a strategy of action for the Communist League, and after the revolutions of 1848 broke out helped form an organisation called the Rhineland Democrats. After the defeat of the revolutions he moved with Marx to London, and in the 1850s published *The Peasant War in Germany* and *Revolution and Counter-Revolution in Germany.* He retired in 1869 and, involved with the German Social Democratic Party, he wrote a fierce critique of a German socialist – *Anti-Dühring*. His *Socialism: Utopian and Scientific* appeared in English in 1892, a popularising work that was widely read, and in 1894 he applied his materialist method to anthropology in the *Origin of the Family, Private Property and the State*. In 1888 he wrote *Ludwig Feuerbach and the End of German Classical Philosophy* and his *Dialectics of Nature* was published posthumously in 1927.

After Marx's death Engels devoted the rest of his life to editing and translating Marx's writings.

- **a theory of history** All societies are basically moulded by the **conflict** between the forces of production (which embrace science and technology) and the relations of production (the system of ownership). These two elements form a basis upon which arises a 'superstructure' that incorporates political institutions, educational systems, culture and ideas. In class-divided societies the conflict between the forces and relations of production creates the need for revolution, so that under capitalism the social character of the forces of production come into sharp and increasing conflict with the **private** relations of production. That is why revolution is inevitable. After this revolution class divisions disappear, and with the disappearance of these divisions the need for a state itself 'withers'.

- **a theory of society** Central to this theory of history is a theory of society which argues that people enter into relations of production 'independent of their will'. This means that although human activity is a conscious activity, the consequences of this activity are never the same as those intended. Capitalism is seen as a system that unwittingly creates the working class, educates them through factory production, goads them into struggle and ultimately drives them to revolution. By way of contrast, 'utopians' do not see capitalism as a contradictory system, a system that is self-destructive. They do not accept the particular role of the workers in providing leadership to a political movement for social **emancipation,** nor do they accept the need for a communist or socialist party to provide leadership for revolution. Socialism, as far as they see it, is merely 'desirable' and not inevitable.

## The Authoritarian Consequences of 'Scientific Socialism'

In our view, there are a number of problems with the theory (and not merely the practice) of 'scientific socialism'. We would list them as

(a) the argument of inevitability – the major problem;

(b) the theory of class war;

(c) a rejection of 'moralism';

(d) the question of leadership – a relatively minor problem.

It will be argued that together these problems explain why Communist Party (CP) states following the theory of 'scientific socialism' have proved vulnerable to popular (even proletarian) protest. We have seen how attempts to make Communist Party states more democratic were resisted by the Soviet leadership in 1968 and today only North Korea, Cuba, China and Vietnam remain as CP states. Former CPs changed their names – usually to include democracy in their title – and they invariably describe themselves as socialist rather than communist. What relationship exists between the hapless fate of these states and the theory of scientific socialism? It is worth giving this question some thought.

## The Inevitability Argument

In Part I of the *Communist Manifesto* the victory of the proletariat is described as 'inevitable', as in the famous comment that 'what the bourgeoisie . . . produces, above all, is its own grave-diggers. Its fall and the victory of the proletariat are equally inevitable' (Marx and Engels, 1967: 94). This has become a central theme of Marxism in general, and Engels was to argue that revolutions are 'the necessary outcome of circumstances, quite independent of the will or guide of particular parties' (Hoffman, 1995: 135). Marxism is 'scientific' because it arises from the real movement of history that compels people to do things whether they like it or not. Revolution is (in some sense of the term) a **natural** process, driven by the antagonistic conflict between the forces and relations of production at the heart of society. It is therefore unavoidable. There are a number of problems with the 'inevitability argument'.

### What happens when revolutions are 'bourgeois' in character?

In the *Communist Manifesto* Marx and Engels declare that 'Communists everywhere support every revolutionary movement against the existing order of things' (1967: 120). Contrary to the 'utopians', who support socialism rather than capitalism, Marxists will support a 'bourgeois revolution' in countries where liberal constitutionalism has yet to prevail: in Germany, as the *Communist Manifesto* points out, communists will fight with the bourgeoisie where the latter are acting in a revolutionary way. This notion is of the utmost importance for it explains the attraction of Marxism in colonial countries or autocratic regimes of a feudal or semi-feudal kind. But what has a liberal revolution to do with communism?

One of the most contentious aspects of the *Communist Manifesto* derives from the argument that once the old absolutist regime has fallen, 'the fight against the bourgeoisie itself may immediately begin'. The argument here focuses on Germany in 1848. Given the much more advanced conditions of European civilisation and 'a much more developed proletariat', 'the bourgeois revolution in Germany will be but the prelude to an immediately following proletarian revolution' (Marx and Engels, 1967: 120). This sentence was seen by the Bolsheviks as giving the October revolution its classical Marxist credentials, since Russia of 1917 was deemed analogous to Germany of 1848, because of the combination of material backwardness and heightened political consciousness. The destruction of Tsarism – the bourgeois revolution – could then be 'the prelude to an immediately following proletarian revolution'.

Hunt has argued at some length that this formulation – which occurs nowhere else in Marx's writing – was put in to appease the members of the Communist League who commissioned the *Manifesto*. They did not like the idea of a bourgeois revolution anyway, but a bourgeois revolution immediately followed by a proletarian one was enough to sugar the pill. Hunt's argument is that this notion of permanent revolution – that a bourgeois revolution becomes relatively quickly a proletarian one – does not square with classical Marxism and the emphasis placed elsewhere in the *Communist Manifesto* on the gradual, step-by-step, education of the proletariat preparing them for revolution and power (Hunt, 1975: 180; 246). Whatever tactical considerations played their part in this fateful formulation, the argument is never actually repudiated by Marx and Engels, although they did later speak of the *Communist Manifesto* as a 'historical document which we have no longer any right to alter' (1967: 54). Whether or not we find Hunt's argument convincing, the point is that the notion that one revolution can immediately follow another has had significant historical consequences, and has come to be seen as part and parcel of Marxist theory.

The implication is that relatively undeveloped countries can become socialist or communist without the lengthy period of preparation which capitalism unwittingly and normally allows the proletariat. Since this period is precisely the one in which workers become familiar with liberal ideas and institutions, it is not difficult to see that the omission or dramatic compression of such a period can only increase the need for the authoritarian leadership of a 'vanguard' party, and authoritarian political institutions themselves. Is it surprising then that the USSR, and later the People's Republic of China, followed a development in which the liberal tradition was suppressed, rather than made the basis for further political advance?

## What happens when revolutions are 'pre-mature'?

see Chapter 4: Anarchism, pp. 86–109 and the box on p. 69

Engels told the German socialist Weydemeyer that 'we shall find ourselves compelled to make communist experiments and leaps which no-one knows better than ourselves to be untimely' (Hoffman, 1995: 135). But if revolution is deemed inevitable then Marxists will 'find themselves' compelled to support 'experiments' and 'leaps' that are not only untimely, but can only be sustained by authoritarian institutions. A good example of this problem can be seen in relation to Marx and Engels's attitude towards the Paris Commune. Because of the heroism of the Communards, Marx extolled the virtues of the Commune. This he did in a book called *The Civil War in France*, which outlined a radical polity that became the basis of Lenin's blueprint in *The State and Revolution* written in 1918.

Yet the Commune was in reality influenced by Blanquism (a rather elitist and coercive **egalitarianism** named after the French socialist Blanqui, 1805–81) and anarchist trends, and reflected what has been called 'an unsophisticated anti-bureaucratism' (Hoffman, 1995: 137) – an anti-bureaucratism that enshrined anti-liberal political practices. Despite his private reservations, Marx felt obliged publicly to support an 'experiment' that could only have succeeded if power had been concentrated in an unambiguously authoritarian manner.

### Rosa Luxemburg, the Bolshevik Revolution and Stalinism

Marx's 'support' for the Paris Commune is not an isolated example. The Polish Marxist, Rosa Luxemburg, was to defend the Bolshevik revolution in the same way and for the same reasons that Marx and Engels had praised the Paris Commune. The Bolsheviks, she argued, have acted with immense heroism: the revolution was an act of proletarian courage, and she supported it. On the other hand, she was alarmed by the authoritarianism of Lenin and Trotsky and she was particularly critical when the two leaders dispersed the Constituent Assembly in 1918, when it was returned with a socialist, but not a Bolshevik majority. She thought that the revolution was bound to fail. In fact, the Russian Revolution succeeded by crushing its opponents, and

## The Paris Commune

The Paris Commune was created in 1871 after France was defeated by Prussia in the Franco-Prussian war. The French government tried to send in troops to prevent the Parisian National Guard's cannon from falling into the hands of the population. The soldiers refused to fire on the jeering crowd and turned their weapons on their officers.

In the free elections called by the Parisian National Guard the citizens of Paris elected a council made up of a majority of Jacobins and Republicans and a minority of socialists (mostly Blanquists – explicitly authoritarian socialists – and followers of the anarchist Proudhon). This council proclaimed Paris autonomous and desired to recreate France as a confederation of communes (i.e. communities). Within the Commune, the elected council members were paid an average wage. In addition, they had to report back to the people who had elected them and were subject to recall by electors if they did not carry out their mandates.

The Paris Commune began the process of creating a new society, one organised from the bottom up. By May, 43 workplaces were cooperatively run and the Louvre Museum became a munitions factory run by a workers council. A meeting of the Mechanics Union and the Association of Metal Workers argued that 'equality must not be an empty word' in the Commune. The Commune declared that the political unity of society was based on 'the voluntary association of all local initiatives, the free and spontaneous concourse of all individual energies for the common aim, the well-being, the liberty and the security of all'.

On 21 May government troops entered the city, and this was followed by seven days of bitter street fighting. Squads of soldiers and armed members of the 'bourgeoisie' roamed the streets, killing and maiming at will. Over 25,000 people were killed in the street fighting, many murdered after they had surrendered, and their bodies dumped in mass graves.

The Commune had lasted for 72 days, and Marx, as President of the International Working Men's Association – the First International – expressed solidarity and support for the action. Yet ten years later Marx declared that the Commune was the rising of a city under exceptional conditions; that its majority was by no means socialist, nor could it be, and that with a 'modicum of common sense' a compromise with the French government at Versailles could have been reached (Marx and Engels, 1975: 318).

## Biography — Rosa Luxemburg (1871–1919)

Born in Zamosc, in the Polish area of Russia. She became interested in politics while still at school and in 1889, emigrated to Zurich where she studied law and political economy.

While in Switzerland she met other socialist revolutionaries from Russia living in exile, and in 1893 helped to form the Social Democratic Party of Poland. As it was an illegal organisation, she went to Paris to edit the party's newspaper, *Sprawa Robotnicza* (Workers' Cause). She criticised the 'revisionism' of Bernstein in her first major work, *Social Reform or Revolution* (1899).

She settled in Berlin, where she joined the Social Democratic Party, and in 1905 she became editor of the SPD newspaper, *Vorwarts* (Forward). During the 1905 Revolution she returned to Warsaw and the following year published *The Mass Strike, the Political Party, and the Trade Unions*. She argued that a general strike had the power to radicalise the workers and bring about a socialist revolution.

Her book on economic imperialism, *The Accumulation of Capital*, was published in 1913. Although she continued to advocate the need for a violent overthrow of capitalism, she took the side of the Mensheviks in their struggle with the Bolsheviks. She opposed Germany's participation in World War I, and was involved in establishing an underground political organisation called *Spartakusbund* (Spartacus League).

In 1916 she wrote the highly influential pamphlet, *The Crisis in the German Social Democracy*, and in the same year she was arrested and imprisoned, following a demonstration in Berlin. It was here that she criticised the dictatorial methods used by the Bolsheviks.

She was released in 1918 and was a founding member of the German Communist Party (KPD). In 1919 Luxemburg helped organise the Spartakist Rising in Berlin. The army was called in, the rebellion was crushed, and Luxemburg (along with Liebkneckt) was executed without trial.

Luxemburg, who was assassinated by German soldiers in 1919, never lived to see how a virtue was made of necessity first by Lenin and then by Stalin.

A whole generation of communists in liberal countries were prepared to support Stalin and Stalinism on the grounds that such rule was 'inevitable'. This position also created a grave dilemma for Stalin's critics such as Trotsky, who supported the Russian Revolution and had shown his own illiberal tendencies. Crick expresses quite a common view when he says that 'it would have made little difference had Trotsky, not Stalin succeeded Lenin' (1987: 62). Engels was to argue (in response to the anarchists) that 'revolution is the most authoritarian thing there is' (Tucker, ed., 1978: 733). A theory that regards such an event as 'inevitable' will produce despotic political practices.

## The Concept of Class War and the Problem of Morality

Let us look at the other factors that arguably demonstrate a link between Marxism as a scientific socialism and the authoritarianism that created the popular upheavals

# Vladimir Ilich Lenin (1870–1924)

Born Ulyanov in Simbirsk, Russia, he was educated at the local Gymnasium. In 1887 Lenin's brother was executed for his part in the plot to kill Tsar Alexander III, and while at university Lenin became involved in politics. Expelled from Kazan University, he studied law in Petrograd (today known as St Petersburg). In 1895 he formed the Union of Struggle for the Emancipation of the Working Class. In 1896 Lenin was arrested and sentenced to three years internal exile, where he wrote *The Development of Capitalism in Russia*, *The Tasks of Russian Social Democrats*, as well as articles for various socialist journals.

Released in 1900, Lenin moved to Geneva and became involved with *Iskra*, the official paper of the Social Democratic Labour Party. In 1902 Lenin published *What is to be Done?* in which he argued for a party of professional revolutionaries dedicated to the overthrow of Tsarism. His long-time friend, Jules Martov, disagreed, believing that it was better to have a large party of activists. Martov won the vote 28–23 but Lenin was unwilling to accept the result and formed a faction known as the Bolsheviks. Those who remained loyal to Martov became known as Mensheviks.

Lenin returned to Russia during the 1905 Revolution but after its failure he called on Bolsheviks to participate in the elections for the Russian parliament or Duma (a legislature with limited powers). In 1913 Lenin moved to Galicia in Austria, but was arrested the following year as a Russian spy. After a brief imprisonment he was allowed to move to Switzerland, where he branded World War I as an imperialist conflict and wrote *Imperialism: The Highest Stage of Capitalism*. Russia's incompetent and corrupt system could not supply the necessary equipment to enable the army to fight a modern war. Food was in short supply and in February 1917 a large crowd marched through the streets of Petrograd breaking shop windows and shouting anti-war slogans.

Attempts to close down the Russian parliament led that body to nominate a Provisional Government, and in March 1917 the Tsar abdicated. Lenin, now desperate to return to Russia, travelled to Petrograd. In his *April Theses* he argued the case for a socialist revolution and Kerensky, head of the Provisional Government, gave orders for Lenin's arrest. Lenin escaped to Finland, where he completed his *State and Revolution*, a pamphlet that made the case for soviet (or council) rule in Russia. Lenin returned to Petrograd but remained in hiding. The Bolsheviks set up their headquarters in the Smolny Institute. When Kerensky moved to crush the Bolsheviks the Winter Palace was stormed and the Cabinet ministers arrested.

In October 1917 Lenin was elected chairman of the Soviet Council of People's Commissars. Land was distributed to peasants. Banks were nationalised and workers' control of factory production introduced. The Assembly elected to draw up a new constitution was closed down, other political parties were banned, and in 1918, with German troops moving towards Petrograd, Lenin ordered Trotsky to sign the Brest–Litovsk Treaty that resulted in the surrender of the Ukraine, Finland, the Baltic provinces, the Caucasus and Poland. This decision increased opposition to the Bolshevik government and a civil war followed. This came to an end in 1918, and the following year there was an uprising against the Bolsheviks at Kronstadt. Lenin now introduced the New Economic Policy that allowed some market trading and denationalisation.

After being shot by a member of the Socialist Revolutionaries Lenin's health declined, and in April 1922 Stalin occupied the new post of general secretary. An operation left Lenin paralysed, three days after dictating a 'will and testament', in which he called for the removal of Stalin from the post of general secretary. Lenin was so rude about all the members of the party leadership that the testament was suppressed and Stalin was confirmed in post. Lenin had a third stroke and died in 1924.

How to read:

*The Communist Manifesto*

This is a relatively short work and can be found in many editions. It is crucial to use an edition that contains all the prefaces since these are an invaluable aid to understanding the *Manifesto* and placing it in historical context. Both the prefaces to the later German edition (1872) and the Russian edition (1883) were written by Marx and Engels and contain fascinating comments that throw light on the character of the state and Marxism as a theory of history. The later prefaces should certainly be skim read. Part 1 of the *Manifesto* itself should be read carefully and it contains many passages that have been quoted frequently. Part 2 is important since here Marx talks about the nature of communists and their character as a 'party'. Part 2 ends with a ten-point programme that throws important light on the relationship in Marxist theory between revolution and reform. Part 3 is somewhat dated and needs only to be skim read, but Part 4 is crucial since it contains the historically important reference to Germany and what is (in fact) the theory of permanent revolution.

in 1989. Marxism embraces a polarising concept of class war, and this can only reinforce its authoritarian consequences. Such a concept has excluded or marginalised a whole series of struggles – for women's equality, gay rights, religious toleration, ecological sensitivity, etc. – that are clearly central to the goal of emancipation, but which do not fit in with the notion that the proletariat, and only the proletariat, has a leading role to play. A disdain for moral argument encourages the view that rights do not matter since we must choose between proletarian morality and bourgeois morality.

Leadership is a problem for all political movements that seek to change society in the interests of the poor and the relatively inarticulate, since people from relatively comfortable backgrounds will tend to monopolise leadership skills. But this problem is aggravated by a belief that utopian ideals are mere fantasies. A 'scientific' attitude ought to be tolerant and empirical, but in Marxism the notion of leaders spearheading revolutionary processes that are deemed inevitable and historically necessary must give a further twist to an authoritarian version of socialism whose state and political institutions are illiberal, and – despite Marxist theory on this point – refuse to 'wither away'.

## The Dilemma of Democratic Socialism

Up until 1914 (as noted above), the term 'social democrat' was widely adopted. It was used both by the Bolsheviks and the British Labour Party. In 1914 a great schism occurred. Some socialists supported World War I, and this divide was deepened when the Bolshevik revolution took place in 1917. Although socialists generally welcomed the fall of Tsarism in February 1917 many, including those who considered themselves Marxists, saw the seizure of power by Lenin in October 1917 as the act of a madman, a coup d'état rather than a genuine revolution, a premature act that ignored the 'unripe' conditions in Russia.

From then on, the concept of a social democrat became a term of differentiation, with the emphasis on *democracy*. Socialists who opposed the Russian Revolution and subsequent Leninist and Stalinist rule invariably called themselves democratic socialists – a term we shall use interchangeably with social democrat. Socialism, it was argued, is concerned with reforms, not revolution: it must develop through parliamentary democracy, not through workers councils or soviets. It must express itself through electoral victory, not a seizure of power: nor should socialists tie themselves to the leadership of the working class. Socialism involves the whole nation – not simply a part of it – and socialism must be realistic, attained through piecemeal reforms and in a manner that works with, and respects, the liberal tradition. As the French socialist Jean Jaures put it, 'the great majority of the nation can be won over to our side by propaganda and lawful action and led to socialism' (Berki, 1974: 91–2).

Social democracy sees itself as everything that Marxism is not: democratic, reformist, realistic, open-minded and concerned with the moral case for socialism. What is its dilemma? It is so anti-utopian that it is vulnerable to the charge that it is no different in essence from liberalism and even more flexible versions of conservatism. Is it a movement in its own right? Berki makes the point that just as in Aristotle aristocracy can turn into its degenerate form, oligarchy, so social democracy can turn into its degenerate form, which is electoralism (1974: 104), i.e. a concern to win elections without worrying about principles at all.

In other words, social democracy suffers from a serious **identity** problem. It is so pragmatic and flexible, so concerned with avoiding divisiveness and outraging, as Durbin puts it, 'the conservative sections of all classes' (Berki, 1974: 103), that it becomes a form of conservatism itself (or liberalism), and cannot be called socialism at all. Socialism, we have argued, is vulnerable to the charge of utopianism: but a forthright rebuttal of utopianism of any kind may mean that the transformative element in socialism is lost, and socialism 'degenerates'.

## Eduard Bernstein and the German Socialists

Eduard Bernstein is a significant figure to examine, for his critique of classical Marxism formed the theory and practice of what came to be called social democracy. He influenced a tradition that was resistant to theory. In his work, social democracy is not only contrasted explicitly and in detail to Marxism, but its own premises are lucidly displayed. Indeed, the book that has the English title *Evolutionary Socialism* was actually called (if one translates the German directly) *The Premises of Socialism and the Task of Social Democracy*.

Bernstein joined the German Socialists in 1872. When the warring groups united the party went from electoral success to electoral success. In 1876 it won 9 per cent of the votes cast (Gay, 1962: 38–9). Bismarck, the German chancellor, used the attempt to assassinate the Emperor (not, it should be said, by socialists) to harass the party. Bernstein, who was in Switzerland at the time, became converted to Marxism.

Despite the problems caused by Bismarck's anti-socialist law (which only lapsed in 1890), the party polled 12 per cent of the vote in the elections of 1881 (Gay, 1962: 52). In 1884 the party sent 24 members to the Reichstag – the German parliament. Under renewed pressure from Bismarck Bernstein was forced to leave

Switzerland, and went to London. In 1890 the party secured nearly 20 per cent of the vote in the national elections and increased its number of MPs to 35. By 1903 the SPD had 81 seats in parliament (Gay, 1962: 230).

## Bernstein, Revisionism and the British Tradition

Engels, who died in 1895, had already expressed his concern over Bernstein's enthusiasm for the Fabians – British socialists who explicitly rejected Marxism and named themselves after the Roman emperor Fabius, famed for his step-by-step approach to fighting war. Engels was to accuse the Fabians (whose society was established in London in 1874) of 'hushing up the class struggle' (Gay, 1962: 106). Bernstein was impressed by the tolerance and liberalism he found in London, so much so that Karl Kautsky, then the great champion of Marxist orthodoxy, was to declare Bernstein 'a representative of English socialism' (Gay, 1962: 80).

In 1899 Bernstein wrote his *Evolutionary Socialism* – described as the 'bible of revisionism'. Bernstein had been asked by Engels to be one of the executors of the Marxist papers, and Bernstein was reluctant to accept that he had – in the theological jargon which Marxists embrace – 'revised' Marxism. He argued that his critique was a way of further developing Marxism: he was not destroying Marxism since, as he put it, 'It is Marx who carries the point against Marx' (Bernstein, 1961: 27). But what he argued was certainly explosive, and a different kind of socialism emerged in his critique.

## Bernstein's Argument

Bernstein's views are as follows:

- Small and medium-sized enterprises were proving themselves viable. Hence members of the possessing classes were increasing, not diminishing (Bernstein, 1961: xxv). Society was not becoming more simplified (as the *Manifesto* declared) but more graduated and differentiated (1961: 49). Moreover, the constantly rising national product was distributed, albeit unequally, over all segments of the population, so that the position of the worker was improving (1961: 207). In agriculture, the small and medium landholding was increasing, and the large and very large decreasing (1961: 71).
- Bernstein followed the Fabians by arguing that the idea of value or surplus value in Marxist theory was unnecessary. Depressions are becoming milder. Modern banking and the internationalisation of trade create adjustment and flexibility in capitalism – not breakdown.
- He saw Marx's emphasis on dialectics (the world consists of opposing forces) as a snare, uncritically taken over from Hegel. Why not assume that cooperation is just as important as struggle? Socialism must be based on the facts, and it is a fact that there is compromise and cooperation between the classes.
- Ethical factors, in Bernstein's view, create much greater space for independent activity than was seen to be the case in classical Marxism (1961: 15). The notion of inevitability – a fusion of what is and what ought to be – must be decisively

rejected. 'No ism is a science' (Gay, 1962: 158). Socialism is about what is ethically desirable: science is about what is.

- Democracy, for Bernstein, is 'an absence of class government' – it avoids both the tyranny of the majority and the tyranny of the minority. Democracy is the high school of compromise and moderation (1961: 142–4). The notion of the 'dictatorship of the proletariat' has become redundant. Socialism seeks to make the proletarian into a citizen 'and to thus make citizenship universal' (1961: 146).

- Socialism, declared Bernstein, is 'the legitimate heir' to liberalism 'as a great historical movement' (1961: 149). There is no really liberal thought that does not also belong to socialism. Industrial courts and trades councils involve democratic self-government (1961: 152). Socialism is 'organising liberalism' and requires the constant increase of municipal freedom (1961: 159). He was devoted to liberal parliamentarism (1961: 299) and, if this parliamentarism becomes excessive, the antidote is local self-government.

- The SPD must fight for all those reforms that increase the power of the workers and give the state a more democratic form (Gay, 1962: 225). Bernstein described the SPD as a 'democratic-Socialist reform party'. Hence the trade unions, far from being schools for socialism (in Marx's revolutionary sense), were concerned with practical and non-revolutionary improvements. Trade unions are, declared Bernstein, 'indispensable organs of democracy' (1961: 139–40).

- He linked the practicality of trade unions with the empirical orientation of the cooperative movement (1961: 204). The class struggle continues, but it is taking ever-milder forms. Cooperatives, particularly consumer co-ops, encourage democratic and egalitarian forms of management.

Bernstein exemplifies the dilemma of democratic socialism. How can the social democratic party navigate between what Gay called the Scylla of impotence and the Charybdis of betrayal of its cause (1962: 302)? How can it be 'realistic' and yet remain socialist?

## The British Labour Party and the Fabians

The British Labour Party has never been a party of theory. Although its members (and some of its leaders!) may not even have heard of Bernstein, it is Bernsteinism that provides the underpinning for its practice.

We have already mentioned the importance of the Fabians. The Fabian Society became a kind of think tank for the Labour Party. The Fabians were influenced by the same kind of theories that so appealed to Bernstein – empiricism, a philosophy which argues that our knowledge comes through the observation of 'facts' – and a belief in piecemeal reform through parliamentary democracy. Socialism was not a philosophy for life, but a highly focused doctrine that concerns itself with the organisation of industry and the distribution of wealth. Examine Fabian pamphlets today and what do you find? Specific proposals on organising the Civil Service, the health service, tax reforms, social security benefits, European Monetary Union, and the like. Beatrice Webb (1858–1943), who played a key role in the Fabian Society and in the formation of the Labour Party, took the view that the whole nation was sliding into social democracy.

## The Labour Party, Constitutionalism and the Trade Unions

The Labour Representative Committee in 1900 was formed by trade unions. These unions felt that they needed a political voice and would cooperate with any party engaged in promoting legislation 'in the direct interest of labour' (Miliband, 1973, 19). The Liberal Party did not oppose the two Labour candidates who won their seats in 1900.

After the formation of the Labour Party in 1906, a Trades Dispute Act was passed that strengthened the right of unions to strike, while the Trade Union Act of 1913 allowed the trade unions to affiliate to the Labour Party. Ramsay MacDonald, the party leader, made it clear that political weapons are to be found in the ballot box and the Act of Parliament – not in collective bargaining (Miliband, 1973: 35).

The party itself received a constitution in 1918 and the famous Clause IV that spoke of common ownership of the means of production was (rather cynically) inserted by the Webbs to give the party some kind of ideological distance from the Conservatives and the Liberals. Sidney Webb would, Tony Blair commented in 1995, be astonished to find that the clause was still in existence some 70 years later (1995: 12). It was not intended, Blair argued, to be taken seriously.

The 1922 programme made it clear that Labour stood for neither Bolshevism nor Communism, but 'common sense and justice' (Miliband, 1973: 94). It is true that it suited the Liberals and Conservatives to present, in Churchill's words, Labour as 'the party of revolution' (Miliband, 1973: 99), but in fact Labour's politics were always of a liberal and constitutional nature. It is revealing that during the crisis of 1936, when MacDonald was expelled from the Labour Party for entering into a national government with the Conservatives, the Tory leader, Sir Herbert Samuel, argued that it would be in the general interest if unpalatable social measures to deal with the economic crisis could be imposed by a Labour government (Miliband, 1973: 176). In the 1930s the Labour leadership was opposed to the Popular Front government in Spain, and contributed significantly to the appeasement of the extreme right.

see Chapter 4:
Anarchism,
pp. 86–109

Although the right-wing publicist Evelyn Waugh saw the country as under occupation after the Labour electoral victory of 1945, in fact Morrison made it clear that the socialisation of industry would only work 'on the merits of their specific cases. That is how the British mind works. It does not work in a vacuum or in abstract theories' (Miliband, 1973: 279). There is a clear link between Sidney Webb's statement to the Labour conference of 1923 that the founder of British socialism was not Karl Marx but Robert Owen – the doctrine underlying the Party is not that of class war but human brotherhood – and Harold Wilson's comment at the 1966 conference that no answers are to be found in Highgate cemetery (i.e. where Marx is buried) (Miliband, 1973: 98; 361).

## Blair's Socialism

The position of Tony Blair follows this tradition of pragmatism, moralism and constitutionalism. Indeed Blair makes it clear that the elimination of the old Clause IV was to facilitate a return to Labour's ethical roots (Wright, 1996: x). We must

## Biography — Eduard Bernstein (1850–1932)

Born in Berlin. The son of Jewish parents, his father was a railroad engineer. Bernstein worked as a bank clerk and in 1872 he joined the Social Democrat Party (SDP). In the 1877 general election in Germany the SDP won 12 seats. This worried Bismarck, and in 1878 he introduced an anti-socialist law that banned party meetings and publications.

After the passing of the anti-socialist law Bernstein emigrated to Switzerland, where he became editor of the underground socialist journal *Der Sozialdemokrat*. After being expelled from Switzerland he moved to England where he worked closely with Engels and members of the Fabian Society.

While living in London Bernstein gradually became convinced that the best way to obtain socialism in an industrialised country was through trade union activity and parliamentary politics. He published a series of articles where he argued that the predictions made by Marx about the development of capitalism had not come true. He pointed out that the real wages of workers had risen and the polarisation between an oppressed proletariat and oppressive capitalist class had not materialised. Nor had capital become concentrated in fewer hands.

Bernstein's revisionist views appeared in his extremely influential book *Evolutionary Socialism* (1899). His analysis of modern capitalism undermined the claims that Marxism was a science and upset revolutionaries such as Lenin and Trotsky. In 1901 Bernstein returned to Germany. This brought him into conflict with the left wing of the SDP which rejected his 'revisionist' views as to how socialism could be achieved. Socialists such as Bebel, Kautsky, Liebkneckt and Luxemburg still believed that a Marxist revolution was possible.

Bernstein was elected to the Reichstag (1902–6 and 1912–18) where he led the right wing of the SDP. However, he sided with the left wing over Germany's participation in World War I and in 1915 voted against war credits.

In April 1917 Bernstein worked with Kautsky and Hilferding to form the Independent Socialist Party. After the war he joined the leadership of the SDP in condemning the attempted seizure of power by the communists. In the government formed by Ebert, Bernstein served as secretary of state for economy and finance.

Elected to the Reichstag in 1920 Bernstein opposed the rise of the extreme right and made several powerful speeches against Hitler and the Nazis.

retain, he argues, the values and principles underlying democratic socialism but apply them entirely afresh to the modern world (Blair, 1992: 3).

The values of democratic socialism are 'social justice, the equal worth of each citizen, equality of opportunity, community'. Socialism is, if you will, social-ism (Blair, 1994: 4). In the 50th anniversary lecture of the 1945 Labour victory, Blair describes socialism as 'the political heir of radical liberalism' (1995: 8). He sees the New Liberals as social democrats, and he defines socialism as a form of politics through which to fight poverty, prejudice and unemployment, and to create the conditions in which to build one nation – tolerant, fair, enterprising and inclusive. Socialists have to be both moralists and empiricists. They need, on the one hand, to be concerned with values, but at the same time they must address themselves to a world as it is and not as we would like it to be (Blair, 1995: 12–13).

## International Social Democrats

These notions have been internationally endorsed. The German SPD has sternly repudiated communism, and in its Bad Godesburg Resolution of 1959 – described by Berki as 'one of the boldest, most impressive "liberal" party manifestoes ever written' – it argues for competition where possible, planning 'as far as it is necessary'. It follows what the Swedish social democrats have called a 'matter-of-fact conception of man' (Berki, 1974: 98–9).

These comments capture the dilemma. Berki suggests that in a way social democracy can be characterised as 'utopian socialism minus utopian expectations', since it does not believe that ideals such as justice, goodwill, brotherliness and compassion could be 'unreservedly realized' (1974: 101). Is social democracy so pragmatic and flexible that it cannot be called socialism at all?

## Can Marxism be Rescued?

The idea of communism as a 'scientific socialism' does, indeed, lead to authoritarianism. But this is not because communism aims to create a classless and stateless society. Rather it is because Marxist theory embraces elements that make it impossible for the state to 'wither away'.

Of the problems that need to be tackled if Marxism is to made credible, the first is discussed below.

## The Notion of Revolution

The concept of revolution as a dramatic element focused around a seizure of power is problematic. Marx uses the term revolution in different ways. He and Engels speak in the *Communist Manifesto* of the constant 'revolutionizing of production' under capitalism (1967: 83) and in that sense, revolutions are occurring all the time. But revolution is also used to denote a transformation of state and class power – an event in which the character of society as a whole changes.

It is true that Marx was to argue that such an event did not have to be violent, and he even puts the view in 1882 that if in Britain 'the unavoidable evolution' turns into a revolution, that would not only be the fault of the ruling classes but also of the working class. Every peaceful concession has been wrung out through pressure, and the workers must wield their power and use their liberties, 'both of which they possess legally'. That suggests that each step forward is a kind of revolution in its own right, and that the notion of revolution as a dramatic event which inevitably changes the character of society is redundant (Hoffman, 1975: 211).

But this is not typical of Marx's view. The notion of revolution as a dramatic event linked to a seizure of power was, it seems to us, inherited uncritically from the French Revolution of 1789. It creates a polarisation that makes the assertion of common interests and consensus more, not less, difficult. Engels is right: revolutions are authoritarian events, and they create a new state that clearly distinguishes between revolution and counter-revolution, and this leads to the kind of insecurity and division that generates despotism rather than democracy.

## The Inevitability Problem and the Liberal Tradition

Clearly the notion of revolution as inevitable creates the problem of supporting revolutions that generate authoritarian states, and the consequent abuse of human rights. A scathing attitude towards morality can only aggravate the problem. But it does not follow from this that all elements of Marxism are authoritarian in orientation. Here the attitude towards **liberalism** is crucial. Not only did Marx begin his political career as a liberal steeped in the ideals of the European Enlightenment, but when he becomes a communist, he seeks to go beyond rather than reject liberal values.

The distinction between 'transcending' and 'rejecting' liberalism is crucial to our argument. To transcend liberalism is to build upon its values and institutions: it is to develop a theory and practice that extends freedom and equality more consistently and comprehensively than liberalism is able to do. Socialism as a **'post-liberalism'** seeks to turn liberal values into concrete realities so that those excluded by classical liberalism – the workers, the poor, women, dependants – become free and equal, as part of an historical process that has no grand culminating moment or climax. Socialism as a 'pre-liberalism', on the other hand, negates liberal values by introducing a system that imposes despotic controls upon the population at large (whatever its claim to speak in the name of the workers), and it is well described in the *Communist Manifesto* as a reactionary socialism because it hurls 'traditional anathemas' against liberalism and representative government (Marx and Engels, 1967: 111).

The problem with Marxism is that it is an amalgam of pre- and post-liberalism. It is post-liberal insofar as it stresses the need to build upon, rather than reject, capitalist achievements. But while (conventionally defined) revolutions make sense in situations in which legal rights to change society are blocked, in societies that have, or are attempting to build, liberal institutions, revolutions lead to elitism, despotism and a contempt for democracy. The notion of class war does not place enough emphasis on the need to create and consolidate common interests, to campaign in a way that isolates those who oppose progress.

Again there is a tension here in Marx's writings between his view that a classless society will eliminate alienation for all, and his argument that the bourgeoisie are the 'enemy' who must be overthrown. This leads to the privileging of the proletariat as the agent of revolution, and hostility to all who are not proletarians.

## The Question of Class and Agency

Socialists are right when they see class as something that is negative; freedom for all, as Marxism argues, is only possible in a classless society. Class privileges come at the expense of others. In liberal societies class encourages an abstract approach to be taken to equality and power so that formal equality coexists with the most horrendous inequalities of **power** and material resources. Class is thus divisive, and it generates the kind of antagonisms that require **force** (and therefore the state) to tackle them.

For this reason Marx is right to argue that if we want to dispense with the need for an institution claiming a monopoly of legitimate force we must dispense with classes. In a well-known comment, Marx argues that in class-divided societies social relations are not 'relations between individual and individual, but between worker and capitalist, between farmer and landlord, etc. Wipe out these relations and you annihilate all society' (Marx and Engels, 1976: 159). But this comment is not concrete enough. For workers also have a gender and national identity, etc., and this materially affects how they relate to others. It is not that the class identity is unimportant: it is rather that it fuses with other identities since these other identities are also a crucial part of the process that creates class. Brown argues that class has become invisible and inarticulate, rarely theorised or developed in the multiculturalist mantra, 'race, class, gender, sexuality' (1995: 61). The point is that we do not need to present these other identities as though they are separate from class.

In our view, class is only *seen* in 'other' forms. Thus we are told (*Independent*, 8 May 2003) that whereas 4.5 per cent of white British men (aged 16–74) are unemployed, this figure rises to 9.1 per cent for men of Pakistani origin, 10.2 per cent of Bangladeshis and 10.4 per cent of Afro-Caribbean men. There are not simply two sets of figures here (black and Asian men *and* unemployment): rather it is that unemployment is integral to the discrimination from which black and Asian men suffer. Class only becomes visible through the position of women, gays, ethnic minorities etc. The diversity of form in which classes express themselves is of the utmost importance, and it is the reason why no particular group should be privileged over any other in the struggle to achieve a classless and stateless society.

Socialists must, in other words, seek to mobilise all those who are excluded by contemporary institutions. This goes well beyond the concept of a 'proletariat', although those who are poor and have to subject themselves to the 'despotic' rules of employers are an obvious constituency in the struggle to govern one's own life. It is impossible to be free and equal if one is subject to aggressive pressures from employers and managers. Democratising the workplace to allow greater security, transparency and participation is critical, and all those who suffer from these problems are natural constituents in the struggle for socialism.

But the point is that we cannot exclude the wealthy and the 'beneficiaries' of the market and state from the struggle for socialism even though it would be foolish and naive to assume that the 'haves' will be enthusiastic proponents for a socialist future! Nevertheless, it has to be said that those who drive cars (however rich they are) are still vulnerable to the health problems associated with pollution. They suffer the nervous disorders linked to congestion and frustration on the roads. Inequalities and lack of social control, whether within or between societies, make everyone insecure, and result in a futile and wasteful use of resources. Wealthy people who try to 'buy' peaceful neighbourhoods are seeking to escape from problems that will inevitably affect them too.

Take another issue. It is becoming increasingly clear to 'establishments' in advanced industrial countries that if nothing is done about the divisions within the international community then liberal traditions will be eroded as refugees move around the globe.

## Ideas and Perspectives:

# The Problem of Determinism and Free Will

Bauman has argued that utopianism is compatible with everything but determinism (1976: 37), and in his hostility to utopianism Marx sometimes gives the impression that he does not believe in free will. When he speaks of his theory of history as one in which people enter into relations 'independent of their will', does this mean that people have no will? What it means, it seems to us, is that what people intend (i.e. humans are beings with purpose and thus will) is never quite the same as what actually happens.

Take the following assertion of Marx's. The capitalist and landlord are 'the personifications of economic categories, embodiments of particular class interests and class relations' so that his or her standpoint can 'less than any other' make the individual 'responsible for relations whose creature he socially remains, however much he may subjectively raise himself above them' (1970: 10). This comment seems to suggest that our will cannot transform circumstances, and therefore we cannot create new relations. Yet Marx's third thesis on Feuerbach had already stated (against mechanical materialism which saw people as passive and lacking in agency) that the changing of circumstances and human activity coincide as 'revolutionary practice' (again – an identification of revolution with ongoing change, not a dramatic one-off event!). This, it seems to us, is the answer to the problem of determinism and inevitability. If we assume that determinism negates free will and that we need to make a choice between them, then clearly determinism is a problem for socialism. For how can we change society if we do not have the will to do so? But what if we go beyond such a 'dualism' and argue merely that determinism means that free will always occurs in the context of relations? Why is this concept of determinism a problem?

Circumstances determine our capacities. Our capacity to change circumstances involves recognising these circumstances and making sure that we correctly appraise their reality. To successfully strengthen the struggle for socialism we need to attend to movements within our existing society which demonstrate that we can regulate our lives in ways which increase our capacity to get the results we want – whether it is in terms of transport policy, cleaning up the environment or giving people greater security and control in the workplace.

Whether these reforms or 'revolutionising activities' are effective depends upon how carefully we have assessed the circumstances that determine the context and the event. This kind of determinism does not undermine free will: on the contrary, it makes it possible to harness free will in a sensible and rational manner. If Marx is suggesting that there was a 'dualism' between free will and determinism, he would simply be turning classical liberalism inside out and not going beyond it. Classical liberalism argues for a notion of freedom independent of circumstances and relationships, and socialists might find it tempting (since they are critical of liberalism) to take the view that since circumstances determine the way people are, therefore people have no freedom or will-power. But if this was the position of socialists like Robert Owen (Hoffman, 1975: 139), arguably it was not the position of Marx's 'new' materialism, even though he and Engels sometimes gave the impression that it was.

We will *all* suffer as a consequence. The British government has just announced measures to place terrorist suspects under 'house arrest'. Although the victims of crime in, say, contemporary South Africa are predominantly the poor who live in the shanty towns, this scourge does not simply affect those who are on the margins of society. Everyone can be the victim of crime. Socialism – making people conscious that they are living in society and that everything they do affects (and may harm) others – is, it could be argued, in everyone's interests. There is an interesting parallel here with measures taken to combat cholera in nineteenth-century British cities. The disease was no respecter of class or wealth: it was in everyone's interests that it was eradicated. What is the point of having wealth and power if your health is devastated?

Marxists might argue that, with divisiveness in the world growing through a kind of globalisation which increases inequality, the notion of a proletariat must be viewed internationally rather than simply nationally. But the danger still remains that such a perspective will take a narrow view of class and underplay the problem of cementing common interests across the globe.

## Socialism and Inevitability

Marx sometimes makes it seem that socialism will arrive come what may. He speaks of 'the natural laws of capitalist production' 'working with iron necessity towards inevitable results', and in a famous passage he likens the birth of socialism to pregnancy (Marx 1970: 10). The development of socialism is as inevitable as the birth of a child. This argument is, however, only defensible as a *conditional* inevitability – not an absolute certainty independent of circumstances. In the *Communist Manifesto* Marx and Engels comment that class struggle might end 'in a revolutionary constitution of society at large' or 'the common ruin of the contending classes' (Marx and Engels, 1967: 79). Not only is it impossible to establish a timescale for socialism, but its inevitability is conditional upon, for example, humanity avoiding a nuclear conflagration that wipes out humans, or the destruction of the environment which makes production impossible. Nor can it be said that liberal societies might not turn to the right before they turn to the left.

What a conditional inevitability merely states is that if humanity survives then sooner or later it will have to regulate its affairs in a socially conscious manner, and that, broadly speaking, is socialism. Only in this qualified and conditional sense can it be said that socialism is inevitable. Marxism can be rescued if it makes it clear that 'inevitability' is conditional, drops a notion of revolution as a concentrated political event and, with it, a polarised and narrow notion of class. Whether it would still be Marxism is a moot point.

## The Problem of Utopianism

We have argued that a credible socialism must draw upon social democratic *and* Marxist ideas. The problem with 'pure' social democrats as well as 'pure' Marxists is that they can be said to either embrace a (liberal) empiricist framework or they simply turn such a framework inside out.

Bernstein is a case in point. On the one hand, he saw himself as a positivist who stuck rigorously to the facts. On the other hand, since he was living in a society that was clearly not socialist, socialism is, he tells us, a piece of the beyond – something which ought to be, but is not (Gay, 1962: 158; 163). Abstract 'realism' coexists with abstract utopianism. The role of ethics is not integrated into a concern with the facts, and Marck has pointed out that such a theory can pay too much attention to 'short-run developments', ruling out in a dogmatic fashion dramatic and unanticipated actions, 'apparently contradicted by the happenings of the day' (Gay, 1962: 162).

Bernstein's position on economic concentration bears this out. As Gay comments, after 1924 German industry centralised and cartelised as never before (1962: 172). The trends he analysed in 1899 were not irreversible. In the same way Bernstein assumed that a new middle class would be democratic and pro-socialist. Yet anyone who knows anything about German history after World War I, comments Gay, 'will recognize the fallacious assumptions of Bernstein's theory'. Inflation and the world depression traumatised large groups within the German middle classes: they saw descent into the proletariat as a horrendous possibility (1962: 215). Bernstein's analysis put into the context of Germany between the wars turned out to be wishful thinking. Whether government through a representative parliament can work depends upon the social structure and political institutions of a country – it allows no dogmatic answer (Gay, 1962: 236).

Once we see that reality is in movement, then we can fuse utopia and realism. Utopia derives from the transformation of existing realities: but this utopia is not to be located outside existing realities, it is part of them. In arguing that socialism must be a 'utopian realism', we avoid the dualism between facts and values, utopia and reality, a dualism that bedevils so many exponents of socialism, whether of the right or the left. Bernstein's argument that socialists should always avoid violence is right under some circumstances. But it could hardly apply when the Hitler leadership in Germany destroyed parliamentary institutions and embraced fascism.

As will be argued in Chapter 4 (Anarchism), we need a state as long as humanity cannot resolve its conflicts of interest in a peaceful manner. For Bernstein, because the state exists, it is here to stay. The 'so-called coercive associations, the state and the communities, will retain their great tasks in any future I can see' (Gay, 1962: 246). But to identify the state with community, and regard its mechanisms for settling difference as only apparently 'coercive', shows how far 'pure' social democracy is still steeped in the abstract aspects of the liberal tradition.

Gay is surely right when he comments that Bernstein's optimism was not well founded: it took short-run prosperity and converted it into a law of capitalist development (1962: 299). If, as A.J. Taylor has said, Marx was a dogmatic optimist (Marx and Engels, 1967: 47), so was Bernstein. Socialism requires a conditional concept of inevitability and a 'dialectical' determinism – one that takes full account of human agency – so that it is neither 'optimistic' nor 'pessimistic' but a utopian realism.

## Summary

Socialism is certainly a 'broad church', but underlying its numerous forms is a concern with cooperation and equality, a belief that human nature can change and that freedom requires an adequate provision of resources. Socialism is peculiarly prone to the problem of utopianism because it seeks to establish a society that differs from the world of the present.

The work of Saint-Simon, Fourier and Robert Owen demonstrates that socialists who were labelled 'utopian' by their Marxist critics did not regard themselves in this light. Marxism is a variant of socialism that leads to authoritarianism insofar as it emphasises an unconditional inevitability, has a particular notion of revolution, and is apparently disdainful of moral judgement. Social democracy or democratic socialism rejects utopianism but runs the risk of a dogmatic adherence to a doctrine of 'realism' that can be at variance with the facts.

Marxism can only be rescued from the problem of authoritarianism if it rejects the notion of revolution as a single political event, and adopts a broader view of class and a conditional notion of inevitability. The problem of utopia in socialism needs to be meaningfully addressed by constructing socialism as a 'utopian realism' so that neither half of this construct is stressed at the expense of the other.

## Questions

1. Are Marxist organisations necessarily authoritarian?
2. Can the notion of revolution play a part within a democratic socialism?
3. Is socialism inevitable?
4. Is parliament a barrier to, or a precondition for, a viable socialism?
5. Is socialism necessarily utopian?

## References

Bauman, Z. (1976) *Socialism as Utopia* London: George Allen & Unwin.

Berki, R. (1974) *Socialism* London: Dent.

Bernstein, E. (1961) *Evolutionary Socialism* New York: Schocken.

Blair, T. (1992) 'Pride without Prejudice', *Fabian Review* 104(3), 3.

Blair, T. (1994) *Socialism* Fabian Pamphlet 565, London.

Blair, T. (1995) *Let Us Face the Future* Fabian Pamphlet 571, London.

Brown, W. (1995) *States of Injury* Princeton, New Jersey: Princeton University Press.

Crick, B. (1982) *In Defence of Politics* 2nd edn Harmondsworth: Penguin.

Crick, B. (1987) *Socialism* Buckingham: Open University Press.

Gay, P. (1962) *The Dilemma of Democratic Socialism* New York: Collier.

Geoghegan, V. (1987) *Utopianism and Marxism* London and New York: Methuen.

Heywood, A. (1992) *Political Ideologies* Basingstoke: Macmillan.

Hoffman, J. (1975) *Marxism and the Theory of Praxis* New York: International Publishers.

Hoffman, J. (1991) *Has Marxism a Future?* Discussion Papers in Politics: University of Leicester.

Hoffman, J. (1995) *Beyond the State* Cambridge: Polity Press.

Hunt, R. (1975) *The Political Ideas of Marx and Engels* vol. 1 Basingstoke: Macmillan.

*Independent*, 8 May 2003: 'Britain Today: A Nation Still Failing its Ethnic Minorities'.

Mannheim, K. (1960) *Ideology and Utopia* London: Routledge & Kegan Paul.

Marx, K. (1970) *Capital* vol. 1 London: Lawrence & Wishart.
Marx, K. and Engels, F. (1967) *The Communist Manifesto* Harmondsworth: Penguin.
Marx, K. and Engels, F. (1968) *Selected Works* London: Lawrence & Wishart.
Marx, K. and Engels, F. (1976) *Collected Works* vol. 6 London: Lawrence & Wishart.
Marx, K. and Engels, F. (1975) *Selected Correspondence* Moscow: Progress.
Miliband, R. (1973) *Parliamentary Socialism* 2nd edn London: Merlin.
Tucker, R. (ed.) (1978) *The Marx-Engels Reader* 2nd edn New York and London: W.W. Norton.
Wright, T. (1996) *Socialisms* London and New York: Routledge.

## Further Reading

- Wright's *Socialisms* (referenced above) is a most valuable summary of different positions.

- Crick's *Socialism* (referenced above) is very useful, with a chapter excerpting texts on British socialism.

- Miliband's *Parliamentary Socialism* (referenced above) is a classic critique on Labourism.

- Geohegan's *Utopianism and Marxism* (referenced above) is a useful defence of the utopian tradition.

- Gavin Kitching's *Rethinking Socialism* London and New York: Methuen, 1983 offers a very challenging attempt to rework socialism during the Thatcher period.

- The David McLellan edition of *Marxism: The Essential Writings* Oxford: Oxford University Press, 1988 includes valuable excerpts from various Marxist traditions and a piece on Eduard Bernstein.

## Weblinks

Very useful on the history of socialism and the various personalities that predominate: http://www.spartacus.schoolnet.co.uk

Allows one to look at original texts on different aspects of socialism: http://www.inter-change-search.net/directory/Society/Politics/Socialism/

Easy to get information of the different 'varieties' of socialism: http://www.the-wood.org/socialism/

Material on Marxism: http://www.marxist.org.uk/htm_docs/princip2.htm

Full text of the *Communist Manifesto*: http://www.socialistparty.org.uk/manifesto/m2frame.htm?manifesto.html

# Chapter 4

# Anarchism

## Introduction

see Chapters 1: Liberalism, pp. 10–32 and 3: Socialism, pp. 56–85

Much is made in the press about the frequent anti-capitalist protests happening in various cities throughout the world, and it is argued that anarchists are behind these demonstrations. The word 'anarchist' is often used as a term of abuse, and is sometimes misused – but what exactly does it mean? What does it stand for, and why have some argued that anarchism has enjoyed a resurgence in recent years? On the face of it, it seems an absurdly self-defeating philosophy, so why does it remain influential? Who does it attract and why?

To answer these questions, in this chapter we will try to establish what anarchism is, and how different varieties of anarchism advocate different strands of argument.

## Chapter Map

In this chapter we will explore:

- The overlap with other ideologies while grasping the distinctive character of anarchism.

- Philosophical anarchism and free market anarchism, while noting their difficulties.

- The views of anti-capitalist anarchists such as Proudhon, Bakunin and Kropotkin.

- An actual experience of anarchism, during the Spanish Civil War.

- The problem of **violence**, and what role it plays in the new social movements.

- The problem that organisation poses for anarchism.

- The difficulties that arise when the distinctions between the state and **government** and force and **constraint** are ignored.

# Death in Genoa

Riot police storm past a dead protester who has been shot and killed by carabiniere, 20 July 2001

On a sunny Italian morning a group of young politics students landed in Genoa to protest against the G8 summit. Before travelling they had been leafleted by anarchist groups and emailed regarding the details of the demonstrations, where they should stay and where preliminary meetings were being held locally to them. They met their rendezvous outside the airport and hitched a lift to the Carlini Stadium. Inside the stadium they first noticed the Italian Ya Basta group, also called *tutti bianci* ('all white').

There is a definite uneasy atmosphere in the stadium – the Ya Basta group want only to stage an act of civil disobedience such as a peaceful march and protest – whereas the anarchists are aiming to dismantle the 'Red Zone' fence that separates delegates from protestors. Although they tell the group that they support the demonstrations against capitalism in principle, they also remind everyone of their own specific demands they want made, maintaining that a revolution against capital must be linked to a revolution against the state and government.

Once the details have been amicably agreed upon, they march to the fence. Almost immediately the protestors are drenched by the Italian police with water cannons. When the increasingly angry crowd try to pull down the fence the police use tear gas against them. Violent confrontations break out between the police and certain groups of protestors. Rumours (later confirmed) start that a protestor has been killed by the police.

Imagine you are a member of an anarchist committee whose job it is to contact the 250 people planning on travelling from Britain to Genoa, placing information on the internet, consulting on leaflets, arranging accommodation etc. How does this level of organisation compare to your initial conception of what it is to be an anarchist?

At the G8 summit, force was answered with force. Imagine you were the Genoan Police Chief responsible for ensuring public order. How would you have tried to counter and control the anarchists?

## The Relationship with Socialism

In her *Using Political Ideas* (1997) Barbara Goodwin has a separate chapter on anarchism and argues that the anarchist is 'not merely a socialist who happens to dislike the state'. She concedes, however, that there is much overlap and that many anarchists have analysed capitalism in a way that resembles that of socialists (1997: 122).

R.N. Berki, however, in his influential book *Socialism*, treats anarchism as a current within **socialism** and notes, for example, that it was Proudhon (a key anarchist as we shall see later in this chapter) who first called his doctrine 'scientific socialism' (Berki, 1974: 12), and that Proudhon's significance for socialism is enormous (1974: 84). Berki makes many acute observations about anarchism in the context of his chapter on the evolution of socialism. In a section on socialist thought at the turn of the century he describes Michael Bakunin as a precursor to both Russian socialism and anarcho-syndicalism, about which more will be said later (1974: 83–8).

see pp. 94–6

Andrew Vincent, as does Goodwin, has a separate chapter on anarchism, and makes the point that the doctrine overlaps with both liberalism and socialism (1995: 114). But whatever the overlap between some kinds of anarchism and socialism, there is also an anarchism that is explicitly non-socialist, and in some of its forms even anti-socialist. It will be useful to say something about these first, since they are dramatically different from 'socialist' forms of anarchism.

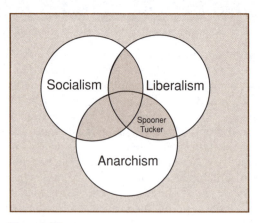

**Figure 4.1**

## Philosophical Anarchists

We will take the view that although anarchism is a very old theory, it only emerged in systematic form in the eighteenth century as part of the Enlightenment. We will begin with what is widely agreed to be the first comprehensive account of anarchist principles, William Godwin's classic *Enquiry Concerning Political Justice* (1793).

Godwin was really a liberal, even though he abandoned the classical liberal view of natural rights and a state of nature. He argues that humans are social beings, are moulded by their environment and are imbued with a capacity to reason. True happiness, as far as Godwin was concerned, lies with the development of individuality. All individuals have a right to private judgement. Everything understood by organisation is 'in some degree evil' and he argued that communal institutions, even theatre and musical performances, could be seen as an invasion of our individuality. Society should be regarded as a 'luxury', rather than a 'necessity' and can never be more than the sum of its parts (Vincent, 1995: 125). Compulsory restraint violates a privately determined pursuit of happiness, and it is said that Godwin ends where Hobbes begins. While Godwin sees the state as vicious, evil and tyrannical, the premises of his theory are militantly individualistic. If this **atomistic** and abstract view of the individual leads to radical insecurity and arbitrariness in Hobbes, in Godwin it generates the 'unspeakably beautiful vision of a world' in which individuals freely exercise their private judgement (Hoffman, 1995: 114).

Godwin was opposed to property, the market and acquisitiveness in general, but he was no socialist. His opposition to the state extends to social relationships, and all individuals retain a sphere of private judgement that shuts society out. He may have hoped that small face-to-face communities would replace the state (with temporary coordinating bodies being transitionally necessary to resolve disputes and repel invaders), but he has been rightly called a 'philosophical anarchist' since his main preoccupation is with principles rather than practice.

Max Stirner is often bracketed with Godwin as a philosophical anarchist, but unlike Godwin Stirner does not see individuals as benevolent and rational. He enthusiastically embraces the argument that consciousness (which is always 'alienated') is the source of our oppression. In Stirner's case, concepts such as humanism, communism and liberalism are inherently oppressive because they are necessarily imposed upon the sovereign individual. The state of nature adhered to by classical liberals was essentially social in character, but individuals constitute the highest reality, and Stirner exhorts them to desert their natural condition. People have no rights of any kind. As a conscious egoist, the individual, in Stirner's view, is beyond good and evil and the oppressiveness of the state is no different in essence from the oppressiveness of all social relationships, indeed of ideologies. All subject the ego to some 'generality or other' (Hoffman, 1995: 115).

Stirner sees the natural world as a war of all against all, but unlike Hobbes who posits a powerful state to tackle this problem, Stirner advocates the formation of an association of sovereign individuals – a union of conscious egoists – who would spontaneously and voluntarily come together out of mutual interest. All 'teleological' categories – goals, purposes and ends – are oppressive even if they are imposed by individuals upon themselves. This means that even a system of direct democracy is unacceptable. His union of egoists would enable individuals to accomplish more than they could on their own, and though Stirner's world is one without rights and morality, the union would create security and put an end to poverty. Marx and Engels in their lengthy critique of Stirner's *The Ego and His Own* point out that Stirner employs a concept of the unique individual that in practice morally obliges other individuals, so that he is in the hapless position of attacking authority from moral premises which are not supposed to exist (Hoffman, 1995: 115).

In a more recent exposition of philosophical anarchism, Wolff argues that all adults are responsible beings who have a capacity for choice and a potential for autonomy that they lose if they obey the dictates of another. A person's primary obligation is to be autonomous. However, unlike Stirner and Godwin, Wolff

## Biography    William Godwin (1756–1836)

The son of a poor Presbyterian minister, Godwin was influenced by Dissenters and became a Presbyterian minister himself in 1768. He did not make a success of this and decided to earn his living from writing.

see her biography box in Chapter 7: Feminism, p. 178

Although this was precarious, he got his publisher to finance him and he produced his major work, *An Enquiry Concerning Political Justice*. This was first published in 1793 and substantially revised for a second (1795) and third edition (1797). In 1794 he wrote his most successful novel, *Caleb Williams*, and three years later he married Mary Wollstonecraft who died in childbirth some five months after their marriage. His *Memoirs* lost him public support and,

although he continued to write, he lived his final 30 years in debt and relative obscurity.

His anarchism was based on a belief that individuals were rational and social beings whose autonomy was necessarily corrupted by government. A representative assembly was only permissible as a transitional expedient.

The capacity of individuals to judge is sacrosanct and, as perfectible beings, they can only progress through knowledge, truth and understanding. Many commentators find his anarchism implausible and concentrate on his utilitarianism, which they see as making an important contribution to the history of political thought.

accepts the case for a direct democracy, and he argues that people are bound by the decisions they have taken. The advantage of such a system is that the authority to which each citizen submits 'is not of himself simply, but that of the entire community taken collectively'. Not only does this sound rather authoritarian, but Wolff argues that each person encounters 'his better self in the form of the state, for its dictates are simply the laws which he has, after due deliberation willed to be

## Biography    Max Stirner (1806–56)

Born Johann Kaspar Schmidt at Bayreuth in Bavaria, he was of poor parents. From 1826 to 1828 he studied at the University of Berlin where he attended the lectures of Hegel.

He returned to Berlin in 1832 and managed to get a teacher's certificate, but the Prussian government refused to appoint him to a full-time post. He married in 1837 but his wife died in childbirth a few months later. He acquired a post at a girls' school and was able to associate with Young Hegelians such as the Bauer brothers.

He wrote an article, 'The False Principle of our Education', for Karl Marx's *Rheinische Zeitung* (Rhineland Gazette) in 1842, and in 1845 published his principal work, *The Ego and His Own*.

Influenced by Hegelianism, he saw history as culminating in his sovereign individual, which is unique and creates everything. Because he argued that sovereign individuals must emancipate themselves from society, he was dubbed 'Saint Max' by Marx and Engels in the ferocious critique they wrote of him (and other left Hegelians) in *The German Ideology*.

He married a member of the Young Hegelian circle and, although he had adopted the *nom de plume* Max Stirner so as not to alarm the head of the school where he taught, he lost his job. He spent the rest of his life in poverty.

To earn a living, he translated the work of English economists. His wife left him, and in 1852, four years before his death, he wrote a *History of Reaction*.

enacted' (cited by Dahl, 1989: 348). As an anarchist, he treats direct democracy as a form of the state!

All philosophical anarchists have the problem of moving from the individual to some kind of collective organisation that, on the one hand, is deemed necessary to realise anarchism, but, on the other, contradicts anarchist principles. We will see if the free market anarchists are better able to tackle this problem.

## Free Market Anarchists

Nineteenth-century Americans such as Spooner and Tucker argued for an anarchism that was an extension of liberalism: if individuals are free and equal, why should they accept the compulsion of the state? Locke's state of nature was seen as a world in which individuals are not subject to external discipline: why should things not stay that way? But whereas nineteenth-century free market anarchists were concerned about the structural inequalities that the market might generate – and they took the view that everyone should be an entrepreneur – more recent free market anarchists have accepted capitalism, arguing that exploitation and **coercion** are simply the product of the state. Substantial inequalities are inevitable in a free society.

Free market anarchists such as Murray Rothbard take the view that state welfare is as pernicious as state warfare. Any attempt to regulate production prevents consumers from purchasing commodities that *they* wish to buy, while goods that everybody wants, such as sanitation, roads, street lighting, are best provided by private enterprise. Disadvantaged groups, for example the elderly, the unemployed and the disabled, should be catered for by charity since state provision is invariably wasteful and open to abuse (Hoffman, 1995: 117).

It is not only the 'positive' functions of the state that ought to be 'privatised'. As far as modern-day free market anarchists are concerned, the market should take over the state's 'negative' role as well. Rothbard contends that people could insure themselves against bodily assault in the same way that they currently insure their possessions against theft. Aggrieved parties could then seek compensation and redress for injury through private tribunals, with the free market ensuring that arbitrators or judges with the best record in settling disputes would be hired.

But how would these judgements be enforced? Recalitrants who refused to abide by tribunal decisions would be subject to boycott and ostracism, and in more serious cases guards and police could be hired to defend injured parties and enforce judgments. People who refused to comply with judgments could be placed in private prisons, and aggrieved individuals might decide (with the help of friends and relatives) to retaliate in person. Rothbard describes the state as 'the great legalized and socially legitimated channel of all manner of social crime', and getting rid of the state would strengthen the 'good' in human nature and discourage the bad (Hoffman, 1995: 118). But humans remain possessive individualists by nature, and it is this assumption that leads the libertarian thinker, Robert Nozick, in his classic work *Anarchy, State, and Utopia* (1974) to make the case for the minimal state.

Nozick's argument is interesting because he seeks to construct his non-anarchist case on individualist anarchist principles. He argues that individuals have natural rights, and their goods and bodies are protected by private protective associations. However, unlike Rothbard and the free market anarchists, he accepts that through competition one of the protective associations will emerge as dominant, and when it protects all who live in its domain, whether they pay privately or not, it then becomes a 'minimal state'.

Some form of government seems to be essential if the problem of 'externalities' or 'spillovers', as they are called, are to be dealt with. Negative externalities arise when, for example, a factory pollutes the environment and the cost that results is much less to the individual than to society at large. Some kind of collective association is needed to bring the offending individual to book, and make him change his ways. But the principle of the minimal state is also necessary to tackle positive externalities as in a situation in which some, but not all, households in a neighbourhood pay for the protection of a policing agency. However, the presence of a policing agency may have a deterrent effect from which *all* households benefit, and premium payers, indignant at the fact that they are paying for services from which 'free-riders' benefit, withdraw from the scheme, which then collapses.

But how does Nozick justify the services of a minimal state that applies to all? Who funds such a service? Nozick argues that a minimal state emerges in a way that violates no one's rights in the process. But how is the dominant protection agency that becomes the minimal state to exist without violating the rights of its competitors? Nozick's argument is that these competitive agencies are compensated because the minimal state provides protective services free of charge. But what happens if the agencies do not accept the monopolistic role of the minimal state? People are being compensated whether they like it or not, so that it is difficult to see how the minimal state avoids compulsion.

## Biography | Murray N. Rothbard (1926–95)

Educated in New York City, and in 1945 studied at Columbia University. His doctoral thesis (1956) was on Welfare Economics and from then on there followed a steady stream of publications.

In 1965 (to 1968) he edited *Left and Right*, and published a biography on the Austrian free marketeer Ludwig von Mises. He was particularly interested in the problem of economic depression, and in 1970 he wrote a book exposing what he called 'The Hoover Myth'. He produced a Libertarian Manifesto, entitled *For a New Liberty,* which was published in 1973. He also wrote on the US colonies in the seventeenth century (1975) and the first half of the eighteenth century (1976), and complained of Nozick's 'Immaculate Conception of the State'. He edited the *Journal of Libertarian Studies* to 1995, and published a major work in 1982, *The Ethics of Liberty.* He was made a Distinguished Professor of Economics at

the University of Nevada, Las Vegas. In 1990 he described Karl Marx as a religious eschatologist.

In all, he wrote 25 books and thousands of articles and Volumes One and Two of his history of economic thought appeared just after his death.

He was devoutly anti-socialist as well as being anti-statist, and in 1993 he declared that 'in an age of galloping statism, the classical liberal, the advocate of the free market, has an obligation to carry the struggle to all levels of society'.

He had been bitterly opposed to Roosevelt's New Deal. He identified with the Confederates, the anti-federalists, and objected to taxation. Indeed he argued that the taxing power defines the state in the same way that theft defines a robber. The only civil rights are property rights. He died in New York in 1995.

## Exercise

You are walking down the street when someone attacks you. Since you are living in a stateless society of an anarchist kind there are no public order offences, since everything has been privatised. There is, however, a tribunal to which you can turn in order to sue the person who assaulted you, for compensation, and this you are determined to do.

A number of problems face you:

- The person who attacked you obviously does not regard you as a fellow human being who deserves respect.

- Will he attend the tribunal hearings and pay up if the ruling goes against him?

- What kind of pressures can be brought to bear upon this person to ensure that he cooperates? The tribunal has officials and you know where this person lives, but they have no powers to compel the person to attend.

- The individual does have friends and family. Can they be relied upon to pressurise him to attend?

Moreover, once this compulsion has been justified, this is a principle capable of infinite extension. After all, if the provision of protection is deemed too 'risky' for competing agencies, why could not one argue, say, that the provision of low-cost housing or accessible medical services are too 'risky' to be left to private agencies? The New Liberals of the late nineteenth century showed just how painlessly the notion of 'protection' can be broadened. Will people feel 'secure' if they are destitute and have no job? Are contracts really respected if the rich invade the security of the poor? Once you have the state, a consistent free market anarchist could argue, how do you stop it from expanding?

Pressures to conform can only really be successful when everyone is, broadly speaking, in the same boat and can change places. There has to be a sense of common interest – freedom *and equality* – and if we begin with an order in which possessive individualism has divided society, how do we move to a condition of equality without regulation and compulsion, and even – horror of horrors – a role for government? Indeed, Marshall argues that 'anarcho-capitalists' should not be called anarchists at all (1993: 565).

## Anti-capitalist Anarchists: Proudhon, Bakunin and Kropotkin

Proudhon was certainly a socialist, although he objected to communism on the grounds that it subordinates the individual to the collectivity (Marshall, 1993: 238). It is the unequal distribution of property that creates disorder, but the answer, as he saw it, was 'mutualism' – a system that avoided the vices of both **private property** and collective ownership, and was based upon exchange and credit. Exchange would occur through associations that calculated the necessary labour time involved in a product. People could start businesses by borrowing from a mutual credit bank, and this economic reorganisation would make the state redundant. In Proudhon's view, parliamentary democracy is futile and counter-productive – 'Universal suffrage is counter revolution' is one of his many celebrated dictums (Marshall, 1993: 244).

Proudhon aroused the wrath of Marx, who wrote his *Poverty of Philosophy* against Proudhon's *Philosophy of Poverty*. Marx objected to Proudhon's opposition to political involvement and trade unionism, and regarded his principles of **justice** and equality as woefully unhistorical. Proudhon's rejection of liberal principles of government meant that he regarded all forms of the state as anathema. He was also strongly nationalistic, patriarchal, and for a period supported the autocratic Emperor Napoleon III who suspended parliamentary **politics**. Proudhon popularised the view that anarchy stood for order – despite the frequent use of the word as a synonym for chaos – and he is widely regarded as the father of anarchism.

Influenced by Proudhon but strongly collectivist in orientation was the Russian anarchist Bakunin. Bakunin declares with an anti-Hobbesian fervour that 'man is born into society, just as ant is born into an ant-hill and bee into its hive' (Marshall, 1993: 291). The analogy with nature is important for Bakunin, since he takes the view that sociability and the desire to revolt is *instinctive*. It is both universal, and stronger among some rather than others. Bakunin took the view that the instinct for revolt was particularly strong among the Latins and the Slavs, and particularly weak among Germanic peoples. He saw **revolution** as a violent process, and what Marshall calls his 'apocalyptic fantasies' (1993: 306) manifest themselves in his belief that to create is to destroy. This slogan reappears during the May events – the student rebellion – in 1968 in Paris, and Berki notes that Bakunin's ideas became very fashionable in the 1970s in Western libertarian socialist circles (1975: 84).

Bakunin clashed with Marx in the First International and he was expelled in 1872. Nevertheless, although he and the 'authoritarian' Marx disagreed over strategy, he greatly admired Marx's critique of capital, and he was opposed not simply to the repressive hierarchy of the state but to the inequalities and exploitation identified with capitalism. He was, however, passionately opposed to Marx's notion of the workers becoming a ruling class and having to control a transitional state. The workers' state, he insisted, would be nothing but a barracks; a regime where working men and women are regimented. We will have 'despotic rule over the toiling masses by a new, numerically small aristocracy of genuine or sham scientists. The people . . . will be wholly regimented into one common herd of governed people. Emancipation indeed!' (Maximoff, ed., 1953: 287). Not only was Bakunin sceptical about the 'authority' of science, but he regarded religion and the notion of God as inherently statist and authoritarian.

Yet Bakunin argued the case for a secret association in which a revolutionary general staff would serve as intermediaries 'between the revolutionary idea and the instincts of the people', and this presumably accounts for his temporary attraction to the notorious Nechaev, a nihilist, terrorist and a man of no scruples. Against one's will, declared Bakunin, one is obliged to use 'force, cunning and deception' (Marshall, 1993: 282–4). Bakunin was hugely influential. Not only did he make an enormous impact upon French labour, Italian revolutionaries and, as we shall see, the socialist movement in Spain, but his anti-capitalism attracted support among those who espoused what was called anarcho-syndicalism.

Bertrand Russell has referred to syndicalism as 'the anarchism of the market place' (Berki, 1975: 87) and it focuses on the role of industrial workers who are to organise themselves into revolutionary syndicates, making 'war on the bosses' and not bothering with politics (Marshall, 1993: 441). The general strike is seen as the best weapon for ushering in the new order. Syndicates should take on social functions as the germ of the stateless, socialist society. But not all anarchists agreed with syndicalism. Emma Goldman feared that syndicalism trampled upon the rights of the individual by accepting a principle of majority rule, while the Italian Malatesta saw syndicalism simply as one of many means to achieve anarchist ends (Marshall, 1993: 444).

The contrast between Kropotkin and Bakunin is striking indeed. Although they were both Russian and both influenced by Marx's critique of capitalism, Kropotkin had great respect for science and was an accomplished geographer. He espoused the ideal of a federal and decentralised society with the land and factories owned by the producers. He was sympathetic to syndicalism and argued that the great gains in the past had been made by the force of popular revolution, not through 'an evolution created by an elite' (Marshall, 1993: 317).

Anarchism must proceed with the method of the natural scientists. Mutual aid was far more important to the evolution of the species than mutual struggle. The species that cooperates the most is most likely to survive. Humans are by nature social and moral, and the greatest individual development comes through practising the 'highest communist sociability'. The socialist notion of a 'people's state' – here Kropotkin agreed with Bakunin – is 'as great a danger to liberty as any form of autocracy' (Marshall, 1993: 321–6). Whereas Bukunin saw distribution as linked to the performance of work, Kropotkin also stressed need: production and distribution are integrated in communal enterprises so as to meet the physical and cultural needs of all (Vincent, 1995: 133).

He was offered a cabinet position (which he turned down) in the Provisional Government of Kerensky after the overthrow of Tsarism in 1917, and was bitterly critical both of the Bolshevik Revolution (he sent letters to Lenin in vain) and the tactics adopted after the Revolution. Kropotkin called himself a communist anarchist; Bakunin preferred to see himself as a collectivist, while Proudhon regarded himself as a mutualist; but all were critical of capitalism, and all saw anarchism as a solution to the kind of inequality generated by a capitalist society.

## How to read:

### Bakunin's *God and the State*

This is a relatively short work and therefore the whole book should be read. Of course, the arguments are presented in a fairly jumbled fashion, since Bakunin moves from philosophy to theology to politics in a very unsystematic way. It is important to suspend criticisms in the face of Bakunin's very strong language in order to try and grasp, as sympathetically as possible, what he is arguing. It is true that Bakunin dismisses religion and idealism as inexplicable stupidity, but it is important (however tempting) not to adopt the same dogmatic tone against Bakunin. The link between religion and the state has been acknowledged by many political thinkers, even if they see something positive where Bakunin sees only the negative. The challenge is to think of condemning slavery and oppression in ways that are more effective than Bakunin's celebrated polemic. His analysis of science, its strengths and weaknesses, raises important points that need an answer. Read the book critically but sympathetically!

## Biography          Pierre-Joseph Proudhon (1809–65)

Born in Besançon near the Swiss border from a peasant background. He went to the best school in the town but when his father became a bankrupt he was forced to drop out of school, and in 1827 he became a printer's apprentice.

Proudhon developed an extensive knowledge of Christian doctrine but this had the effect of making him an atheist who identified God with tyranny and property. In 1838 he won a scholarship to the Academy of Besançon. After winning a prize for an essay for the *Sunday Observance,* he wrote his *What is Property?* in which he espoused anarchy as 'the true form of government' and developed his famous paradox, 'Property is Theft'. His target was large-scale property and collectivism, and although he was prosecuted for his *Warning to Property Owners* that followed in 1842, he was acquitted on the grounds that the book was too complicated for ordinary people to understand!

He became interested in dialectical philosophy, went to Paris in 1844–45 where he clashed with Marx – whom he described as 'the tapeworm of socialism' – and published his two-volume *System of Economic Contradictions* in 1846. He described communists as 'fanatics of state power'. He issued a manifesto in 1848, having being elected as a deputy to parliament.

After Napoleon's *coup,* he was sent to prison for three years. Here he wrote *Confessions of a Revolutionary,* but his greatest work on ethics, *Justice in the Revolution and Church* (1858), brought him another three-year sentence. He fled to Belgium, where he wrote about war and art, and after his return he urged abstention in the presidential elections of 1863. Although he became increasingly conservative, espousing nationalism, patriarchy and anti-Semitism, he retained great influence over French workers, and his followers were the largest group to support the Paris Commune six years after his death.

see Chap Socia pp. 5

## Biography          Michael Bakunin (1814–76)

Born north-west of Moscow, Bakunin was the son of a retired diplomat who had liberal sympathies. At 15, he was sent to the Artillery School at St Petersburg. He was posted to a brigade in Poland but resigned from the army in 1836 in order to teach philosophy in Moscow.

Influenced by Fichte and Hegel, Bakunin went to Berlin in 1840 and joined the Young Hegelians. He travelled to Zürich where Weitling, a German communist, made a deep impact upon him. In Paris, he met Marx in 1844 but preferred Proudhon. Expelled from Paris under Russian pressure – he advocated the independence of Poland from Russia – he took part in the French Revolution of 1848 and wrote a fiery *Appeal to Slavs* in Prague in the same year. He participated in the insurrection in Dresden in 1849. Captured by Prussian troops, he was eventually deported to Russia and spent eight years in prison. When Alexander II became Tsar in 1855, Bakunin was banished to Siberia, where he married and remained until 1861.

When he moved to Italy, he began to advocate social rather than national revolution, and developed his theory of anarchism. He established a secret revolutionary brotherhood, hierarchical and centralised, while calling for the destruction of the state and for the organisation of society by free association and federation. He joined the First International but in 1869 clashed with Marx, who accused him of trying to set up an International within the International. He worked for a short time with Nechaev, a Russian nihilist, and in so doing damaged the reputation of anarchism. He hoped that the defeat of Napoleon in the Franco-Prussian war of 1870 would lead to a French uprising, and he was involved in the short-lived insurrection in Lyon.

Bakunin was enthusiastic about the Paris Commune of 1872 and wrote his first and last book, *The Knouto-German Empire and the Social Revolution* between 1870 and 1872.

## Biography          Peter Kropotkin (1842–1921)

Born into an aristocratic family. His father was an officer in the imperial army, and Kropotkin attended the most select military academy in Russia. He then became a military administrator in Eastern Siberia, concluding in his close observations of the natural world that cooperation is the most important factor in evolution.

It was in Siberia that Kropotkin became an anarchist. He returned to St Petersburg in 1867 and enthusiastically welcomed the Paris Commune in 1871. His views were confirmed by Marx's handling of the dispute with Bakunin in the First International. For two years he worked closely with a populist group called the Chaikovsky circle, publishing a manifesto in 1873 entitled *Must We Occupy Ourselves with the Ideal of a Future System?* He was imprisoned for three years but escaped and wrote a number of pamphlets and helped set up the journal *Le Révolté.*

In 1882 he was sentenced to five years' imprisonment by the French authorities, but was released in 1886 following an international outcry. The following year he wrote *In Russian and French Prisons,* having settled in London. He was active in anarchist politics and had a high reputation as a scientist. He opposed indiscriminate violence but was not a pacifist. In 1892 he published *The Conquest of Bread* in Paris, and seven years later his *Memoirs of a Revolutionist.*

Kropotkin supported Britain and France during World War I. He returned to Russia after the Revolution, and although he was opposed to the 'dictatorial tendencies' of the Bolsheviks he argued against foreign intervention. When he died he was offered a state funeral, but his family refused.

## The Argument So Far . . .

**Godwin** believed that individuals should be allowed to express freely private judgements.

**Stirner** thought that individuals were sovereign and form a voluntary and spontaneous union of like-minded beings.

**Rothbard** was a free marketeer who took the view that the market could replace the state.

**Nozick** argued that a state was needed, but a minimal state that would protect property and enforce contracts.

The following were not only against the state, but against capitalism as well:

**Proudhon** believed in 'mutualism' – a scheme that allowed individuals to exchange goods and secure credit without the need for political involvement or trade unions.

**Bakunin** argued that humans should work together collectively and they had a natural instinct for revolt and solidarity.

**Kropotkin** believed that a communist society was possible through mutual cooperation and revolution.

## Republican Spain and the Anarchist Experience

The Spanish Republic has become a valuable historical laboratory for trying to understand anarchism because this is the only example in the twentieth century in which anarchism succeeded in constructing a new society, at least in particular regions and for a few years. As Thomas comments, 'the Spanish Anarchists are the only Anarchists in European history to have made any mark upon events' (1965: 279).

The liberal tradition was weak in Spain. During the nineteenth century the Church and the army had intervened to prevent or paralyse a liberal constitution and this had strengthened the widespread scepticism towards conventional political processes. Anarchist strength centred in Barcelona in the north where it was reinforced by separatist sentiments among the Catalans (and took the form of anarcho-syndicalism), and it was also strong among the impoverished peasantry in the south. When a Spanish Communist Party was formed in 1921 the anarchists were four times more numerous than the socialists. In Spain the mass of workers and peasants had followed Bakunin when he broke with Marx. The Confedacion National del Trajbajo (CNT) had over a million members at the time of World War I, and in 1933 the anarchist weekly *Tierra y Libertad* declared grandly:

> Workers! Do not vote! The vote is a negation of your personality . . . All the politicians are enemies . . . we need neither state nor government . . . Do not be concerned whether the Right or the Left emerge triumphant from this farce . . . Parliament . . . is a filthy house of prostitution . . . Destroy the ballots! Destroy the ballot boxes . . . hack off the heads of the ballot supervisors as well as of the candidates . . . (Thomas, 1965: 95)

One could well argue that revolutions do not have to be violent but this was not how Spanish anarchists saw the issue. The communists had, following the Seventh Comintern Congress, thrown their weight behind the idea of a Popular Front (an alliance of liberal and left-wing forces), and in 1936 the left won a substantial electoral victory on a programme of radical reform. Franco, with the army mostly loyal to him, led a rebellion. The socialists (and communists) were strong in Madrid but the anarchists retained control of Barcelona where all large industries passed to the CNT, and expropriation was considered the rule. Large numbers of people belonging to the old order were killed, and churches were destroyed. In some places money was replaced by coupons, while in Andalusia in the south, where the anarchists were also strong, each town acted on its own responsibility. By 1937 some 3 million people were living in rural collectives.

The anarchists adopted military methods of organisation, and Miller cites Borkenau's comment that in one of the villages of Aragon the agrarian revolution was almost the automatic consequence of executions (1974: 106–7). In September 1936 the anarchists entered the Catalan government, calling it the Revolutionary Defence Council so as to avoid giving the impression 'to their already alarmed extremist followers' that they had joined a real government (Thomas, 1965: 367). Marshall argues that in so doing they had started down the slippery slide to parliamentary participation and this meant sacrificing the social revolution to the war against Franco (1993: 461).

As the crisis continued, the anarchists entered the government in Madrid, with the anarchist Garcia Oliver becoming Minister of Justice and the CNT recognising the republican state as 'an instrument of struggle' (Thomas, 1965: 404). The defence of this action by the CNT's daily paper is regarded by Marshall as 'an unparalleled bout of dissimulation' (1993: 465). Oliver, 'for all his devotion to Bakunin', proceeded to establish a new code of state laws and defended the need for iron discipline in the popular army (Thomas, 1965: 470; Marshall, 1993: 465). In late April 1937 a civil

## Orwell comments that:

I had come to Spain with some notion of writing newspaper articles, but I had joined the militia almost immediately because at that time and in that atmosphere it seemed the only conceivable thing to do. The Anarchists were still in virtual control of Catalonia and the revolution was in full swing . . . it was the first time that I had ever been in a town where the working class was in the saddle. Practically every building of any size had been seized by the workers and was draped with red flags or the black and red flag of the Anarchists; every wall was scrawled with the hammer and sickle and with initials of the revolutionary parties; almost every church had been gutted and its images burnt . . . Every shop and café had an inscription saying it had been collectivised . . . Waiters and shop-walkers looked you in the face and treated you as an equal. Servile and ceremonial forms of speech had temporarily disappeared . . . There were no private motor cars, they had all been commandeered . . . And it was the aspect of the crowds that was the queerest thing of all. In outward appearance it was a town in which the wealthy classes had practically ceased to exist.

(Orwell, 2001: 32)

war between the anarchists and the communist-backed government broke out in Barcelona, and some 500 were killed. Anarchist influence ebbed away, and although the CNT continued to collaborate with the government they no longer took even nominal responsibility for its actions (Thomas, 1965: 558).

On 18 March 1938 the CNT signed an agreement with the socialist Union General Trabajadores (UGT) to subject industry to central economic planning – collectivisation everywhere was giving way to state control (Thomas, 1965: 671). In Madrid, the anarchists backed attacks on the communists, putting the blame for the perilous military position on the Popular Front government (Thomas, 1965: 750). By the end of March, Franco's victory was secured.

**Influences and Impact:**

## Anarchism and the Spanish Civil War

What does the civil war reveal about anarchism as an ideology? Leaving aside its fierce opposition to Marxism that had already been evident in the nineteenth century, the civil war points to a paradox at the heart of anarchism. In order to be effective, the militias had to adopt more conventional methods of organisation and the anarchists had to agree to enter into governments, trying in the Catalan instance to disguise the character of this institution. This points to a wider predicament. Anarchism is only likely to flourish in deeply divided conditions. A revolutionary situation inevitably throws up counter-revolutionary forces so that anarchists are likely to find themselves in positions of power in civil war-type situations. Dramatic changes are called for, but how is it possible to carry these through without organisation and a state? It takes a state to get rid of a state – that in essence seems to be the lesson of the events in Spain.

This argument conflicts with Marshall's view that the defeat of the anarchist movement in Spain arose from the failure to carry through the social revolution. The latter was sacrificed for the war effort, and if this and the seizure of power by the communists had not taken place the outcome would have been very different. The failure, he suggests, was not a failure of anarchist theory and tactics (1993: 467).

## The Problem of Violence

The question of violence is linked to the question of transition – how gradual is the movement towards a stateless society to be? Can a dramatic transformation of society take place bit by bit?

Godwin believed that it would take considerable time before society became sufficiently enlightened to adopt anarchist institutions, and Marshall has suggested that different types of anarchist organisation could be taken to secure progression towards the anarchist goal. Thus Proudhon's mutualism (involving the regulation of different private producers) could give way to Bakunin's collectivism (where people are rewarded according to their work), which in turn might yield to the more egalitarian idea of Kropotkin's communism where each is rewarded according to their need (Hoffman, 1995: 124).

It is true that many anarchists have seen that violence involves an intolerable conflict between ends and means. The Russian anarchist and novelist, Leo Tolstoy (1828–1910) rejected all forms of violence, whether revolutionary or statist: is there any difference, he asked, between killing a revolutionary and killing a policeman? 'The difference is between cat-shit and dog-shit . . . I don't like the smell of either' (cited in Marshall, 1993: 377). Gandhi, influenced by Tolstoy, also espoused a militant pacifism. But Carter argues that there are elements within anarchism that are peculiarly receptive to violence. The belief that many anarchists held, that a golden age might be realised through one apocalyptic outburst, an all-embracing revolution, can only encourage what Bakunin called the 'poetry of destruction' (Carter, 1978: 337).

see the box in Chapter 3: Socialism, p. 69

Part of this 'utopianism' is the shunning of political organisation in its conventional form, for it might be argued – as we saw with the anarchists in Spain – that it is worse to cast a ballot than fire a bullet. If constitutional procedures are identified with 'statist' liberalism, then the alternative may have to be despotism and violence. It is revealing that Robert Michels turned from anarchism to authoritarianism, arguing that because the German Social Democratic Party was too hierarchical, all organisation is oligarchical in character. One sympathetic commentator has argued ruefully that 'a streak of pathological violence' runs through anarchism (Hoffman, 1995: 126). We see how after the crushing of the Paris Commune in 1871, many anarchists resorted to a 'propaganda by deed' – dramatic action designed to shake the masses out of their passivity – and these propagandist deeds often degenerated into acts of terror. The agonised slogan of radical black youth in the South African townships in the 1980s – 'liberation before education' – echoes comments by Italian followers of Garibaldi and Proudhon in the 1870s. A belief that everything is right that is not 'legal' can easily lead to violence even if it is justified as a way of avenging wrongs against the people, inspiring fear in the enemy and highlighting the evil practices of the state (Miller, 1974: 98–9).

Marshall quotes a passage from the CNT constitution printed on the membership card which states that 'the adversary does not discuss: he acts' (1993: 457), and even Kropotkin, whose personal life is often described in saint-like terms, displays what Marshall calls 'an uncomfortable mixture of quietism and aggressive elements'. Indeed, at one point in his life, Kropotkin supports the arguments of the anarcho-syndicalist Sorel that violence is the revolutionary whirlwind that energises 'sluggish hearts' (Hoffman, 1995: 126).

The problem of abolishing the state and authority seems to us to lead inevitably to the resort to violence; the perpetuation of the state in a new form, and a legacy of division and mistrust. But how are people to free themselves when they are oppressed? Oppression arises when a person is deprived of material and social resources and lacks esteem. But how is this emancipation to be secured without organisation? Marshall argues that anarchists only reject authoritarian organisation, but it could be argued that all organisation requires some form of **hierarchy** and leadership – the very political qualities that anarchists reject (Hoffman, 1995: 124).

Miller cites the sad reflections of Emma Goldman as she compares the weaknesses of Russian anarchists when set against the organisational strengths of the Bolsheviks. The work of the anarchists, she remarks, 'would have been of infinitely greater value had they been better organized' (Miller, 1974: 97–8). But she fails to ask herself whether these weaknesses were a product of anarchist theory itself. What are anarchists to do if the masses fail to rise in revolt? Two responses are possible. Either anarchists simply wait (as Godwin seems to argue) until the spirit of rational enlightenment takes root in the minds of the masses, or (as in Bakunin's case) the people need a helping hand. He advocates, as we have seen, an 'invisible dictatorship' that seems flagrantly to contradict anarchist ideals.

Certainly it is difficult to see how anarchists can combine revolutionary effectiveness without resort to force, given the fact that politics in terms of organisation, representation, leadership and compromise are ruled out in terms of the theory adopted. This is a problem not only for left-wing anarchists, but it also afflicts anarcho-capitalists who see the market as a source of freedom, but have the problem (among others) of tackling those who have vested interests in perpetuating concentrations of state power. Rothbard notes that anarchists have to contemplate 'the extremely difficult course of a revolution against a power with all the guns in its hands' (Hoffman, 1995: 124).

Despite Marshall's argument that the civil war in Spain demonstrated the strengths and not the weaknesses of anarchist theory, it is difficult not to see that event pointing to the fact that anarchists in practice can only operate in contradiction to their own theory. Those who see anarchism as having a built-in propensity to violence, whatever the pacifist claims of some of its adherents, are right. The theory cannot be understood without seeing a contradiction between ends and means.

## Anarchism and the New Social Movements

Anarchism continues to be influential, with adherents such as Herbert Read stressing the relevance of anarchism to the struggle for peace, secularism, a respect for art and the democratising of education. Comfort argues the case for sexual freedom, while Paul Goodman before his death in 1972 influenced many who took part in the counter-culture movements of the 1960s and 1970s. The relevance of anarchism to green movements and a concern about the deterioration of the urban and rural environment has been memorably stressed in the work of Murray Bookchin. Nature, he argues, is a 'complex of life', charged with ethical meaning. Nature is essentially creative, directive, mutualistic and fecund (Marshall, 1993: 605–6). This confirms the sociability and decency of humans. Without anarchism, there will be ecological disaster.

Bookchin's work is particularly important, because many of his positions have been adopted in the new social movements by people who may be unfamiliar with anarchism and would not regard themselves as anarchists. The new social movements concern themselves with a wide array of causes – animal rights and ecology; peace and women's rights; road building and private transport; to name just some. New social movements are characterised, in our view, by a general anti-authoritarianism which sees conventional politics as stifling and treacherous; by a concern with breaking down barriers between the personal and political, and adopting a style of campaigning that unites ends and means and links enjoyment to efficiency. All this suggests that particular anarchist ideas have made a huge impact, even if anarchism considered as a comprehensive philosophy and systematic movement has not.

Green parties, such as that in Germany, have enjoyed some electoral success, and have built into their procedures a libertarian distrust of authoritarianism, and what are regarded as the dangers inherent in conventional political organisation. But at the same time they have not ignored parliament or the state, and they have treated anarchism less as a dogma and more as a set of values, some of which are more relevant and valid than others.

The philosophy of direct action – that laws and private property are not sacrosanct – stems from an anarchist suspicion of the state. When people in Britain refused to pay their poll tax in the 1980s or occupied military and nuclear bases they were acting according to anarchist values – understood in the sense of particular attitudes that may be appropriate for particular situations. Writing to your MP is all very well – but much more immediate action may be called for. A commitment to social justice; a belief in the worthiness of human nature; adherence to equality; a dislike of repressive hierarchy; a concern with the destruction of the environment; anxiety about poverty in the so-called Third World – these and many other movements are inspired by parts of anarchism, though not by anarchist philosophy as a whole.

Classical anarchism is seen as being in the same boat as classical Marxism: rigid and dogmatic; old-fashioned; weak on issues of women, children's rights and the environment – too concerned with ideological rectitude and theoretical 'rigour'. Anarchists often link their dislike for large organisations to a belief that the market is corrupting and capitalism unfair. Turner argues that the natural supporters of anarchist values are those who are excluded from consumerist society and who see politicians as an elite incapable of engineering real change. He speaks of anarchism having a more receptive and permanent home among an underclass that might include 'disaffected youth, the long term unemployed and inner-city dwellers in perpetual poverty' (1993: 32). Anarchism and anarchist values are clearly the price society pays for a conventional politics that fails to ameliorate inequality and ecological damage.

## The Problem of Organisation and Relationships

It has been said that anarchism 'owes more to conventional liberalism than some of its adherents are willing to admit' (Hoffman, 1995: 113). It is not only philosophical and free market anarchists who embody the problems of the liberal tradition, so too do the anti-capitalist anarchists. The problem is that even when liberalism is militantly opposed liberal values are turned inside out – they are inverted, but never meaningfully transcended, or moved beyond.

Marshall captures the problem in a graphic way when he criticises Bookchin and Kropotkin for committing the naturalistic fallacy of deriving an 'is' from an 'ought'. 'There is', he argues, 'no logical connection to make us move from fact to value' (1993: 620). But this is a misuse of the notion of a 'naturalistic fallacy'. The 'naturalistic fallacy' should, it seems to us, refer to an erroneous belief in the timelessness of nature and of human links with nature. It is however quite another thing to argue that we cannot move from facts to value. This is a positivist (or empiricist) dictum that arises because thinkers cannot see that facts themselves embody relationships. Indeed, it is the **relational** nature of facts that gives them their evaluative or normative content. Thus, the fact that there are many women lawyers but few women judges tells us something about the relationship between men and women in our society, and therefore it would be erroneous to assume that such a fact has no ethical implications.

## Biography — Murray Bookchin (1921– )

Born in New York, Bookchin entered the communist youth movement in the 1930s. Deeply involved in organising activities around the Spanish civil war (he was too young to participate directly), he drifted away from the communists because of their role in Spain and the occurrence of the Moscow trials. After the Stalin–Hitler pact of September 1939, he was formally expelled from the Young Communist League for 'Trotskyist–anarchist deviations'.

After returning from service in the US Army during World War II, Bookchin participated in the great General Motors strike of 1946, but he began to question traditional Marxist ideas about the 'hegemonic' role of the industrial proletariat. In the late 1940s and early 1950s Bookchin wrote agitational literature that opposed not only nuclear weapons but also the peaceful uses of the atom because of radioactive fallout. In 1956 he demanded US intervention on behalf of the uprising in Hungary against the Soviet Union.

He started publishing articles on ecological issues, and in his *Our Synthetic Environment* he calls for a decentralised society and the use of alternative energy sources as part of an ecological solution. *Ecology and Revolutionary Thought* (1964) argues for a political marriage of anarchism and ecology, while *Towards a*

*Liberatory Technology* (1965) asserts that alternative technologies could provide people with the free time necessary to engage in civic self-management and a democratic body politic. These articles laid the groundwork for the body of ideas that Bookchin called social ecology.

At the same time, in the 1960s, Bookchin was deeply involved in both the counter-culture and New Left and worked to fuse the two movements. Bookchin's essays from the 1960s have been anthologised in *Post-scarcity Anarchism*. In the late 1960s he taught at the Alternative University in New York, and later at City University of New York. In 1974 he co-founded the Institute for Social Ecology and became its director; in the same year he began teaching at Ramapo College of New Jersey, where he eventually became a full professor and retired in 1981 with emeritus status.

Bookchin has also written extensively on urban issues, and his 'libertarian municipalism' is a politics based upon the recovery or creation of direct-democratic popular assemblies on municipal, neighbourhood and town levels. He has continued to publish, and is currently working on a three-volume history of popular movements in the classical revolutions, called *The Third Revolution*.

This argument suggests that Marshall, an enthusiastic anarchist, is still committed to a liberal methodology, and to a liberal opposition to understanding individuals in terms of the relationships that identify them. We see this position in anarchist attitudes to organisation. Marshall may insist that he does not reject organisation per se, but only authoritarian organisation. The fact remains, however, that he accepts a philosophical standpoint which makes it impossible to see organisation as deriving from the relational character of humans. Even anarchists such as Kropotkin and Bookchin fail to go along with the full implications of seeing humans as relational beings. By arguing that anarchism is based upon 'a mechanistic explanation of all phenomena' (Marshall, 1993: 318), Kropotkin accepts a static view of humanity – to which (as does Bakunin) he ascribes an 'instinct' for sociability. His notion of the natural sciences is positivist and he appears to argue that because humans have evolved from nature they are simply the same as other natural beings. The specificity of human relationships is not understood.

While Bookchin does stress that humans have a 'second nature' – different from but linked to their biology and their 'first nature' – it is revealing that he calls his blending of anarchism and ecology an 'ecotopia'. He proclaims that 'our Science is Utopia' without seeing that (traditionally defined) utopias 'on their own' are static and ahistorical, and postulate some kind of final end of history (Marshall, 1993: 621). This emphasises the ideal at the expense of the facts and ignores the dynamic and fluid nature of the real world. This abstract approach makes it impossible to account for relationships and the need for organisation – not simply to achieve a 'utopia' – but as an ongoing expression of human relationships.

## The Problem of Hierarchy

Anarchists in general use the term 'hierarchy' in a negative way. But hierarchy itself is part and parcel of human relationships.

Turner notes the work of A.S. Neil, who believed that education was possible without any hierarchy. Neil was the founder of the 'free school' movement, whose designs for education modelled at his Summerhill school conformed to anarchist prescriptions. There were to be no compulsory lessons; no authority of teachers over pupils; an emphasis upon self-development rather than 'instruction'; no testing of knowledge against prescribed targets; and no need to attend anything (1993: 31).

But while Summerhill school may have avoided authoritarianism, did it really avoid hierarchy as such? It is certainly true that the use of force in relationships is counter-productive and is incompatible with the nature of relationships themselves. Hence *repressive* hierarchy is inherently undesirable. But it does not follow from this that hierarchy in itself is wrong or oppressive. On the contrary, it exists in all relationships. The term 'authority' can be taken to assume persuasion and consent, but an authoritative relationship is one based on hierarchy. Surely when you go to a doctor you accept her 'authority', not because you are unwilling to question her advice, but because *in this situation* there is a hierarchy born of the fact that the doctor has a specialist knowledge of health that you lack. This is not a static hierarchy – you may become more knowledgeable yourself – nor is it a comprehensive hierarchy. If you are a motor mechanic the doctor may well come to you for help, and the hierarchy is reversed.

But, in our view, it is impossible to conceive of a relationship without hierarchy. Each party is different, and it is this difference that creates the hierarchical character of relationships. There is clearly a hierarchical relationship between parents and children. This does not mean that they are not equal, for equality, in our view, means sameness *and* difference. The hierarchy is fluid and interpenetrating: sometimes the parent teaches the child; on other occasions the parent learns from him. It is difficult not to conclude that anarchist opposition to hierarchy arises from what is essentially a liberal view that equality can only mean sameness, and that freedom is a spontaneity born of the complete absence of restraint – an abstraction that derives from the classical liberal view of individuals who 'originate' in a 'natural' world without constraint or relationship.

## The Question of Self-determination and Constraint

Anarchists argue for self-determination and this is a valid objective to aim at. But it is misleading to imagine that self-determination, as with autonomy or emancipation (to take just two related concepts), is a condition that we 'finally' reach, for like the notion of 'perfection', emancipation would turn into a nightmare if it ever 'arrived'. For what would happen to those deemed unemancipated? They would inevitably be 'forced to be free'.

What makes emancipatory concepts absolute as well as relative is the fact that our relationships with other humans, as with our relationships with the wider world of nature, are continually changing. We are absolute in the sense that all humans are the same – they must relate to nature and to one another in order to survive. But we are also relative to one another. The way we relate depends upon the world we find ourselves in, and the world we construct, and this makes us different.

Not only are humans both absolute and relative in their rights, but we are agents whose freedom derives from the recognition and transformation of necessity. This is why we are both free and constrained at the same time, for this world of necessity constrains us. Marx and Mill use the term 'coercion' to embrace morality and circumstances, but we favour a narrower view of coercion: coercion involves the threat of credible force. The kind of pressures that arise from being in society is better conceived of as a constraint and these constraints arise out of relationships, and are part and parcel of the price we pay as social beings, who can only become conscious of our individuality through relationships with others.

It is crucial to make the distinction that anarchism fails to make, between force and constraint. Force disrupts relationships, because one party loses their subjectivity and becomes a mere 'thing'. Constraint on the other hand, while sometimes unpleasant, is unavoidable and a condition for freedom. It is not possible to be free without recognising and transforming the constraints that act upon us, and even the most spontaneous act can only succeed if it acknowledges and works to change a world of constraint. When Bakunin took part in the uprising in the French city of Lyon and proclaimed 'that the administrative and governmental machinery of the state' have been abolished (Marshall, 1993: 286), he learnt that it takes more than

Ideas and Perspectives:

## Utopianism and Realism

Anarchists are right to see the state as problematic. But to look beyond the state, the state has to be presented in a way that is realistic. Why should we assume that if an idea is realistic it cannot also be utopian? Utopianism and realism need to be creatively combined, but this is only possible if one makes distinctions of a kind that break with the liberal tradition.

Of course, it is wrong to force a person to act against her will. But it does not follow from this that force can simply be abolished. The use of force as a way of addressing conflicts of interest can only be dispensed with when people have sufficient in common that they can 'change places'. An opposition to force under all circumstances constitutes utopianism without realism, for we need to work to create the conditions under which force becomes redundant.

Moreover, realism requires us to face the fact that relationships constrain as well as empower. This constraint becomes severe when used deliberately as a punishment, and although we would accept that the less of these kind of constraints the better, it is unrealistic to imagine that people can relate to one another and to the wider world of nature without some kind of constraint being employed and involved. Hence the attempt to eliminate force as a way of tackling conflicts is strengthened by the distinction between constraint and force. Society is inconceivable without constraint and hierarchy, and anarchists weaken their arguments against the state by refusing to accept this.

words to overthrow a despotic state and, unsurprisingly, the rising was speedily crushed. The point is that alliances must be formed; existing institutions utilised; the people must be prepared and feel that such an action is justified, and the forces of the opponent must be marginalised and neutralised – all the things which require organisation and the acknowledgement of constraints are crucial if a political action is to meet with hope of success.

## Anarchism and the Distinction between State and Government

The distinction between force and constraint translates into the opposition between state and government, and by condemning both anarchists again leave themselves open to the charge that they are being utopian without at the same time being realistic.

The distinction between state and government is a crucial one. Anarchists tend to regard the two as synonyms. Godwin finds that government is opposed to society. It is static and oppressive – 'the only perennial causes of the vices of mankind' – and looks towards its 'true euthanasia' (Marshall, 1993: 206–7). Kropotkin makes a distinction between state and government, but considers both equally oppressive and that both should be abolished. Representative government is no more than rule by the capitalists (Marshall, 1993: 325). It is not difficult to see that this negative view of government, as well as the state, is linked to a failure to distinguish between force and constraint.

Godwin saw public opinion as oppressive and as irresistible as whips and chains. Orwell is cited sympathetically as an anarchist who found Tolstoy's pacifism potentially coercive, while Gandhi's doctrine of non-violence has coercive overtones that Marshall sees as bullying and constituting a 'totalitarian danger' (Marshall, 1993: 650). It is one thing to warn (as J.S. Mill did) that public opinion can be intolerant and needlessly intrusive. But it is quite another to suggest that moral pressures are a kind of 'coercion' and as unacceptable as brute force. If the constraints imposed by Mill's natural penalties and the use of moral pressures are deemed authoritarian, then constitutionalism and the rule of law have to be rejected, even when these institutions operate in a purely governmental, as opposed to an oppressively statist, way (Hoffman, 1995: 127).

Government, it could be argued, is inherent in organisation and relationships. It involves the use of constraint in order to resolve conflicts that arise from the fact that each of us is different from the other. For this reason conflict is inevitable and so is government, but just as a sharp distinction needs to be drawn between constraint and force, so a distinction needs to be made between state and government. To link the state and government as twin enemies of freedom is to ignore the fact that stateless societies have governments, and that even in state-centred societies the role of government is positive and empowering. With the rise of new liberal and socialist administrations significant programmes of social reform have been introduced; the power of the trade unions has been strengthened; the health and security of the most vulnerable sections of society has been improved; and a modest redistribution of income and resources has been introduced. But these reforms are vulnerable and can be reversed, and force employed in an increasingly divisive way by the state. Indeed one radical theorist has protested that were the state to disappear overnight, 'there would be an orgy of unlimited repression and exploitation by capitalism', but this comment rests upon a confusion of state and government. It is crucial to see that many of the activities undertaken in the name of the state are not necessarily and intrinsically statist in character (Hoffman, 1995: 123).

Anarchist attacks on the 'welfare state' as bureaucratic and oppressive can only be legitimately described as *anti-statist* if they are able to show that the provision of welfare and security undermines self-development and is thus part and parcel of the state's exercise of force. If this cannot be shown, then the provision of welfare and security – to the extent that it is genuinely developmental – is governmental rather than statist in character. The existence of 'interference' and constraint is not in itself evidence of oppression since such attributes are inherent in all organisations and in relationships.

Carter is right to argue that administration in itself does not require the use of violence (1978: 324), although, of course, administrators may act in a high-handed and undemocratic fashion and thus contribute to the alienation which causes the use of force, both by the opponents of the state and by the state itself. Nevertheless, we need to keep government and the state conceptually separate, since it is wrong and counter-productive to identify government with oppression, simply because it involves pressures and sanctions of a constraining kind. Without a distinction between state and government, it is impossible to move beyond the state.

## Summary

Anarchism is often analysed as part of socialism, but anarchism is so distinctive that it deserves treatment in its own right. Philosophical anarchists are concerned with the autonomy of the individual as a theoretical problem, while free market anarchists argue the case for replacing the state with an unfettered market.

Anti-capitalist anarchists are critical of Marxism either because, as does Proudhon, they dislike collectivist solutions to the problem of inequality, or because, in the case of anarchists such as Bakunin and Kropotkin, they are unconvinced by the need for a dictatorship of the proletariat in the transformation of capitalism into communism. The Spanish civil war constitutes a veritably historical laboratory in understanding anarchism since anarchists were extremely influential during this period and their clashes with other sections of the left, and the tactics they adopted, are extremely instructive.

Anarchism is unable to handle the problem of violence, but it has played a significant role in the formation of new social movements. Anarchism runs into particular difficulty in its treatment of the problem of hierarchy and organisation. It is weakened through its failure to distinguish between state and government, and force and constraint.

## Questions

1. Should those who seek to replace the market with the state be called 'anarchists'?
2. Discuss the proposition that the new social movements, such as the movement for peace, **environmentalism** and women's rights, embrace part of anarchism rather than anarchism as a whole.
3. What do anarchists understand by 'hierarchy' and does it interfere with the demands of political organisation?
4. What do you see as the lessons of the Spanish civil war?
5. Is the notion of a stateless society a mere anarchist fantasy?

## References

Berki, R.N. (1975) *Socialism* London: Dent.

Carter, A. (1978) 'Anarchism and Violence' in J. Pennock and J. Chapman (eds), *Anarchism* New York: New York University Press, 320–40.

Dahl, R. (1989) *Democracy and its Critics* New Haven, Conn. and London: Yale University Press.

Goodwin, B. (1997) *Using Political Ideas* 4th edn Chichester and New York *et al.*: John Wiley and Sons.

Hoffman, J. (1995) *Beyond the State* Cambridge: Polity Press.

Marshall, P. (1993) *Demanding the Impossible* London: Fontana.

Maximoff, G. (ed.) (1953) *The Political Philosophy of Bakunin* New York: The Free Press.

Miller, D. (1974) *Anarchism* London: Dent.

Nozick, R. (1974) *Anarchy, State, and Utopia.* New York: Basic Books.
Orwell, G. (2001) *Orwell in Spain* (ed. P. Davison) Harmondsworth: Penguin.
Thomas, H. (1965) *The Spanish Civil War* Harmondsworth: Penguin.
Turner, R. (1993) 'Anarchism: What is it?' *Politics Review* 3(1), 28–32.
Vincent, A. (1995) *Modern Political Ideologies* Oxford: Blackwell.

## Further Reading

- Marshall's *Demanding the Impossible* (referenced above) is a detailed and highly readable account of anarchist doctrines and personalities.

- Turner's short piece on 'Anarchism: What is it?' (referenced above) is very clear and comprehensive and raises the question as to why anarchists still continue to make an impact.

- Orwell's *Homage to Catalonia* (within *Orwell in Spain*, referenced above) provides a vivid account of the way in which the anarchists operated in Spain, and the difficulties under which they worked.

- Carter's piece on 'Anarchism and Violence' (referenced above) is both thoughtful and rigorous, and raises important theoretical problems within anarchism.

- Chapter 3 in Dahl's *Democracy and its Critics* (referenced above) contains an amusing and instructive dialogue between characters he calls 'Demo' and 'Anarch' that is both critical and fair.

- Shatz's edition of *The Essential Works of Anarchism* London, New York and Toronto: Bantam Books, 1971, contains extracts from classical and more recent anarchists so that you can read the arguments 'in the original'.

- A useful exposition of anarcho-capitalism can be found in C. Stone, 'Some Reflections on Arbitrating our Way to Anarchy' in J. Pennock and J. Chapman (eds), *Anarchism* New York: New York University Press, 1978.

## Weblinks

This is very comprehensive. A1 & 2 are particularly valuable, as is A4 and some of A5: http://www.anarchistfaq.org

Used selectively, something of value here: http://www.anarchism.ws/

For anyone who wants a more detailed analysis of anarchism in Spain: http://www.struggle.ws/spaindx.html

# Chapter 5

# Nationalism

## Introduction

Nationalism has been a powerful force in modern history. It arouses strong feelings – for some, nationalism is tantamount to racism, but for others nationalist sentiment creates solidarity and stability, which are preconditions for freedom. These two perspectives are informed by history: in its most extreme form nationalism was at the root of the genocidal policies of Nazi Germany, and yet it has also been the basis of liberation movements in such regions as Eastern Europe, Africa and Asia. The challenge for political theorists is to explain how the 'nation' can be a source of value and an object of allegiance. And this is indeed a challenge: most liberals (and many anarchists) hold that the *individual human being* is the ultimate source of value, and the individual has claims against collective entities, such as the nation; many socialists are collectivists, but for them it is *class*, or *humanity* as a whole, that is the proper object of concern.

## Chapter Map

In this chapter we will:

- Outline the debate around the origins of the 'nation' and of 'nationalism'.

- Discuss the relationship between nationhood and nationalism.

- Consider the ethical implications of nationalism by reference to the distinction between **civic nationalism** and **ethnic nationalism**.

- Analyse the role of nationalism in the work of two liberal thinkers (Mill and Herder), and in the work of Marx and Engels.

# Mountains, Muesli, Cuckoo Clocks and Yodellers

Switzerland has an unusual citizenship law. It is based on three principles: (1) triple citizenship level; (2) *jus sanguinis*, or determination of citizenship through the family line, as distinct from *jus soli*, or determination of citizenship through place of birth; (3) prevention of statelessness. With regard to the first principle, every Swiss is a citizen of her commune of origin, her canton of origin, and of the Confederation. Children born to Swiss parents living abroad will lose their citizenship by the age of 22 unless they indicate to the authorities they wish to retain it, although 'reinstatement' is a possibility, especially in order to prevent statelessness.

The most controversial aspect of Swiss citizenship law is the rejection of *jus soli*: it is possible to be a third-generation resident and still be denied citizenship. Naturalisation requires approval by a local citizenship committee; individual applications may be put to a local referendum in which voting information includes pictures of the applicants. One native-born 'foreigner', 23-year-old Fatma Karademir, whose parents are Turkish, applied for citizenship through her local village citizenship committee, but was rejected and told she had to live another ten years in Switzerland before the committee could really judge her suitability for citizenship. She complains that longevity in the country counts for less than the answers she gives to the committee: 'They'll ask me if I can imagine marrying a Swiss boy . . . or if I like Swiss music, or who I'll support if Switzerland play Turkey at football – really stupid questions' ('Long Road to Swiss Citizenship', BBC website, 20 September 2004). In 2004, a proposal to ease the naturalisation process was defeated by 57 per cent to 43 per cent in a national referendum; a separate proposal to grant the right to citizenship to grandchildren of immigrants was defeated by 52 per cent to 48 per cent.

• Do you think the Swiss law is valid?

## Nations and Nationalism

In the period from around 1850 to the start of World War I in 1914 there was a marked rise in popular nationalist consciousness across Europe, with the unification of Italy in 1861 and Germany in 1871, and the so-called 'scramble for Africa' pitting the European nations against one another on that continent, while a precarious balance of power was maintained within Europe. After its defeat in World War I the Austro-Hungarian Empire fragmented into 'new' nations such as Czechoslovakia and Hungary. There was much discussion of the right to national self-determination. But in the period after World War II there was less theoretical interest in nationalism, with ideological debate centred on the struggle between liberal capitalism and state **socialism**; this was despite the fact that it was a period of significant nation building in Africa and Asia in the wake of decolonisation. Since the dramatic events in Eastern Europe in 1989 there has been an extraordinary resurgence of interest in nationalism; in large part, this has been due to the recognition that powerful nationalist sentiments survived 40 years of state socialism in Eastern Europe. So while nationalism is a 'traditional ideology' it is very much one the study of which is in the ascendant.

## Definitions

Over-reliance on dictionaries for definitions of concepts in political theory should be avoided: while it can be useful to trace the etymology of words, everyday usage is too diverse and conflicting to provide guidance on the correct employment of concepts, the meanings of which are bound up with particular theories. The word 'nation' is a good example of the dangers of dictionary definitions. Dictionaries trace the word 'nation' to the Latin *natio*, and the Latin term was certainly used in the medieval period. For example, there is a debate about whether Scotland was really a nation before the Act of Union with England in 1707; one of the documents used in favour of the claim that Scotland was a nation is the Declaration of Arbroath (1320), which was written in Latin and uses the term *natio*. The difficulty with this argument is that *natio* can be translated as 'place of birth' – note the English word 'natal' – and the 37 signatories when they make reference to themselves as a 'nation' may not necessarily have possessed the modern consciousness of nationhood (Davidson, 2000: 48–9). The point is that words do not, in themselves, settle arguments over the nature of nationalism. Meanings are embedded in theories, and we will discuss different theories in the course of this chapter. However, it is useful to set out a variety of *competing* definitions of 'nation' and of 'nationalism', and try to identify commonalities and divergences. We start with 'nation':

- **Otto Bauer** The totality of people who are united by a common fate so that they possess a common (national) character. The common fate is . . . primarily a common history; the common national character involves almost necessarily a uniformity of language (Bauer in Davis, 1967: 150).
- **Max Weber** A nation is a community of sentiment that could adequately manifest itself in a state of its own: hence a nation is a community which normally tends to produce a state of its own (Weber in Hutchinson and Smith, 1994: 25).

- **Anthony Smith** [A nation is] a named human population which shares myths and memories, a mass public culture, a designated homeland, economic unity and equal rights and duties for all members (Smith, 1991: 43).

- **Benedict Anderson** [A nation] is an imagined political community – and imagined as both inherently limited and sovereign . . . all communities larger than primordial villages of face-to-face contact (and perhaps even these) are imagined. Communities are to be distinguished, not by their falsity/genuineness, but by the style in which they are imagined (Anderson, 1991: 6).

- **James Kellas** A nation is a group of people who feel themselves to be a community bound together by ties of history, culture and common ancestry. Nations have 'objective' characteristics that may include a territory, a language, a religion or common descent (though not all of these are always present), and 'subjective' characteristics, essentially a people's awareness of its nationality and affection for it (Kellas, 1998: 3).

All five definitions begin with the idea of a 'collective': 'totality of people', 'community of sentiment', 'named human population', 'imagined political community', 'group of people . . . community'. But disagreement exists on how this collective is held together. Bauer maintains the nation possesses a 'common character' or 'common fate', which necessarily entails a shared language. Weber argues that sentiment – or fellow feeling – holds the collective together, but that it also has a political project, namely the drive to create a state. Smith is more pluralistic in his understanding of what makes the collective cohere: myths, memories, mass public culture, homeland, economic unity, rights and duties. The last basis is, however, distinctly political: the nation has a legal dimension. Anderson maintains that we 'imagine' the nation: because we will never meet more than a tiny fraction of our fellow citizens the national community is imaginary, constructed above all through the medium of literature. Finally, Kellas draws attention to the objective *and* subjective dimensions of nationhood – nations require 'objective materials' such as territory or language, but there must also be a corresponding consciousness of belonging to a nation. It may be that, for example, Switzerland's multilingual character increases the necessity of a populist mechanism for citizenship, even if the Swiss are open to the charge of racism. An important issue is raised by these competing definitions: what are the origins of the nation? If, as Bauer implies, there is an ethnic basis to nationhood, then, to use a cliché, does not the nation have its roots in the 'mists of time'? If, however, the nation is a distinctly political project, and political structures change over time, then nationhood would appear to be a relatively recent phenomenon. We pursue this issue in more detail in the following section. What then of 'nationalism'? Again, we have competing understandings of nationalism:

- **Ernest Gellner** It is a theory of political legitimacy, which requires that ethnic boundaries should not cut across political ones, and in particular, that ethnic boundaries within a given state . . . should not separate the power holders from the rest (Gellner, 1983: 1).

- **Elie Kedourie** Nationalism is a doctrine invented in Europe at the beginning of the nineteenth century. It pretends to supply the criterion for the determination of the unit of population proper to enjoy a government exclusively of its own, for the legitimate exercise of power in the state and for the right organisation of a society of states. Briefly, the doctrine holds that humanity is naturally divided into nations, that nations are known by certain characteristics which can be ascertained, and that the only legitimate type of government is national self-government (Kedourie, 1993: 9).

- **Montserrat Guibernau** By nationalism I mean the sentiment of belonging to a community whose members identify with a set of symbols, beliefs and ways of life and have the will to decide upon their common political destiny (Guibernau, 1996: 47).

Whereas the term 'nation' refers to some kind of entity, 'nationalism' would appear to be a body of doctrine, theory or beliefs about the nation, its historical signif-icance and moral importance. Common sense would suggest that nations precede nationalism: there must exist this entity we call a 'nation' in order to develop attitudes or beliefs towards it. This view is, however, challenged by 'modernists', who maintain that nations are the product of nationalism. Against them, 'perenni-alists' argue that nations do exist before the development of nationalism: the former are **pre-modern**, while the latter is modern.

## Modernism versus Perennialism

Most of the discussion of nationalism has been between political scientists rather than political theorists. While it is acknowledged that nationalist sentiment has been a powerful political force, political theorists, who tend to operate with *universalist* concepts such as human nature, freedom, equality and justice, have found it difficult to explain nationalism, which is, essentially, *particularist* – that is, it assumes that national boundaries are morally significant. At best, nationalism has been incorporated into other ideologies, such as liberalism or socialism, as a subsidiary or derivative concern. For example, liberals or socialists may argue that all human beings are equally worthy of moral concern, but the world is a better place if it is organised into nations – world government would be inefficient, or dangerous, because it would concentrate rather than disperse power. Given this relative neglect of nationalism within the history of political thought the best approach is to consider the political science debate and see whether it has implications for the ethical issues that are at the heart of political theory.

Within political science attention has focused on explaining the origins of *nations* and, distinct from nations, *nationalism*. As suggested above, two positions can be identified on the question of the origin of the nation: modernist and perennialist. For modernists, the nation is a modern creation, dependent on certain features of **modernity**, such as the unification of territory and the rise of a popular consciousness of belonging to this entity called a 'nation'. Nationalism – the ideology of nationhood – precedes the creation of nations. Perennialists accept that *nationalism* is modern, and that the nation itself has undergone significant changes in the modern period, but that the nation is continuous with an older community, which may have an ethnic, linguistic or cultural basis: nationhood can be 'forgotten' but it can also be 'recovered'. Anthony Smith provides a useful summary of the differences between modernism and **perennialism** (Smith, 1998: 22–3), as shown below.

The terms modernism and perennialism are broad categories encompassing a number of different theories, and to make sense of the two positions we need to say more about these particular theories.

| Perennialism | Modernism |
|---|---|
| 1. **Cultural community:** the nation is a politicised ethno-cultural community – a community of common ancestry that stakes a claim to political recognition on that basis. | **Political community:** the nation is a territorialised political community – a civic community of legally equal citizens in a particular territory. |
| 2. **Immemorial:** the history of the nation stretches back centuries, or even millennia. | **Modern:** the nation is recent and novel – a product of modern conditions. |
| 3. **Rooted:** the nation is 'rooted' in place and time and embedded in a historic homeland. | **Created:** the nation is consciously and deliberately 'built' by its members, or segments of its membership. |
| 4. **Organic:** the nation is a popular or demotic community – a community of 'the people' and mirroring their needs. | **Mechanical:** the nation is consciously constructed by elites who seek to influence the emotions of the masses to achieve their goals. |
| 5. **Qualities:** belonging to a nation means possessing certain qualities – membership is a state of 'being'. | **Resources:** belonging to a nation means possessing certain resources – membership is a capacity for 'doing'. |
| 6. **Seamless:** nations are seamless wholes, with a single character. | **Divided:** nations are typically riven and divided into a number of (regional, class, gender, religious, etc.) social groups. |
| 7. **Ancestry based:** the underlying principles of the nation are of ancestral ties and authentic culture. | **Communications based:** the principles of national solidarity are to be found in social communication and citizenship. |

## Modernist Theories

Although there are many non-Marxist modernist theories of nationhood, it is the writings of Marx and Engels that have been the most influential in the formation of the modernist perspective on nationalism. Recall that for Marx and Engels class is the central concept in history – history is, at base, class conflict. Nation, unlike class, does not have an objective existence; whereas your class is determined by your objective position in the relations of production, independently of whether or not you recognise yourself as belonging to that class, membership of a nation is, in large part, determined by consciousness of membership of it. In the case of class, we move from an objective reality to a subjective consciousness of that reality; in the case of nations we move from subjective consciousness to objective reality. A few qualifications are, however, required to this distinction between class and nation:

- There must be a significantly large group for national consciousness to develop – individuals cannot, at will, create nations.
- An individual may be recognised as a member of a nation without recognising herself as a member; for example, her language or religion or family origin may mark her out as a member of a particular nation, even if she does not recognise herself as a member.
- There must be some 'objective materials' in order to construct a national consciousness.

The construction of the nation can be likened to the selection of ingredients for a meal: there is a choice to be made, such that the ingredients are akin to fragments of nationhood, which are then put together to make a single thing. Examples of such 'fragments' might include a particular language, or a dialect raised to a linguistic standard; a constructed history, with significant dates, myths, stories and interpretations; a common ancestry based on phenotypical similarity (how people look); a territory; religion; political institutions. The inclusion of the last item may seem odd: surely, having political institutions presupposes the existence of a nation, rather than being an ingredient in the construction of nationhood? We consider the distinction between 'state' and 'nation' in a later section, but the point to make here is that for modernists the existence of 'national' political institutions does not necessarily indicate the existence of national *consciousness*: such institutions could be 'elite', and thus not the object of a *popular* consciousness.

For Marx and Engels the growth of a national consciousness, and thus a nation, is bound up with the development of capitalism, which requires determinate legal institutions, a bounded territorial market, a shared means of communication, flexible labour markets and so relatedly a certain level of education, a single unit of currency, trade agreements and so international recognition of independent nation-states. On top of these economic requirements there is a need to legitimate the state, and this necessitates the development of a psychological identification with the nation. To generate that legitimacy may require drawing on pre-modern bases of group identification, such as ethnic symbolism. Neil Davidson, in his book *The Origins of Scottish Nationhood* (2000), arguing from a particular Marxist perspective, claims that Scotland only became a nation after the union with England in 1707, and the process involved the 'Celtification' of Scotland: prior to the defeat of the Jacobite Highlands in 1745, Scottish nationhood had been unable to develop precisely because there had existed a deep division of Highland and Lowland marked by geography, language, religion, and the absence of a single market. After the defeat of the Highlands, its symbols – tartanry, bagpipes, the kilt, Celtic myths – were disseminated throughout Scotland, such that they came to symbolise what it meant to be Scottish, and be the means by which a group of people identified one another as Scottish. Pre-modern symbols were pressed into service to create *for the first time* a Scottish nation (Davidson, 2000: 139).

We will consider the more normative aspects of Marx and Engels's views of nationalism in the section on Socialism and Nationalism, but at this stage we are concerned to identify the basic elements of the Marxist and non-Marxist modernist view of nationalism. Modernists talk in general terms about the relationship between modernity (capitalism, industrialism) and nationhood, but more detailed theories are required if we are to explain the differences between nations and, in particular, why some nations appear to have a stronger 'ethnic' character than others. Space prevents more than a selection of the most influential theories:

- **Tom Nairn** explains nationalism in terms of the uneven development of capitalism: marginalised 'elites' on the periphery of industrialised regions mobilise the masses so as to create 'a militant, inter-class community . . . strongly (if mythically) aware of its own separate identity vis-à-vis the outside forces of domination' (Nairn, 1977: 340). The wealthy centre has no need for such romantic, ethnic nationalism because it derives pride and confidence from its economic achievements. Such an analysis could be used to explain 'regional' nationalisms in Europe, but also nationalisms in the 'developing world', where the 'core' is the developed world.

- **Michael Hechter** offers a 'rational choice' analysis of nationalism (Hechter, 1988: 271). For Hechter, nations are no different to other groups, and individuals join groups in order to gain benefits. Nations are 'solidarity groups' that apply sanctions to prevent individuals gaining the benefits of membership while evading the costs. Because secession from the group carries a very high cost, it will only succeed if enough people want to secede, and the benefits of secession outweigh any costs imposed on those who attempt to secede. It follows that existing nations must provide inducements as well as impose sanctions if they wish to avoid secession. Rational choice theory cannot, however, explain the *passion* with which many people identify with the nation.

- **Eric Hobsbawm** and **Benedict Anderson** offer rather different explanations of nationalism, but are both part of a tradition of theorising the nation as involving 'invented traditions' (Hobsbawm) or being an 'imagined community' (Anderson). For Hobsbawm, the memory of having belonged to a political community is extended by an elite to the masses, and in the process 'traditions' are 'invented' which give rise to a consciousness of the nation as 'ancient' (Hobsbawm and Ranger, 1983: 13–14). Anderson argues the nation is 'imagined' because its members will never meet; in the absence of meeting, each member imagines the nation as limited, bounded and sovereign. Print communities, facilitated by capitalism, permitted the development of a linguistic standard, and a literary imagination (Anderson, 1991: 6).

Anderson's argument draws attention to an important dimension of nationalism: language. It is commonplace to trace the development of the system of nation-states back to the Treaty of Westphalia (1648), which was the final 'settlement' of the Wars of Religion which had raged in Europe in the previous 100 or more years, and which had been caused in part by the schism with Christianity between the Reformers ('Protestants') and the Church of Rome ('Catholics'). Most modernists would claim that 1648 is too early a date from which to mark the beginning of the

Ch 1:
Liberalism,
p. 15

nation-state; many would, however, acknowledge the importance of Protestantism in the development of nationalism. As was argued in Chapter 1, a significant aspect of Protestantism was the translation of the Bible into the vernacular languages of Europe. In many cases these translations set a *national standard* for the languages concerned, and led to a process of linguistic unification within a particular territory.

## Perennialist Theories

Hans Kohn, writing in 1944, distinguished two forms of nationalism: organic and voluntarist, with voluntarism corresponding to modernism. Organic nationalism assumes that the world consists of 'natural' nations, and has always done so, and that nations are the primary actors in history. Each nation is an 'organic whole', with a distinct character (Kohn, 1944: 3–24). Many such nations have, however, lost their 'self-consciousness' as nations, along with their political independence, and so nationalism is a 'restoration project' rather than a 'construction project': the creation of Hungary and Czechoslovakia in the wake of the collapse of the Austro-Hungarian empire after its defeat in World War I exemplifies the restoration project.

While the normative task of nationalists is to restore both consciousness and independence, the theoretical challenge for such perennialist nationalism is twofold: explaining the basis of such *natural* nations, and accounting for the loss of consciousness. There are a variety of accounts of such nations:

- **Pierre van den Berghe** argues that a nation is an extended kinship group. Human sociality is based on three principles: kin selection, reciprocity and **coercion**. Nations originate from tribes, or 'super-families', defined by territory; he does not claim that there is necessarily a genetic *identity* – migration and conquest rule that out – but what holds the group together are powerful sentiments of kinship, which give rise to a drive for genetic reproduction within the group. Human beings need markers for discriminating 'our kin', and these include language, dress and other cultural traits (van den Berghe, 1978: 403–4).

- **Clifford Geertz**, in his study of post-colonial nations in Africa and Asia, argues that such nations are caught between the 'modern' demand for economic success and a 'primordial' desire to belong, based on 'assumed blood ties' (Geertz, 1993: 259–60). Given that the boundaries of these nations encompass a plurality of 'assumed blood tied groups' they tend to instability, as groups struggle with one another for control of the state.

- **Joshua Fishman**, in his analysis of ethnicity and language in Eastern Europe, argues that nationalism can be understood only 'from the inside' – that is, by considering how the participants themselves view it. Ethnicity is the basis of nationhood, but it is not primarily a matter of biology, rather ethnic identification is achieved through a process of 'authentification', meaning that nations change, but the change has to be compatible with how the citizens of that nation see themselves (Fishman, 1980: 84–5). In essence, nationalism answers a deep psychological need for belonging.

Few perennialist theorists claim that nations equate to biological groups, although that belief certainly has been at the basis of racist theories of nationhood. But what then distinguishes perennialism from modernism? After all, many modernists accept that people value the nation because it appears to correspond to an ethnic group, and that the process of nation building entails drawing on that ethnic loyalty. What distinguishes perennialism from modernism is a belief that the 'building blocks' of the modern nation are pre-existing communities grounded in kinship relations; the smallest such community is the family.

## Nationalism: the Ethical Debate

### Implications of the Modernist–Perennialist Debate

While we need to be careful about drawing conclusions for political theory from what are descriptive theories, it is not difficult to see how competing modernist and perennialist explanations of nationalism *may* carry moral–political implications. Using Smith's table, set out in the box on p. 115, we can turn each of his points into a moral–political question:

1. **Who belongs to the nation?** What does a person have to do, or what qualities must he possess, in order to be the citizen of a particular nation-state?

2. **What is the purpose of the nation?** If the nation is 'recent' and 'novel' then there is an implication that it was created, or came about, to fulfil specifically modern functions, and if it fails then it should be dissolved or in some way reconstituted. If, however, the nation is 'ancient', then it may be that continuity and survival are what matter – simply existing is what matters.

3. **What is the relationship of the nation to 'land' or 'soil', as against the struggle for resources?** Politics is, in large part, a struggle over resources, including territory, but if 'land' has historical resonance, then territory is not simply an interchangeable resource. Although the most striking example of the struggle over symbolically charged territory is that between Israel and Palestine, it might also be argued that there is a struggle over resources, such as access to water, and that an overemphasis on the symbolic elements of the Israel–Palestine conflict obscures the more 'mundane' aspects of that conflict.

4. **What role does the nation play in engendering loyalty to the state?** To what extent is a person's *individual* identity bound up with membership of a particular nation? If, as modernists argue, the nation is constructed by elites, then national loyalty would seem to be shallow. If, however, nations are not created but develop 'organically' from more basic kinship groups, then loyalty to the state, as the political expression of the nation, is 'deep'.

5. **Is the nation an end-in-itself – that is, intrinsically valuable?** If a person's identity is bound up with the nation, and human beings are 'ends in themselves', then it follows that nations must be intrinsically valuable. But modernists would argue that nations are simply means for acquiring and securing resources.

6. **Does loyalty to nation 'trump' all other loyalties?** For a modernist, the nation is one loyalty among others, but for a perennialist it is a seamless whole. The most extreme perennialist position maintains that the nation is an 'organic' whole, such that the value of its parts is derivative from their relationship to the whole.

7. **What is the basis of national solidarity – why care about fellow nationals, as against other people?** This question raises issues of international justice – in a world of nations, what obligations does one nation have to another? Indeed, should international obligations hold between *nations*, or between *individual human beings*?

We have expressed the ethical issues raised by the perennialism–modernism debate in somewhat abstract terms, but answers to these questions carry implications for more concrete matters of political organisation and public policy. These include the following:

- the treatment of minorities within a national territory;
- the possible conflict between the rights of the individual and the rights of the nation;
- immigration policy;
- the relationship between nation-states, including conflict over resources;
- the tension between respecting the sovereignty of a nation-state and militarily intervening on humanitarian grounds in the affairs of that state.

The debate within political theory tends to focus on the conflict between the rights of individuals and sub-national groups as against the rights of the nation, and on the conflict between nation-states within the international system of states. And corresponding closely, but not completely, to the distinction between perennialism and modernism is a distinction between civic (or civil) nationalism and ethnic nationalism.

## State versus Nation

Before considering civic and ethnic nationalism it is important to highlight a conceptual distinction implicit in the preceding discussion: we have used the terms 'nation', 'state' and 'nation-state' interchangeably. The state is a complex and allusive concept, but is associated with the organisation of power, or coercion, and those who exercise such power make an implicit or explicit claim to legitimacy in exercising it. Whether or not those subject to such power accept it as legitimate, we can at least say that the state is bound up with the concept of legality. Certainly, in international law, the state is an 'artificial person', bearing rights and duties. If we were to define a nation as a state we would encounter two problems: first, we would be unable to account for the phenomenon of nationalist consciousness, because not all groups who make claims to nationhood possess the attributes of statehood. Possible examples of stateless nations include Palestine, Scotland, Kurdistan, Tibet, Kosovo and Quebec. Second, by identifying nations with states, we encounter an ethical problem, namely that many nationalist conflicts are about a claim to statehood on the basis of the existence of nationhood. Such a claim depends on a conceptual distinction between state and nation. That said, there is a close relationship between the concepts of nation and state: even if we reject Weber's definition of the nation as 'a community which tends to produce a state of its own', most nationalists do express a demand for political independence – they want to turn their 'nation' into a 'nation-state'.

## Civic Nationalism and Ethnic Nationalism

Michael Ignatieff defines a civic nation as 'a community of equal, rights-bearing citizens, united in patriotic attachment to a shared set of political practices and values' (Ignatieff: 7). For a civic nationalist 'belonging' to a nation entails a rational choice rather than an inheritance. In contrast, an ethnic nationalist maintains 'that an individual's deepest attachments are inherited, not chosen' (Ignatieff: 7). The distinction between the two forms of nationalism has been attributed to Hans Kohn, who, in his discussion of nationalism in the nineteenth century, defined 'Western' nations, such as France, Britain and the United States as civic, and 'Eastern' nations, such as Germany and Russia, as ethnic. Indeed, our discussion of Swiss citizenship law at the beginning of this chapter appears to lend plausibility to this categorisation, with the principle of *jus sanguinis* suggesting ethnic criteria for citizenship, while *jus soli* implies a civic conception. But this is an oversimplification.

Drawing on the discussion of citizenship laws (pp. 122–3) consider, for example, those of Germany. Germany was unified relatively late, and it is argued that national consciousness preceded the formal creation of Germany as a political entity, albeit Prussia had existed as a significant power since the late seventeenth century and, in addition, there emerged a federation of German states and principalities after Napoleon Bonaparte's defeat in 1815. Despite this gradual unification of Germany, only in 1871 was there achieved an approximate correspondence of national and political boundaries, such that Germany was, prior to 1871, in effect a stateless nation. We have to say 'approximate' because the cultural boundaries of Germany, defined above all by the German language, did not correspond to the political boundaries even of post-1871 Germany. The consequence was that the newly unified Germany had serious difficulty in defining citizenship, and it was only in 1913 that the citizenship law was codified. The self-understanding of the German nation as primarily a cultural entity, which had been given political identity as a state, fundamentally affected that law. On the face of it, German nationalism would appear, therefore, to be 'ethnic' rather than 'civic', and the overtly racist laws passed during the Nazi years appear retrospectively to reinforce this perception of German nationalism. Much of the discussion in the German and international media in the late 1990s of the German citizenship law reforms focused on what appeared to be archaic 'blood-line' notions of citizenship. However, it is quite possible to interpret the 1913 German citizenship law as a response to modern conditions: a developing nation with indeterminate boundaries requires criteria for citizenship, and some idea of culture or ethnicity seemed the most appropriate. In modernist terms, the available ingredients of nationhood meant that Germany had to rely on 'ethnic' criteria in order to create a *modern* nation. This is not to say that there is no connection between the 1913 law and the citizenship laws promulgated by the Nazis in the 1930s, but simply that the use of apparently ethnic criteria does not preclude the possibility that Germany was – Nazi years apart – basically a civic nation. Conversely, those nations described by Kohn as 'civic' are not free of ethnic criteria for citizenship.

As with Germany, the development of British and US citizenship laws were a response to their specific geographic and historic conditions. As Samuel Huntington argues, the United States can be considered a settler society rather than an immigrant society, and those original settlers defined themselves as British and Protestant; while post-Independence America sought to distance its political institutions from any particular Christian denomination, a belief in God was implicit in being American, and the structures of the Protestant world-view were deeply embedded in the nation. The large numbers of non-Protestants who migrated to the USA in the period between the civil war (1861–5) and World War I were 'assimilated' into the existing value system (Huntington, 2004: 95–8). In the case of Britain, the very loose citizenship laws that operated until 1981 were a response to the specific historical conditions of British nation building and transformation; in particular, the need to cement the relationship between England and Scotland, which was achieved to a significant degree through the building of an empire. The point is that 'being British' relied on ethnic criteria just as much as 'being German' did; what made British identity appear more 'civic' was that loyalty to the nation was expressed through loyalty to a constitutional monarchy, rather than to the 'British people'.

## Citizenship Law: Germany, Britain and the USA

We started this chapter with a discussion of Swiss citizenship law. It is useful to compare Swiss law with those of Germany, Britain and the United States, and then reflect below on what these laws say about each of the countries.

### Germany

The traditional basis for acquiring German citizenship was through descent (*jus sanguinis*), meaning that you had to prove that one or more of your parents was German, with the possibility of restoration of citizenship to those stripped of it by the Nazi regime, or to their descendants. A law passed in 1953 extended the concept of membership of the nation (*Volkszugehörigkeit*) to all ethnic Germans in Eastern Bloc countries. Thus the law was highly inclusive of anyone who could prove German descent. On the other hand, until the year 2000 millions of 'guest workers' were denied the right to citizenship because the law did not recognise the principle of acquisition of citizenship by place of birth (*jus soli*), except under certain circumstances and at the discretion of the state. The new law, which came into effect on 1 January 2000, allowed the children of non-German parents to acquire, by right, citizenship if one parent has had a minimum legal residence in Germany of eight years and has held an unlimited residence permit for at least three years. Under most circumstances, the child who acquires citizenship in this way must, before the age of 23, revoke any other nationality – in principle, Germany does not tolerate multiple citizenship. In addition, new citizens must demonstrate competence in the German language, and swear allegiance to the principles of the Constitution.

### Britain

In theory, loyalty to the British monarch, as expressed through the holding of a British passport, has been the primary determinant of 'nationality'; however, there are different categories of passport, not all of which grant *citizenship*. In the period from 1948 to 1981 Britain moved closer to other European countries in adopting a citizenship law, partly based on *jus sanguinis* and partly on *jus soli*. Compared to many countries, the proof of integration required as part of the naturalisation process is light: basic competence in English (or Welsh, or Scots Gaelic), being of 'good character', and swearing (or affirming) that you will 'be faithful and bear true allegiance to Her Majesty Queen Elizabeth the Second her Heirs and Successors according to Law'. Citizenship ceremonies were introduced in 2004, and since then new citizens have also been required to pledge loyalty to the country's rights, freedoms and democratic values. Multiple citizenship is permitted.

## United States

The United States sees itself as, historically, a 'country of immigration'. For that reason, the principle of *jus sanguinis* might be thought weak; however, as in most countries, a family connection does provide a person with a privileged access to citizenship. That said, historically, naturalisation has been an extremely important route to citizenship; perhaps unsurprisingly, the symbolic dimensions are very important. In addition to legal residency requirements, an applicant must be of 'good moral character', and there is a long list of criminal offences that preclude a person from citizenship. He must show attachment to the principles of the Constitution, be competent in the English language, demonstrate knowledge of US history and government (a pass of 6 out of 10 questions from a battery of 100 is required). Finally, the applicant must swear an oath of allegiance – this takes rather longer than the seven-second British oath.

## The Debate over German (Re-)unification

The fall of the Berlin Wall in 1989 and the 1990 (re-)unification of East and West Germany generated an interesting debate between three German intellectuals: philosopher Jürgen Habermas, cultural critic Karl-Heinz Bohrer and novelist Günter Grass. Each presented a distinct position on the nature of the German nation, and more broadly on the role of nationalism in political life. Grass argued against unification mainly on the grounds that 'there can be no demand for a new version of a unified nation that in the course of barely 75 years, although under several managements, filled the history books, ours and theirs, with suffering, rubble, defeat, millions of dead, and the burden of crimes that can never be undone' (Grass in James and Stone, 1992: 57–8). The division must remain as a tangible symbol of those crimes. Bohrer, on the other hand, argues that the crimes to which Grass refers have their roots, in part, in the parochialism of the 'police states' which constituted the pre-1871 Germany; what Germany needs is a sense of nationhood. He accepts that the Holocaust is the 'great, unavoidable fact of our modern history', but a cultural regeneration of Germany – nationalism rather than parochialism – is the best guarantor of liberal democracy. Habermas, while accepting the legitimacy of unification – and it is unification rather than reunification, for the 'two Germanys' in no way correspond to the Germany of 1937 – argues for a form of civic nationalism, based on what he calls 'constitutional patriotism'. His argument revolves around a complex debate concerning the legal nature of the 1990 unification: in effect, it extended the West German 'constitution' (1949 *Grundgesetz* – Basic Law) to East Germany, rather than creating a new constitution (*Verfassung* – this word was not used in 1949 because it was always assumed that the division of East and West would be temporary). Had there been a new constitution, endorsed by a referendum, the German people would quite literally have 'constituted' themselves rather than seeing the unified nation as the product of 'pre-political imponderables like linguistic community, culture, or history' (Habermas in James and Stone, 1992: 97).

Note: This debate is reproduced in Harold James and Marla Stone (eds) (1992) *When the Wall Came Down: Reactions to German Unification*.

## Nationalism and Exclusivity

There is some validity in the distinction between civic nationalism as based on allegiance to political institutions and ethnic nationalism as entailing a belief in unity through blood or culture. But the distinction is overstated. In the post-World War II period the – justifiable – concern with Nazism resulted in a strong focus on the racist aspects of nationalism to the detriment of a concern with the conflict between nations over resources. All nations are, by definition, exclusive: each must determine its membership. A civic nation may do so, first, by accepting the existing population of a territory, irrespective of its ethnic and cultural identity, and, then, by granting citizenship to those who can demonstrate allegiance to the nation. But to demonstrate allegiance you have to live in the country, and immigration controls prevent people entering the country. It is possible to have a 'colour-blind' immigration policy, but then some other criteria are required. One possibility is entry on the basis of skill, but the result of such a policy is to poach the most able members of poorer countries. Every nation must answer the question 'who belongs?', and there is no answer to that question that does not generate some form of political conflict.

## Liberalism and Nationalism: Mill and Herder

## Liberalism versus Nationalism

At first sight liberalism and nationalism appear odd bed-fellows: for nationalists the most significant moral entity is the nation, whereas for liberals the most significant is the individual human being. Where there is a conflict between the claims of the individual and those of the nation, liberals and nationalists will diverge over which should take precedence. Furthermore, the priority given to the individual by liberals normally rests on features all human beings share, such that the logic of liberal individualism is moral *universalism* (individualism might also lead to egoism, but we will ignore that possibility here). In contrast, nationalists are *particularists*: although some nationalists will argue that there is a universal need to belong to a nation, nationalism entails regarding one's own nation as 'special'. The differences between liberalism and nationalism can be expressed in the following way:

| Entity | Moral attitude or response |
|---|---|
| Humanity | Universalism |
| Nation | Particularism |
| Individual | Universalism (or Egoism) |

The difficulty with this apparent rejection of nationalism is that historically liberalism and nationalism have often been combined into a single political programme: the struggle for national self-determination has been expressed in the language of freedom, self-government and accountability. The question is whether the apparent affinity of liberalism and nationalism is simply a historical accident, or whether there is a deeper philosophical compatibility that is not captured by an oversimplistic derivation of **universalism** from individualism.

Jean-Jacques Rousseau can be taken as the first significant liberal thinker to make an explicit case for nationalism. His defence of nationalism was based on the importance of a 'people' possessing a general will, the recognition of which supposedly guarantees individual freedom; the general will is not reducible to the wills of individuals, or to a simple aggregation of wills. Rousseau's theory is highly abstract, and seems unconnected to the political realities of his time, but it has been influential in the development of a popular nationalism based on democratic self-government. What provides the link between liberalism and nationalism in Rousseau's theory is the idea of democracy, such that a better understanding of the relationship between the individual and the nation is:

Nation ◄—► Sovereign People (democracy) ◄—► Individual

However, there are still difficulties involved in reconciling nationalism and liberalism. First, as we have argued, democracy and liberalism, while closely related, can conflict: democracy does imply that each person's interests should be given equal consideration, but to make decisions we have to rely on a voting system, such that some people's preferences will almost inevitably be overridden. To protect individual freedom, we need rights that cannot be removed by the majority. The threat from majorities exists whether or not there is strong nationalist sentiment, but it is deepened by the existence of such sentiment. Second, even if we can guarantee the rights of individuals within a democracy, a world divided into nation-states raises issues of international justice: there are strong and wealthy nations, and there are weak and poor nations. If individuals matter then they matter irrespective of their nationality.

While the nation *may* be a threat to **liberty** and to international justice, there are grounds for holding that a world of nation-states is more likely to guarantee liberty and justice than some other form of political organisation. Two quite different lines of argument suggest themselves; both are liberal but, in fact, correspond respectively to civic and ethnic forms of nationalism. The first – civic – argument is that the world is more stable and efficient if organised around nation-states, where each nation respects the territorial integrity of the others. This argument attaches *instrumental* value to the nation: that is, the nation serves the purposes of individuals. The second – ethnic – argument maintains that individuals need culture as a means of self-expression, and the nation-state is the embodiment of culture. Such an argument assumes that nations have *intrinsic* value – valuing individual lives means respecting an individual's culture, the political expression of which is the nation-state. In terms of the history of political thought, John Stuart Mill was an important exponent of the first position, while Johann Gottfried von Herder defended the second position.

## John Stuart Mill

In his book *Considerations on Representative Government* (published 1859) Mill argues that 'free institutions are next to impossible in a country made up of different nationalities' (Mill, 1991: 428). A 'nation' Mill defines as a portion of humankind united 'among themselves' by common sympathies, which make them cooperate with each other more willingly than with those of other nations. These common sympathies may be based on 'race and descent', language, religion, shared memory and political antecedents. Mill states that the last of these is the most important, and yet his brief discussion of nationalism actually focuses much more on the need for a shared language than the existence of historic political institutions. Without a shared language a 'united public opinion' cannot exist; if, say, two major languages coexist, then public life is vertically divided, with each group reading different newspapers, books and pamphlets, and each looking to its own political class, which speaks to them in their own language.

The danger with a 'multi-national' – meaning, a multilingual – state is that the army, as the security wing of the state, is held together by obedience to its officers, and not by a shared sympathy. Although Mill does not argue for a popular militia, he does imply that the army, and other security forces, must have popular legitimacy. Faced with popular discontent, an army made up of one particular ethnic-linguistic group will just as soon 'mow down' the members of another group as they will 'foreigners' (429). In a multi-national state the objective of the government will be the maintenance of stability, and that will entail balancing competing linguistic groups, such that instead of developing fellow feeling differences will become institutionalised. Mill concedes that there are successful multi-national states, the best example being Switzerland, and he also accepts that geographical 'intermingling' can be such that some states must be multi-national. But he considers it preferable that 'peripheral' minorities be absorbed by larger nations: a Breton is better to share 'the advantages of French protection, and the dignity and prestige of French power, than to sulk on his own rocks, the half-savage relic of past times' (431). Similarly, Wales and the Scottish Highlands are better absorbed into Britain. Today, these remarks seem anachronistic: the emphasis now is on respecting differences within the nation-state, and ensuring that 'threatened' languages such as Breton, Welsh and Scots Gaelic survive – note, for example, that the British naturalisation process requires competence in English *or* Welsh *or* Gaelic. However, the anti-ethnic basis of Mill's argument is significant: the 'admixture' and 'blending' of nationalities is to the benefit of humanity, because it softens the extremes between people (432). In essence, Mill's nationalism is 'assimilationist' – nations are culturally hybrid, but the political project must be to create fellow feeling, because this guarantees the development and reinforcement of individual freedom.

## Johann Gottfried von Herder

Herder is a major point of reference within the tradition that takes the nation to be a pre-modern ethnic community. For this reason it might be thought that he cannot also be a liberal. Yet, in fact, Herder has been influential among those liberals who see human beings as necessarily cultural beings. At the heart of culture is language, and Herder anticipates one of the dominant themes of twentieth-century philosophy in arguing that human self-consciousness is dependent on language: the very capacity to think presupposes language. Furthermore, language is necessarily collective, and while it is possible to identify universal features, languages are

## Johann Gottfried von Herder (1744–1803)

Herder was a major influence on the formation of German nationalism; his reflections on the importance of culture inspired the Grimm Brothers (Jacob and Wilhelm) in their collection of Germanic folk stories.

Herder was born in Mohrungen in Prussia (it is now in Poland, and in Polish is called Morag). He studied at the University of Königsberg. In 1764 he went to Riga as a preacher and teacher; in his 1770 essay 'On the Origins of Language' he wrote that no man lives for himself alone, he is 'knit into the whole texture' of society. That essay received some critical notice, and it brought him into contact with the great German writer Johann Wolfgang von Goethe (1749–1832), and many intellectual historians locate the beginnings of the Sturm und Drang (Romantic) movement to their meeting.

In 1771 Herder became pastor at Bückeburg, moving in 1776 to Weimar, where Goethe was resident. He published *Stimmen der Völker in ihren Liedern* (*Voices of the People in their Songs*) (1773), which was used later by poets and composers under the title *Des knaben Wunderhorn* (*The Boy's Magic Horn*).

particular; a language is not simply a means by which we name things, but in writing, reading and speaking a particular language, such as English or German, we locate ourselves and others in a particular world of emotion and sentiment. (For a modern application of Herder's reflections, see Breuilly, 1993: 55–9.)

Herder attempts to reconcile Enlightenment and Romanticist views of human nature. Under the influence of the former, he argues that to be free, autonomous agents we need language, but under the influence of the latter, he maintains that language summons up an emotional world. Herder also attempts to reconcile progress and tradition: the transmission of culture from one generation to another involves both the preservation of culture, or tradition, and the confrontation of the old with the new. This has implications for his understanding of nationalism: since newness is part of tradition, and can come from outside a culture as a 'foreign influence', nations should not be chauvinistic. However, while Herder distances himself from extreme nationalism, he also maintains that cultures cannot be manufactured out of nothing, and that each culture – or nation – has a distinct character which should be preserved.

While language is one of the most fundamental capacities of human beings, the roots of political organisation lie in the family, and this is what gives rise to his organic view of the nation: the nation is not an organism in the sense that there is a **hierarchy** of parts, as the metaphor of the human body would imply, but rather the nation develops from its most basic unit of organisation. And Herder draws an egalitarian and non-authoritarian conclusion from this: elites cannot create nations, and they must not impose their wills on individuals, but rather individuals must be free to develop themselves. Like the growth of an oak tree from an acorn, national development must come from 'within'. The difficulty with Herder's argument is that the family inevitably has paternalistic, if not **patriarchal**, overtones, and derivation of the nation from the family is problematic, for citizenship involves relationships with people you have never met and will never meet. Ethnic nationalism embodies all the limitedness of the family without preserving its positive features as a small-scale, 'face-to-face' community, based, at its best, on ties of affection.

## Socialism and Nationalism: Marx and Engels

Marx and Engels make various comments on nationalism in the *Communist Manifesto*: responding to the charge that communists want to abolish the nation-state Marx and Engels argue that the workers have no nation of their own, and that national divisions have become increasingly irrelevant as capitalism has developed – the capitalists have created a single world bound together by free trade. Marx and Engels were 'collectivists', but the historically significant 'collective' was the working class, as the most advanced, and first 'truly revolutionary', class. Although they avoid using the language of morality, believing that moral beliefs are the product of existing (capitalist) society, and the task is to create a new society, it is possible to discern a moral message in their work: the task is to create a classless society in which human beings recognise their common humanity. In his early work, Marx called this 'species consciousness'. So the historical task is to develop (proletarian) class consciousness, and the ultimate moral aim is to overcome human alienation. This appears to leave little room for nationalism.

Marx and Engels do, however, argue that during the revolutionary phase the workers must 'make themselves into a nation': 'since the proletariat must first of all acquire supremacy, must rise to be *the* national class, must constitute itself the nation, it is, so far, itself national, though not in the bourgeois sense of the word' (Marx and Engels, 1967: 23). During what they call the 'dictatorship of the proletariat' it is necessary to take hold of the state and use it both to defeat counter-revolutionaries and to transform the relations of production. But this is a temporary phase, and just as the aim is for the state 'to lose its political character', that is, its coercive character, so it is necessary that the nation lose what might be termed its 'particular' character – in the latter phases of the process the national revolutions will become international. Because Marx and Engels said very little about what a classless society – or world – would look like, it is unclear what place nationalist consciousness would have in such a society, or world. Cultural differences would not necessarily disappear, but they could not determine the distribution of resources. Nonetheless, even if the future of nationalism is unclear, nationalist consciousness does play a role in the revolutionary period, and broadly speaking Marx and Engels argued that if nationalist movements serve the class struggle, then they should be supported. More specifically, they maintained:

1. Nations must have a certain *minimum size* and large and powerful ones were to be encouraged – what Engels called the 'miserable remnants of former nations' should dissolve. A distinction is drawn between historic and non-historic nations, where 'history' is understood as actions and movements possessing class significance. The 'miserable remnants', examples of which include the Basques, Bretons and Gaels, have no historic significance. They argue that after a workers' revolution there will always be the danger of counter-revolution, led by 'conservative' elements in society, and that these 'rotting remnants' would be among them. Interestingly, Mill also maintains that these peoples are better absorbed into larger nations.

2. National self-determination was to be encouraged if it helped revolution. In the main Marx and Engels believed that national struggles should only be encouraged in the big nations of Central and West Europe: France, Britain and Germany. Struggles on the 'edge of Europe' were not generally supported. This means, for example, that they did not in 1848 support the Irish struggle against the British – they later changed their views, and the reasons for the shift in their position are briefly discussed below.

3. They opposed Russia, which they saw as the primary source of reaction in Europe, and so tactically supported the Habsburg (Austro-Hungarian) Empire – which meant opposing nationalist movements among, for example, the Czechs, Slovaks and Serbs (Mill supported these struggles). Basically, their attitude to the nationalisms of their time was determined by the role that they played in the historic class struggle.

4. Ireland: from an orthodox Marxist perspective Ireland in the nineteenth century appears backward – Engels describes it as the agricultural appendage of Britain, or more specifically England. It had not developed capitalism (except in a small north-eastern corner of the country) – which was a precondition of a workers' revolution. What is more, the Catholic Church was a source of 'false consciousness'. But Marx and Engels gradually shifted to the view that the liberation of Ireland was a condition for revolution in Britain: Britain (or England) was the nation most likely to experience revolution, but the Irish constituted a source of competition to British workers, which worsened the conditions of the latter, but without fuelling revolution, because British workers saw their struggle against Irish labour as nationalist (and religious) in character. Paradoxically, through granting Ireland independence British and Irish workers would develop class solidarity, and recognise that the bourgeoisie was their true enemy.

## Conclusion: Banal Nationalism

Michael Billig argues that the central thesis of his book *Banal Nationalism* is that 'there is a continual "flagging", or reminding of nationhood' (Billig, 1995: 8). Political leaders in France, the United States or Britain do not define themselves as 'nationalist' – nationalism is a term applied to those on the 'fringe', whether fighting for independence from a larger nation or seeking to radicalise the consciousness of a nation through, for example, racism. But those leaders *are* nationalist, for they daily remind their citizens of the importance of nationhood through 'banal' – that is ordinary, everyday – acts. Political and cultural discourse is suffused with nationalist rhetoric: the word 'national' appears in official titles of state bodies, along with visual symbols; newspapers have 'national' and 'international' news; the promotion of tourism rests on a few identifiable 'signifiers'. Sport itself is organised around the nation-state. The 'cricket test' ('Tebbit test') is a prime example of consciously elevating the banal to the status of a supposedly essential criterion for allegiance to the nation-state. As Billig says, 'the metonymic image of banal nationalism is not a flag which is being consciously waved with fervent passion; it is the flag hanging unnoticed on the public building' (1995: 8). A metonymic image is one that locates a person in relation to something else, in this instance a collective entity – the nation.

While Billig's argument can be criticised it is a useful way of concluding our discussion on nationalism. Billig argues that nationalism is a powerful force, but most of the time we do not realise its force; only at times of crisis does it 'erupt'. Political theorists, operating with universalist concepts, find nationalism a difficult phenomenon to understand, let alone use as a justification; they cannot, however, ignore it. The question is whether we should be so concerned about nationalism – does it matter which team a person supports so long as he or she obeys the law? After all, millions of people do not support any cricket, football or rugby team, professing themselves utterly bored with sport. The most compelling argument for taking nationalism seriously is, as Mill observed, that it does provide connections between people that, at a time of crisis, may be essential for the maintenance of liberal-democratic institutions. Those ties may be sporting, or linguistic, or based on an appreciation of cities and landscape, and it is possible that we do not need to share all of them – we can be bored by sport – but we need some of them. The danger is that those who quite justifiably do not share such ties will suffer when there are crises – in the 1930s Italian restaurants were the only decent places to eat out in for most people in Britain; when Italy declared war on Britain in 1940 suddenly Italian restaurants were burned out, possibly by the same people who had frequented them. To address this 'dark side' of nationalism requires a theory of culture and **multiculturalism**, and that is a topic for a later chapter.

## Summary

For political theorists nationalist sentiment is problematic because it seems to resist universalist concepts. While it is possible to talk about universal rights to national self-determination and assert that all nations are equal, both the reality of international politics and, perhaps more importantly, the concept of nation undermines that claim. Even the softest, most 'civic', nationalist will be forced to concede that his nation is special, for how else can he explain the value of nationhood? Of course, if we say, as liberals do, that the individual is the ultimate source of value and focus of concern, a similar objection can be raised: your individual life is especially valuable to *you*. However, because the nation-state entails a massive concentration of power the ethical particularism within nationalism is of special concern. On the other hand, a world of nation-states may offer the best way to realise values such as freedom, justice and equality, and a history of nationalism that focused on the extremism of Nazi Germany or the virulent nationalisms of some contemporary states – thinking here of the Balkans in the 1990s – may fail to do justice to nationalism as a liberationist ideology.

## Questions

1. Is the 'nation' a product of 'modernity'?

2. Is a multilingual nation inherently unstable?

3. Are nationalism and socialism compatible?

4. What are the arguments in favour of the abolition of nations and the creation of a world government?

5. A Scottish nationalist, bemoaning the lack of majority support among Scots for independence, labelled Scots '90-minute nationalists'. Is it possible to be a strong supporter of a national football team but reject political nationalism?

## References

Anderson, B. (1991) *Imagined Communities: Reflections on the Origin and Spread of Nationalism* London: Verso.

Berghe van den, P. (1978) 'Race and Ethnicity: A Sociobiological Perspective', *Ethnic and Racial Studies* 1(4).

Billig, M. (1995) *Banal Nationalism* London: Sage.

Breuilly, J. (1993) *Nationalism and the State* Manchester: Manchester University Press.

Davidson, N. (2000) *The Origins of Scottish Nationhood* London: Pluto Press.

Davis, H. (1967) *Nationalism and Socialism: Marxist and Labor Theories of Nationalism to 1917* New York: Monthly Review Press.

Fishman, J. (1980) 'Social Theory and Ethnography: Language and Ethnicity in Eastern Europe' in Peter Sugar (ed.), *Ethnic Conflict and Diversity in Eastern Europe* Santa Barbara, Calif.: ABC-Clio.

Geertz, C. (1993) *The Interpretation of Cultures: Selected Essays* London: Fontana Press.

Gellner, E. (1983) *Nations and Nationalism* Oxford: Basil Blackwell.

Guibernau, M. (1996) *Nationalisms: The Nation-State and Nationalism in the Twentieth Century* Cambridge: Polity.

Hechter, M. (1988) 'Rational Choice Theory and The Study of Ethnic and Race Relations' in John Rex and David Mason (eds), *Theories of Ethnic and Race Relations* Cambridge: Cambridge University Press.

Hobsbawm, E. and Ranger, T. (1983) *The Invention of Tradition* Cambridge: Cambridge University Press.

Huntington, S. (2004) *Who Are We?: America's Great Debate* London: Free Press.

Hutchinson, J. and Smith, A. (eds) (1994) *Nationalism* Oxford: Oxford University Press.

Ignatieff, M. (1993) *Blood and Belonging: Journeys into the New Nationalism* London: BBC Books and Chatto & Windus.

James, H. and Stone, M. (eds) (1992) *When the Wall Came Down: Reactions to German Unification* New York and London: Routledge.

Kedourie, E. (1993) *Nationalism* Oxford and Cambridge, Mass.: Blackwell.

Kellas, J. (1998) *The Politics of Nationalism and Ethnicity* Basingstoke: Macmillan.

Kohn, H. (1944) *The Idea of Nationalism: A Study on its Origins and Background* London: Macmillan.

Marx, K. and Engels, F. (1967) *The Communist Manifesto* (introduction and notes A.J.P. Taylor) London: Penguin.

Mill, J.S. (1991) *On Liberty and Other Essays* (ed. John Gray) Oxford: Oxford University Press.

Nairn, T. (1977) *The Break-Up of Britain: Crisis and Neo-nationalism* London: NLB.

Smith, A. (1991) *National Identity* London: Penguin Books.

Smith, A. (1998) *Nationalism and Modernism: A Critical Survey of Recent Theories of Nations and Nationalism* London: Routledge.

## Further Reading

There are several good introductions to the study of nationalism. From the above references Kellas (1998), Smith (1991) and Smith (1998) are useful overviews (also by Anthony Smith: *Nationalism: Theory, Ideology, History*, Cambridge: Polity Press, 2001). Other books in the references very much argue a line – the most influential are Anderson (1991), Gellner (1983), Hobsbawm and Ranger (1983), and Kedourie (1993). General – and brief – introductions not listed in the references include: Kenneth Minogue, *Nationalism* (London: Batsford, 1967) and Fred Haliday and Umut Özkirimli, *Theories of Nationalism: A Critical Introduction* (Basingstoke: Palgrave Macmillan, 2000). For a useful collection of essays: Umut Özkirimli, *Nationalism and its Futures* (Basingstoke: Palgrave Macmillan, 2003). Books focusing on the ethical aspects of nationalism include Yael Tamir, *Liberal Nationalism* (Princeton, New Jersey: Princeton University Press, 1995); David Miller, *On Nationality* (Oxford: Clarendon Press, 1995); Andrew Vincent, *Nationalism and Particularity* (Cambridge and New York: Cambridge University Press, 2002); Margaret Moore (ed.), *National Self-Determination and Secession* (Oxford: Oxford University Press, 1998).

## Weblinks

An article with an extensive bibliography: http://plato.stanford.edu/entries/nationalism/

A very extensive list of (largely academic) links: http://www.nationalismproject.org/

Another extensive list of links, although more of a mix of 'popular' and academic: http://www.socresonline.org.uk/2/1/natlinks.html

A more history-oriented site: http://www.fordham.edu/halsall/mod/modsbook17.html

# Chapter 6

# Fascism

## Introduction

The word 'fascist' is often used as a word of abuse. Fascists are seen as people who act in authoritarian ways and seek to impose their views and values on others. But fascism is more complicated than this. First because fascism needs to be more precisely defined and, second, the question arises as to whether it is a movement of the past, or can it be said that fascist movements still exist today? Everyone has heard of Hitler (1889–1945) but Hitler called his party the National Socialist German Workers Party: can he still be called a fascist? Not many movements have come to power since 1945 that can unambiguously be called fascist – but can we describe movements in these terms when they do not necessarily declare themselves in favour of Hitler or the founder of Italian fascism, Mussolini?

This chapter will explore these issues, and those listed below, in order to tackle the questions: what is fascism; is it an ideology at all; and can a grasp of it help us in understanding certain political movements in today's world?

## Chapter Map

In this chapter we will examine:

- A definition of **fascism** – a task that is clearly crucial if the question of whether it is a general movement or simply an Italian movement of the inter-war period is to be tackled.

- The development of fascism in Italy: this was the particular movement that gave the general movement its name.

- The relationship of Nazism to fascism – it will be argued that Hitler's National Socialism was an extreme form of fascism.

- The relationship of fascism to capitalism and class. This not only throws light on the relationship between fascism and socialism but is important if we are to explain the rise of fascism.

- The view taken by fascists towards liberal ideas and the European Enlightenment in order to gauge the depth of the rejection of 'reason', liberty and equality.

- The fascist view of the state.

- Fascism today, the form that it takes, and the conditions under which it is likely to become increasingly influential.

# 'Never Again': Contemporary Forms of Fascism

Gypsy woman suffering from typhus at Bergen Belsen concentration camp waiting with other gypsies for medical treatment, Germany, April 1945

see
apter 10:
Funda-
entalism,
240–261

You are conscious of considerable media coverage given to the 60th anniversary of the destruction of the Nazi concentration camp at Auschwitz and of the existence of Holocaust Day, a day that commemorates the murder by the Nazis of millions of European Jews, the killing of travellers (Gypsies) and of political opponents.

Interviews with victims bring tears to your eyes, and former concentration camp attendants explain why they were able to kill inmates. You are horrified at the information you receive – the starvation, brutality, the killing and the sophisticated methods used to nefarious purposes – and you can only agree with the general theme of 'never again'. At the same time you have read about the **genocide** of the Tutsis in Rwanda in Africa, and the grisly ethnic cleansing in former Yugoslavia where whole communities were wiped out, women raped and men placed in concentration camps. The media is full of the following: Jewish cemeteries have been desecrated, black people killed by gangs and even by the police, Muslims are 'blamed' for terrorist atrocities such as the destruction of the Twin Towers in 2001 because these actions were committed in the name of Islam, and extreme right-wing movements such as the British National Party or the Freedom Party in Austria are campaigning to have immigrants expelled from the countries in which they have settled. At the same time you read about left-wing regimes denounced as fascist when they violate the human rights of political opponents. Inevitably a number of questions suggest themselves.

- Are we witnessing the re-emergence of fascism in our modern world?
- When does a racist become a fascist? Are the two synonymous and if not, how do we differentiate between them?
- Can we call people who support nationalism, fascists?
- Is opposition to immigration fascist in character?

## Defining Fascism

see Chapter 3:
Socialism,
pp. 56–85

Fascism is sometimes used as a word of abuse – against movements or individuals who are intolerant or authoritarian. Fascism is certainly intolerant and authoritarian, but it is more than this. It is a movement that seeks to establish a dictatorship of the 'right' (i.e. an ultra-conservative position that rejects liberalism and anything associated with the 'left'). It targets communists, socialists, trade unionists and liberals through banning their parties and their members, so that these groups cannot exercise their political, legal or social rights. It is anti-liberal, regarding liberal values as a form of 'decadence', and seeing them as opening the floodgates to socialist, communist and egalitarian movements.

Defining fascism raises a problem. Fascism as a movement extols action and practice over ideas and theory. It uses ideas with considerable opportunism, mixing socialist ideas, avant-garde positions, anti-capitalist rhetoric, ecological argument and pseudo-scientific ideas to do with '**race**' and **ethnicity** in a veritable pot-pourri. Is it an ideology at all? Trevor Roper described fascist ideology as 'an ill-sorted hodge-podge of ideas', and Laski has argued that any attempt to find a 'philosophy of fascism' is a waste of time (Griffin, 1995: 1; 276). Kitchen contends that the 'extraordinary collection of half-baked and cranky ideas certainly did not form a coherent whole' (1976: 28). We shall argue, however, that while fascism is peculiarly 'flexible' as an ideology, there are particular features that characterise it, so that a general view of fascism can be created. Vincent argues that fascism 'often occupies a middle ground somewhere between rational political ideology on the one hand and opportunist adventurism on the other' (1995: 142).

see the box,
p. 137

The term derives from the 'fasces' – the bundle of rods carried by the consuls of ancient Rome and the word 'fascio' was used in Italy in the 1890s to indicate a political group or band, usually of revolutionary socialists (Heywood, 1992: 171). National defence groups organised after the Italian defeat at Caparetto in 1917, also called themselves 'fasci' (Vincent, 1995: 141).

Fascism is, however, essentially a twentieth-century movement although it draws upon prejudices and stereotypes that are rooted in tradition. Italian fascism saw itself as resurrecting the glories of the Roman Empire and Rocco, an Italian fascist, saw Machiavelli as a founding father of fascist theory. Nazism (which we will argue is an extreme form of fascism) was seen by its ideologues as rooted in the history of the Nordic peoples, and the movement embodied anti-Semitic views that go back to the Middle Ages in which Jews, for example, were blamed for the death of Christ, compelled to be moneylenders, confined to ghettos and acquired a reputation for crooked commerce.

## Fascism and Communism

Fascism appeals particularly to those who have some property but not very much, and are fearful that they might be plunged by market forces into the ranks of the working class. We would, however, agree with Griffin that there is nothing 'in principle' that precludes an employed or unemployed member of the working class,

## Battle of Caparetto

This battle involved some 600,000 Italian casualties and was the worst disaster in the history of the Italian armed forces. Ernest Hemingway based his *A Farewell to Arms* (1929) on the war between Austria and Italy between 1915 and 1917, reading military histories and first-hand reports to flesh out the background. His novel centres around an American, Frederic, who speaks Italian, and fights for the Italians. He lived, we are told, 'in Udine' and saw that things were going 'very badly' (Hemingway, 1985: 10).

Frederic tells the priest (whom he befriends): They (the Italian army) were 'beaten to start with. They were beaten when they [the military authorities] took them from their farms and put them in the army. That is why the peasant has wisdom, because he is defeated from the start. Put him in power and see how wise he is' (1985: 157).

In October 1917 Italy was occupied by Germany. Germany reached Udine on 28 October 1917 and the Italians lost about 600,000 men in a week. This is the lowest point in the war and Frederic deserts.

see Chapter 5: Nationalism, pp. 110–132

an aristocrat, city dweller or peasant, or a graduate 'from being susceptible to fascist myth' (1995: 7). Fascism is particularly hostile to communism, since it is opposed to the cosmopolitan contentions of Marxist theory, and its belief in a classless and stateless society. It is a movement that dislikes universal identities of any kind, although of course fascists may call for unity with kindred spirits in other countries. Nevertheless, it is intensely nationalistic, and takes the view that the people must be saved from enemies whose way of life is alien and threatening. Differences are deemed divisive and menacing, and war extolled as a way of demonstrating virtue and strength. The idea that people are divided by class is rejected in favour of the unity of the nation or people, so that industry is to be organised in a way that expresses the common interest between business and labour. In practice, this did not happen, and Kitchen argues that the social strata which provided the mass basis for fascism did not actually gain from its policies (1976: 65).

## Fascism and Religion

Fascists vary in their attitude towards the Church (extreme fascists may see religious organisations as a threat to the state) but they regard religion in a loose sense as being a useful way of instilling order and loyalty. Certainly they use a religious style of language in invoking the need for sacrifice, redemption and spiritual virtue and attacking materialism, consumerism and hedonism as decadent and unworthy. Although women can be fascists as well as men, fascism is a supremely patriarchal creed, by which we mean that women are seen as domestic creatures whose role in life is to service men, to have children, to be good mothers and wives, and to keep out of politics.

## Fascism and Liberalism

Fascism is hostile to the liberal tradition, and its dislike of the notion of 'reason' makes it difficult to pin down (as we have commented above) as an ideology. It stresses 'action' as opposed to words and yet propaganda and rationalisation are crucial to the movement. It regards the **individual** as subordinate to the collectivity in general, and the state in particular. Liberal freedoms are seen merely as entitlements that allow the enemies of the 'nation' or the 'people' to capture power. Fascist regimes are highly authoritarian, and use the state as the weapon of the dominant party to protect the nation, advance its interests and destroy its enemies. They are strongly opposed to the idea of democracy (although fascists may use democratic rhetoric to justify their rule or use parliamentary institutions to win access to power), and regard the notion of self-government (the idea that people can control their lives in a rational way and without force) as a dangerous myth. As a movement based upon repressive hierarchy, fascism argues that all institutions should be controlled by 'reliable' leaders, and the 'leadership principle' comes to a climax with the supreme leader, seen as the embodiment of the nation and the people. Fascist leaders may be civilians, but they are closely identified with the army and police, since these institutions are crucial to rooting out opponents. Fascist movements extend beyond the state, but the violence of these movements is condoned and encouraged by the state and, given tight control over the media, this violence is then justified in the light of fascist values.

## Fascism and Conservatism

Fascists see themselves as revolutionary in that they are concerned to 'rejuvenate' a tired and decadent society, and some fascists speak of creating a 'new man' in a new society. They are, therefore, anti-conservative as well as anti-liberal, although, as we shall see, they may form tactical alliances with other sections of the right where they can establish momentary common ground. Many regimes, loosely called fascist, are in fact conservative and reactionary systems – Franco's Spain, Petain's 'Vichy' France (a regime that collaborated with the Nazis who occupied the country), Japan under Tojo etc. They may have fascist elements within them, but they are not really anti-conservative in character.

## Fascism in Italy

Commentators generally agree that there was no fascism before World War I and that it began in 1922–3 with the emergence of the Italian fascist party. The fascist movement was in power in Italy for 18 years (1925–43). Benito Mussolini, the leader of the Italian fascists, had campaigned for Italy's entry into World War I. The parliamentary Fascio of National Defence was formed in 1917 and drew heavily upon veterans from the war to make up its extra-parliamentary forces. The movement took off when the left organised factory occupations in Milan during the 'red years' of 1919–20, and in November 1920 a fascist party was formed. In October 1922 Mussolini persuaded the king, Victor Emmanuel III, by means of a threatened putsch (dramatised by the march on Rome) to allow him to become prime minister of a coalition government.

The 'action squads', veteran soldiers from an elite battalion, were in theory absorbed into the Voluntary Militia of National Security, but in June 1924 dissatisfied elements killed the socialist deputy, Matteotti, who was a major parliamentary critic of Mussolini. Mussolini then suppressed all the other parliamentary parties and created a regime made up purely of fascists. Until 1929 Mussolini was concerned to consolidate the new system, and in the next decade he embarked upon the conquest of Abyssinia and formed an alliance with Hitler's Germany. Although Italy joined World War II on Hitler's side, in July 1943 Mussolini was ousted by the king and disaffected fascist leaders and Italy sued for peace with the anti-German allies. Mussolini was 'rescued' by German troops and in a small town near Lake Garda an Italian Social Republic was proclaimed that lasted from 1943 to 1945.

## Nationalism and War

Mussolini had argued strongly for intervention in World War I, and war was treated by the fascists in Italy as a force for rejuvenation and life. War enabled the nation to constitute itself as a vital, living force, hence Maronetti (1876–1944), leader of the Futurist movement, spoke of the need for a nationalism that was 'ultra-violent, anti-traditionist and anti-clericalist', a nationalism based on 'the inexhaustible vitality of Italian blood' (Griffin, 1995: 26). World War I was crucial to win the battle for civilisation and freedom. Maronetti believed that this war would enrich Italy with 'men of action', while in 1914 Mussolini broke with the 'cowards' who opposed the war, and declared in 1917 that those who fought in the trenches were the 'aristocracy of tomorrow', 'the aristocracy in action' (Griffin, 1995: 26–8). The regime's slogans were 'believe, obey, fight'.

The war was regarded by Roberto Farinacci (1892–1945) as the creator of a new Italian nation, and in Mussolini's view World War I brought about a 'profound psychological transformation' among the peasants in the countryside, with veterans becoming leaders in the rural areas. In Hemingway's *Farewell to Arms* Frederic says to the priest that the Italian army 'were beaten to start with' when they took the peasants from their farms 'and put them in the army. That is why the peasant has wisdom, because he is defeated from the start. Put him in power, and see how wise he is' (1985: 157). Clearly, Mussolini would not have agreed with Hemingway!

Physical exercise was to develop skills, according to the Italian leader, 'which may be necessary in a future war'. War was linked to nationalism. The nation, Mussolini declared shortly before the march on Rome, is a myth to which all must be subordinated, and Costamagna (1881–1965) insisted that from a cultural point of view only the individual nation constitutes a *universum*, a concrete universal. The Italian nation, argued the National Association in 1920, embraces people of the future as well as the present, in a venture that is both domestic as well as international in character: the nation either perishes or dominates. War has, said Luigi Federzoni (1878–1967) of the same Association, 'regenerating properties' that 'have taken effect miraculously and mysteriously in the soul of the Italian people'. War is 'the sole hygiene of the world' (Griffin, 1995: 38; 41–2; 44–5; 71; 85).

## Corporativism, Violence and the State

There is a strong economic imperative for fascism. D'Annunzio, a fervent nationalist and military leader who had occupied the Adriatic port of Fiume in September 1919, argued for a corporate structure that embraced employees and employers, **public** and private, within a state that expressed the common will of the people. Mussolini organised the whole country into 22 corporations. Lyttelton argues that these were held up as fascism's 'most imposing creation': in fact they served no serious function except as a front for groups of leading industrialists to control raw material allocations and investment decisions (Lyttelton, 1979: 97).

The trade unions were seen as contributing loyal employees within this structure – strikes and lockouts were banned – and syndicalists such as Sergio Panunzio (1886–1944) saw in revolutionary trade unionism or syndicalism a force that would transcend its adolescent phase by building up the state. A new national class was to be created – the essence of a civilisation that is neither bourgeois nor proletarian. Mussolini spoke of 'conscious class collaboration', and although the regime attacked both liberalism and socialism, the tiny Italian Social Republic declared that it aimed to abolish the whole internal capitalist system (Griffin, 1995: 47; 49; 64; 87). In practice employers were regulated by the Italian state, but anti-capitalism was more rhetoric than reality.

Maronetti spoke of 'violence, rehabilitated as a decisive argument', and when links were forged with Hitler's Germany Mussolini declared that both fascists and Nazis believe in violence 'as the dynamo of their history'. The work of the French anarcho-syndicalist, Sorel, was hugely influential because he had extolled both the importance of myth and the need for violence (Griffin, 1995: 36; 45; 79).

Not surprisingly, the state was given a pivotal role, a spiritual and moral entity that, Mussolini declared, is the conscience of the nation. The state is the foundation of fascism: the state organises the nation and is concerned with the growth of empire. Giovanni Gentile (1875–1944) was the key intellectual of the regime and, drawing upon a version of Hegelian idealism, he pronounced the fascist state to be an 'ethical state': it is the state of 'man himself'. The leader is revered with a capital 'L'. Mussolini ridiculed the 'demo-liberal' civilisation, while praising Hitler for creating 'a unitary, authoritarian, totalitarian state, i.e. a fascist one', although he acknowledges that Hitler operated in a different historical context. Oneness is asserted with a vengeance: in Mussolini's words, the 'order of the day is a single, categorical word which is imperative for all' (Griffin, 1995: 63; 70; 72–3; 79; 82).

Reason is rejected: as an anonymous fascist put it, 'blood is stronger than syllogisms'. (A syllogism is a logical statement in which a conclusion is drawn from two propositions, e.g. all dogs are animals, all animals have four legs, and therefore, all dogs have four legs. A false syllogism!) Mussolini was likened to a Messiah who evangelised millions and, despite the anti-clericalism of some fascist supporters, a pact with the Vatican was signed. Irrationalism and mysticism expressed itself in racism. It is a myth to think that racism was only developed by the Italian fascists at the insistence of the Nazis. The invasion of Ethiopia was presented as the salvation of the Italian race, and even before the alliance with Hitler Mussolini had spoken of the danger that the (so-called) 'coloured races' posed to the 'white race' with their fertility and rate of multiplication. Miccari (1898–1989), one of the key fascist intellectuals, warned against the kind of modernity that is a racket manipulated by 'Jewish bankers, war-profiteers, pederasts, brothel keepers', and Volpe (1876–1971), official historian of fascism, argued that the voice of anti-Semitism was not entirely new in Italy (Griffin, 1995: 60; 80). It is true that a much more systematic racism developed as a result of Nazi pressure (many Jews had actually been recruited to the party and were now expelled), but we can certainly say that fascism built upon a racist culture that is integral to fascism.

## Intellectual Roots

Although fascist intellectuals drew upon Machiavelli, Nietzsche and Hegel, there was an important tradition of elitism in Italian political thought that was more recent and more influential.

Mosca (1858–1941) had taught constitutional law at the University of Palermo between 1858 and 1888, and at the Universities of Rome and Turin. In 1884 he published *Theory of Governments and Parliamentary Government*, but is best known for his *The Ruling Class*, which appeared in 1896. All societies, he argued, are governed by minorities whether these are military, hereditary, priestly or based on merit or wealth. He accepted that ownership of property could be a factor in accounting for elite rule, but he rejected the Marxist account that sought to privilege this particular factor. The ruling class or elite owes its superiority to organisational factors, he argued, and its skills alter according to circumstance. What he called the 'political formula' or the ideological mechanisms of rule varied, but whatever the form, all states are necessarily elitist in character, whether their legitimating myth is the divine right of kings, popular sovereignty or the dictatorship of the proletariat.

Democracy, in his view, is simply a more subtle form of manipulation, and the parties offered inducements for people to vote for them. The 'political class' need to be distinguished from other sections of the elite, such as industrialists, but in 1923 Mosca introduced in his work the argument that elites could compete through rival political parties. People of lower socio-economic origin can be recruited in order to renew elites. Unlike other elitists he was, however, fiercely critical of Mussolini, and his theory is best described as conservative rather than fascist.

Rather more hawkish was Pareto (1848–1923). Pareto had taken the chair in political economy at the University of Lausanne in 1894, publishing his *Cours d'économie politique* (1896, 1897). In 1900 he declared himself an anti-democrat, arguing that the political movements in Italy and France were simply seeking to replace one elite by another. While he approved of Marx's emphasis upon struggle, he rejected completely the notion that a classless society was possible. In 1906 Pareto published his *Manual of Political Economy*, where he presented pure economics in mathematical form.

As far as he was concerned, human action is mostly non-logical in character, and stems from non-rational sentiments and impulses: what Pareto called underlying 'residues'. In his most important political and sociological work, the *Mind and Society* that he wrote in 1916, he distinguishes between Class I residues, inventive, imaginative capacities, and Class II residues, conservative, persistent tendencies.

All government is government by an elite who use a combination of coercion and **consent**. Class I residues predominate when 'foxes' are in control – manipulative politicians who create consent – and Class II residues when violence is necessary. Each of these residues has its strengths and weaknesses, and the 'circulation of

## Biography | Benito Mussolini (1883–1945)

Born in Forli, Italy. His father was a democrat and a socialist, and Mussolini was expelled from the first school he attended. He went to Switzerland in 1902 in order to evade military service, but returned two years later to become first a journalist with and then the editor of the socialist paper *Avanti*. Initially a socialist and an opponent of war, he resigned from the party, becoming a strong nationalist and supporter of the war. He fought in the war but was wounded and returned to Milan to edit the right-wing *Il Popolo d'Italia*.

He was angered by the fact that the Peace Treaty failed to support Italy's demands, and he helped to found the Fascist Party. After the march on Rome he was appointed prime minister by the king, and headed a coalition of fascists and nationalists until the murder of Matteotti in 1924. Left-wing parties were then suppressed and Italy became a one-party state in 1929. After seeking to reorganise the economy, he sent the army into Ethiopia in 1935. Some 400,000 troops fought in this campaign: the capital was captured, poison gas was used and the Emperor of Ethiopia fled to Britain.

League of Nations sanctions were ineffectual (and opposed by Britain and France), and Mussolini formed a pact with Hitler in 1936. He supported Franco's 'nationalists' and sent troops to support him during the Spanish civil war (1936–9). In 1939 Albania was invaded, and in 1940 war (with Nazi Germany) was declared on Britain and France.

Fighting broke out in North Africa but attempts to invade Greece ended in failure, and Tobruk in Libya was seized by the British in 1941. Italy was now becoming increasingly dependent on Nazi Germany, and Britain and the United States decided to invade Sicily. Although German troops cut off the mainland, the fascist state got the king to dismiss Mussolini, but in 1943 he was freed by German commandos and he set up a fascist regime in northern Italy.

Rome was captured by the allies in 1944, the German resistance disintegrated, and in 1945 Mussolini was captured and shot by partisans while trying to escape to Switzerland.

elites' can be explained as 'lions' – those who rule through brute force – replacing 'foxes'. He saw in Mussolini a politician with a lion-like character who had displaced wily politicians.

But perhaps most important of all in analysing the intellectual roots of fascism was the work of Michels (1876–1936), a disillusioned German socialist who gained an academic position in Turin, and was greatly influenced by syndicalism. In 1911 he published *Political Parties*. Here he argues that all societies and all organisations are subject to 'an iron law of oligarchy' (i.e. a small group controlling the masses). Struck by what he saw as the contrast between the official statements of the German Social Democratic Party and the timidity of its political practice, he argued that oligarchy is present even in parties apparently committed to the norms of democracy. The fact that leaders are in practice autonomous from their followers derives from the constraints of organisation. Although he wrote a good deal about psychology, Michels argued that oligarchical tendencies are based upon organisational rather than psychological factors. The complexity of organisations can only

Born in Sicily, he was greatly influenced by Hegel, and held chairs of philosophy in Palermo, Pisa, Rome and Florence.

His theory of 'actualism' represented an extreme form of idealism, and he argued that by linking thought and will, objective knowledge was possible.

He was appointed Minister of Public Instruction under Mussolini, and his studies in education have proved hugely influential and are still read today. He contended that Italy had developed its own philosophy as part of a European tradition reflecting the unity of human consciousness. He

had joined the Fascist Party in 1923 and a year later drafted a 'Manifesto of Fascist Intellectuals'. He wrote the entry on party philosophy for the *Italian Encyclopaedia* to which Mussolini appended his name.

Gentile saw humans as social in nature, and argued that their will harmonised with the structure of the state, so that the state itself became an ethical institution. His *Genesis and Structure of Society* was written in 1943, and he continued to support fascism, even when it was confined to the German-controlled statelet in the north. He was assassinated by partisans in Florence.

be grasped by professional leaders who have communication skills, and who understand the rules of elections and other external pressures. This leadership is made all the more entrenched by what Michels regarded as the incompetence and emotional vulnerability of their mass membership.

In 1914 Michels wrote a study of Italian imperialism and published widely on politics and sociology. In 1930 he wrote the entry on 'Authority' for the *Encyclopaedia of the Social Sciences*. He admired fascism and argued that, as with Bolshevism, it was a reflection of the general tendency to oligarchy. Michels also wrote a good deal on nationalism, with his later writings becoming increasingly anti-democratic in tone (Beetham, 1977).

## Fascism in Germany

see Ideas and Perspectives box, p. 150

Nazism is, in our view, a form of fascism. Despite historical and cultural differences, both Hitler and Mussolini saw striking similarities in each other's regimes, and the Nazis were greatly influenced by Mussolini's theory and tactics. It is true that Hitler's movement was more extreme than that of Mussolini's. Its racism was more aggressive, its hatred of democracy more intense, and its expansionism more grandiose. But, as will become clear from the analysis of its features, it was a form of fascism, and there is no need to take the position that the differences between Hitler and Mussolini's regimes outweighed their similarities.

### A Brief History

The collapse of the German war effort saw the creation of a republic: an uprising of the left had been smashed by a socialist government that cooperated with the army and the employers. As Griffin has shown in detail, there were German fascists whose version of nationalism, idealisation of war, anti-liberalism and anti-Semitism was at variance with the Nazi view (1995: 104–15). Hitler had made contact with the German Workers' Party (DAP or Deutsche Arbeiterpartei), a fanatical nationalist grouping. Since the clauses of the Versailles Treaty limited the Reichswehr (the German army) to 100,000, Hitler was demobilised in 1920. He became leader of the DAP, which was then renamed the National Socialist German Workers' Party (NSDAP). A putsch was attempted in 1923, and Hitler was given a short prison sentence by a sympathetic court. Nazis had been regarded as isolated fanatics until 1930: yet in 1933 the movement seized power. In 1928 the NSDAP won only 2.6 per cent of the popular vote. The Versailles Treaty that ended World War I, had punitive effects on Germany: all colonies were lost, while it is calculated that the reparations bill equalled 1.5 times the total GNP of Germany in 1929. Although the economy had improved in the 1920s, the depression had catastrophic effects. Investment and industry collapsed, and unemployment was officially estimated at some 30 per cent: the real figure was nearer half.

The Social Democratic Party of Germany (SPD) had headed a coalition government until 1930: when this fell apart the president ruled by decree for three years, real wages were halved, and Hitler had meanwhile stressed the need for a party capable of winning elections and conducting effective mass propaganda. In the elections in 1930 the Nazis came second to the SDP, and two years later they received 37 per cent of the vote. Large employers began to support the Nazis and, although many thought Hitler 'tactless' and his economic policies 'utopian', his militant anti-Bolshevism appealed to them, and they backed him for chancellor. He was appointed to the position in 1933, and the Nazis received 3 posts in an 11-strong cabinet. Goebbels vowed that 1933 would strike the French revolutionary year of 1789 out of history.

By July 1934 Germany had become a one-party state, and the Nazis embarked on their task of building a 'Third Reich' and New European Order. War broke out in 1939 and the defeat of the Nazis was secured in 1945.

## Anti-capitalism

Although virulently anti-Marxist, the Nazi movement was in the 1920s strongly anti-capitalist as well. The first programme of the party spoke of the need to share profits, nationalise the trusts, increase pensions and provide free education. Hitler referred to the need to make the working people national, while Strasser (1892–1934), killed in the purges of 1934, attacked capitalism and argued for the **emancipation** of the worker through 'participation in profits, property and management'. Gründel saw the creation of a new type of human being as constituting the end of the property-owning bourgeoisie (Griffin, 1995: 117; 123; 128), while Goebbels had said in 1928 that 'no honest thinking person today would want to deny the justification of the workers' movements'. Indeed he had complained in 1926 that Hitler wanted to 'compensate the aristocrats' and not 'disturb private property. Horrendous! . . . we are Socialists. We don't want to have been so in vain!' There is evidence to suggest that those who supported the Nazis were less likely to be unemployed, but rather threatened with unemployment, i.e. the middle and lower middle classes rather than the industrial workers.

The body particularly concerned with advancing Nazi interests among trade unionists (the Nationalsozialistiche Betriebszellen-organization, NSBO) became an increasing embarrassment to the Nazi leadership. The 'Night of the Long Knives' that saw the liquidation of the leadership of the SA (stormtroopers) was justified by Hitler on the grounds that a second **revolution** had to be avoided at all costs. Socialism continued in the party's title, but it was mere rhetoric. The Nazi economic programme was presented as a form of 'soldierly socialism', but the real target was Marxism and democracy. Marxism, it was said, 'always follows capitalism as its shadow'. Steding (1903–38) spoke contemptuously of 'the purely mercenary capitalism of the stock exchange' (Griffin, 1995: 141; 152). These policies often involved taking away certain freedoms from employers. For example, the introduction of some labour-saving machinery was banned and government permission had to be obtained before reducing their labour force. The government also tended to give work contracts to those companies that relied on manual labour rather than machines.

see Anti-Semitic Propaganda, p. 146

The German economy remained capitalistic, although with extensive state control. The attack on the Jews was clearly linked to the virulent opposition to Marxism and internationalism, and although Germany had a potent anti-Semitic tradition to draw upon, it has been argued that before 1933 the Nazis placed relatively little emphasis upon anti-Semitism.

Hitler had attacked Jews in *Mein Kampf*, but he had toned down his anti-Semitism while gaining power since he was anxious not to alienate Jewish business leaders. Henry Ford had been compelled to stop publishing anti-Semitic attacks in the United States after the Jewish community organised a boycott of Ford cars in the late 1920s. In the same way Lord Rothermere, owner of the *Daily Mail*, had been forced 'to toe the line' when Jewish businessmen had withdrawn advertising from the newspaper. Hitler began to leave out anti-Semitic comments from his speeches during elections, and during the 1933 general election Jewish businessmen even contributed money to his party.

However, after 1933 Jews were increasingly excluded from mainstream life, and the Nuremburg laws of 1935 stripped Jews of their citizenship and made intermarriage illegal. During Crystal Night over 7,500 Jewish shops were destroyed and 400 synagogues burnt down; 91 Jews were killed and an estimated 20,000 sent to camps. The only people who were punished for the crimes committed on Crystal Night were members of the SA who had raped Jewish women (since they had broken the Nuremberg Laws in so doing). The numbers of Jews wishing to leave the country increased dramatically, and it has been calculated that between 1933 and 1939 approximately half the Jewish population of Germany (250,000) left the country. This included several Jewish scientists (such as Albert Einstein) who were to play an important role in the fight against fascism during the war. Speer recalls that the Ministry of Education was not inclined to support nuclear research on the grounds that nuclear physics was seen as the product of the Jewish mind (1970: 228).

By the beginning of 1942 over 500,000 Jews in Poland and Russia had been killed by the SS, and at the Wannsee Conference in 1942 a final solution was proposed that led to the systematic termination of Jewry. It has been estimated that between 1942 and 1945 around 18 million were sent to extermination camps. Of these, it has been suggested that between 5 and 11 million were killed.

## Statism, Women and Colonialism

The Nazis extolled the principle of oneness. The party was Germany, with a single will, faith, flag and leader. Although the Nazis opposed organised religion, a concordat was signed with the pope (the Catholic Church could continue if it did not 'interfere' in politics) and Himmler (1900–45), head of the SS, told the SS that they must believe in God. The religion of the Jews is godless.

Goebbels spoke of 'forging the German nation into a single people'. Benn, who ceased to support the Nazis after the purges of 1934, had declared that Nazi rule manifested itself in the 'total state' – an institution that asserts the complete identity of power and spirit, individuality and the collective. 'It is monist, anti-dialectic, enduring, and authoritarian'. The strong state, argued Schmitt, transcends diversity: every atom of its existence is ruled and permeated by the principle of leadership (Griffin, 1995: 134–5; 138–9; 147).

see Women in
Nazi Germany,
p. 149

The Nazis, of course, espoused an explicit and militant patriarchy. Paula Siber, acting head of the German Association of Women, argued that 'to be a woman means to be a mother'. The woman belongs wherever care is required and she manages 75 per cent of the nation's income by running the home. Hitler disliked women who were interested in politics. By introducing measures that would encourage women to leave the labour market, the level of unemployment could be further lowered. Women in certain professions such as medicine and the Civil Service were dismissed, while other married women were paid a lump sum of 1,000 marks to stay at home.

## Anti-Semitic Propaganda

It is worth noting that before 1933 Streicher's virulently anti-Semitic *Der Stürmer* was opposed by some Nazis, and it was only after Nazis took office that its circulation reached half a million. As is argued in the Comenius History Project, a survey of NSDAP members and their reason for joining found that 60 per cent of respondents made no reference at all to anti-Semitism, while 4 per cent openly expressed disapproval of it.

Analysis of Nazi posters in the period from 1928 to 1932 has revealed the following:

**Table 6.1** Enemy groups targeted by NSDAP posters, 1928–32

|  | Total no. of posters | Percentage |
| --- | --- | --- |
| The 'system' | 15 | 12.1 |
| 'November-parties' | 25 | 20.1 |
| SPD/Marxism | 39 | 31.5 |
| Centre Party/allies | 10 | 8.1 |
| KPD | 6 | 4.8 |
| Jews | 6 | 4.8 |
| Miscellaneous | 23 | 18.6 |

The subjects chosen for front-page headlines in the official daily, the *Volkische Beobachter*, between the crucial July 1932 election and Hitler's installation in power, confirm the picture. Between 1932 and 1933 anti-Semitism only featured in just over 3 per cent of the cases: the paper was much more concerned with the 'threat' of Bolshevism, Marxism and the trade unions, and the economic problems facing people. (http://www.stevenson.ac.uk/comenius/articles/totalitarianism/uk_dg/naz_1h.htm)

## Biography — Adolf Hitler (1889–1945)

Born in the Austrian town of Braunau on 20 April 1889. His parents had come from poor peasant families.

He was deeply religious as a child and contemplated going into the Church. Instead of joining the Civil Service as his father hoped, he became an artist, volunteering for the German army at the outbreak of World War I, and was decorated with the Iron Cross for bravery and boldness. After the war he was stationed in Munich, Bavaria, and was bitterly opposed to the decision to declare Bavaria a socialist republic. The republic was overthrown in May 1919, and Hitler was identified as an enthusiastic supporter of the military. It was the Jews and Marxists, he argued, who had undermined the war effort.

He became a leading figure in the German Workers' Party (a nationalist and anti-Semitic organisation that the army had feared might foment communist revolution). He established a reputation as an orator, and in 1920 the National Socialist German Workers' Party was created, and a year later he became leader. After being sent to prison for being involved in violence towards a rival politician he established his own private army – the SA. The members were invariably veterans from the war. The attempt to overthrow the government in Bavaria failed dismally, and Hitler received (an extremely lenient) five-year prison sentence. The prison authorities allowed him to have his autobiography ghost written. *Mein Kampf*, a passionate diatribe against Jews, socialism and liberalism, made the case for empire: Hitler was released after serving a year of his prison sentence.

His *Road to Resurgence* was written in 1927 in order to assure industrialists that he supported private enterprise and was opposed to any social and economic reconstruction of Germany. Unemployment soared during the Depression, and by 1930 the Nazi Party was the second largest party. Two years later it was the largest party in the parliament. In 1933 Hitler was appointed chancellor: in the elections of 1933, despite his persecution of communists and socialists, the Nazis only received 43 per cent of the vote, and with the support of the Catholic Centre Party an Enabling Act was passed giving Hitler dictatorial powers. By the end of 1933 150,000 people were in concentration camps. The inmates included beggars, prostitutes and anyone incapable of working.

Ernst Roehm, as head of the 4.5 million strong SA, was feared particularly by the army. After his murder and the purges, the SS became dominant. In October 1933 Hitler withdrew from the League of Nations; the army trebled in size and military conscription was introduced. The Rhineland was reoccupied, and in 1938 Austria was united with Germany. Hitler marched his troops into the German-speaking part of Czechoslovakia, the Sudetenland, and in 1939 the army was ordered into Poland. With the declaration of war Norway, the Netherlands, Belgium and France were occupied.

Britain was bombed, and in 1941 the invasion of the USSR began. German advances were halted, and the German army suffered massive losses. Hitler's health deteriorated, but attempts to assassinate him were unsuccessful. Soviet troops took Berlin in May 1945, and he committed suicide.

| Biography | Ernst Roehm (1887–1934) |
|---|---|

Born in Munich, he joined the army in 1906 and became a major during World War I.

Roehm became active in right-wing politics after the war, recruiting Hitler to spy on the German Workers' Party. When assured that it was not communist, he joined this party and helped to fund it with army resources.

He took part in the putsch in Munich, and although found guilty of treason he was released and dismissed from the army, becoming a military instructor in Bolivia. In 1931 he returned to Germany, where Hitler placed him in charge of the SA. He increased its numbers, and by 1934 it had a membership of 4.5 million. The army and Hitler's own minister of war became concerned about SA influence, particularly as Roehm argued, as a member of the National Defence Council, that the SA should be responsible for war and was more important than the army itself.

A dossier was assembled on Roehm and the SA, and evidence was created to suggest that Roehm had been paid by the French to overthrow Hitler. Hitler was unmoved by these arguments since Roehm and the SA had played a crucial role in tackling his political opponents and helping him to state power.

On the other hand, Roehm had upset not only the army but industrialists. The latter were unhappy with Roehm's argument that the economy needed to be organised on socialist lines and that a real revolution had yet to take place. The SA leaders were ordered to attend a meeting in Wiesse, and on 29 June 1934 Hitler, accompanied by the SS, personally arrested Roehm. Although many of the SA leaders were shot, Hitler sought to pardon Roehm, but was persuaded by Goering and Himmler that Roehm had to die. When he refused to commit suicide he was shot by the SS.

The purge of the SA was justified by Hitler on the grounds that their leaders were guilty of treason. Eleven years later Goebbels described Roehm as 'a homosexual and an anarchist' and incapable of reforming the army.

Hitler argued that the slogan 'emancipation of women' had been invented by Jewish intellectuals. The woman's world is her husband, her family, her children and her home. The distinction between the two worlds was natural and necessary. 'The woman', he declared, 'has her own battlefield. With every child that she brings into the world, she fights her battle for the nation'.

A mystical belief in the state went hand in hand with a contempt for democracy and a belief in colonialism. The pursuit of colonies was defended as a source of raw materials and as an activity that was vital for Germany's living space. It was not, Ritter argued in 1937, 'an expression of imperialism' but a 'vital natural necessity' (Griffin, 1995: 137; 145).

> By rejecting the authority of the individual and replacing it by the numbers of some momentary mob, the parliamentary principle of majority rule sins against the basic aristocratic principle of Nature . . .

> The receptivity of the great masses is very limited, their intelligence small, but their power of forgetting is enormous. In consequence of these faults, all effective propaganda must be limited to a very few points and must harp on these in slogans . . .

> *Adolf Hitler,* Mein Kampf (1925) *London: Radius Books/Hutchinson,*
> *p. 24; p. 165.*

## Women in Nazi Germany

Women were seen as inferior beings who must procreate for the good of the nation. They were to give up work in order to fulfil this biological purpose. During the election campaign of 1932 Hitler promised to take 800,000 women out of employment within four years. In August 1933 a law was passed that enabled married couples to obtain loans to set up homes and start families, which meant that single men and childless couples were taxed more heavily. Married women doctors and civil servants were dismissed in 1934 and from June 1936 women could no longer act as judges or public prosecutors. Women were ineligible for jury service since Hitler believed that they were unable to 'think logically or reason objectively, since they are ruled only by emotion'.

However, during the war it proved necessary to allow women to work in artillery factories and on farms. Medals were provided for women who had large families. The number of women in universities fell significantly. Girls were educated into becoming mothers – women were not to smoke or diet in case this affected their health as mothers.

In 1934 the *Ten Commandments* for the choice of a spouse were propagated:

1. Remember that you are a German.
2. If you are genetically healthy you should not remain unmarried.
3. Keep your body pure.
4. You should keep your mind and spirit pure.
5. As a German choose only a spouse of the same or Nordic blood.
6. In choosing a spouse ask about his ancestors.
7. Health is also a precondition for physical beauty.
8. Marry only for love.
9. Don't look for a playmate but for a companion for marriage.
10. You should want to have as many children as possible.

This was a common rhyme for women:

'Take hold of kettle, broom and pan,
Then you'll surely get a man!
Shop and office leave alone,
Your true life work lies at home.'

Information from  http://www.historylearningsite.co.uk/Women_Nazi_Germany.htm
http://www.germanculture.com.ua/library/weekly/aa080601b.htm
http://www.spartacus.schoolnet.co.uk/GERwomen.htm

## Fascism and Capitalism

There can be little doubt that fascists were anti-capitalist in their rhetoric. Radek, one of the communist leaders, was to describe fascism as the 'socialism of the petty bourgeois masses' (Kitchen, 1976: 2). Ramos (1905–36), a Spanish fascist, blamed the bourgeoisie and its 'agents, advocates and front men' for fragmentation, impotence, exhaustion and egoism. Rivera argued that fascism was neither capitalist nor communist: he advocated a national syndicalism that would pass surplus value, as he called it, 'to the producer as a member of his trade union'. La Rochelle, a French fascist, spoke of 'annihilating' liberalism and capitalism. A

## Ideas and Perspectives:

# Nazism and Fascism

A fiercely debated question relates to the relationship between Nazism and Italian fascism. Is there a general fascism of which Nazism is an example, or is Nazism so unique and particular that it cannot be categorised in this way? As Griffin has pointed out (1995: 93), a number of scholars have argued that Nazism is *sui generis,* unique to the history of Germany. Allardyce, a US scholar, took the view that a generic fascism does not exist (Griffin, 1995: 302):

| Similarities | Differences |
|---|---|
| Impact of World War I | Attitude to organised religion |
| Hatred of liberalism and Marxism | Degree of anti-Semitism |
| Rejection of parliamentary democracy | Global aspirations |
| Belief in leadership principle | Use of socialism to describe party. |
| Commitment to colonialism | |
| Admiration for the state | |

Not only do we have the profound influence exercised over Hitler and the Nazis by the success of Mussolini in Italy, but the conditions that contributed to the rise of fascism in Italy exercised their influence in Germany as well. The list above shows that Kershaw is right to argue that the similarities between Nazism and other brands of fascism are 'profound' (cited by Griffin, 1995: 93).

Nazism is better understood by seeing it as a variant of fascism – of course with its own particular features. The idea that racism was a German import into Mussolini's Italy is untrue, even though German fascism was much more extreme (and competent) than its Italian counterpart, and the genocidal policies towards the Jews were not part of the anti-Semitism of Italian fascism. Nevertheless, the case for considering Nazism as a form of fascism is overwhelming, and bears upon the important question of other forms of fascism that arose, not only in the inter-war years, but in the post-war period. Griffin's collection of documents is noteworthy for its inclusion of non-Nazi forms of German fascism. Spanish fascists such as Primo De Rivera denied that they were imitating Hitler and Mussolini: he argued that 'by reproducing the achievements of the Italians or the Germans we will become more Spanish than we have ever been' (Griffin, 1995: 188).

Latvian fascist made it clear that 'we acknowledge private enterprise and private property' but are opposed to anarchy (Griffin, 1995: 186; 189; 203; 218).

see her biography in Chapter 7: Feminism, p. 181

Zetkin influenced the Comintern in its argument that fascism 'by its origin and exponents' 'includes revolutionary tendencies which might turn against capitalism and its state' but in fact it is counter-revolutionary, supporting capitalism in a situation in which the old, allegedly non-political apparatus of the bourgeois state 'no longer guarantees the bourgeoisie adequate security' (Griffin, 1995: 261). The argument echoes Marx's comment in *The Eighteenth Brumaire of Louis Bonaparte* that when the parliamentary system seems to aid the socialists, then 'the bourgeoisie confesses that its own interest requires its deliverance from the peril of its own self-government' (Marx, 1973: 190). The merits of this argument are that it indicates the dangers which an explicitly illiberal regime poses to the bourgeoisie, and that in 'normal times' a liberal parliamentary system would be much more congenial to a 'bourgeois' regime than an explicitly authoritarian one. It is only when there is the fear that a parliamentary system might help the enemies of capital to power in a situation of crisis and revolutionary threat that 'deliverance' is sought. Miliband stresses that capitalists had to pay a high political price for a system that advantaged them: they had no real control over a dictatorship which arguably served their interests (1973: 85).

Miliband argues that the 'anti-bourgeois resonances' (1973: 80) are important, if only to enable fascist movements to acquire a mass following, nor need we deny that supporters of these movements believed that an anti-capitalist revolution was under way. It is not only Jewish capitalists we will hang, but all capitalists! declares a poster in the museum at the Dachau concentration camp. But Miliband cites Mussolini in 1934 defending private property, and notes that big business under Hitler was given a key role in managing the economy. There was a dramatic increase in the power of capital over labour and an increase in profits. Miliband concedes that businesses under fascism had to submit to a greater degree of intervention and control than they would have liked, and put up with policies they found disagreeable. Kitchen points out that industrialists disliked particular aspects of Nazi policy (the use of foreign slaves rather than women in the factories, for example, or the economic inefficiency involved in the mass murder of Jews), but he argues that, in broad terms, the industrialists were satisfied with Nazi policy (1976: 59).

As for fascism's supposedly revolutionary character: Miliband contends that the state not only does not significantly change in the composition of its personnel (except to purge it of 'traitors', liberals, etc.), but in Nazi Germany, for example, there were fewer people in the state from working-class origin than before (1973: 82–4). This is why it is not satisfactory to describe fascism as 'a party of revolutionaries' (Linz, 1979: 18), since fascism sought not to transform society and the state but to prevent it from being transformed. It is thus counter-revolutionary rather than revolutionary in character. It is impossible to agree with Eugen Weber that fascism is not a counter-revolution but merely a rival revolution (to communism) (Weber, 1979: 509).

The orthodox communist position – enshrined in the theses of the Comintern or Third International – was that fascism represented 'the most reactionary, most chauvinist, and most imperialist elements of finance capital' (Griffin, 1995: 262). It was only in the mid-1930s that communists dropped the notorious argument that social democrats were 'social fascists' and the enemy of the working class. 'Finance capital', in the orthodox definition cited above, refers to Lenin's argument in *Imperialism* that bank capital has merged with industrial capital, but it seems less contentious to accept Miliband's point that fascism represented industrialists as well as bankers in a situation in which threat of left 'extremism' made right 'extremism' a necessary, if far from ideal, choice. The Coles argued that fascism is state-controlled capitalism 'operated in the interests of the broad mass of property owners'. Horkheimer, a key figure in the neo-Marxist Frankfurt School, declared that 'whoever is not prepared to talk about capitalism should also remain silent about fascism' (Griffin, 1995: 267; 272).

Psychoanalysts argued that fascism is rooted in the human character – it is a form of personality structure, an authoritarian character. But this does not mean, as Adorno acknowledged, that such a structure can only be modified by psychological

How to read:

**Kitchen's *Fascism***

Kitchen's short book starts with an introduction that should be read carefully. His next two chapters – dealing with orthodox communist theories and psychological theories of fascism – contain useful information and can be skim read. The same is true of the following two chapters – dealing with the theory of totalitarianism and Ernst Nolte's theory of fascism. Both are powerful critiques but skim reading should enable the reader to get the gist of the argument.

Chapters 5 and 6 deserve closer attention. Kitchen's examination of the links between fascism and industry and fascism and the middle classes are exceptionally compelling, and merit a close reading. The chapter on Bonapartism is useful but again can be skim read, while the conclusion contains a valuable summary of his argument, and deserves a careful look.

means (Griffin, 1995: 289), and it could well be argued that we still need to refer to capitalism and crisis to understand why fascism arises in certain societies and at certain historical periods, and not at others. Reich, who was expelled from the German Communist Party in the 1930s for his dissident views, had argued that fascism is the result of thousands of years of warping in the human structure: a number of later studies contended that fascism was an attempt to compensate for mothering and family life (Kitchen, 1976: 13; 23).

## Fascism, Liberalism and the Enlightenment

'1789 [the year of the French Revolution, and the inauguration of the era of Liberty, Equality and Fraternity] is abolished' (Heywood, 1992: 174). This was how the Nazis proclaimed their victory in 1933. Although fascists specifically targeted Marxism, they saw it as an ideology that built upon, and was thus rooted in, the assumptions of liberalism and the Enlightenment. Dunn quotes the words of Hitler: 'National Socialism is what Marxism could have been had it freed itself from the absurd, artificial link with the democratic system' (1979: 21).

### The State of Nature, Equality and the Individual

Fascists not only deny that humans have ever lived outside of society, but they interpret 'nature' in a repressively hierarchical manner. Although the idea that humans are self-contained atoms who are naturally separate and unrelated to one another constitutes a mystification of social reality, fascism attacked abstract individualism because of its universal and egalitarian claims. It dramatically threw the baby out with the bathwater.

Classical liberalism sees individuals as naturally free and equal. Fascism takes the view that nature is a force that embodies violence, instinct and superiority: hence it rejects the whole notion of equality, even as a formal attribute. Individuals are created by the community, and the community is interpreted in statist terms. It is

true that Nazi ideologists gave a specifically racial and *völkisch* (peoples')
dimension to the notion of community so that the community constituted a kind of
soul. But all fascists see the community as 'natural', animated by some kind of life
force – it is an emotional organism, not a rational construct – and it assigns
superiority to the few and inferiority to the many.

The notion of humanity was attacked for two reasons: first because it ignored
what was deemed to be racial superiority – of Aryans over Jews, whites over
blacks, etc. – and second because it implied that the mass of humans mattered. The
progress and culture of humanity, declared Hitler, 'are not a product of the
majority, but rest exclusively on the genius and energy of the personality' (Vincent,
1995: 157). The individual denotes not the ordinary and everyday human being,
but the leader, the genius, the person who must be obeyed.

## Nationalism

Liberalism has an ambivalent position towards nationalism because it has an
ambivalent position towards the state. In the state of nature individuals are deemed
cosmopolitan – they are outside both nation and state – but as they become
conscious of the 'inconveniences' of such a position they not only form a state but
acquire a national identity. Liberal nationalism, as does the liberal state, seeks to
reconcile universal freedom and equality with the 'necessary evil' of particular
institutions that divide the world. Liberal nationalists argue that all nations are
equal, and the liberal state seeks to provide security for the free citizen. Just as
fascism sees the community as somehow prior to the individual (an inversion of the
liberal abstraction), so it sees the nation as the embodiment of superiority and
domination.

Nationalism necessarily takes an explicitly xenophobic form, based on hatred.
Hatred of foreigners, aliens, the weak, the vulnerable, the disabled, the needy, the
female, and a characterisation of 'lesser' peoples and nations in terms of these
'despised' categories. Mussolini challenged those who saw Machiavelli as the
founder of fascism, on the grounds that Machiavelli was insufficiently contemptuous
of the masses – the herd, as Mussolini liked to call them – who gratefully accepted
inequality and discipline (Vincent, 1995: 156).

## Rationality

Liberalism and the Enlightenment see all individuals as rational, and thus capable
of governing themselves. Fascism regards 'reason' as inherently abstract, and extols
action as a force based upon instinct and feeling. You should 'think with your
blood', and de Rivera of the Spanish Falange (a fascist movement that Franco
tolerated and used) declared that the movement is not a way of thinking but 'a way
of being' (Vincent, 1995: 155). It is the soul, not the mind, emotion and instinct,
not reason and logic that ultimately count. Again fascism challenges, in a spirit of
negative inversion, the abstractions of the Enlightenment. Reason is rejected – not
made historical and concrete. Fascism dismisses not merely the weaknesses of
liberalism (its chronic tendency to abstraction), but its conceptual strengths (its
argument for the individual, universality, reason and self-government).

Colin Jordan, who founded the White Defence League in 1958 and the National Socialist Movement in 1962, declared himself in revolt against liberalism, singling out for particular mention its 'cash nexus', 'its excessive individualism', 'its view of man as a folkless, interchangeable unit of world population', its 'sickly humanitarianism' and its 'fraudulent contention' that the wishes of the masses are 'the all-important criteria' (Griffin, 1995: 325–6).

## Fascism, Stalinism and the State

Fascism identifies the individual and the community with the state. Fascism inverts the classical liberal thesis, that humans dwell in a stateless order of nature, by arguing that humans derive their very nature and being from membership of the state. Although the Nazis liked to speak of the community in racial terms, they too held that the repressive hierarchies of the state are central to human identity.

Hence the explicit and dramatic **statism** of the fascist analysis. By arguing that humans are statist in essence, fascists reject the idea that freedom and force stand as mutually exclusive entities. On the contrary, force becomes something that ennobles and distinguishes humans and, since the exercise of force implies the existence of a repressive hierarchy, fascism rejects the notion of equality. The individual is a person who stands out from the mass, so that the leadership principle is woven into social analysis. Leaders are outstanding individuals who dictate to and mould the formless and ignorant masses.

It follows from this avowedly statist doctrine that the nation has enemies both from without and within who threaten its purity and cohesion. War and violent conflict are the only viable responses so that the crushing of the other is the way to affirm the self. Xenophobia and racism are built into the statism of fascist premises, and so is male chauvinism. The superior individual must be a 'he' since the notion of the female is identified with passivity and cowardice.

It is important not to see the state as itself a fascist institution, since states can be liberal and anti-authoritarian in character in which, through devices such as the rule of law and parliamentary representation, state force is regulated and limited. On the other hand, it is also important to see the continuities as well as the discontinuities between fascism and the state. The use of force polarises, and can only be justified against those who are deemed 'enemies' of society. The nationalism that reaches its extreme form in fascism is inherent in the state, and it could be argued that there is a real tension between the state as an institution claiming a monopoly of legitimate force and the notion of democracy as self-government.

## Stalinism

Can one describe Stalinism – authoritarian communism – as a form of fascism? There are of course similarities. The concept of dictatorship is central to Stalinism and a particularly vicious and exclusionary form of class struggle is used to justify purges, mock trials and authoritarian practices in general. But there are also significant dissimilarities, so that, however tempting, it is, in our view, erroneous to see left and right authoritarianism, Stalinism and fascism as interchangeable.

## Stalin's Purges

Stalin was admired by Hitler, and the latter told Speer that if Germany won World War II Stalin would remain in charge of Russia (Speer, 1970: 306). The famine in the early 1930s that followed collectivisation killed between 6 and 7 million people. The purges that began in the mid-1930s were directed against dissidents within the party and in society at large, and took millions of lives. About 35,000 military officers were shot or imprisoned. Robert Conquest has estimated that by 1938 there were 7 million victims in the labour camps, where the survival rate could drop to some 2 or 3 per cent. The purges have been summarised as follows:

Arrests, 1937–38 – about 7 million
Executions – about 1 million
Died in camps – about 2 million
In prison, late 1938 – about 1 million
In camps, late 1938 – about 8 million

By the time Stalin died (in 1953), the camps' population had increased to some 12 million.

Source: www.gendercide.org

In other words, the argument that became widespread during the cold war, identifying communism and fascism as forms of **totalitarianism**, is superficial and misleading. Mommsen makes the point that this theory glosses over the structural features peculiar to the fascist party. The theory of democratic centralism may have operated to strengthen the leadership of communist parties but it was a theory of

## Exercise

You are having a cup of coffee in a crowded coffee shop in your Students' Union when four young men sit at your table and begin talking. Because you are on your own you cannot but hear their conversation. 'There are too many blacks around here', says A. 'I agree, they should all be sent back to their place of origin', comments B. 'But some of them were born here', interjects C. 'That's irrelevant', says D. 'Whether they were born here or not, they are not part of our race, and they just don't fit in'. 'Indeed', declares A, 'I have noticed that the lecturers make a fuss of them, as though they are more important than us whites'. 'Yeah', says B, 'what do you expect when most of the lecturers are communists and Jews? I think that the university should only employ decent-minded Christians – people with sensible views'. C protests: 'That would be undemocratic'. 'So what', says D. 'Our democracy is a farce anyway – we need strong rule by someone we can look up to. This notion of majority rule is an idiotic liberal idea anyway'. 'In fact', comments A, 'there are blacks in my street and tonight a group of us are going to show them what we think of them with something hard and large through their windows'.

A, B and D are clearly right-wing extremists. They are racists.

• Which would you say is a fascist?

• Although you find their views deeply upsetting, would you call the police?

organisation alien to fascism (Mommsen, 1979: 153). Moreover, fascist and communist ideology are poles apart. Stalinism seeks to build a world that is ultimately stateless and classless in character – it draws upon a Marxist heritage to argue that under communism people, all people, will be able to govern their own affairs.

This is not to deny the authoritarianism that existed (and still exists) in Communist Party states, but it could be argued that the 'cult of the personality', the denial of democracy, the male chauvinism, etc. in these societies stand in contradiction to the theories of communism. In fascism, on the other hand, these features are not in contradiction with the doctrine: they are explicitly enshrined in the theories and movements. This argument may not seem of much comfort to the inmate of a 'gulag' who is worked to death in inhuman conditions, but it points to a qualitative difference between the **statism** of fascism and statism of Stalinism. Moreover, as Kitchen points out, communism sought to radically change the means of production, whereas fascist regimes did not, and this throws further doubt on the proposition that similarities between fascism and communism outweigh the differences (1976: 31).

## Fascism Today

One of the objections that Kitchen makes to the German thinker Ernst Nolte's theory of fascism is the view that fascism belongs only to the past. It does not exist today. This is not only a complacent view of fascism, it confuses a movement with its historical manifestations (Kitchen, 1976: 40–1). It is true that fascism arose in the inter-war period, and that one of the problems of identifying post-war fascism is that the revulsion of most of the world against Nazism in particular has meant that contemporary fascism generally avoids too close an identity with the 'models' of the past. Fascists in Europe have had the problem in the post-war period of getting to grips with the defeat of Mussolini and Hitler in World War II. There have been a variety of responses.

### The Unrepentant Apologists

Some have taken the view that Hitler and Mussolini were correct in their policies although they were defeated by the Allied forces. Jordan, who founded the White Defence League in 1958 and the National Socialist Movement in 1962, took the view that fascism (even in its extreme Hitlerian form) is as relevant as ever, and the West European Federation set up in 1963 espoused explicitly Nazi doctrine. The New European Order established in Switzerland supported similar views (Griffin, 1995: 326–8).

### The Holocaust Deniers

Some fascists try to undercut the argument of their critics by denying that the Nazis had in fact brought about the Holocaust. The leader of the Belgian fascist movement during World War II, Degrelle, argued to the Pope in 1979 that

Auschwitz could not have exterminated large numbers of Jews, travellers, etc. and that anyway, the terror bombing of the Allies and the gulags of Stalin put into perspective any human rights abuses the Nazis might have caused. The term 'final solution' did not mean extermination – this is another of the deniers' contentions – and that during the war other nations had concentration camps too (Griffin, 1995: 330–7). Irving, an historian who has built his reputation on 'reassessing' the Holocaust, admits the terrible atrocities of the camps, but argues that these took place against the instructions of Hitler, who merely wanted to have Jews transported to Madagascar, an island off the African coast (Griffin, 1995: 330–5). To deny the existence of the Holocaust is a criminal offence in Germany, although it could be argued that obnoxious contentions such as these should be exposed through argument rather than crushed by law.

## The Critical Fascists

Mosley, the leader of the British Union of Fascists, before World War II, argued that Hitler had overreached himself – tried to achieve too much – and this was the reason for his downfall. The concentration camps and the sacrifice of the youth tarnished an otherwise noble ideal. Mussolini had badly miscalculated when he entered the war, but the harshness of his *squadristi* can be excused by 'the incredible savagery and brutality of the reds'. Chesterton, the first chair of the National Front, admits that fascism failed disastrously, and the 'excesses' of Hitler, in particular, discredited the cause (Griffin, 1995: 323–4).

Some, such as Ernest Niekisch (1889–1967), argued that the fascist revolution had been hijacked by demagogues (i.e. leaders who appeal to prejudices for support) such as Hitler, who was a travesty of the spiritual elite really required (Griffin, 1995: 319).

## Eurofascism

The European Social Movement, founded in 1951, sought to unite Europe against 'communism', with Evola, an Italian fascist, arguing that such a Europe must be an empire. Mosley, on the other hand, spoke of the need for Europe to become a 'nation', with a pan-European government using Africa as a resource base (Griffin, 1995: 333–5). A number of those associated with what can be called a 'New Right' (not to be confused with the neo-liberalism of free marketeers) speak of the need to regenerate Europe so that it stands apart from communism and capitalism that in its liberal form eradicates identity and imposes a vulgar and soulless 'rule of quantity' upon life (Griffin, 1995: 351).

## Nationalist Salvation

Some fascists have turned to nationalism, arguing that a national revolution is necessary as a 'cleansing fire of purification'. Ultra-nationalists have utilised punk rock, heavy metal music and football hooliganism (Griffin, 1995: 360; 363). However, parties such as the British National Front claim to stand for democracy, and accuse their opponents of not being supporters of 'genuine democracy'.

Ideas and Perspectives:

## South African Apartheid

There is no doubt that the South African National Party and its policies of apartheid were widely admired by the extreme right elsewhere, including explicit fascists. A Mosley supporter, Webster spoke of the South African nationalists as following 'the same path as Hitler did, but they will not be as hasty as he was' (Bunting, 1969: 71). During World War II, the National Party (NP) communicated with Nazis over their campaign to withdraw South Africa's support from the Allies. The NP had cordial links with the Ossewabrandwag (the Ox-wagon Sentinel), which also had connections with the Nazis and whose paramilitary wing sought to overthrow the government. Vorster, a future prime minister, declared in 1942 that his Christian nationalism 'was an ally of national socialism' (Bunting, 1969: 98).

When Germany and Italy were defeated, the National Party began to distance itself from anti-English and anti-Semitic policies, and concentrated on developing the doctrine of apartheid. All those serving sentences for wartime offences were released after the Nationalist electoral victory in 1948. The stripping of Africans and (so-called) coloureds of their political rights, the outlawing of sexual relations between the 'races', the Suppression of Communism Act (which banned the party and imposed house arrest on opponents of the regime), the reservation of skilled jobs for whites, the control imposed on the trade unions – all these and many more acts had been envisaged by the National Party during the war period (Bunting, 1969: 110).

Bunting's detailed account of what he calls the Nuremberg Laws of grand apartheid and the title of his book, *The Rise of the South African Reich*, raises the question whether apartheid South Africa can be considered a fascist regime. The regime certainly resorted to terror against its opponents, and was brutal, explicitly racist and authoritarian. On the other hand, it was a parliamentary system for whites, and allowed limited liberalism in its treatment of the press, judiciary and opposition parties, provided they were relatively conservative in character. It comes close to being a fascist regime, and certainly Griffin is right to regard Afrikaner nationalist organisations such as the Afrikaner–Weerstandsbeweging (the Afrikaner Resistance Movement), which developed in the post-apartheid period, as fascist in practice (Griffin, 1995: 376).

Nevertheless we would say that, although apartheid was extremely right wing, it was not technically fascist, despite its pre-war and wartime roots.

Nationalism is presented as a doctrine for the equality of nations. The National Front (NF) sees itself 'as a radical party seeking deep and fundamental changes in British society. Unlike many other radical parties, particularly those of the past, we do not seek to impose our views on the population'. The implication is that such a party distances itself from the explicit authoritarianism of inter-war fascism. (See http://www.nfne.co.uk/nfsop.html.)

In 1982 John Tyndall formed the British National Party (BNP) and, although he speaks of the 'degenerative forces' poisoning national life linked to liberalism and internationalism, the party speaks of wishing to extend democracy (go to http://www.bnp.org.uk/mission.htm), and objects to the idea that it is fascist or

## Oswald Mosley (1896–1980)

Educated at Winchester and Sandhurst, Mosley fought in World War I. In 1918 he was elected to Parliament as a Conservative MP for Harrow, but broke with the Conservatives and won a seat as an independent in 1922.

Two years later he joined the Labour Party and in 1927 he was elected to the party's National Executive Committee. He was appointed by the Labour leader to the post of Chancellor of the Duchy of Lancaster when Labour won the election in 1929. In 1930 Mosley proposed a programme that he believed would help deal with the growing unemployment in Britain. Using ideas derived from the economist John Maynard Keynes, Mosley proposed that the state should stimulate foreign trade, direct industrial policy and use public funds to promote industrial expansion. When these proposals were rejected he resigned his post.

In 1931 he founded the New Party, but despite his influential supporters the party failed to secure a seat in the election of 1931. The following year he met Mussolini and, impressed by the Italian regime and its leader, he dissolved the New Party and set up the British Union of Fascists (BUF) in its stead.

The BUF was strongly anti-communist and argued for a programme of economic revival based on government spending and protectionism. By 1934 Mosley was organising marches through Jewish districts in London. The 1936 Public Order Act outlawed the wearing of political uniforms, and private armies were also made illegal. Threatening and abusive words were made a criminal offence, and the Home Secretary was given powers to ban marches. This seriously affected the activities of the BUF.

In October 1936 Diana Mitford secretly married Mosley in Nazi propaganda minister Joseph Goebbels's drawing room in Berlin, with Hitler one of the guests at the ceremony. Mosley's party lost further support with the outbreak of World War II and in 1940 Mosley was arrested and, along with other prominent members of his organisation, sent to prison. The British Union of Fascists was dissolved and its publications banned.

Mosley and his wife were treated extremely leniently in prison, and in 1943 he was released, despite protests, with Mosley's own sister-in-law describing the release as 'a slap in the face of anti-fascists': 'a direct betrayal of those who have died for the cause of anti-fascism'.

After the war Mosley ran a publishing house for right-wing authors, and in 1947 he formed the Union Movement, which argued for an integrated Europe and an end to Commonwealth immigration.

In 1949 Mosley went to live in France, close to the Duke of Windsor who had been forced to abdicate as king some 13 years earlier. He published *The European Situation* in 1950, arguing that the union of Europe needed to be accompanied by a national government able to act rapidly and decisively and be subject to parliamentary control. In 1958 he wrote *Europe: Faith and Plan*. Mosley stood for parliament in 1959 (for Kensington North) and in 1966 (for Shoreditch and Finsbury). He was unsuccessful on both occasions.

authoritarian. It is difficult to avoid the conclusion that parties such as the BNP and the NF are parties of the extreme right rather than fascist in the way we have defined the term. On the other hand the BNP, for example, has links with and invites speakers from explicitly fascist groups, so that the 'democratic' appearances of such organisations should not be taken at face value. La Oeuvre France, founded in 1968, describes itself as 'a strictly nationalist movement' and treats the accusation of 'fascism' and nazism' as slurs against French people 'of good stock' (Griffin, 1995: 371–2). Of course ultra-nationalist movements will be sensitive to the idea that they are the derivatives of other movements, and hence are likely to resist the label of fascism on that score as well.

However, groups on the far right that have sprung up in former Communist Party states, such as Romania, may espouse more explicitly fascist positions. The New Right movement, founded in 1993 in Romania, speaks of the need for an 'ethnocratic' state that it explicitly contrasts to a democratic state. The National Democratic Party of Germany, eclipsed in the late 1980s by the Republican Party and the German People's Union, espouses Germany as a *völkish* national entity, but calls for social justice and equality within Germany's borders. The Italian Social Movement which won 12.7 per cent of the vote with the National Alliance (in March 1994), seeks to reconstruct the Italian state and regards Mussolini as the greatest statesman of the twentieth century (Griffin, 1995: 379; 382; 387).

## Summary

Although fascism is a chaotic and opportunist movement, it can and should be defined. There are a number of characteristics – anti-liberalism, ultra-nationalism, the extolling of violence, militant statism, mass support, etc. – that distinguish this twentieth-century movement from other movements.

Fascism arose first in Italy. The development of fascism in Italy needs to be explained, since this was the particular movement that gave the general movement its name. Contrary to widely held views, Mussolini's regime was racist, although it is true that systematic anti-Semitism only developed after the alliance with Hitler.

Nazism is seen as a form of fascism, and not simply as a historically unique movement. It is an extreme kind of fascism, emphasising the racial character of nationalism in a more aggressive and systematic manner. Its anti-capitalism was ultimately rhetorical, as the liquidation of the leaders of the Nazi 'left' in 1934 demonstrates. Although fascism acquired mass support through espousing a rhetorical anti-capitalism, once in power fascist movements consolidated their links with big business. It is true that fascist leaders directed businesses and implemented policies that were not always to the satisfaction of the business community, but it is also true that backing from large capitalist corporations was crucial for fascism's success.

Fascism rejects liberalism and the Enlightenment. Ideas of reason, equality and emancipation are contemptuously dismissed in a specifically negative manner. Although there are problems with the ideas of liberalism and the Enlightenment, fascism unceremoniously throws the baby out with the bathwater. Fascists see the state itself as central to human identity and vital to the idea of community. The violence that the state both exercises and seeks to regulate is extolled by fascists, and although the liberal state is significantly different from the fascist one there are similarities as well as differences in all forms of the state. Similarly, all left-wing authoritarianism is also statist in character; it is not correct to describe Stalinism, say, as a form of fascism. There are similarities, but these are outweighed by their differences.

Fascist movements exist today, but there are a number of problems in identifying them. Fascism was discredited by the defeat of Nazi Germany and fascist Italy in World War II, and of course by the atrocities committed by the Nazis in the concentration camps. Post-war movements of the extreme right often deny that they are fascist in character – they may even claim to espouse democracy, although these claims should be approached with caution. The other problem with identifying post-war fascism is that extreme nationalist movements (which are not German or Italian) feel that to express allegiance to fascism would compromise their own claims to 'authenticity' and national uniqueness.

## Questions

1. Can fascism be defined and, if so, how?
2. Is fascism a purely Italian phenomenon?
3. Why does fascism reject liberalism and the Enlightenment?
4. 'Stalinism is a form of fascism.' Discuss.
5. Comment on the argument that fascism is a movement of the inter-war period.

## References

Beetham, D. (1977) 'From Socialism to Fascism: The Relation between Theory and Practice in the Work of Robert Michels', *Political Studies* 25, 3–24, 161–81.

Bunting, B. (1969) *The Rise of the South African Reich* Harmondsworth: Penguin.

Dunn, J. (1979) *Western Theory in the Face of the Future* Cambridge: Cambridge University Press.

Griffin, R. (1995) *Fascism* Oxford and New York: Oxford University Press.

Hemingway, E. (1985) *A Farewell to Arms* London: Heinemann Educational.

Heywood, A. (1992) *Political Ideologies* Basingstoke: Palgrave.

Kitchen, M. (1976) *Fascism* Basingstoke: Macmillan.

Linz, J. (1979) 'Some Notes towards a Comparative Study of Fascism in Sociological Historical Perspective' in W. Laqueur (ed.), *Fascism: A Reader's Guide* Harmondsworth: Penguin, 13–78.

Lyttelton, A. (1979) 'Italian Fascism' in W. Laqueur (ed.), *Fascism: A Reader's Guide* Harmondsworth: Penguin, 81–114.

Marx, K. (1973) 'The Eighteenth Brumaire of Louis Napoleon' in D. Fernbach (ed.), *Surveys from Exile* Harmondsworth and London: Penguin and New Left Review, 143–249.

Miliband, R. (1973) *The State in Capitalist Society* London: Quartet.

Mommsen, H. (1979) 'National Socialism: Continuity and Change' in W. Laqueur (ed.), *Fascism: A Reader's Guide* Harmondsworth: Penguin, 151–92.

Speer, A. (1970) *Inside the Third Reich* London: Weidenfeld & Nicolson.

Vincent, A. (1995) *Modern Political Ideologies* 2nd edn Oxford: Blackwell.

Weber, E. (1979) 'Revolution? Counter-Revolution? What Revolution' in W. Laqueur (ed.), *Fascism: A Reader's Guide* Harmondsworth: Penguin, 488–531.

## Further Reading

- Griffin's reader on fascism (referenced above) is an invaluable source of material with acute introductions and prefaces.

- Kitchen's *Fascism* (referenced above) is comprehensive and readable, short and incisive.

- Fromm's *Fear of Freedom* (London: Routledge & Kegan Paul, 1942) is a classic interpretation of fascism that draws upon psychoanalysis for its explanation.

- For detailed analyses of fascism in the inter-war period see *The Fascism Reader*, ed. A. Kallis, London and New York: Routledge, 2003.

- Albert Speer *Inside the Third Reich* (referenced above) is a fascinating read.

## Weblinks

For information about the Holocaust: http://www.thinkequal.com

For useful sites on fascism: http://dictionary.reference.com/search?q=fascism

For further information and bibliography: http://en.wikipedia.org/wiki/Fascism

**Part 2**

# New Ideologies

We have argued that an ideology is a belief system focused around the state. The 'classical ideologies' discussed in Part 1 took the legitimacy of the state to be a central concern, and this is true even of anarchist theories: although most anarchists reject the claim to legitimacy made on behalf of the state, one of their main objectives is to challenge the state, and in this sense anarchists are 'state focused'. Despite talk of **'globalisation'** and the 'hollowing out of the state', the state remains important in political theory, and the new ideologies discussed in Part 2 do not dismiss it. They do, however, challenge the *sharp* distinction between domestic and international politics. For example, multiculturalists argue that cultures do not equate to nations, and therefore allegiance to the state does not, as the British politician Norman Tebbit claimed, require that British Asians support the English cricket team against Pakistan. Similarly, an important feature of **feminism** is the linking together of women's experience across the world. While a traditional ideology, such as socialism (or Marxism, as one variant of socialism), stressed that the workers 'know no nation', and therefore class solidarity should transcend the state, the focus of socialist (communist) political action was capture of the state. Feminists, on the other hand, while prepared to work through state structures to achieve legal change, identify power relations at both sub-state and supra-state levels: women can be oppressed through family structures as well as by global forces. **Ecologism** represents an even more radical challenge to the significance of the state as the central focus of political thought. Ecologists – as distinct from environmentalists – see 'nature' as an interconnected whole, protection of which requires both small-scale organisation and global action. Small-scale, quasi-anarchistic communities are required as a means of avoiding environmentally damaging transportation of goods, while global agreements are necessary to tackle problems that by their nature do not respect state boundaries. **Fundamentalism** may also represent a challenge to the state: Islamic fundamentalism regards the state as a corruption of Islam (US fundamentalism and Zionism do, however, appear highly nationalistic, although some variants of Zionism conceive of the Jewish state as a religious, rather than a secular, entity, and thus as quite different to the traditional state).

But the challenge to the distinction between national and international politics is not the only significant divider between classical and new ideologies. In trying to understand what is 'new' about the new ideologies three differences – or 'discontinuities' – can be identified. The first we have already identified – the challenge to the significance of the state. The second may appear trite: the 'new ideologies' are recent in origin. This point can, however, be expressed in a more sophisticated way: the new ideologies have emerged as a response to fundamental changes in the social and economic structures of advanced industrial societies. The third difference relates to the intellectual relationship of the new ideologies to the traditional ones: the former engage *critically* with the latter.

## Social and Economic Change

The four ideologies that we discuss in Part 2 emerged after World War II. While they have intellectual roots predating the war, and indeed the roots go back centuries – think of Mary Wollstonecraft – *consciousness* of each as a *relatively unified system of thought* has only developed in the last 40 or so years. While it is crude to date an ideology simply from its first usage in public debate, the employment of these labels – these -isms – in everyday debate is of some significance and, roughly speaking, the terms 'feminism' and 'ecologism' (environmentalism, Green thought) became current in the 1960s, multiculturalism in the 1970s, and fundamentalism (which had been employed in debates within US Protestantism in the 1920s) began to achieve wider application in the 1970s and 1980s. Without reducing these new ideologies to social and economic changes we suggest that they are, in part, the product of certain new socio-economic structures.

We have seen that the traditional ideologies themselves changed in response to the massive social and economic change of the nineteenth century: John Stuart Mill's defence of representative democracy is a response to the rise of 'mass society', as is his concern with the 'tyranny of the majority'. Mill's political world is very different to that of, say, John Locke. Similarly, Mill's near-contemporary Karl Marx contrasts his own socialism with that of earlier 'utopian' socialists. And conservatism, the ideology that above all others claims to be 'historical' – in the sense of responding to the world as it is, rather than providing a model of an alternative world – has undergone considerable adaptation from the eighteenth-century thinkers Hume and Burke to twentieth-century thinker Oakeshott. Given the extent of social 'rationalisation' which Oakeshott so bemoans, his thought has an elegiac quality when compared with that of earlier conservative thinkers. Fascism is, of course, a response to specific social and economic conditions, most especially a perceived mismatch between the development of state and economic structures. By entitling the first part of this book 'Classical Ideologies' we are not suggesting that these ideologies are 'dead': they are continually developing as ideologies, and indeed some thinkers have argued that we are all liberals now (Fukuyama, 1992). Rather than seeing the contrast between classical and new ideologies as a distinction between 'dead' and 'living' we understand new ideologies as distinct systems of thought that have emerged out of, and in response to, changing social and economic structures, and those changes have also affected the classical ideologies.

What then are these changes? One way of addressing this question is to consider what might be termed the 'crisis of Marxism'. The development of this 'crisis' can be understood in terms of historical events, of which the final and most spectacular was the overthrow of state socialism in Eastern Europe in 1989 followed by its collapse in the Soviet Union in 1991. In the period dubbed 'the short twentieth century' (Hobsbawm, 1995) – 1914–91 – there were a series of key events that arguably presaged the final collapse of the socialist project: the Molotov–Ribbentrop Pact between the USSR and Nazi Germany in 1939, the Soviet invasions of Hungary (1956) and Czechoslovakia (1968), and the imposition of martial law in Poland in the early 1980s. But in parallel to these concrete political events there was a deeper intellectual crisis. The central problem for Marxists has been the failure of the working class to develop a truly 'revolutionary consciousness'. Far from rising up as one, the working class (or classes?) splintered. In, for example, Weimar Germany (1919–33) there was a major split between the communists and the social democrats, as well as between left and right, with a significant section of the working class attracted to the far right Nazi Party (or NASDP). And, as critics of Marx point out, those countries such as Russia that underwent proletarian revolutions were not the ones 'marked down' for it because they lacked sufficient industrial development. The fragmentation of Marxism into different streams of thought (McLellan, 1979) was a response to the crisis, but so was the adoption of Marxist categories of thought by (essentially) non-Marxist theorists. These theorists use the language of collective agency, oppression and liberation, but they are no longer applied to the working class, and the strategy of liberation is much more 'particularistic' – whereas the root idea of Marxism was that the transition to a classless society ultimately resulted in the liberation of humankind, and not simply one oppressed socio-economic class new social movements, be they feminist, multiculturalist or ecological, do not *necessarily* make such a claim. We say 'not necessarily' because there is still a hint that women's liberation is good for men, or that human beings are part of 'nature', and so 'ecological **justice**' is also 'human justice'. Fundamentalism – or, at least, Islamic fundamentalism – can also be understood as a response to the crisis of Marxism: many parts of the Arab-Islamic world embraced Marxist ideology in the 1960s as a form of development, or 'catch-up', ideology. The failure of state-led socialism opened a space for another ostensibly egalitarian ideology – Islamic fundamentalism.

We have suggested that the four new ideologies are, in part, a response to the failure of Marxism, but conversely at least two of them – feminism and ecologism – have emerged due to rising levels of economic well-being (of course the survival of capitalism, against Marx's predictions, is part of the explanation of the crisis of Marxism). This may seem a strange claim, given that both are concerned with oppression. However, that feminism and ecologism emerged in the 1960s is significant. If we consider gender relations, even prior to the 1960s there were social changes taking place that fundamentally affected the balance of power between men and women: the wartime mobilisation of women to work in factories and on the land is generally regarded as significant in breaking down the distinction between the 'private' (home) and the 'public' (work and the civic sphere). The development of household appliances and a general improvement in living conditions reduced to some extent the pressure on women as the chief source of 'domestic labour'. By the 1960s the speed of change had picked up, with Western industrialised countries experiencing significant economic and social changes: a shift from manufacturing ('blue-collar') jobs to service ('white-collar') jobs; greater availability of contraception, especially the 'pill' (oral contraception); increasing educational opportunities; and the narrowing of the gap between men and women in educational attainment. Certainly feminism does champion oppressed women, but the leadership of women's organisations, as well as academic feminist theorists, are drawn disproportionately from relatively privileged social groups. This is not in any way to denigrate feminism – our concern here is simply to identify the reasons why feminism emerged as a fully fledged ideology when it did.

Turning now to ecologism, the link between rising prosperity and ecological consciousness may seem much more tenuous. However, political scientist Ronald Inglehart identified the emergence in the 1970s of a generation born during or just after World War II – sometimes called the generation of '68 (with '68 a reference to the student disturbances of 1968) – that espoused 'post-materialist values': questioning of authority, liberal attitudes to human relationships, rejection of job security, importance of 'self-realisation' and individuality (Inglehart, 1977). The preceding generation, which had directly experienced the inter-war depression, World War II and the hardships of the immediate post-war period, were much more inclined to hold 'materialist values'. The word 'materialist' should not be read as 'selfish' – the war generation simply wanted an end to the deprivations of the war, and so were strongly committed to job security and rising prosperity. The post-war generation might be thought more selfish because they took for granted the opportunities provided by the welfare state and economic growth policies. Nonetheless, the post-war generation did, according to Inglehart, display a distinct set of values, and it is not difficult to see how these values might lead that generation to reject traditional political ideologies and movements in favour of an ecological consciousness.

The socio-economic conditions that gave rise to the development of multiculturalism are slightly different, but are still connected to rising levels of prosperity among certain key groups. The post-war period was characterised by increasing levels of economic migration from South Asia and the Mediterranean fringe to the countries of central and northern Europe. For example, the so-called 'economic miracle' (*Wirtschaftswunder*) in West Germany was made possible by 'guest labour' from (especially) Turkey. And large numbers of South Asians came to Britain in search of work. These groups – disproportionately made up of men – tended to seek protection in their own communities, especially as tensions rose in the late 1950s. However, by the 1960s there emerged organisations that campaigned against discrimination. It is, however, significant that 'race' rather than 'culture' was the central concept, with the emphasis on overcoming 'skin prejudice'; this was paralleled on a much larger scale in the United States, with the emergence of a powerful Civil Rights Movement (although, of course, the African-American community had a quite different history to European immigrant communities). It is only in the 1970s and 1980s that there emerges a shift from the language of race, and the idea of a *multiracial* society, to culture, and the notion of a *multicultural* society. Certainly, some of the advocates of multiculturalism were first-generation immigrants, but many were the children of first-generation immigrants who argued that the recognition of pluralism required an analysis of society centred on culture rather than race. Again, as with feminism, while the aim was to overcome disadvantage, the political and intellectual leadership of this movement was relatively advantaged.

## Critique of Classical Ideologies

We have already suggested that the new ideologies emerged, in part, as a response to the failure of Marxism. And we have also argued that rising prosperity changed the expectations and outlook of certain groups – women, the post-war generation and 'ethnic' (cultural) minorities. The combination of a recognition of the crisis of Marxism and the underlying socio-economic conditions which have given rise to these new ideologies means that there is a need to reconsider liberalism. With the collapse of state socialism it may be argued that liberalism lacks any competitor. This is the claim Francis Fukuyama made in his 1992 book *The End of History*; his thesis is contentious but were we, for the sake of argument, to accept that liberalism is the last (effective) ideology, it is still possible to see three of the new 'ideologies' – feminism, multiculturalism and ecologism – as critical responses to the liberal tradition (fundamentalism stands opposed to liberalism, but there are few societies that can be described as *effectively* organised around fundamentalist ideas). These three ideologies are engaged in a *critique* of liberalism. It is important to use that word carefully: to engage in a critique of liberalism does not entail rejecting it but, rather, drawing out its truth. In particular, the central ideas of freedom and equality are taken up from the liberal tradition and turned against it. It might also be argued that the new ideologies employ the 'fragments' of competing classical ideologies – socialism, anarchism and even conservatism and nationalism – and seek to revitalise them through integration into a new kind of liberal ideology. How this is achieved will become clearer in our discussion of the particular ideologies, but it is useful to identify a couple of examples of critical engagement with the classical ideologies.

First, feminists and multiculturalism in particular have sought to challenge the liberal claims to freedom and equality. The dual claim to freedom and equality is subjected to an analysis of how *informal* power relations operate in society, and how formal legal and political relations, despite the appearance of impartiality, actually serve to reinforce informal inequalities. Of course, this line of attack is not new: Marxists have argued that material inequality restricts the effectiveness of the economic freedoms guaranteed by the liberal–capitalist state. But Marx still operated with a universalist model of liberation, whereby the abolition of capitalist relations of production would ensure equal treatment. The model of a classless society – which admittedly Marx failed to outline in any detail – did not adequately account for 'difference', that is, the apparently paradoxical idea that equal treatment of men and women, or of cultural groups, requires recognition of the differences between them. Ecologists are even more radical in their adoption of the ideals of freedom and equality in that they extend the 'moral community' to include non-human animals and even plant life.

Second, drawing on socialism (in particular, Marxism), the new ideologies take up the idea of collective oppression and collective action. Just as Marx argued that there was a revolutionary process of 'consciousness raising' whereby workers achieve, first of all, workplace consciousness, and then trade union consciousness, followed by national, and international, class consciousness, so feminists, multiculturalists, ecologists and fundamentalists argue for a process whereby the oppressed – women, cultural minorities, non-humans, co-religionists – come to recognise their oppression and, crucially, the causes of that oppression. Obviously the ideologies – and different streams within each ideology – will define the causes of oppression in their own way. Our linking together of these four ideologies is not intended to suggest mutual sympathy between them: many feminists regard multiculturalism as, in the words of Susan Okin, 'bad for women' (Okin *et al.*, 1999), and fundamentalists of all hues consider multiculturalism to be the political expression of the moral and cultural relativism which they are fighting. The affinities between the four ideologies relate to the historical conditions under which they have emerged, and the style in which they engage with the classical ideologies.

## References

Fukuyama, F. (1992) *The End of History and the Last Man* London: Penguin.

Hobsbawm, E. (1995) *Age of Extremes: The Short Twentieth Century, 1914–1991* London: Abacus.

Inglehart, R. (1977) *The Silent Revolution: Changing Values and Political Styles among Western Publics* Princeton, New Jersey: Princeton University Press.

McLellan, D. (1979) *Marxism after Marx: an Introduction* London: Macmillan.

Okin, S. *et al.* (1999) *Is Multiculturalism Bad for Women?* Princeton, New Jersey: Princeton University Press.

# Chapter 7

# Feminism

## Introduction

Feminism is an ideology that has always been highly controversial. It asks such questions as: do women have too much or too little power? It is not only controversial as far as traditional defenders of the status quo are concerned. Some women feel that they are in favour of equality with men, but do not like the idea of feminism. It has been said that we live in a 'post-feminist' age and some contend that the main goals of feminism have been realised, so that it is quite unnecessary for feminists to continue their argument against male domination.

Feminism, however, is also controversial in the sense that different feminists mean different things by the term. There are different varieties that seem to have little in common. Just as writers have spoken of 'socialisms', so feminism has also been presented in the plural in order to indicate the diversity involved. In this chapter we shall follow the example of many writers in trying to explain these different feminisms, and also try to suggest a way of extracting some kind of unity out of this formidable diversity.

## Chapter Map

In this chapter we are going to explore:

- The immense variety of different kinds of feminism:

- Liberal feminism; its strengths and its weaknesses:

- Radical feminism, and its claim to be a 'true feminism':

- The meaning of socialist feminism and its limitations:

- Black feminism:

- 'Philosophical feminisms' and postmodern feminism in particular.

# Women's Work?

A huge amount of attention has been devoted in the media to the changing roles of women. An example of this can be found in a 2003 cover story of the *Observer* magazine, in which women who had become corporate executives were questioned as to how they perceived both *their* position, and those of women in general, in society.

- Sunita Gloster is head of an advertising agency and argues that more and more women are facing reality head-on. 'Success', she says, 'used to be defined by a traditional male standard – rising up the corporate ladder, with rewards of money and status. Now women define success by a more feminine standard: satisfaction, fulfilment, making a difference – and that can come in many forms'.

- Sahar Hashemi, who co-founded a chain of companies and who runs her own consultancy, insists that women want equality with, and not superiority over, men, and that they should celebrate being women, 'not try to disguise it'. 'It's about being women in our own right and doing things on our own terms.'

- Patricia Hewitt, as a member of the British cabinet, argues that things are getting better but too many women who work outside the home feel that it is impossible to have children. 'An unofficial "parent bar" is operating, and I think that's the biggest issue for working women.'

- Caroline Plumb, who developed a graduate recruitment and research agency, notes that women need to be stronger on self-promotion, declaring that 'success for me is about having an interesting life, and being exposed to a wide range of experiences and people'.

- Ronnie Cook, a New Yorker running her own design consultancy in the United Kingdom, compares the 'warrior spirit' of American women with the more laid-back approach she finds in London.

- Dr Laura Tyson, Dean of the London Business School, finds that 'women are talented team players, and the need in business now is for individuals who can lead and inspire through influence rather than by dictating. Women are more consensual, and the old power hierarchies are crumbling'.

- Helen Fernandes, the first ever female surgeon at Addenbrooke's Hospital, Cambridge, argues that 'medicine has changed and the old sexism is dying out, but perception and archetypes still put women off'.

Do the testimonies above suggest to you that women should pursue careers outside the home? How possible do you think it is to combine outside work and parental responsibilities?

Make a list of men you know, and see whether you agree with the point that younger men are more egalitarian than older men.

Now make a list of women you know, and ask yourself whether they seek:

- equality with men;
- superiority over men;
- a position of subordination to men.

One of the respondents in the article took the view that 'there are only superficial differences between the sexes'. Do you agree? List the *social* differences between men and women, and see whether they are the result of biological differences, or differences in conditioning, or both.

## Liberal Feminism

Liberal feminism would appear to be the earliest form of feminism. Feminism has a particular relationship to **liberalism**, and it has been said that all feminism is 'liberal at root' (Eisenstein, 1981: 4). We are assuming here not only that earlier treatments of women were anti-feminist in character, but that the ancient Greek philosopher, Plato, does not count as a feminist although his views on women were remarkably atypical at the time.

Plato argues in *The Republic* that women can be among the elite who rule philosophically in his ideal **state**. Whereas Aristotle had contended that 'the relation of male to female is naturally that of superior to inferior, of the ruling to the ruled' (Coole, 1988: 44–5), Plato adopted (at least in *The Republic*) a gender-free view of political capacities. On the other hand, what makes his feminist credentials suspect is his explicit elitism. Only a tiny number of women would have been 'eligible' to become rulers, and those that did, would (it is said) have to act just like men.

The position of women in medieval theory is depicted in explicitly hierarchical terms with women being seen as more sinful than men, inferior to them, and not equipped to take part in political processes. Aquinas follows Aristotle in arguing that a wife 'is something belonging to her husband', although she is more distinct from him than a son from his father or a slave from his master (1953: 103). Had not the Bible made the inferiority of women clear?

## Mary Wollstonecraft

What is remarkable about the liberal tradition is that it challenges the notion that repressive hierarchies are natural. It thus opens the way for the feminist argument that if all are free and equal individuals, why can women not be equal to men? It is true that Mary Astell had contended, as early as 1694, that women should be educated instead of being nursed in the vices for which they are then upbraided (Brody, 1992: 28). But Mary Wollstonecraft is rightly regarded as the first major feminist, and in her famous *Vindication of the Rights of Women* (first published in 1792), she argues for women's economic independence and legal equality. At the time she wrote, a married woman could not own property in her own right, enter into any legal contract or have any claim over the rights of her children. History, philosophy and classical languages were considered too rigorous for women to learn; botany and biology were proscribed from their educational curriculum, and physical exercise thought unsuitable.

Wollstonecraft directs her argument to middle-class women – women in what she calls the 'natural state'. The middle-class woman is the woman who is neither dissipated by inherited wealth nor brutalised by poverty. Wollstonecraft had taken from Richard Price the Enlightenment principle that all people are rational. The problem lay with the environment. Physical frailty derives from a cloistered upbringing, and this was thought to impact negatively upon intellectual ability. She tackles in particular Rousseau's traditionalist view that women are inferior, seeing this as a betrayal of the liberal assumptions of his political theory. What Rousseau thought charming, Wollstonecraft considered immoral and dangerous. It is inconsistent to value independence and autonomy in men but not in women, particularly as patriarchy, or male domination, degrades men as well – 'the blind lead the blind' (1992: 104).

Women, Wollstonecraft argues, are placed on a pedestal but within a prison (Brody, 1992: 50–1). Women ought to be represented in government and have a 'civil existence in the State' (Wollstonecraft, 1992: 265; 267). They should not be excluded from civil and political employments (1992: 291). The enlightened woman must be an 'active citizen' 'intent to manage her family, educate her children and assist her neighbours' (1992: 259). Friendship rather than gentleness, docility and a spaniel-like affection 'should prevail between the sexes'. The emancipation of women is, in Wollstonecraft's view, part and parcel of the case against autocracy and arbitrariness in general: why contest the divine right of kings if one continues to subscribe to the divine right of husbands (1992: 118; 119)?

Wollstonecraft's position has a number of shortcomings that we will deal with later, but it is generally acknowledged that she tended to juxtapose reason to feeling, identifying feelings with animal appetites that men exploited. Moreover, she saw perfection as a realisable ideal, a position undoubtedly influenced by the intensely religious character of her argument. But Wollstonecraft's position was complex – and she has been seen by some writers as 'ambivalent, contradictory and paradoxical' – reformer and revolutionary, rationalist and woman of feeling (Brody, 1992: 67; 70).

## John Stuart Mill

John Stuart Mill (influenced by his partner Harriet Taylor) wrote *The Subjection of Women* in 1869. In it he argues that women should enjoy equal rights with men – including the right to vote. Women, he contended, were still slaves in many respects, and to argue that they are inferior by 'nature' is to presume knowledge of nature: until equality has been established, how do we know what woman's nature is? It cannot be said that women are housewives and mothers by nature, although Mill does say – and this position is controversial among feminists today – that they are 'most suitable for this role', and he feels that female suffrage can only assist women in supervising domestic expenditure (Coole, 1988: 144; Bryson, 1992: 55–63). Mill, it is suggested, contributed to liberal feminism by extending his liberal principles to the position of women (Shanley and Pateman, 1991: 6), and, as did Wollstonecraft, he argued that the family must become a school for learning the values of freedom and independence.

## Liberal Feminism in Britain and the United States

Throughout the nineteenth century liberal feminism had developed often as an extension of other emancipatory movements. In the United States, figures such as Elizabeth Cady Stanton (1815–1902) and her lifelong friend, Susan Anthony (1820–1906) raised the issue of women's freedom and equality as a result of experience in anti-slavery movements. Both edited a feminist journal in the 1860s

## Exercise

You meet a woman who describes herself as a feminist. 'All women should be equal and be free to choose their own lifestyle', she argues.

You feel uneasy. You note the following factors in your mind:

- Her mother is an MP and her father a headmaster.

- The woman concerned went to a very good school and has had a university education.

- She has a job outside the home that is well paid.

- She has young children and can afford to put them all day in a nursery.

- Because her and her partner are both employed and are on good salaries, they employ someone to clean their house twice a week.

How important are these 'other' factors? The feminist you have met argues that 'all' women should be equal to men, but how many other women are in her relatively privileged position?

called *The Revolution*. A National Women's Suffrage Association was set up after the civil war and women's suffrage was attained in the United States as a result of the 19th amendment to the Constitution in 1920. In Britain, Mill's classic work had been preceded by the campaign against the Contagious Diseases Act (1864) that gave the police draconian powers to arrest prostitutes and those considered prostitutes, and when limited suffrage for women was achieved after World War I, the struggle for its further extension was consolidated in the National Union of Societies for Equal Citizenship.

British liberal feminism appeared to have its greatest triumph when all women became eligible to vote in 1928 in Britain. In other countries this was attained later – in France after World War II, while in Switzerland women only received the vote in 1970. In Britain the Sex Discrimination Act and the Equal Opportunities Commission were established in the late 1960s.

Liberal feminism identifies itself, in the words of Winifred Holtby, 'with the motto Equality First' (Humm, 1992: 43) and it extended its concerns with the publication of Betty Friedan's *The Feminine Mystique* (1963), which argued that middle-class American women suffered from depression and alienation as a result of giving up a career outside the home. They were incarcerated in a 'comfortable concentration camp' – Friedan's dramatic name for the home. She was instrumental in setting up the National Organization of Women in 1966 that not only campaigned for equal rights (including 'reproductive rights' – a right to abortion and birth control), but also assisted American women in re-entering the labour market, and supported the establishment of childcare facilities in workplaces.

## Problems with Liberal Feminism

Liberal feminism has been criticised on a number of grounds.

## Radical Feminist Critique

Radical feminists protest that liberal feminism is too superficial in its approach. All feminisms agree with the extension of liberal principles to women in terms of the vote and civil liberties, but radicals argue that the notion of equality is too abstract to be serviceable. The point about women is that they are different from men, and to argue for equality implies that they aspire to be like men. But why?

Men not only oppress women but they are responsible for war, **violence**, hierarchy and the exploitation of nature and their fellows. Is this the model to which women should aspire? Radicals argue that it is not equality that women should want, but liberation – and freedom for women means being separate and apart from men. It means celebrating their difference from men and their own distinctive sexuality. Liberal feminists not only regard sexuality as irrational and emotional, but they uncritically accept that feelings should be transcended and they adopt a notion of reason that reflects male experience. Feminism is not an extension of another ideology. It is concerned with the interests of women, and a new set of words needs to be developed to reflect the separateness of women. Some radicals, such as Mary Daly, adopt a different style of writing, so as to make it clear that feminism represents as total a break as possible with male-constructed society. Politics is not simply about the law and state, as liberals think. It is about human activity in general and the celebrated slogan – 'the personal is political' – captures the radical feminist argument that inter-personal relations are as 'political' as voting in elections. Radicals encourage women to meet separately – to voice their problems without men – and to take personal experience much more seriously than the liberal tradition allows.

Radicals see themselves as sexual revolutionaries, and thus very different from liberal feminists who work within the system. We shall see later that radicals have very different views from liberals on questions such as prostitution and pornography.

## Socialist Feminist Critique

The socialist critique of liberal feminism argues that liberal feminists ignore or marginalise the position of working-class women and the problems they have with exploitation and poor conditions in the workplace. The question of gender needs to be linked to the question of class – and legal and political equality, though important, does not address the differential in real power that exists in capitalist society.

Marxist feminists in particular want to challenge the view of the state as a benevolent reformer, and to argue that the state is an expression of class domination. The freedom of women has to be linked to the emancipation of the working class in general, with a much greater concentration on the social and the economic dimensions of gender discrimination. Why should the right to join the armed forces and the police be a positive development if the police are used to oppress people at home and the army to oppress peoples abroad? Liberal feminism neglects the question of production and reproduction that lies at the heart of human activity.

## Other Critiques

The black feminist critique takes issue particularly with the tendency of liberal feminists to treat women in abstract fashion, and to assume that women are not only middle class, but white as well. Many of the objections that liberal feminists raise to the hypocritical politeness of men hardly apply to women who are subject to racist abuse and treated in a derogatory fashion because they are black.

The feminisms looked at so far can be called 'ideological' feminisms, and they overlap with what can be labelled 'philosophical feminisms': feminist empiricism, standpoint feminism and postmodern feminism.

Feminist empiricists take the view that feminism should be treated as an objective science that concentrates on the *facts* relating to discrimination. Feminist empiricists feel that it is unnecessary and counterproductive to hitch feminism to an ideological position, and that the norms of liberalism involve a value commitment which narrows the appeal of feminist analysis.

Standpoint feminists take the view that the position of women gives rise to a different outlook, so that liberal feminists are wrong to argue simply for equality with men, and to concern themselves only with legal and political rights.

As for postmodern feminists, they consider the tradition of the Enlightenment and liberalism to be hopelessly abstract. Not only is liberalism oblivious to the importance of difference – both between women and men and within women themselves – but the notion of freedom and autonomy as universal values reflects a prejudice that is part of the modern as opposed to the postmodern tradition.

---

| Biography | **Mary Wollstonecraft (1759–97)** |
|---|---|

Born in Spitalfields, London. In 1784 she became friends with Richard Price, a minister at the local Dissenting Chapel. At Price's home she met the publisher, Joseph Johnson, who commissioned her to write *Thoughts on the Education of Girls.* In 1788 she helped Johnson found the *Analytical Review.*

Edmund Burke's *Reflections on the Revolution in France* was written in response to a radical sermon by Richard Price. Wollstonecraft's *A Vindication of the Rights of Man* not only supported Price but also criticised the slave trade, the game laws and way that the poor were treated.

In 1790 she published *A Vindication of the Rights of Women,* and as a result was described as a 'hyena in petticoats'. In 1793 Burke led the attack on The London Corresponding Society and the Unitarian Society (both of which Wollstonecraft supported) describing them as 'loathsome insects that might, if they were allowed, grow into giant spiders as large as oxen', while King George III issued a proclamation against seditious writings and meetings.

In June 1793 Wollstonecraft decided to move to France with the American writer, Gilbert Imlay. After her relationship with Imlay came to an end she returned to London. She married William Godwin in March 1797 and soon afterwards, Mary (the author of *Frankenstein*), was born. The baby was healthy but as a result of blood poisoning, Wollstonecraft died on 10 September 1797.

How to read:

**Wollstonecraft's *A Vindication of the Rights of Women***

Her 'Introduction' and 'Dedication' contain useful summaries of her overall position and should be read carefully. Chapters 1–2 are important and it is vital that you pay particular attention to the critique of Jean-Jacques Rousseau. The section on Gregory can be skim read, but Chapter 3 continues the critique on Rousseau and deserves careful attention. The poetry cited in Chapter 4 can be skim read. Chapter 5 returns to Rousseau and Gregory – and you can remind yourself about Wollstonecraft's response to these two authors (though references to Rousseau are more important than those to Gregory). Chapters 6 and 7 stress the importance of education and deserve a careful read. Chapter 12 is devoted to education. Chapters 8–9 are also important, and if you are concerned about the impact of the family on women read Chapter 11 carefully. The final chapter, though interesting, can be skim read.

## Socialist Feminism

Socialist feminism arose out of the belief that feminism is not simply a legal and political question – though socialists (by which we mean socialist feminists) do support the case for the legal and political emancipation of women. Socialists take the view that women's emancipation is also – and primarily – a *social* question so that the movement for women's freedom needs to be linked with the struggle to transform capitalism itself.

Early socialists such as the Frenchman Charles Fourier saw the liberation of women as integral to redefining the labour process so that it becomes pleasurable and fulfilling, and he saw, as Marx did, the position of women as symptomatic of the level of civilisation of a given society. Marx tended to see women as the victims of market forces, and he argues in an early text that the prostitution of women is only a specific expression of the general prostitution of the labourer (Marx and Engels, 1975: 295). In the *Communist Manifesto*, for example, Marx takes the view that women under capitalism are mere instruments of production. But Marx showed little interest in the position of women and regarded the relation of men and women as 'natural' rather than moulded by class relationships.

### Engels's Contribution

Engels was much more interested in women, and in his celebrated work, *The Origin of the Family, Private Property and the State*, published in 1894, he argues that in early tribal societies men, women and children lived together as part of larger households in which production was for use rather than exchange. Decision making involved both men and women and, because paternity or the position of a particular man as father could not be established in group marriage, collective property descended through women (i.e. matrilineally). 'The world-historical defeat of female sex', as Engels graphically describes it, occurs when men begin to domesticate animals and breed herds. Women seek monogamous relations in marriage (one wife–one husband) and the family is privatised. In the later bourgeois family, the woman's formal right to consent to marriage is neutralised by her lack of economic independence, and in the working-class family the husband represents the bourgeois and the wife the proletarian – what nineteenth-century socialists liked to call the 'slave of a slave'.

In Engels's view, male domination would only disappear with the socialisation of production. With women involved in paid employment outside the home, housework itself would become a public and collectivised activity (Sacks, 1974: 207).

## Bebel and Later Socialists

August Bebel of the German Social Democratic Party wrote a much more influential book than that of Engels – *Woman Under Socialism* (1878) – which followed the argument that women could only be emancipated through a proletarian **revolution** that resulted in their economic independence and the collectivisation of housework and childcare. However, unlike Engels, he was also conscious of the problems that were peculiar to women. Capitalist employment resulted in women being paid less than men, and women suffered from the problem of having to do all or most of the housework. Bebel also noted that economic subordination was linked to non-economic forms of oppression, such as double standards of sexual morality and inconvenient forms of dress (Bryson, 1992: 121).

Clara Zetkin, a German socialist who was to be a founder member of the German Communist Party, argued that class must take primacy over gender interests. She refused to cooperate with other women in campaigns for improved education, employment prospects and legal status, on the grounds that proletarian and 'bourgeois' women had nothing in common. Lenin was to declare at the time of the Russian Revolution that 'the proletariat cannot have complete liberty until it has won complete liberty for women' (Rowbotham, 1972: 163) but this did not prevent him from extracting a pledge from Zetkin that personal matters would not be raised in political discussions (Bryson, 1992: 125). It is true that the new Soviet government was the first in history to write women's emancipation into the law (in 1918), but the right to abortion was removed in 1936 and the family which radical Bolsheviks had sought to 'abolish', was idealised under Stalin as a crucial part of the disciplinary mechanism of the state.

Alexandra Kollontai was commissar or minister of social welfare in the first Bolshevik government and she sought to encourage women to set up, with state help, nurseries, laundries and educational campaigns. But she fell from power in 1921 and the Women's Department that she headed was abolished in 1929. She is also interesting because she argued for a new kind of relationship between men and women – one that would be less exclusive and not monogamous (Bryson, 1992: 137–40).

## Women in the Communist Party States

In terms of more recent developments in Communist Party states, the regime in Romania was particularly oppressive, with Ceauşescu stating in 1986, some 20 years after an anti-abortion law had been passed, that those 'who refuse to have children are deserters, escaping the law of natural continuity' (Funk and Mueller, 1993: 46). In the German Democratic Republic (East Germany) abortion was legal and used as the main means of birth control, while 90 per cent of women of working age were in paid employment, and 87 per cent had completed vocational training (Funk and Mueller, 1993: 139). Despite the authoritarian character of these Communist Party states, the position of women in post-communist societies has worsened as reproductive rights have been scaled down (although in Poland the attempt to pass an anti-abortion law was blocked in 1991). Women have left the workforce, are much less represented in legislatures and have suffered as state nurseries have been closed; the gender gap in pay has widened, and pornography and prostitution have dramatically increased (Hoffman, 2001: 141).

## The Domestic Labour Debate

Of course many socialists disagreed vehemently with the Communist Party states, even while they maintained a loyalty to Marxism. The domestic labour debate that took place in the pages of the British journal, *New Left Review*, sought to examine the position of women in the home and their relationship to the capitalist economy. Some argued that domestic labour produces value in the same way that other labour does, and therefore women who work at home should be paid. Despite controversy on this point, there was general agreement that the family is linked to capitalism, and that domestic labour, and who does it, is an important issue for feminists to tackle (Bryson, 1992: 241).

Even socialists who disagree with Marxism have accepted the need to ensure that women in the workforce are paid equally and should be able to combine domestic

| Biography | **Clara Zetkin (1857–1933)** |
|---|---|

As Clara Eissner she studied at Leipzig Teacher's College for Women and became a socialist and feminist.

In 1881 Zetkin joined the Socialist Democratic Party, and married Ossip Zetkin, a Russian revolutionary living in exile. The couple had two children before Ossip died of tuberculosis in January 1889.

In 1891 Zetkin became editor of the party's journal, *Die Gleichheid* (Equality). A strong campaigner for women's suffrage, she was appointed secretary of the International Socialist Women in 1910.

In December 1914 she joined with Liebknecht and Luxemburg in an underground organisation called *Spartakusbund* (Spartakus League). She supported the Russian Revolution and joined the Independent Socialist Party in 1917. In January 1919 she took part in the Spartakist uprising in Berlin. The rebellion was crushed, and a year later she helped to form the German Communist Party (KPD).

Zetkin was elected to the Reichstag (the German parliament) in 1920 and served on the Central Committee of the KPD. She was also appointed to the executive committee of Comintern, which meant she spent long periods in the Soviet Union. In 1932, Zetkin was once again elected to the Reichstag. Here she took the opportunity to make a long speech in which she denounced the policies of Hitler and the Nazi Party. Clara Zetkin died on 20 June 1933.

and professional duties. Women and men may receive the same pay for the same job, but where there are occupations in which women predominate (such as nursing and primary school teaching), workers in these occupations receive relatively low pay. Women in Britain earn about 75 per cent of men's pay – whereas the average over Europe is 79 per cent (http://news.bbc.co.uk/1/hi/business/1962036.stm). Socialist feminists feel that the market and free enterprise do impact upon women's lives, and that improving pay, employment prospects and conditions of work are crucial questions for feminism to consider.

## Problems with Socialist Feminism

### Liberal Feminist Critique

Liberal feminists, such as Betty Friedan and Naomi Wolf (who wrote *Fire with Fire* in 1993), feel that socialist feminists are divisive in not accepting that some women might go into, and make a success of, business. Their dynamism and entrepreneurial flair should be both rewarded and acknowledged, and to regard feminism as a class question is unhelpful and narrowing. All women will benefit from a free system of production, based on the market and capitalism.

Women are individuals who should be entitled to exercise choice, and the tendency by socialist feminists to see work outside the home as crucial for emancipation is not borne out by the many women who choose to stay at home and live fulfilled and happy lives. Liberal feminists are not opposed to reforms that facilitate working outside the home, but they are opposed to an ideological position which seems to privilege this.

Liberal feminists would (as would many other feminists) point to the authoritarian character of Communist Party states as evidence not only of the generally problematic character of socialism, but of the negative way in which it impacts upon women's lives.

### Radical Feminist Critique

Radicals are sceptical that the problems facing women are simply to do with capitalism. It is true that some socialist feminists have argued that there is a dual system that oppresses women – capitalism *and* patriarchy. Capitalism may reward men as 'breadwinners', thereby creating a division of labour that disadvantages women, and writers such as Ann Ferguson see patriarchy as semi-autonomous – sexual oppression exists alongside class oppression and is not 'reducible' to it (Bryson, 1992: 243–5). But radicals feel that this argument merely serves to deepen the theoretical crisis faced by socialist feminists, since there is no reason to believe that pornography, prostitution and male chauvinist attitudes are specifically linked to a particular mode of production.

Indeed, many radical feminists developed their position as a result of experience in socialist movements where they were expected by socialist men to take menial and 'feminine' roles. Attempts to introduce the concept of patriarchy alongside the analysis of capitalism fail to get to grips with the fact that the former is wholly independent of the latter, and that when Marx treats the relations between men and women as natural, this is symptomatic of an inadequate methodology which cannot be rectified by simply tacking a critique of sexism on to Marxism or socialism. Catherine MacKinnon, in a much-quoted comment, argues that 'sexuality is to feminism, what work is to marxism' (Humm, 1992: 117). The logics of the two are quite different, and any attempt to 'synthesise' Marxism and feminism, or feminism with socialism more generally, is bound to fail.

## Black Feminists and the Philosophical Feminist Critique

Black feminists believe that socialist emphasis upon class is as abstract as liberal emphasis upon the individual. Socialist feminism does not take the question of ethnicity seriously: it suffers from the problem of abstract **universalism**, that means that it unthinkingly privileges a particular group or culture.

Feminist empiricists see in socialism the problem of ideological bias, and although some standpoint feminists such as Nancy Hartsock are sympathetic to Marxism, standpoint feminism in general is unhappy with any privileging of class. After all, women experience oppression as women, and Gilligan argues in *In a Different Voice* (1992) that because women are socialised differently from men they grow up with quite different notions of morality and relationships. This occurs in both working-class and 'bourgeois' homes.

As for postmodern feminists, socialism has what they call an emancipatory 'metanarrative' – particularly strident in Marxism – that stems from the Enlightenment and expresses an absolutist prejudice. The belief in progress, equality and autonomy, though different from the views of liberal feminists, still reflects a belief in a 'philosophy of history' that is ultimately arbitrary and implausible.

## Radical Feminism

Radical feminism, as indicated from its critiques of other positions, takes the view that feminism ought to deal with the position of women independently of other ideological commitments. As MacKinnon argues, 'feminism is the first theory to emerge from those whose interests it affirms' (Humm, 1992: 119).

Radical feminists argue that women are oppressed because women are women, and men are men. Male domination permeates all aspects of society – from sport to literature, dress to philosophy, entertainment to sexual mores. As Mary Daly argues, 'we live in a profoundly anti-female society, a misogynistic "civilization" in which men collectively victimize women, attacking us as personifications of their own paranoid fears' (Humm, 1992: 168).

This ubiquity of 'maleness' extends to the state itself. Weber's view of the state as an institution which claims a monopoly of legitimate force is too limited in MacKinnon's view, since this monopoly 'describes the power of men over women in the home, in the bedroom, on the job, in the street, through social life' (1989: 169). Patriarchy is a comprehensive system of male power and it arises from men.

Oppression, as the *Manifesto of the New York Redstockings* in 1969 declared, is total, 'affecting every facet of our lives' (Bryson, 1992: 183–4).

Moreover, the radicals argue that women's oppression is the oldest and most basic form of oppression, and whether it arises from socialists who expect women to make tea while men develop political strategy, or it is expressed through black men such as Stokely Carmichael, who see women as having only bodies and not minds, the same point holds: all men oppress women, and all receive psychological, sexual and material benefits from so doing. Germaine Greer argues that her proposition in *The Female Eunuch* (1970) still holds 30 years later – men hate women at least some of the time. Indeed she reckons that in the year 2000 'more men hate more women more bitterly than in 1970' (1999: 14). Greer gives as good as she believes that women get, and argues that 'to be male is to be a kind of idiot savant, full of queer obsessions about fetishistic activities and fantasy goals' – a freak of nature, fragile, fantastic, bizarre (1999: 327).

Why does the antagonism between men and women arise? Brownmiller appears to suggest that the root is biological, and she speaks of the 'anatomical fact that the male sex organ has been misused as a weapon of terror' (Humm, 1992: 73), but radical feminists are aware of the dangers of a naturalist argument that reduces male domination to biology. Although MacKinnon speaks highly of Robert Dahl and endorses his view of politics as a system of power, authority and control, she almost certainly would not endorse his once-expressed view that women's subordination arises from the superior physical strength of males (Hoffman, 2001: 97). The relation of men and women is a social product, she argues, and a 'naturalist' view fails to see these relationships as historical and transitory (MacKinnon, 1989: 56). Nevertheless, radical feminists reject Marxist accounts that male domination arose historically from class divisions, and they argue that patriarchy has always been around. Although radicals disagree as to how and when patriarchy came about, they all agree that it exists and it has done so in every known society (Bryson, 1992: 188).

What can be done about it? Radical feminists developed in the late 1960s the idea of an all-women's 'consciousness-raising' group. Indeed, MacKinnon describes 'consciousness raising' as the 'feminist method' (Humm, 1992: 119) – a coming together by women to describe problems collectively so that the existence of oppression can be confirmed. The solution can only be separatism, for the consequence of the fact that the personal is political (and by political is meant the exercise of repressive power) is that men and women should live their lives as separately as possible. As Greer puts it rather wittily, 'both could do without each other if it were not for the pesky business of sexual reproduction' (1999: 68).

One radical actually famously argued that the basis of women's oppression lies with childbearing, as well as child rearing, and the conception of love (Bryson, 1992: 204; 201). Others are doubtful that this 'pesky business' can be so easily avoided. But sexuality is seen as an expression of power so that the distinction between rape and sexual activity is not a meaningful one, and the reason why radical feminists are so passionately opposed to pornography and prostitution is that they see these institutions as fundamentally linked to a demeaning view and treatment of women. Whether men intend to oppress women is beside the point: patriarchy is a structural system of male oppression that operates whether men are conscious of oppressing women or not.

Radical feminists have sometimes advocated lesbianism as a solution to the problem of oppressive encounters with men. Feminists in general would accept that lesbianism is a legitimate lifestyle choice, but radicals often go further and argue that it is a necessary way of preventing male domination. Rich advocates a broader notion of lesbianism so that it does not have to embrace genital activity, but denotes a rejection of a compulsory heterosexuality imposed to prevent women from being individuals in their own right (Humm, 1992: 176–7). Because patriarchy is seen as a comprehensive system of male domination, even the most intimate of relationships becomes a matter for political scrutiny.

MacKinnon sees the whole notion of the public/private divide as oppressive and nothing more than a dangerous myth. The public is the private, just as the personal is political. Women's interest lies in overthrowing the distinction itself (1989: 120–1). Radical feminism is revolutionary. It is averse to differentiating one kind of patriarchy from another, and it is opposed to the kind of reforms that do not tackle the problem at its root. Radical feminists tend to identify pornography with sexual violence, and they regard prostitution as an act of force (Hoffman, 2001: 193).

Women, in the view of radical feminists, do not want equality with men. They want liberation, and liberation is only possible if patriarchy is overthrown.

## Problems with Radical Feminism

### Liberal Feminist Critique

Liberal feminists disagree with radical feminists on a range of grounds. The first is that they see the idea that there is a war between the sexes as unfruitful. Men can be sympathetic to feminism (as J.S. Mill famously was), and it is wrong to assume that men cannot become adherents to the feminist cause. The notion of separatism is pessimistic and self-defeating.

Nor are liberal feminists persuaded by the arguments for patriarchy. The notion that male domination enters into the very fibre of relationships ignores the importance of privacy and choice. Women are, or can be, agents, and the notion that the personal is political is a totalitarian credo that does not allow individuals to decide matters for themselves.

Some liberal feminists argue that prostitutes are sex workers who choose a profession that others dislike, and the legalisation of prostitution would enable women who wish to pursue careers in this area to do so without hindrance and condemnation. Liberal feminists see the campaigns against pornography as oppressive and authoritarian. Not only do such campaigners find themselves working with extremely conservative pressure groups, but the attempt to ban pornography leads to censorship – the prevention of people acting in unconventional ways that, liberal feminists insist, do not harm others.

Their attitude, in the eyes of liberal feminists, towards the state and legal reform is generally negative, and radical feminists suffer from an absolutist outlook which prevents them from seeing that gradual change, based upon rational discussion, is far more effective than utopian fantasies.

## Socialist Feminist Critique

Socialist feminists have no difficulty in extending the notion of politics at least to workplaces and the family. But they see the idea of sisterhood as dangerously abstract. Socialist feminists want to stress that women belong to different classes and their interests vary according to their class position. Socialist feminists are not necessarily opposed to the notion of patriarchy, but they insist that it is much more complex than the radicals imagine.

In the first place, it is a system that arises historically, and even if Engels's account is not wholly plausible he is correct to assume that patriarchy has not always existed, and that it is connected with private property and the state. Second, socialist feminists want to distinguish between different kinds of patriarchy. There is an important distinction to be made between the kind of explicit patriarchy that exists in medieval and slave-owning societies, and a liberal patriarchy in which male domination coexists with liberal notions of consent and freedom. In fact, it is the gulf between theory and practice that makes the socialist critique possible, for women in developed liberal societies enjoy formal rights that contrast with their lack of real power. This kind of analysis is only possible if patriarchy itself is placed in a very specific historical context.

Socialist feminists, as do liberal feminists, see no problem in forming alliances with men, since men can be in favour of emancipation just as privileged women can be opposed to it. It is true that men benefit from patriarchy, but the socialist emphasis upon *relationships* means that men have their own lives limited and warped as a result of patriarchal prejudices which regard women, for example, as the natural guardians of children.

Even though socialist feminists would not accept extreme left-wing strictures against feminism as being inherently 'bourgeois' and a distraction from class struggle, they tend to see the concern of radical feminists with lifestyle and sexuality as the product of a middle-class outlook that ignores the problems faced by women workers.

## Black Feminists and the Philosophical Feminist Critique

Black feminists are sceptical about a supra-ethnic notion of sisterhood. All women are not the same, and the notion that they are fundamentally oppressed by men could only be advanced by those who have never suffered from racist stereotyping. Women themselves can be racists and oppress black women (as well as black men), and the experiences of subject women under slavery and colonialism demonstrate very different patterns of family and economic life to those assumed by radical feminists.

Rape is a case in point. The view of a black man as a potential rapist has been a formidable racist stereotype (particularly in the southern states of the United States) and black women who report assaults to racist-minded police have a very different experience from white women who have been raped. Audre Lorde puts the matter in a nutshell in her open letter to Mary Daly when she comments: 'The oppression of women knows no ethnic nor racial boundaries, true, but that does not mean that it is identical within those differences' (Humm, 1992: 139). A feminism that ignores ethnic or 'racial' differences is a feminism which unthinkingly privileges one group over others.

Feminist empiricists reject the notion that science and objectivity are somehow male activities. It is true that patriarchal prejudices can claim scientific warranty, but this is poor science. Science is not to blame for male domination but is a powerful weapon for exposing and combating it. Facts that point to discrimination and inequality are crucial to the arsenal of feminist argument, and make it much more difficult for unsympathetic men to dismiss feminism as a 'man-hating', irrational doctrine.

Standpoint feminists are, it seems to us, more likely to be influenced by radical feminists, and they can only distance themselves from radical feminism where they defend an argument that a woman's standpoint depends upon the particular social experience she has.

Postmodern feminists hold to the fact that power is exercised at every level in society, and it would seem, therefore, that they should be sympathetic to the radical feminist argument that male domination extends to apparently private as well as public institutions. In reality, however, postmodern feminists are particularly hostile to radical feminism since, as we shall see, they regard the whole notion of a 'woman' as problematically universalist in character. Radical feminism, in their eyes, suffers from deep-rooted binary divides – between men and women, reason and emotion, etc. – which leads these feminists to invert patriarchal arguments by accepting that there is a fundamental sexual divide. Instead of demonising women, they demonise men, but the same absolutist logic is at work.

## Ideas and Perspectives:

## The Pornography Debate

Andrea Dworkin and Catherine MacKinnon, two radical feminists in the United States, campaigned against pornography on the grounds that it harmed the interests of women everywhere.

They secured the passing of the 'MacKinnon–Dworkin' ordinances in Minneapolis and Indianapolis in 1983 and 1984. These would have made it possible for women who considered that they had been harmed to sue producers, distributors and retailers of pornography. The first ordinance was vetoed by the mayor and the second overruled by the federal courts.

These attempts were seen as a model for use elsewhere. Campaigners have sought to achieve restrictions on pornography in Britain, and in 1986 Clare Short sought to introduce the 'Page Three Bill' that would have banned 'naked or partially naked women in provocative pages in newspapers' and fined offending publishers. The attempt failed. The Campaign Against Pornography was launched in the House of Commons in 1988. These campaigns have been challenged by other feminists who argue that pornography is a symptom rather than a cause of women's oppression; a legal attack on pornography, they argue, allies feminists with right-wing fundamentalists who are opposed to any portrayal of explicit sexual material through art and the media. The US liberal feminist Nadine Strossen sees both obscenity laws and feminist proposals to restrict pornography by law as violations of free speech (Bryson, 1999: 174–7).

Biography

## Germaine Greer (1939–)

Well-known radical feminist who was born in Australia and educated at the universities of Melbourne, Sydney and Cambridge. A rigorous Catholic education helped her on her way to renouncing the Church and embracing sexual liberationism.

*The Female Eunuch* (1970) created an enormous stir, and in *The Obstacle Race* (1979) she discusses the social and financial difficulties faced by women painters. Her book *Daddy We Hardly Knew You* (1989) is a family memoir, while her more recent *Whole Woman* (1999) (which her contemporary Camille Paglia called 'seriously unbalanced' in the *New York Times*) shows that her views in many respects have not changed.

She is seen by many feminists as outdated and an anachronism who relies upon media coverage to keep her brand of 1960s and 1970s feminism alive. In her latest work, *Boy*, she includes an attempted defence of under-age sex tourism guaranteed to raise as many moral hackles as her contention that female circumcision is no different in principle from an operation for breast cancer.

She is currently professor of English and comparative literature at the University of Warwick, and appears frequently in media programmes on both literature and sexuality. A respected academic, she has written about art, literature, abortion and infertility, and the menopause. Her appearances on cultural chat shows lead to feisty confrontations. Angela Carter described her as 'a clever fool'. Margaret Cook called her 'paranoid' and 'a bit obsessive' and Edwina Currie called her 'a great big hard-boiled prat'. In 1989 she resigned from teaching at Newnham, Cambridge when a male-to-female transsexual was appointed Fellow at her women-only college.

## Black Feminism

Black feminists are acutely aware of the question of difference. Indeed, the very existence of a 'black feminism' is a protest against the idea that women are all the same. Beneath the supposedly universal notion is to be found women who are often white, university-educated and of middle-class background.

Black feminists argue that there is sufficient in common in Britain between Afro-Caribbean women, African women and Asian women to assert a common identity. Of course each of these categories is itself extremely diverse, but black women are considered to have a common experience. In the case of Britain, they are all 'outsiders', regarded as 'invisible' by the dominant culture, and judged to be 'ethnic' and abnormal, as though the majority community is itself without an ethnic identity and embodies normality.

Black feminism is a protest against marginalisation and the belief in monolithic identities. It rejects the idea that black women have to choose whether they want to be humiliated as women by patriarchal black movements or disregarded as blacks by a feminist movement that really speaks for white women. When the Nation of Islam marched in the United States in 2002, many black women found it very painful to decide between their dislike of patriarchy (which the Nation of Islam explicitly represented) and their concern about racism.

It is true that many white women turned to feminism as a result of their experience in anti-slavery and civil rights movements, but they failed to see that oppression is never simply universal – it always takes differential and particular forms. The notion that there is an *analogy* between women and blacks (Gayle Rubin wrote an essay in 1970 entitled *Woman as Nigger*) assumes that somehow black women do not exist!

The specific existence of black feminism contributes significantly to feminist theory as a whole by stressing the importance of a concrete approach that takes account of people's real-life situations and differences. By noting that some women are black in societies where whiteness is seen as the 'norm', one is more likely to observe that women may also be poor, disabled, illiterate, etc. Black feminism alerts us to the dangers of privileging one identity over others.

The assumption that the family is problematic for women is invariably made without taking account of the particular features of the black family that, in the United States for example, is often headed by women who have also to work outside the home. Barrett and McIntosh have conceded that their own study of the family ignored the very different structures which exist in the families of Afro-Caribbean and Asian people in Britain (Bryson, 1992: 254). As for rape and sexuality, quite different assumptions are made of black women and, in Whelehan's view, black women suffer from poorer mental health than their white counterparts (Whelehan, 1995: 117).

Black feminists have argued that it is not just a question of disadvantages accumulating alongside one another – as independent entities – so that a black woman may suffer from gender, ethnic and class attributes. It is a question of developing a theory of oppression in which these 'multiple oppressions' reinforce one another, and lie at the root of stereotyping. Indeed, it is remarkable how similar class, 'racial' and gender stereotyping are. This warns us against absolutising one kind of oppression, and opens the way to multiple alliances – of some women with some men for specific purposes. As the African-American writer bell hooks has argued, black feminism stresses the value of solidarity – which unites similarity and difference – over the oppressively homogenous notion of sisterhood (Bryson, 1999: 35).

Whelehan has noted that during the 1970s it was commonly felt by radical feminists that analysis of 'related' issues needed to be shelved, so that full attention could be given to the question of women. As she comments, this kind of argument ignores the fact that women can also suffer oppression as a result of their class, racial, gender and sexual orientation (1995: 111). Not only does black feminism provide a challenge to a theory of domination, it poses a challenge to political theory as a whole. It invites a reconceptualisation of the notion of power and freedom, since those who are the subjects of black feminism have no, in Bryson's words, 'institutionalised inferiors' (1999: 34). Given the fact that there are relatively few black feminist academics, black feminism also poses the challenge of mobilising the considerable knowledge which the community has but has not produced in what Whelehan calls 'high theoretical' form (1995: 120).

## Problems with Black Feminism

### Liberal, Socialist and Radical Feminist Critiques

Liberal feminists are concerned about what they see as the divisiveness of black feminism as a distinct variety of feminist argument. Black feminists are rightly opposed to racism but the answer to exclusion and marginalisation is to expand the notion of the individual so as to incorporate groups such as blacks whose experience of repression has been very different.

Lynne Segal speaks for many socialist feminists who express concern at the fragmentation that has taken place within the women's movement, and she notes in particular the problem of the growth of 'Black feminist perspectives' (Whelehan, 1995: 121). What about the real class differences that exist within black communities – will they not be ignored if a feminism is created which highlights blackness as the defining criterion?

Radical feminists are concerned that the opposition to male domination is diffused by a concern with difference. Although MacKinnon does not address herself to black feminism as such, she is suspicious of the argument about difference. Inequality comes first, she insists; difference comes after: difference, she says, is the velvet glove on the iron fist of domination (1989: 219). In other words, difference can distract us from the force and repression inherent in patriarchy, and distinguishing between black and white women, can – radical feminists argue – play into the hands of men who are anxious to downgrade the plight of all women.

## The Critique of Philosophical Feminisms

Feminist empiricists believe that anything that 'ideologises' feminism is a mistake. The statistic that 80 per cent of the mortality rate of illegal abortions came from women of colour (slightly broader than 'black' women) in the years preceding its decriminalisation in the United States (Whelehan, 1995: 117) is a revealing fact, and the danger is that it will not be as widely known as it deserves to be if it is presented by a feminism perceived to be 'separatist' and 'extremist'. Standpoint feminists would acknowledge that different experiences are important and need to be taken into account, but this should not be juxtaposed to the common experiences which all women have and which mould their particular outlook.

Although postmodern feminists are sympathetic to the point about difference, they argue that 'blackness' represents another form of '**essentialism**', i.e. the belief in an abstract 'essence'. Some black women might not only reveal class differences, as the socialists warn: what about hierarchies in the communities that lead black Americans to be suspicious of Asian-Americans? Differences such as these are simply swept under the proverbial carpet if blackness becomes the criterion for a particular kind of feminism. Whatever black feminists may say in theory, in practice the notion of a black feminism inevitably privileges 'blackness' over other differences, while the idea that 'race' must be explored in relation to gender and class ignores the other differences – of sexual orientation, region, religion, etc. – which problematise the very existence of the notion of woman.

## Philosophical Feminisms

### Feminist Empiricism

Feminist empiricists take the view that sexist and 'andocentric' (or male chauvinist) biases can be eliminated from scholarship and statements if there is a strict adherence to existing norms of scientific inquiry. If projects are rigorously designed, hypotheses properly tested and data soundly interpreted, then sexist prejudices can be dealt with alongside all other prejudices – as thoroughly unscientific in character (Hoffman, 2001: 55).

The more female researchers there are in the profession, the better, since women are likely to be more sensitive to sexist prejudices than men. However, the question is not one of female science, but of sound science. The fact is that women are dramatically underrepresented in the decision-making structures of the UN or in legislative bodies or in the world of business – indeed in the 'public' world in general, except perhaps in certain new social movements such as the peace movement and in certain professions. These facts can only be established through sound statistical techniques, and they establish the existence of discrimination in ways that cannot be ignored.

Feminist empiricism ensures that feminism has come of age, entering into mainstream argument and debate.

## Standpoint Feminism

Standpoint feminism arose initially as a feminist version of the Marxist argument that the proletariat had a superior view of society because it was the victim rather than the beneficiary of the market. Standpoint theorists argue that because women have been excluded from power – whether within societies or in international organisations – they see the world differently from men.

Standpoint theorists differ in explaining *why* women have an alternative outlook. Do women have a more respectful attitude towards nature than men because they menstruate and can give birth to children, or is it because they are socialised differently, so that nature seems more precious to them than it does to many men? Peace activists may similarly differ in accounting for the fact that women in general are more likely to oppose war than men.

But whatever the emphasis placed upon nature or nurture, standpoint feminists generally believe that women are different to men. One of the reasons why standpoint feminists see women as more practically minded than men is because they often have to undertake activity of a rather menial kind. Bryson refers to Marilyn French's novel *The Women's Room* (quoted by Hartsock) in which a woman has the job of washing a toilet and the floor and walls around it: an activity, says French, that brings women 'in touch with necessity' and this is why they 'are saner than men' (Bryson, 1999: 23). Indeed Hartsock seeks to redefine power as a capacity and not as domination, arguing that women's experience stresses connection and relationship rather than individuality and competition (Hartsock, 1983: 253).

## Postmodern Feminism

Some make a distinction between postmodern feminism and feminist postmodernism. The distinction, it seems to us, is not a helpful one and we use the two terms indistinguishably. Those who say they are postmodern feminists but not feminist postmodernists sometimes define postmodern feminism as 'postmodernism with a standpoint bent' (Hoffman, 2001: 63), and we would suggest that the question of a 'standpoint bent' is best understood by looking at the section preceding this one.

Postmodernists seek to overcome the dualistic character of traditional theory. We should refuse to accept that we are either critical (and want to overturn everything) or conservative (and want to keep things as they are). We need to be both subjective or objective, valuing the individual *and* society. In this way we avoid making the kind of choices that postmodernists call 'binary' and absolutist. This leads postmodernists to stress the importance of difference and plurality, and this is why postmodern feminists or feminist postmodernists argue that the notion of feminism as the emancipation of women is doubly problematic. First because emancipation sounds as though at some privileged point in time women will finally be free and autonomous, and second because the very term 'woman' implies that what unites women is more important than what divides them.

This, postmodernists argue, violates the logic of both/and, since it privileges sameness over difference. Indeed Kate Nash argues that because postmodernism (we use the term interchangeably with poststructuralism) commits us to arguing that woman 'is not a fixed category with specific characteristics', we have to be committed to the concept of woman as a 'fiction' in order to be a feminist at all (Hoffman, 2001: 78).

## Problems with the Philosophical Feminisms

### Liberal Feminist Critique

Liberal feminists are sympathetic to feminist empiricism. Indeed, one writer has described feminist empiricism as the 'philosophical underpinning of liberal feminism' (Hoffman, 2001: 56), and naturally liberal feminists are attracted to the stress on rationality, science and evidence. On the other hand, liberal feminists argue that questions of freedom and autonomy, the rule of law and individual rights involve values, and feminist empiricists seem to be committed to a notion of science that excludes values, basing their hypotheses and findings simply on facts.

Standpoint feminists suffer from the same one-sidedness that afflicts radical feminism. By probing woman's experience in general, it does not respect the division between the public and the private, and by arguing for the superiority of the female standpoint it makes alliances with well-meaning men more difficult. Both factors make standpoint feminists liable to embrace an authoritarian style of politics.

As for postmodern feminism, liberal feminists feel that its aversion to absolutes and modernism leads to scepticism and renders problematic the whole concern with women's rights.

### Socialist, Radical and Black Feminist Critiques

Socialist feminism challenges the feminist empiricist notion of science as value free and not itself ideological. An emphasis upon relationships leads to the view that facts do not speak for themselves but imply evaluation, and therefore it is naive to imagine that a purely scientific (rather than explicitly ideological) presentation of feminism will be more persuasive.

As for standpoint feminism, socialists argue that an emphasis upon women's experience needs to take more specific account of the impact of class and capitalism, while postmodern feminism leads to a kind of academic conservatism that makes emancipatory politics impossible.

Radical feminists feel that the emphasis upon science is male-oriented and feminist empiricists underestimate the extent to which male mores have penetrated the academy. Radicals are more sympathetic to standpoint feminism, particularly where the difference and even superiority of women is emphasised, while postmodernist feminism is seen as a betrayal of women's interests and a rejection of the need for feminism at all.

To black feminists, feminist empiricism seems elitist and very 'white' since most black women find it difficult to obtain academic positions. As for standpoint feminism, it speaks (as does radical feminism) of women in abstract terms, and therefore unthinkingly adopts the position of white women. Postmodern feminism is seen as indulgent and sceptical, and for all its emphasis upon difference, ignores the problems that black women face, and which make the notion of emancipation a meaningful ideal. Deconstructing modernity seems a rather hollow enterprise when women who are black have yet to obtain 'modernist' goals of equality and autonomy.

---

### Ideas and Perspectives:

## Feminism and Diversity

It could be argued that the emphasis upon different strands of feminism is itself counter-productive. If feminism is defined broadly as the emancipation of women, then it becomes possible to see each of the different feminisms making a positive contribution to the development of feminism overall, while betraying a certain one-sidedness that needs to be discarded. A recent work has spoken of the need to recover 'feminisms from the intolerance of other feminisms' (Zalewski, 2000: 142) and it seems to us that we do not need to choose between one feminism and many feminisms. Feminism can only be constructed as a viable and dynamic theory through multiple feminisms.

Thus liberal feminism stresses the importance of people as free and equal individuals but, as Steans argues, 'liberal feminism is not merely feminism added onto liberalism' (1998: 17), while socialist feminists rightly emphasise the importance of class and capitalism as social institutions that negatively impact upon women. Despite its weaknesses, radical feminism argues for a notion of patriarchy that extends into all areas of life and it invites attention to relationships as the location of conflict.

Black feminists warn us eloquently against the dangers of ethnocentrism. Women can be black as well as white, and analyses, say, of the family and sexuality that might apply to white women will not necessarily apply to black women. As for the philosophical feminisms, feminist empiricists stress the importance of a sophisticated presentation of the facts, while standpoint feminists are concerned with the way in which women's experience impacts upon their behaviour and outlook. Postmodernist feminism helpfully warns against static and ahistorical views of women that ignore the differences between them.

There is no need to juxtapose separate feminisms from the development of a feminism that is sensitive to difference, sees the need for alliances with men, acknowledges the problems from which all women suffer (albeit in different ways), and seeks to make feminism as convincing and well researched as possible.

Exercise

## The Problem of Prostitution and Pornography

To many people (who would not necessarily call themselves feminists at all) prostitution is scandalous and unacceptable. Surely it is right that soliciting and brothels are illegal even if prostitution as such is not. Prostitution is an affront to freedom, marriage and the dignity of women. To others, this is a moralistic position that ignores the reasons why women become prostitutes. Prostitute women need help and recognising them as sex workers who should work in safer conditions (and pay tax!), would be a just and humane way of tackling the issue.

Draw up a list of arguments for and against the decriminalisation of prostitution and say why *your* solution to the question would meet the interests of both prostitutes in particular and women in general.

Pornography also arouses strong feelings. Is it merely a portrait of sexuality to which the prudish and puritanical object, or does pornography harm the interests of women and should it be 'cleansed' from society?

How would you define pornography? Of course it can hurt people (think of the exploitation in which children may be involved), but does it have to? Based on your definition of pornography, consider the pros and cons of banning pornography.

## Summary

Liberal feminism seeks to give women the same political and legal rights that men enjoy so that women can be regarded as rational and autonomous individuals. Liberal feminists are accused by their critics of disregarding the negative impact that capitalism and the market make upon women's lives, of ignoring male oppression in the so-called private sphere, and of embracing an ideology that is abstract and absolutist in tone.

Socialist feminism argues that questions of gender must be considered alongside questions of class. Marxist feminism particularly emphasises the problem posed by capitalism to the interests of women. Liberal critics contend that women can legitimately display their equality through becoming executives in business, and argue that it is wrong to assume that all women should work outside the home. Other feminists feel that socialists ignore the general problems faced by women in all societies, while postmodernists feel that the socialist 'metanarrative' is as abstract as the liberal one.

Radical feminists pride themselves on concentrating exclusively on women's problems, and insist that male oppression manifests itself in inter-personal relations as well as in more conventionally political arenas. They are accused by their critics of an authoritarian disregard for the individual and a prejudice against men. The differences between women, whether 'racial' or class based, must be taken into account, and it is wrong to assume that a scientific view expresses masculinist values.

Black feminists take the view that ethnic 'outsiders' must be explicitly considered, and generalised views of women are unacceptable. Their critics feel that black feminists focus one-sidedly upon what is one form of oppression among many, and that they are guilty of 'essentialising' blackness.

The philosophical feminisms stress either the importance of rigorous scientific methods (the feminist empiricists), the need to understand the distinctive character of a woman's outlook (the standpoint feminists), or the importance of plurality and difference (the postmodern feminists). Their critics feel that empiricism is vulnerable to the argument that facts themselves imply values, that a woman's standpoint varies dramatically according to circumstance, and that an excessive emphasis upon difference casts doubt upon the whole feminist project.

These divisions can be resolved by a notion of feminism that seeks to incorporate the strengths of each of the feminisms and exclude their weaknesses.

## Questions

1. Is feminism still relevant in today's world?
2. Which theory of feminism – the liberal, the socialist, the radical or the black – do you find the most persuasive?
3. Can men become feminists or is feminism an ideology that only relates to women?
4. Do the biological differences between men and women have any social significance?
5. Are some women more likely to favour emancipation than others?

## References

Aquinas, St T. (1953) *The Political Ideas of St. Thomas Aquinas* (ed. D. Bigongiari) New York: Hafner.

Bebel, A. (1904) *Women under Socialism* New York: Labor Press.

Brody, M. (1992) 'Introduction' in M. Wollstonecraft, *A Vindication of the Rights of Women* London: Penguin, 1–73.

Bryson, V. (1992) *Feminist Political Theory* Basingstoke: Macmillan.

Bryson, V. (1999) *Feminist Debates* Basingstoke: Macmillan.

Coole, D. (1988) *Women in Political Theory* Hemel Hempstead: Harvester Wheatsheaf.

Eisenstein, Z. (1981) *The Radical Future of Liberal Feminism* London: Longman.

Engels, F. (1972) *The Origin of The Family, Private Property and the State* London: Lawrence & Wishart.

Friedan, B. (1963) *The Feminine Mystique* Harmondsworth: Penguin.

Funk N. and Mueller, M. (eds) (1993) *Gender Politics and Post-Communism* New York and London: Routledge.

Greer, G. (1970) *The Female Funuch* London: Paladin.

Greer, G. (1999) *The Whole Woman* London: Doubleday.

Hartsock, N. (1983) *Money, Sex and Power* New York and London: Longman.

Hoffman, J. (2001) *Gender and Sovereignty* Basingstoke: Palgrave.

Humm, M. (ed.) (1992) *Feminisms* New York and London: Harvester Wheatsheaf.

MacKinnon, C. (1989) *Toward a Feminist Theory of the State* Cambridge, Mass.: Harvard University Press.

Marx, K. and Engels, F. (1975) *Collected Works* vol. 3 London: Lawrence & Wishart.

Mill, J.S. (1869) *The Subjection of Women* Cambridge, Mass. and London: MIT Press.

Plato (1953) *The Republic* Harmondsworth: Penguin.

Rowbotham, S. (1972) *Women, Resistance and Revolution* London: Allen Lane/Penguin.

Rubin, G. (1970) 'Woman as Nigger' in L. Tanner (ed.) *Voices from Women's Liberation* New York: Mentor.

Sacks, K. (1974) 'Engels Revisited: women, the organization of production and private property' in M. Rosaldo and L. Lamphere (eds), *Women, Culture and Society* Stanford Calif.: Stanford University Press, 207–22.

Shanley, M. and Pateman, C. (1991) 'Introduction' in M. Shanley and C. Pateman (eds), *Feminist Interpretations and Political Theory* Cambridge: Polity Press, 1–10.

Steans, J. (1998) *Gender and International Relations* Cambridge: Polity Press.

Whelehan, I. (1995) *Modern Feminist Thought* Edinburgh: Edinburgh University Press.

Wolf, N. (1993) *Fire with Fire* London: Chatto & Windus.

Wollstonecraft, M. (1992) *A Vindication of the Rights of Women* London: Penguin.

Zalewski, M. (2000) *Feminism after Postmodernism* London and New York: Routledge.

## Further Reading

- Bryson's *Feminist Debates* (referenced above) is particularly useful. It is comprehensive and written accessibly. Chapters 1 and 2 contain a valuable introduction to the feminist 'landscape'.

- Nicholson's *Feminism/Postmodernism* London and New York: Routledge, 1990 contains a series of essays (Nicholson is the editor) written at a time when postmodernism was beginning to make an impact. Yeatman and Hartsock's essays are especially useful.

- Greer's *The Whole Woman* (referenced above) is lively and gives the reader a very good flavour of feminism as it emerged in the 1960s and 1970s.

- Engels's *The Origin of the Family, Private Property and the State* (referenced above) has been much commented upon, but is worth reading in the original.

- Shanley and Pateman's *Feminist Interpretations and Political Theory* (referenced above) contains critiques on a wide range of classical political thinkers and more recent theorists. Accessible and full of insights.

- Funk and Mueller's *Gender Politics and Post-Communism* (referenced above) has articles on the position of women after the collapse of the Communist Party states. Some very useful material here.

## Weblinks

Have a look at: http://news.bbc.co.uk/1/hi/business/1962036.stm. Up-to-date material on women's pay in relation to men.

For a survey of different feminisms, see: http://www-lib.usc.edu/~retter/lst2.html

# Chapter 8

# Multiculturalism

## Introduction

Beliefs and values, language and family traditions, dress and diet are central to an individual's sense of identity. Most people would say that these things should be respected, and liberalism has developed into an ideology that places great stress on respecting diversity of belief and lifestyle. A fully human existence entails the freedom to live according to your cultural traditions. But what if a particular cultural tradition is hostile to liberalism? What if, for example, it holds that girls should be educated to fulfil a subservient role, limited strictly to the private sphere of the family? What if it advocates discrimination, or even violence, against adherents of other religions, or homosexuals, or different ethnic groups? These are questions raised by multiculturalism, an ideology that has emerged since the 1960s, but which – arguably – has roots in the religious struggles of the sixteenth and seventeenth centuries.

## Chapter Map

In this chapter we will:

- Disentangle various concepts that often get run together in debates over multiculturalism; in particular, we will distinguish between culture, race, ethnicity and religion.

- Consider the historical development of multiculturalism and, in particular, its relationship to the older ideology of liberalism.

- Set out a number of theories – what we term 'models' – of multiculturalism, and thereby show the diversity of thinking within multiculturalism.

- Apply these theoretical perspectives to 'real-life' case studies.

# Religious Dress Ban: Equality or Oppression?

Muslim girls demonstrate in Marseille against a ban on wearing Islamic headscarves in French public schools, 14 January 2004

In February 2004 the French National Assembly voted 494–36 in favour of banning 'conspicuous' religious symbols in schools. The ban came into effect in September 2004, at the beginning of the new school year. France has a long tradition of *laicitie* (secularity), which is intended to draw a strict line between the state and religion; some advocates of the ban argue that it is necessary to protect the French state – of which the public education system is a part – from the 'threat' of Islamic fundamentalism. Others offer a more subtle defence: the ban ensures that Muslim girls and young women receive equal treatment as French citizens. By preventing those women wearing a veil (*hijab*), or other Muslim dress, they are being protected from their families who are intent on denying them equality in educational provision. Against the charge that the ban discriminates against Muslims it is stressed that the law applies also to Jewish skullcaps, large Christian crosses and Sikh turbans.

This case draws attention to questions of identity and equality: does treating people equally mean treating them in the same way? Most French people – 70 per cent of whom supported the ban – are either committed or nominal Christians, or have no religious beliefs and adherence; for them there is no injunction to wear a particular form of dress. For Muslims, on the other hand, there are requirements, although there are different interpretations of those requirements among Muslims. Apart from conspicuous crosses, the new law does not have any impact on Christians and non-believers, whereas clearly it does affect Muslims. On the other hand, it could be argued that Islam treats men and women unequally, and this is manifested in gender-differentiated dress codes; the French parliament is, therefore, striking a blow for gender equality.

• What do you think: was the French parliament justified in passing this law?

## What is Multiculturalism?

The term 'multiculturalism' has gained wide currency in both academic and popular debate, and its employment is not restricted to political theory or political science: there are multicultural perspectives not only in other social sciences, but also in the humanities, and even in the natural sciences. For this reason it is important to demarcate the debate in political theory, and this requires making some distinctions:

(a) **Multiculturalism as an attitude** Although it is more usual to describe a person as 'cosmopolitan' than 'multicultural', the two can be taken as synonyms, which define either a positive and open attitude to different cultures or, at least, respect for people, where such respect means recognising their rights to make choices about how they live their lives.

(b) **Multiculturalism as a tool of public policy** If you conduct an online search of university library holdings using the word 'multiculturalism' most items will be concerned with education policy, followed by other areas of public policy such as health and social services. Multicultural education policy is concerned with school organisation and curriculum; health and social policy focuses particularly on social inclusion and identifying the special needs of particular cultural groups.

(c) **Multiculturalism as an aspect of institutional design** Whereas policy questions assume the existence of a particular set of political institutions, the question here is what kind of institutions we should have. Examples of institutional design that make explicit the concern with cultural diversity include the power-sharing Assembly and Executive created in Northern Ireland as a result of the 1998 Belfast Agreement, and the constitutional arrangements for Bosnia-Herzegovina which resulted from the 1995 Dayton Peace Accords.

(d) **Multiculturalism and moral justification** Institutions are important, but political theory is not concerned merely with what political institutions should exist, but with how they are justified. It is possible for institutions to be respected for bad reasons, so 'justificatory multiculturalism' is concerned with reasons that all reasonable people can accept. What constitutes 'reasonableness' is, of course, central to the debate.

## Culture, Race, Ethnicity and Religion

### Culture

A difficulty that runs through the multiculturalism debate is the failure to explain what is meant by culture. Will Kymlicka, for example, in the opening lines of his book *Multicultural Citizenship*, makes the following claim:

> Most countries are culturally diverse. According to recent estimates, the world's 184 independent states contain over 600 living language groups, and 5,000 ethnic groups. In very few countries can the citizens be said to share the same language, or belong to the same ethnonational group. (Kymlicka, 1995: 1)

In a few short sentences it is implied that 'culture' equates to a language group, an ethnic group and an ethnonational group. Kymlicka goes on to define the kind of culture with which he is concerned as an 'intergenerational community, more or less institutionally complete, occupying a given state territory, sharing a distinct language and history' (1995: 18) and further suggests that a culture provides 'meaningful ways of life across the full range of human activities' (1995: 76). The problem is that there is a proliferation of concepts with which culture is equated but this simply shifts the strain of definition on to these other, equally problematic, concepts. Other political theorists, such as Tully (1995), do make explicit their reliance on a particular theory of culture – in Tully's case Clifford Geertz's semiotic theory – but they fail to discuss fully the implications of such commitments. And in popular discussion 'culture' is frequently run together with race, ethnicity and religion; while there are important connections between these concepts they are not synonyms. The structure of a religion is quite different to the structure of, say, a linguistic community, and each generates distinct political claims. (Race and ethnicity, and religion, are discussed later in this section.)

If we want to find a serious discussion of culture we have to turn to anthropologists, for whom arguably 'culture' is the central, defining concept of their discipline. Edward Tylor's definition of culture as 'that complex whole which includes knowledge, belief, art, morals, law, custom, and any other capabilities and habits acquired by man as a member of society' (Tylor, 1871: 1), while very broad, does capture the notion of culture as something artificial, in contrast to 'nature' that is a 'given'. We can characterise the anthropologists' discussion of culture as an attempt to answer the question: given a shared biological nature and largely similar physical needs, why is there such cultural diversity? From Tylor onwards responses have fallen into two categories: universalist and relativist. These categories contain, of course, a huge variety of different theories. In the universalist camp we find those Marxists who argue that 'forms of consciousness' (culture) are to be explained by underlying material forces, and cultural change is derivative of changes in the relations of production. For such Marxists culture is a secondary phenomenon, and not the true 'subject of history'. But a universalist can hold culture to be basic, maintaining that cultural diversity is explained by different rates of evolution. Nineteenth-century anthropologists, Tylor included, viewed what they termed 'primitive cultures' as of the same type as earlier European cultural forms. This has clear imperialist overtones, and it is no coincidence that anthropology developed on the back of colonisation. Evolutionism could, however, take a liberal form, if one maintained, as John Stuart Mill did, that human beings have innate rational capacities that can only be realised under particular cultural conditions (Mill, 1991: 231). These Marxist, 'imperialist' and liberal theories are all evolutionary, but universalism need not be evolutionist. One might argue that there are underlying non-cultural needs that are satisfied by diverse cultural forms; such a *functionalist* view explains culture in terms of something non-cultural without a commitment to the evolutionary superiority of one culture over another (Malinowksi, 1965: 67–74).

In its early phase anthropology was dominated by universalist theories, but by the late nineteenth and early twentieth centuries it came under sustained attack by relativists, such as Franz Boas (Boas, 1940: 290–94), and his students Ruth Benedict (Benedict, 1935: 1–14) and Alfred Kroeber (Kroeber, 1952: 118–35).

Benedict, in her book, *Patterns of Culture*, quotes Ramon, chief of the Californian Digger Indians, who laments that with colonisation American Indian culture had died and, taking Ramon's analogy of a cup, Benedict maintains that his culture could not be preserved by 'tinkering with an addition here, lopping off something there', rather, 'the modelling had been fundamental, it was somehow all of a piece' (1934: 16). A culture, Benedict suggests, is as an integrated pattern of intelligent, albeit sometimes unconscious, behaviour. It involves an apparently arbitrary selection of ways of being that are reinforced over time; the correlative of such selection is the implicit rejection of other ways of being. There are no underlying non-cultural needs, drives or capacities, nor is a particular culture, following Hegel, an instantiation of a process of cultural change. Pattern theory implies that there can be no cultural *diversity* within a society, for culture is integral, and it is perhaps not surprising that those political theorists, such as Tully (1995), who make explicit their anthropological commitments, appeal to an alternative and more recent form of cultural relativism, that advanced by, among others, Geertz (1993). Culture for Geertz is a complex of signs, whose meaning is dependent upon perspective, not in the sense that an 'outsider' cannot understand the signs, but rather that such understanding – *interpretation* – must make reference to the context of the participants. For Geertz one does not 'have' a culture in the sense that culture is predicated upon a subject, but rather culture is a shorthand for a 'multiplicity of complex conceptual structures, many of them superimposed upon or knotted into one another, which are at once strange, irregular, and inexplicit' (Geertz, 1993: 10).

## Race and Ethnicity

Race and ethnicity are concerned with somatic, or phenotypical, differences between people: that is, how other people look or sound, or any other way in which they are *perceived* to be different. There is a considerable sociological literature on race and ethnicity, but very little intellectual exchange between sociologists of race and political theorists of multiculturalism. The terms race and ethnicity are used interchangeably. Ethnicity denotes a group of people bound by 'blood-ties', and has its etymological roots in the Greek word for 'nation' – *ethnos* (although some Biblical commentators translate it as Gentile). Although most sociologists reject the notion that racial differences have a biological basis – there is greater genetic variation *within* groups perceived to be the same than *between* such groups – they accept that the discourse of race affects human attitudes and behaviour. Because it has social effects, race is 'real'.

Until relatively recently, race (or ethnicity) rather than culture was the dominant concept in debates about citizenship and immigration. This is reflected in law. British legislation intended to outlaw discrimination were titled Race Relations Acts – of which there were three: 1965, 1968, 1976. The 1976 Act, which superseded the previous ones, defined a 'racial group' as 'a group of persons defined by reference to colour, race, nationality or ethnic or national origins' (Macdonald, 1977: 49). There is no mention of culture, or indeed religion. A complex relationship exists between anti-racist **politics** and multiculturalism. Since a person can be defined as 'different' by a range of characteristics, including language (and accent), bodily characteristics, dress, religion and diet, where the salience of each varies from one situation to another, legislation designed to protect that person cannot easily slot discrimination into a single category, such as racial, or religious, or cultural, or ethnic. In this sense race and culture are inextricably linked. However, race is relatively fixed as against culture – even if we reject race as a biological category, a person's race is *perceived* as fixed. Culture, because it is concerned with beliefs and lifestyle, possesses a greater fluidity. The danger which some anti-racists see in multiculturalism is that, in the name of respecting difference and fighting discrimination, multiculturalists deny people autonomy – they assume that cultural traits are fundamental to that person's identity.

## Religion

Ch 1: Liberalism as Toleration, pp. 14–18

Much debate about cultural diversity is really about the relationship of religion and politics – that is, of the consequences of the existence of conflicting belief systems, including secular ones, within a political territory. As such, multiculturalism has its roots in debates going back to the sixteenth century: the appearance in the same political territory of rival, mutually exclusive, authoritative and comprehensive belief systems caused a political crisis, which was 'settled' with the development of conceptions of religious toleration. The extent to which contemporary debates over, for example, the role of Islam in Western societies, are a continuation of these older debates is something we shall discuss in the last section of this chapter. Here we make a few general remarks about religion and multiculturalism.

The first point to make is that religion is a highly complex phenomenon. Eric Sharpe identifies four 'modes' of religion, that is, ways in which human beings are religious:

1. the *existential* mode, in which the focus is on faith;
2. the *intellectual* mode, which gives priority to beliefs, in the sense of those statements to which a person gives conscious assent;
3. the *institutional* mode, at the centre of which are authoritative organisations that maintain and transmit doctrines;
4. the *ethical* mode, which stresses the behavioural relationships between members of a religious community, and those outside it (Sharpe, 1983: 91–107).

What differentiates different religions and sects is the centrality of one mode relative to another. For example, many Protestant Christians place personal experience (mode 1) at the centre of their religion, and their interpretation of scripture (mode 2), allegiance to the Church (mode 3), and personal behaviour (mode 4) are determined by their religious experience. There are other traditions within Protestantism which make scriptural interpretation (mode 2) central, and the other modes derivative. Catholicism stresses Church teaching and authority (mode 3). Some work in comparative religion contrasts Christianity as a religion of orthodoxy, with Islam, along with Judaism, as a religion of orthopraxy. There is, for example, no equivalent in Islam to the Nicene Creed; while the first of the Five Pillars of Islam – *Shahada* – is a declaration of faith, the remaining four pillars stress correct practice. This simple distinction is open to challenge, but insofar as it holds, the central mode for Muslims is 4.

Ch 1:
Liberalism,
pp. 17–18

## Exercise

If you were to leave the society in which you were brought up and live in another, what aspects of behaviour, belief and lifestyle would you give up first, and which would you give up last, or not give up at all? How you approach this exercise may depend on a number of factors:

- the age at which you emigrate;

- the circumstances of your emigration – it may be relatively 'free', or forced on you by persecution, or economic circumstances;

- the differences between the community from which you emigrate and the community of immigration;

- your gender may be relevant.

You may, in fact, have experienced migration. In that case, you can draw on your experience.

Each of these modes can contain considerable diversity. For example, most religions stress the importance of experience, but that experience can be focused on a divinity, expressed through doctrines, and possibly mediated through religious institutions, such as a priesthood, or a very diffuse and 'free' mysticism. Many great religions have mystical traditions, and those who express their faith through a mystical existential mode may have more in common with one another than with those who are nominally their co-religionists. Again, the three great monotheistic religions – Judaism, Christianity and Islam – place emphasis on scripture, but there are divergent approaches *within* each of these religions. Some claim there is a literal and accessible truth to scripture; others claim that truth is only recoverable by reconstructing the context in which scripture was formed; yet others maintain that truth is relative, or that there are plural sources of truth. In passing, it should be said that the extent to which a religion is 'literate' – that is, stresses reading scripture – as against 'audio-visual' is undoubtedly a reflection of the level of development of society: popular religion in a largely illiterate society will likely be audio-visual, although alongside it there may exist an 'elite' literate religion.

When considering the relationship of religion and politics in contemporary society it is important to keep in mind the dominant mode of a particular religion or sect, as well as the particular content of its beliefs or practices. As we have argued, the development of liberalism depended both on toleration of religious difference and the recognition of a distinction between public and private. One of the central questions for multiculturalists is whether that distinction reflects a particular mode of religion, and therefore a specific religion, or whether liberalism has a broader reach.

## Multiculturalism, Liberalism and Modernity

Liberalism and multiculturalism stand in a close but complex relationship to one another. Liberals accept that we live in a pluralistic society – there is no single good way to live your life, or if there is, there is no means of persuading others that you have found it – and diversity of culture is one expression of that pluralism. But the compatibility of liberalism and multiculturalism turns upon the conceptualisation of pluralism. If by 'pluralism' we mean an irreconcilable difference over the good, then allegiance to the state might simply be understood as a willingness not to impose upon others our conception of the good, and the justification for such 'toleration' of 'difference' is nothing more than social peace. If, however, we see pluralism as a natural outcome of the exercise of human freedom then the justification for tolerance of other conceptions of the good is grounded in something that is itself a good, namely, personal autonomy. Once personal autonomy takes on the status of a political value, the question arises as to whether the political order depends upon the existence and sustenance of particular cultural forms to the exclusion of others.

Biography, p. 206

Multiculturalists argue that 'traditional' liberalism fails to recognise the role that culture plays in the self-worth of individuals. Charles Taylor, who is both a liberal and a multiculturalist, argues that the sense of who we are is constructed in the eyes of others, so that to fail to be recognised by others is to be denied the basis of one's identity: 'non-recognition or misrecognition can inflict harm, can be a form of oppression, imprisoning someone in a false, distorted, and reduced mode of being' (Taylor, 1994: 25). The politics of recognition is a modern concept, developing out of the collapse of hierarchies in the eighteenth century. Hierarchies were the basis of honour, and honour was linked to distinction, and hence inequality; against honour we have dignity, which Taylor takes to be the basis of a liberal–democratic society. At the same time as we shift from honour to dignity, we also experience individualisation: morality is no longer to be understood in terms of mores but is a matter of individual conscience, either in the form of a moral sense or, following Kant, the capacity of an individual to will the moral law. However, after Kant we get what Taylor terms a 'displacement of the moral accent': the inner voice is no longer primarily concerned to tell us what to do – to connect us to an objective moral order – but has become an end in itself. It is the terminus of identity. We have to be true to our 'inner voice' if we are to be 'full human beings'. The conjunction of inwardness and authenticity – following that inner voice – creates a danger that we lose sight of the fact that one's identity is only possible through other people's recognition of us. Somehow we need to reconcile the inwardness of authenticity with the 'outwardness' of recognition. In the days of 'honour' the two were unproblematic because 'general recognition was built into the socially derived identity by virtue of the very fact that it was based on social categories that everyone took for granted' (34). Inwardly derived, as distinct from externally imposed, identity does not enjoy this automatic recognition, but must win it, and that process may fail, such that 'what has come about with the modern age is not the need for recognition but the conditions in which the attempt to be recognized can fail' (35). Recognition is recognition of *difference*, but this is combined with a traditional liberal emphasis on equality:

> The politics of difference often redefines non-discrimination as requiring that we make these distinctions the basis of differential treatment. So members of aboriginal bands will get certain rights and powers not enjoyed by other Canadians . . . and certain minorities will get the right to exclude others in order to preserve their cultural integrity, and so on. (39–40).

The conflict between 'traditional' liberalism and identity politics would be less severe were it not for the fact that 'the demand for equal recognition extends beyond an acknowledgement of the equal value of all humans potentially, and comes to include the equal value of what they have made of this potential in fact' (42–3).

What is interesting about this presentation of multiculturalism is that 'culture' is conceptualised not as an imposition or constraint, but as something we *identify with*, and in the process it becomes our *identity*. Despite Taylor's criticisms of traditional liberalism, his historical reconstruction of the development of multiculturalism as one strain of the politics of recognition – another is feminism – owes a huge amount to a liberal conception of the human subject. Culture is not, for Taylor, something set apart from human beings, but rather it is through culture that we acquire the recognition of other people, and so self-respect. Although there are different models of multiculturalism – we discuss some in the next section – they share what may be called a 'post-liberal' emphasis: that is, they have absorbed liberal conceptions, but at the same time engage in a critique of them. A consequence is that multiculturalism *as an academic debate* cannot be understood as a return to early liberal debates about religious toleration, debates rooted in a quite different conception of human nature. And it is striking that, with the exception of Rawls's contribution, religion is not in the foreground of these models of multiculturalism. The difficulty is that the *popular debate* – in, for example, the media – does tend to focus on religion, and especially the relationship of Islam to liberal–democratic values. We will make some observations on this disjunction between the academic and popular debates in the last section.

## Models of Multiculturalism

In this section we survey five 'models' of multiculturalism. One of the aims of this presentation is to show that although the field of multiculturalism is diverse, there are common concerns with human identity, rationality, freedom and equality.

## Biographies

**Charles Taylor** (1931–). A leading Canadian political theorist. He has written an important book on Hegel, and made significant contributions to contemporary political philosophy.

**Jeremy Waldron** (1953–). A New Zealander, he has taught legal and political philosophy in Britain and the United States.

**Will Kymlicka** (1962–). Another Canadian academic, he has written extensively on multiculturalism. His first book, *Liberalism, Community and Culture*, was a defence of Rawls against communitarian critics, such as Michael Sandel.

**James Tully** (1946–). Also a Canadian academic – the interest among Canadians in multiculturalism reflects, in part, the culturally fragmented nature of their country. Tully's background is in the history of political thought. His reflections on multiculturalism were first given in lectures at Cambridge University in the mid-1990s.

**John Rawls** (1921–2002). An American, widely regarded as one of the most important philosophers of the twentieth century. His main works are *A Theory of Justice* (1971) and *Political Liberalism* (1993).

**Edward Said** (1935–2003). Born into a wealthy Arab-Christian family in Jerusalem during the British Mandate, as a teenager he was sent to school in the United States, and went on to spend most of his life in that country, becoming Professor of Comparative Literature at Columbia University (New York).

## Jeremy Waldron: Hybridity

Waldron takes as his starting point the controversy surrounding Salman Rushdie's novel *The Satanic Verses*. That novel, published in 1988, offended many Muslims, and resulted in a *fatwa* being proclaimed the following year against the author by the Ayatollah Khomeini. Waldron quotes from an essay in which Rushdie describes *The Satanic Verses* as a 'migrant's-eye view of the world'. It is, Rushdie says, written from the experiences of 'uprooting, disjuncture and metamorphosis'. He goes on to say that 'the Satanic Verses celebrates hybridity, impurity, intermingling, the transformation that comes of new and unexpected combinations of human beings, cultures, ideas, politics, movies, songs' (Rushdie, cited in Waldron, 1995: 93). Rushdie argues that 'mongrelization' is the way that 'newness enters the world'.

The concept of hybridity is at the heart of Waldron's understanding of multiculturalism, which, he argues, must be 'cosmopolitan'. Understood in this way, multiculturalism represents a challenge to both liberalism and **communitarianism**. Against liberalism it implies a less 'rigid' conception of what it means to live an autonomous life: 'if there is liberal autonomy in Rushdie's vision, it is a choice running rampant, and pluralism internalized from relations *between* individuals to the chaotic coexistence of projects, pursuits, ideas, images, and snatches of culture *within* an individual' (Waldron, 1995: 94).

Communitarians, on the other hand, fail to define 'community': is it a neighbourhood or the whole world? For the purposes of his argument Waldron defines community as an 'ethnic community' – 'a particular people sharing a heritage of custom, ritual, and way of life that is in some real or imagined sense immemorial' (96). Although we may need culture in a wide sense, we do not need to exist in a single culture, such as an ethnic community. Indeed, he goes further and argues that the only authentic response to modernity is the recognition of cultural hybridity: 'from a cosmopolitan point of view, immersion in the tradition of a particular community in the modern world is like living in Disneyland and thinking that one's surroundings epitomize what it is for a culture really to exist' (101).

Waldron does recognise the counter-charge to cosmopolitanism: that living with fragments of culture generates incoherence. As Benedict argued, the meaning of a particular item of culture depends on the whole, for a culture is all of a piece. Waldron argues, however, that real communities are disparate and overlap and are nothing like the aboriginal hunting bands or the 'misty dawn in a Germanic village' (102). Respecting culture does not entail valuing an entire culture, as if a culture were a self-contained thing, but rather 'meaningful options' come from a variety of cultural sources, and 'cultural erosion' is the key to cultural evaluation: the failure of a culture to survive indicates that one culture – or cultural trait – is better than another. Waldron's argument can be read either as a critique of multiculturalism or a particular model of multiculturalism. It is a critique if by multiculturalism is meant a deliberate policy of maintaining, either through financial support or the restriction of individual freedom, a particular culture, where culture is understood as an organic whole. It is a model of multiculturalism insofar as it presents a model of political society in which cultural diversity is valued.

## Will Kymlicka: Right to Cultural Membership

In his first book, *Liberalism, Community, and Culture*, Kymlicka argued that Rawls's theory of justice could, with a few revisions, accommodate the value of community. In subsequent work he has sought to defend cultural diversity within a Rawlsian framework: he argues that as individuals we have (moral) rights to cultural membership. He argues that culture provides a 'context of choice'. This is problematic, for it is unclear whether culture is instrumentally or intrinsically valuable: does value reside in what we choose or in the fact that we have chosen it? If the ends we choose are of instrumental value then it would not much matter with which culture you identified, although the more compatible with liberal values the better.

Although Kymlicka makes clear that it is the ends we choose which matter, rather than our capacity to choose, the idea of culture as a context of choice does suggest that oppressive and illiberal cultures are less valuable than those which permit freedom, and so human autonomy – the capacity to choose – must have some intrinsic value. Kymlicka avoids addressing this tension within his theory and instead appeals to empirical examples to show that culture need not be oppressive. He cites Quebec as a culture that has 'liberalised':

> Before the Quiet Revolution [1960–66], the Québécois generally shared a rural, Catholic, conservative, and patriarchal conception of the good. Today, after a period of liberalization, most people have abandoned this traditional way of life, and Québécois society now exhibits all the diversity that any modern society contains . . . to be a Québécois today, therefore, simply means being a participant in the francophone society of Quebec. (Kymlicka, 1995: 87)

In the absence of an adequate theorisation of culture it is not clear whether the example of Quebec can help us to see whether 'cultural membership' enhances or diminishes freedom. After all, the struggle within Quebec is fundamentally over language, and although the freedom of one linguistic community is threatened by the other, the capacity to use language, whether it is French or English, is fundamental to human autonomy. Other dimensions of culture, such as religion, may not contain the same freedom-enhancing potential. Quebec shows that a culture *can* be liberal, but it does not establish that a culture is *necessarily* liberal.

Kymlicka argues that individuals should have rights to cultural membership. Rights are central to a liberal polity, and for the purposes of this discussion we can define a right as an advantage held against another (or others). Kymlicka distinguishes between three different types of right: self-government rights, polyethnic rights, and special representation rights. Self-government rights usually entail the devolution of power to a political unit 'substantially controlled by the members of an ethnic minority' (30). Examples of polyethnic rights would be state funding of 'cultural institutions' and exemptions from certain policies, such as those relating to the slaughter of animals (31). Special representation rights are intended to ensure the 'fair' representation of minority groups (32). Each of these types of rights, but especially the first two, can take the form of an 'internal restriction' or an 'external protection' (35–44). Kymlicka maintains that empirical evidence shows most campaigns for cultural recognition take the form of a demand for external protections from wider society, rather than restricting the freedom of the members of that culture, and so are compatible with liberalism (1995: 38–40). The basic problem is that rights are a specific cultural form, and the effects of rights on a culture depend on how one conceptualises culture. If cultures are integral patterns (Benedict, 1935; Kroeber, 1952) then rights may well upset those patterns. If, on the other hand, we conceive culture(s) as overlapping semiotic relationships (Geertz, 1993) then we have a different problem: rights imply a uniform legal system and yet a semiotic theory of culture suggests that interpretation may be relativistic.

## James Tully: Constitutional Diversity

Tully's work has the virtue of making explicit its anthropological and philosophical presuppositions: from anthropology he defends the semiotic theory of Geertz against what he calls the 'stages' – that is, evolutionary – theory of nineteenth-century 'imperialists', and from philosophy he draws on Ludwig Wittgenstein's later language theory.

Constitutional uniformity (or modern constitutionalism) is the object of Tully's attack, and modern political thinkers are (largely) its proponents. Modern constitutionalism stresses sovereignty, regularity and uniformity, and this contrasts with the implied rejection of sovereignty and the irregularity and pluralism of 'ancient constitutionalism'. Although there are notable exceptions, Tully maintains that the process of colonisation entailed the confrontation of these two forms of constitutionalism, and contemporary cultural conflicts in, for example, the Americas have their roots in the imposition of an alien constitutional form on Native Americans (Tully, 1995: 34). This imperial legacy is still with us, not simply in political practice, but also in political theory. Writers such as Rawls, Kymlicka and Habermas, while arguing for cultural diversity, do so in the language of modern constitutionalism (44).

Drawing on Geertz and Wittgenstein, Tully contrasts two models of intercultural communication (he prefers the term 'interculturalism' to multiculturalism). The first requires shared terms of reference – so, for example, we might disagree about what rights people have, but we implicitly assume that rights have certain features (85). The second is based on 'family resemblances' between cultures: we find common ground not through an implicitly agreed, shared language, but by a piecemeal case-by-case agreement, based on affinities between our different cultural traditions (120). This suggests that constitutional formation cannot be understood from an abstract standpoint, such as Rawls's original position. And Europeans have resources within their own culture(s) to engage in such case-by-case communication; English Common Law is an example of an ancient constitution, and Tully considers it significant that there were examples of interaction between Europeans and Native Americans based on recognition of the *affinities* between their legal systems.

Tully's argument, while interesting and provocative, has a number of weaknesses. First, there is a tension between his espousal of a semiotic theory of culture, which stresses looseness of cultural boundaries, and his talk of 12,000 'diverse cultures, governments and environmental practices' struggling for recognition (3) (he provides no source for that figure) and '15,000 cultures who demand recognition' (8) (again, no source). To count something you have to identify it, and identification implies 'hard boundaries'. Second, he says very little about how cultural conflicts can be mediated in the contemporary world, despite the underlying purpose of his work being to show the relevance of ancient constitutionalism. It is not clear what institutional forms would express cultural diversity, especially for geographically dispersed minorities. Third, and most important, he fails to address the charge that protection of culture can have detrimental consequences for individual freedom. He does maintain that culture is the basis of self-respect, such that to be denied recognition is a serious thing, but he offers only metaphorical observations to support the claim that interculturalism is not a threat to individual freedom (189).

## John Rawls: Overlapping Consensus

The focus of Rawls's first, and best known, book, *A Theory of Justice*, was the articulation and justification of principles of justice; in that book he operated with a broadly Kantian and contractarian method for deriving principles. In a later book, *Political Liberalism* (first published 1993), Rawls engages in a critique of the earlier work, arguing that it did not fully account for the 'fact of reasonable pluralism'. The idea that principles of justice are generated from a moral standpoint occupied by autonomous moral agents is a form of comprehensive liberalism, and as such is controversial. Reasonable people can deny that people are autonomous, or that political values derive from such autonomy. As the title of his later book indicates, what he came to defend was a *political*, rather than a *comprehensive*, liberalism.

Rawls lists a number of features of human interaction that explain why reasonable people can disagree: evidence is conflicting and complex; different weights can be attached to different considerations; concepts are vague; there are conflicts between different moral considerations, such as duties to family and duties to strangers; no society can contain a full range of values. He then goes on to define a 'reasonable conception of the good':

1. It entails the exercise of theoretical reason.
2. It entails the exercise of practical reason.
3. 'While a reasonable comprehensive view is not necessarily fixed and unchanging, it normally belongs to, or draws upon, a tradition of thought and doctrine'. It is not subject to 'sudden and unexplained changes, it tends to evolve slowly in the light of what, from its point of view, it sees as good and sufficient conditions' (Rawls, 1993: 59).

From the idea of reasonable pluralism Rawls offers an explanation of how citizens, from a variety of different reasonable comprehensive conceptions of the good can come to respect liberal political institutions. We develop an 'overlapping consensus': it is for citizens as part of their liberty of conscience individually to work out how liberal values relate to their own comprehensive conceptions, where a 'comprehensive conception' could be a religious belief system. Each reasonable comprehensive doctrine endorses the political conception from its own standpoint. Individuals work towards liberal principles from mutually incompatible comprehensive perspectives, and respect for those principles is built on the 'overlap' between them.

Rawls does not give concrete examples of how such an overlapping consensus can be achieved, so to illustrate his argument we provide an example of our own: how might Muslims embrace, from *within* their comprehensive conception of the good, liberal political principles? Some possible grounds are as follows:

- Islam has a long history of toleration of Jews and Christians, grounded in the belief that Islam is an aboriginal and natural form of monotheism, which incorporates the Prophets of the Jews and the Christians.

- So long as secular law is not incompatible with holy law (*Shariah*), then the former should be obeyed. There are arguments in Islam for obeying secular rulers.

- *Jihad* (exertion, struggle) has been misinterpreted: a believer is required to carry out *jihad* by 'his heart; his tongue; his hands; and by the sword'. *Jihad* can be an individual, spiritual struggle.

- 'Islam' is often defined as 'submission' or 'self-surrender'. Submission understood as self-imposed discipline is not incompatible with respect for human freedom – a person might *choose* to submit.

- For Muslims, behaviour is classified as: (a) required – includes prayer, alms-giving, fasting; (b) prohibited – theft, illicit sex, alcohol consumption; (c) recommended – charitable acts, additional prayers and fasts; (d) discouraged – might include unilateral declarations of divorce by men; (e) morally indifferent. From the perspective of respect for secular law, only (b) might raise difficulties – but much will depend on what penalties are imposed for prohibited acts.

- Requirements on women to cover themselves can be interpreted as symbolic – in the Arab–Islamic world there is huge variation in what is required of women. Men are also required to be 'modest'.

Each of these points can be contested, but it is at least plausible to argue that Muslims can be *politically* liberal. Other citizens – Christians, Jews, Hindus, atheists and so on – will, of course, produce different lists of reasons for endorsing liberal principles. The task is not to agree on a set of reasons – reasonable people will always disagree – but to converge on a set of institutions from diverse standpoints.

## Edward Said: Critique of Orientalism

Said does not offer a positive model of multiculturalism, but rather a critique of Western views of 'the Orient'. Nonetheless, it is possible to discern in his writings claims about the value of culture that are relevant not only to relations between states and societies, but relations within particular political communities between different cultural groups. Said was hugely influential in the development of 'post-colonial' studies. That term denotes not simply what comes after colonialism, but rather it suggests a transformation of colonialism – the 'post' can be read in much the same way as the 'post' in 'postmodernism'.

Confrontation with alien cultures engenders dissonance – the inability to incorporate experiences into one's 'conceptual framework'. With the expansion of European empires in the nineteenth century there was a demand placed on the colonisers to 'make sense' of the 'other'. In his most famous book – *Orientalism: Western Conceptions of the Orient* (1991) – Said is concerned with the confrontation of European imperialists with a specific region, which itself is an imperial construction. The Orient was defined as the Arab-Islamic and Indian regions. Anthropologists and other scholars, whose work depended on the colonial enterprise, were forced to accept the kinship of the Orient and the Occident (Europe), and indeed the prior achievements of the former, among which were the technical innovations of ancient Egypt, the existence of complex urban societies, and the fact that the European languages were derived from the ancient Indian language Sanskrit. They had to acknowledge the close relationship between Islam, Judaism and Christianity, and the fact that the Christian 'Holy Lands' were located in the Orient, and that ancient Greek texts survived thanks to medieval Arab scholars (Said, 1991: 74).

Said argues that Orientalists adopted an 'objectifying' attitude to the Orient. While they accepted that Europe had its roots in the Orient, they claimed the achievements of the Orient had been taken over by Europeans. To use Marxist language, Europe was now the historical (or revolutionary) subject, whereas the Orient was static. Said describes the Orient as a (theatre) 'stage' affixed to Europe, with the 'locals' dressed up in costumes (63). And because Europe was now the historical subject, it could understand the Orient better than the 'Orientals'.

Post-colonialism is concerned with 'deconstructing' this binary opposition of subject (knower) and the object (known). In denying themselves, and seeking to be objective, the colonisers were less enlightened than those they sought to enlighten. In a later work, *Culture and Imperialism*, Said argues that the 'other' (the colonised) does appear in French and British cultural life, and there is an implicit, although admittedly negative, recognition of the cultural (as well as material) dependence of the metropolitan centre on the 'periphery'. Joseph Conrad's *Heart of Darkness* is taken by Said as the most important literary example of this recognition, but novels, such as those of Dickens, which do not have an explicit imperial setting, recognise that empire structures the domestic context (Said, 1993: 13–14). Darkness, fear and instability are the themes, but this at least recognises the impenetrability of the 'other' – that which is not Western (33–4). The next step would be to acknowledge heterogeneity, which is distinct from pure negativity ('not us').

Where there might appear to be a more positive recognition of the 'Orient' is as the 'hidden self' of the West. The Romantic movement of the early nineteenth century was a reaction to the rise of scientific rationalism, but equally was a product of modernity. The Orient was a kind of storehouse for Romantic material (or a theatre stage, to use Said's analogy). But just as Romanticism implied controlled sensuality, so the Orient was to be 'experienced' at a distance. The 'correct' attitude was melancholy: a sense of loss of sensuality. While the stress on Oriental sensuality appears superficially positive, in fact it reinforces the 'scientific' objectification of the Orientalists. Indeed, the more 'sensual' the Arabs were, the less 'rational' they were: sensuality went hand in hand with lawlessness and cruelty.

There are several general points to be gained from Said. First, although the world has been decolonised we are dealing with the legacy of empire, not merely in the obvious sense of global conflict and inequality, but in a deeper cultural sense: there are structures of thought generated by colonialism that persist and that affect domestic politics. Second, the colonists' denial of their own culture persists in European countries. The 'majority community' may be conscious of its values, but not of their cultural pedigree – 'culture' appears to be what others possess. Third, we continue to use the language of modernisation: progress versus stasis. While Islamic society is often judged by quotations (in translation) from the Qu'rān and other holy texts, and by practices that are extinct in most parts of the Islamic world, Western society is not judged by a selective and uncontextualised reading of the Bible. In other words: 'they' haven't changed since 632, but 'we' have. An alternative version of this argument is that they have adopted our technology, but not our rationality.

One final point should be made about post-colonialism – if identity is important, then the colonial experience must be acknowledged as part of the identity of both coloniser and colonised. The desire in many parts of the colonised world to expunge that experience and seek a pure pre-colonial identity can be oppressive. Said recalls a meeting he had in the United States with an Arab Christian clergyman who was on a mission on behalf of Arab Protestants, of which Said himself was one. These communities had developed from the 1860s as a result of Christian proselytisation. Most converts were from the Eastern Orthodox Church. The cleric was concerned that the policy now (in the 1980s) was to disband these churches – withdraw financial support – and in the interests of Christian unity and survival encourage the followers to rejoin the Orthodox Church. The policy of the 1860s was now deemed a mistake. The cleric could see the point but felt aggrieved that 100 years of experience was being bureaucratically wiped away.

## Assessment: Identity, Reason and Freedom

We have presented a number of theories of multiculturalism: can any general conclusions be drawn from them?

(a) **Agency and identity** We argued in the section on Multiculturalism, Liberalism and Modernity that multiculturalists draw on the liberal conception of the human agent as a free being capable of shaping his or her identity, but criticise liberals for offering an 'empty' or 'a-cultural' conception of human agency. To varying degrees, the thinkers discussed in the previous section offer what they claim is an improved model of human identity and human agency.

(b) **Culture versus rationality** If culture is something we are born into and take for granted, then reason, which entails conscious evaluation and criticism, would appear hostile to culture. Again, insofar as liberalism stresses a rationalist approach to politics it is perceived as hostile to multiculturalism. Much of the work of multiculturalists is concerned with reconciling culture and reason. Although they offer very different conceptions of reason, for Waldron, Kymlicka, Tully and Rawls the way we reason about just institutions is central to the defence of multiculturalism.

(c) **Freedom** Whereas liberals tend to discuss freedom in abstract terms, exemplified by charters of fundamental freedoms, multiculturalists contextualise freedom. Certainly many of the thinkers we have discussed defend the traditional liberal freedoms, but they also argue that liberalism can be intolerant, and it is most often intolerant when it claims to be defending freedom. For example, Muslim women 'forced' to wear the *hijab* may claim that Western, non-Muslim women are not free if they are continually the object of the male sexualised gaze. Of course this claim can be challenged, especially when Muslim women are indeed forced to wear the *hijab*, but the claim is at least provocative: freedom is enjoyed *in a cultural context*. You can be formally free but oppressed by social mores.

(d) **Difference and equality** Both feminists and multiculturalists have forced liberals to re-evaluate their idea of equality. For liberals, human beings are morally equal, and that moral equality translates into a certain political equality, and a rather limited material equality. Men and women, as well as different cultural groups, may be morally equal, but they are still different – how we translate that conjunction of equality in difference into political principles and political institutions is a major challenge.

## Multiculturalism: the New Wars of Religion?

We have argued that debates about cultural diversity suffer from a lack of conceptual clarity: religion, culture, race and ethnicity are run together. One justification for avoiding a sharp distinction between these phenomena is that discrimination can take many forms; the precise cause of discrimination can only be determined in context. Nonetheless, there is a difficulty that becomes most apparent in the distance between popular debates and academic debates about 'multiculturalism'. By 'popular debates' we mean discussions in newspapers, on radio, television and (perhaps) the internet; the models of multiculturalism discussed above are representative of the academic debate. Race and religion dominate popular debate, whereas culture, or cultural identity, is the focus of academic work. Sometimes academics do influence the wider debate: the most widely discussed contribution to that debate over the last decade has been Samuel P. Huntington's article 'The Clash of Civilisations?' (1993). Huntington argues that with the end of the cold war the 'great divisions among humankind and the dominating source of conflict will be cultural' (Huntington, 1993: 22). He lists seven current civilisations, and argues that there will be 'micro-conflicts' at the interface of these civilisations, and 'macro-conflicts' between power blocs for control of international institutions. The most significant conflict, according to Huntington, will be between Western and Islamic civilisations.

Huntington's thesis has, unsurprisingly, come under sustained attack, most especially for ignoring the cultural diversity that exists within societies characterised as belonging to a single civilisation. What is significant, however, is the influence of his article. The title has a slogan-like quality well suited to popular consumption. If Huntington is right then the post-cold war world is returning to something akin to the Wars of Religion of the sixteenth and seventeenth centuries, the settlement of which established the philosophical foundations of liberalism. It is not a picture of the world accepted by defenders of multiculturalism; for them, there are no monolithic 'civilisations' but complex social systems in which individuals form their identities from diverse sources. In this sense multiculturalism

Ch 1: Liberalism, pp. 14–18

is not a return to the Wars of Religion but a critical development of the liberal ideology that emerged from those wars.

## Summary

Multiculturalism emerged in the 1960s as a distinct area of academic debate, and over the following decades the language of 'cultural diversity' supplanted that of race and religion. Given the dominance of liberalism as an ideology, much discussion in the field of multiculturalism has revolved around the relationship between liberalism and multiculturalism, with the two standing in a complex relationship to one another. Multiculturalists reaffirm the values of freedom and equality but rearticulate these as equality in difference, and freedom in context. Although there are continuities with earlier debates over religious difference and toleration – debates that dominated political discourse in the seventeenth and eighteenth centuries – multiculturalism cannot be understood as simply a return to these earlier disputes, but rather multiculturalism is 'post-liberal', in the sense that it has absorbed the liberal emphasis on human self-expression, but challenges liberals to provide a more adequate understanding of self-expression, one that places much greater emphasis on cultural identity.

## Questions

1. Does treating people equally mean treating them in the same way? Can you think of situations in which cultural difference may be a legitimate basis for difference in treatment?
2. Is it possible to 'pick and mix' cultural traits?
3. Is separatism the only way to respect cultural difference?
4. Is there a 'clash of civilisations'?

## References

Benedict, R. (1935) *Patterns of Culture* London: Routledge & Kegan Paul.
Boas, F. (1940) *Race, Language, and Culture* New York: Free Press.
Conrad, J. (1995) *Heart of Darkness* (ed. D. Goonetilleke) Peterborough, Ont.: Broadview Press.
Geertz, C. (1993) *The Interpretation of Cultures: Selected Essays* London: Fontana Press.
Huntington, S. (1993) 'The Clash of Civilizations?', *Foreign Affairs*, Summer 1993.
Kroeber, A. (1952) *The Nature of Culture* Chicago, Ill.: Chicago University Press.
Kymlicka, W. (1989) *Liberalism, Community and Culture* Oxford: Clarendon Press.
Kymlicka, W. (1995) *Multicultural Citizenship* Oxford: Clarendon Press.
Macdonald, I. (1977) *Race Relations: The New Law* London: Butterworth.
Malinowski, B. (1965) *A Scientific Theory of Culture, and Other Essays* Chapel Hill N. Caro.: North Carolina University Press.

Mill, J.S. (1991) *On Liberty and Other Essays* (ed. John Gray) Oxford: Oxford University Press.

Rawls, J. (1972) *A Theory of Justice* Oxford: Clarendon Press.

Rawls, J. (1993) *Political Liberalism* pbk edn New York: Columbia University Press.

Rushdie, S. (1988) *The Satanic Verses* London: Viking.

Said, E. (1991) *Orientalism: Western Conceptions of the Orient* Harmondsworth: Penguin.

Said, E. (1993) *Culture and Imperialism* London: Chatto & Windus.

Sharpe, E. (1983) *Understanding Religion* London: Duckworth.

Taylor, C. (1994) 'The Politics of Recognition' in Amy Gutmann (ed.), *Multiculturalism: Examining the Politics of Recognition* Princeton, New Jersey: Princeton University Press.

Tully, J. (1995) *Strange Multiplicity: Constitutionalism in an Age of Diversity* Cambridge: Cambridge University Press.

Tylor, E. (1871) *Primitive Culture* London: John Murray.

Waldron, J. (1995) 'Minority Cultures and the Cosmopolitan Alternative' in Will Kymlicka (ed.) *The Rights of Minority Cultures* Oxford: Oxford University Press.

## Further Reading

A general book on the importance of culture in people's lives is Michael Carrithers, *Why Humans have Cultures: Explaining Anthropology and Social Diversity* (Oxford: Oxford University Press, 1992). Two fairly straightforward discussions of culture are provided by Geertz (1993) – read the first essay in the book – and Benedict (1935), Chapters 1–3. On religion, read Sharpe (1983). On the historical development of multiculturalism – or the 'politics of recognition' – read Taylor (1994). For various competing theories of multiculturalism you should read Waldron (1995); Tully (1995); Rawls (1993), especially the preface to the 1996 paperback edition; Said (1991), Chapter 1. See also Jürgen Habermas, 'Struggles for Recognition in the Democratic Constitutional State' in Amy Gutmann (ed.), *Multiculturalism: Examining the Politics of Recognition* (Princeton, New Jersey: Princeton University Press, 1995), and other essays in that volume.

## Weblinks

Websites on multiculturalism – especially those originating from the United States – tend to be highly polemical. Nonetheless, they do provide a flavour of the passions aroused by the multiculturalism debate.

- A right-wing libertarian website against multiculturalism is: http://multiculturalism.aynrand.org/
- Kenan Malik attacks multiculturalism from a Marxist perspective: http://www.kenanmalik.com/essays/against_mc.html
- A US website dedicated to disseminating information on multiculturalism and with many links to other sites: http://members.aol.com/lacillo/multicultural.html
- UNESCO have an online journal: *International Journal on Multicultural Societies*: http://www.unesco.org/most/jmshome.htm
- A discussion of the Canadian Multiculturalism Act: http://laws.justice.gc.ca/en/C-18.7/

# Chapter 9

# Ecologism

## Introduction

Ecologism has only emerged as a fully fledged ideology since the 1960s. As with all recent ideologies it has intellectual roots stretching back centuries, but the construction of a relatively autonomous set of ideas and prescriptions for action is a very recent occurrence. Ecologism should be distinguished from environmentalism – for environmentalists, concern for the environment is based primarily on concern about the consequences of environmental degradation on human beings, whereas for ecologists, something called 'ecology', or 'nature', is the source of value. It follows from this distinction that whereas environmentalism can be combined with other ideologies, ecologism is distinct. In terms of political practice, politicians from across the political spectrum have embraced the rhetoric, and sometimes the policies, of environmentalism.

## Chapter Map

In this chapter we will:

- Distinguish ecologism from environmentalism.

- Outline the so-called 'ecological crisis'.

- Discuss the thought of two ecologists: Aldo Leopold and Arne Næss.

- Discuss the arguments of one – controversial – environmentalist: Garrett Hardin.

- Explore criticisms of ecologism.

# Nuclear Power? Yes Please!

In the 1980s plastered on cars and on lapel badges was the German slogan around a smiley 'sun' face: 'Atomkraft? Nein Danke' ('Nuclear Power? No Thanks'). Central to the German Green movement – and virtually all Green movements – is the rejection of nuclear power as expensive, dangerous, and inextricably linked to the nuclear weapons industry. It therefore came as a shock to many Green activists when one of its leading theorists, James Lovelock – the man who had coined the word 'Gaia' to describe the mutual dependence of all life forms – came out in favour of nuclear power. Lovelock argued that the threat from global warming is now so great that 'nuclear power is the only green solution' (*Independent*, 24 May 2004). The 'great Earth system' – Gaia – is, he says, 'trapped in a vicious circle of positive feedback': extra heat from any source is amplified and its effects are more than additive. This means that we have little time left to act. The Kyoto Protocol, which aimed to cut omissions, is simply a cosmetic attempt 'to hide the political embarrassment of global warming'. If we had 50 years to solve the problem then it might be possible to switch from fossil fuels to 'renewables' such as wind and tide power, but realistically those sources will only make a negligible contribution to the world's energy needs over the next 20 or so years. There is, Lovelock claims, only one immediately available source of energy which does not contribute to global warming, and that is nuclear power. Opposition to nuclear power is based on an 'irrational fear fed by Hollywood-style fiction, the Green lobbies and the media'. These fears are, according to Lovelock, unjustified: 'we must stop worrying about minuscule risks from radiation and recognize that a third of us will die from cancer, mainly because we breathe air laden with "that all pervasive carcinogen, oxygen"'.

- Is Lovelock right? (for background information on nuclear power see weblinks)

## Ecologism or Environmentalism?

Of the four chapters on 'new ideologies' in this book, this one has proved to be the most difficult for which to find an appropriate title. As we saw in Chapter 7, while there are feminisms the general label 'feminism' is broadly accepted by radical, socialist and liberal feminists. At least three possibilities suggest themselves for this chapter – ecologism, environmentalism and green (or Green) thought. And these differing possibilities carry distinct ideological implications. In the view of those who call themselves ecologists, environmentalism denotes an attitude compatible with almost all the competing ideologies. Environmentalists attach value to the 'environment' or 'nature' but only in relation to human consciousness and human concerns, and as such the environment is slotted in as a subordinate component of alternative ideologies, such as liberalism, socialism or feminism. Environmentalism is anthropocentric – that is, human centred. Ecologists, on the other hand, assert that 'nature' has intrinsic value, and that the task of ecologism is to engage in a critique of the anthropocentric world-view, which in socio-economic terms manifests itself as industrialism. Ecologism is 'eco-centred'. This does not mean that ecologists do not embrace values and perspectives derived from other ideologies, but rather those perspectives are assessed from the standpoint of the eco-system, or earth, as an irreducible and interdependent system. Whereas environmentalists share a post-Enlightenment belief in the uniqueness of the human perspective on the world – that is, they place human beings above, or outside, nature – ecologists challenge that philosophical position, maintaining that human life only has value insofar as it is 'knot' in the 'net' of life, a net which connects together not only non-human animals, but non-sentient entities, such as trees, rivers and mountains. Indeed it is the net rather than the knots that is of ultimate value.

Students of politics are most likely to have encountered the political face of the '**green movement**' rather than be aware of the underlying philosophical differences within environmentalism and ecologism, and one of our aims in this chapter will be to connect the philosophical ideas to the political movements (we discuss the rise of the Green movement in the section on Green Politics). The links are less direct than some writers on environmentalism recognise. To illustrate this, consider the idea of an 'environmental crisis' (discussed in the section of the same name). Many people maintain that industrialisation, urbanisation and population growth have either brought about, or threaten to bring about, irreversible changes to the natural environment such that the future of life on earth beyond more than 100 or 200 years is in jeopardy. Some writers maintain that the difference between ecologism and environmentalism rests, in part, on attitudes to the seriousness of this crisis, with ecologists being very pessimistic, and environmentalists being more optimistic. There is some validity in this characterisation of the differing attitude, in that ecologists maintain that the causes of the crisis are not simply scientific–technical; the roots of the crisis lie in human attitudes to nature – we see nature as a resource to be 'exploited' for our benefit. However, a human-centred approach to the environment could also explain the crisis; without condemning human attitudes to nature it could be argued that environmental degradation is the collective consequence of rational individual behaviour. Microbiologist and environmental theorist Garrett Hardin argued that overpopulation will have catastrophic consequences, and that food aid to the Third World should be ended so that population levels can be allowed to fall 'naturally' (his argument is discussed later in this chapter). Hardin is often thought of as an ecologist, and his misanthropic argument is used against ecologism, but, in fact, Hardin reasons from straightforwardly human-centred premises: human beings will suffer from overpopulation.

Although ecologism (also called '**deep ecology**') is the primary focus of this chapter, we will also consider environmentalism. We begin with a brief discussion of the idea that there is an environmental crisis. As suggested above, both ecologists and environmentalists accept such a notion, but they differ fundamentally over its causes, and its solution. After a brief consideration of Green politics, we discuss ecologism as a philosophical position, with the aim of connecting philosophy to politics. We analyse the writings of two of the most important figures in ecological thought: Aldo Leopold and Arne Næss. The third thinker we consider – Garrett Hardin – is hard to categorise as an ecologist, because his philosophical premises are clearly anthropocentric, but his proposed solution to what he regards as one of the fundamental causes of the ecological crisis – exponential population growth – has been so controversial that it is important to give it consideration. After a summary of ecologism, we discuss some major objections to it.

## Environmental Crisis and Green Politics

### Environmental Crisis

Most popular discussion of environmentalism – and ecologism – takes place within the context of a discussion of the so-called 'environmental crisis'. The first point to note is the singularity of the phrase: there is a crisis. This is controversial, for it may be that there is a series of distinct environmental problems. However, virtually all ecologists, and many environmentalists, argue that these problems are interconnected, and a coherent engagement with the environment must recognise this fact. Among the specific environmental problems are the following:

- **Global warming** This is acknowledged by most, but not all, scientists as the most serious environmental problem facing the planet. The earth's temperature is maintained by the 'greenhouse effect' – a layer of gases in the atmosphere traps a small percentage of the sun's radiation – but the burning of fossil fuels increases the greenhouse effect, with the result that sea levels will rise due to the melting of the ice caps, with some fairly obvious consequences for low-lying land areas. At a certain point in the process of global warming life-forms will be threatened.

- **Resource depletion** Some resources, such as fish, are, with careful stewardship, naturally replenished; other resources, such as coal and gas, are not. Both types of resource are threatened by excessive demand and so overproduction (this raises the question of the 'tragedy of the commons', discussed in the section on Garrett Hardin).

- **Localised pollution** This may not cause a 'global crisis', but poor air in places such as Mexico City can have a debilitating effect on inhabitants.
- **Decline in species** Although the effects of species loss – or decline in bio-diversity – are unclear, many ecologists would argue that the loss of species is bad in itself, regardless of its wider impact. The use of agricultural chemicals and the genetic modification of crops are identified by some environmentalists as the cause of the decline in bio-diversity.
- **Nuclear war** This will not, of course, be a direct environmental problem unless nuclear weapons are actually used (although nuclear weapons testing has had environmental consequences). In the 1980s, when consciousness of the threat of nuclear war was much higher than it is today, scientists speculated that the use of intercontinental ballistic missiles could result in a 'nuclear winter': atmospheric pollution caused by dust, soot, smoke and ash would prevent the sun's rays from penetrating for a period of time long enough to eradicate most plant life and create a new ice age. Since the 1980s there has been a proliferation of states with nuclear weapons.

Students of political theory cannot be expected to be experts on the scientific causes of environmental problems, and the focus of this chapter is on the philosophical ideas behind ecology, many of which can be understood without reference to the 'environmental crisis'. However, the 'crisis' does raise interesting questions about the relationship between science and politics. Ecologists are critical of scientific rationality, and yet employ scientific evidence to support their arguments. We consider this apparent incoherence in a later section (Summary and Criticisms of Ecologism). Furthermore, while there is widespread distrust of scientists employed by multinational companies, and to a lesser extent by government agencies, scientists who speak on behalf of environmental groups enjoy a high level of trust.

## Green Politics

Green political parties and movements emerged in the 1970s. In terms of political influence the most successful Green party is the German Green Party (Die Grünen/Bundnis 90). By 1982 they were represented in the parliaments of six of West Germany's regions (Länder), and they entered the Federal Parliament (Bundestag) in 1983, winning 5.6 per cent of the vote. In the following election their support rose to 8.3 per cent, and other parties began to adopt environmental policies. However, during the 1980s it became clear that there was a major schism between Realos (realists) and Fundis (fundamentalists); the former wanted power within the existing political system, while the latter challenged that system. Opposed to German unification in 1990, the Greens fell below the 5 per cent of the vote required for seats in the Bundestag (although their Eastern equivalent – Bundnis 90 – won 6 per cent of the Eastern vote, and thus seats). The internal dispute within the party was won by the Realos and the party – now in alliance with Bundnis 90 – grew in strength through the 1990s. In 1998 they formed a government with the Social Democrats. Although their support held steady they lost power in 2005, as the Social Democrats lost votes and seats.

## Environmental Movements

The Green movement encompasses more than just Green political parties – conservation and environmental pressure groups are also important. Indeed, as membership of political parties declines, so the membership of pressure groups increases. Figures from Britain indicate the importance of such groups, as shown in Table 9.1.

**Table 9.1**

| Membership (in thousands) | 1971 | 1991 | 1997 | 2002 |
|---|---|---|---|---|
| Royal Society for the Protection of Birds | 278 | 2152 | 2489 | 3000 |
| World Wide Fund for Nature | 12 | 227 | 241 | 320 |
| Wildlife Trusts | 64 | 233 | 310 | 413 |
| Friends of the Earth | 1 | 111 | 114 | 119 |

Source: http://www.statistics.gov.uk/StatBase/ssdataset.asp?vlnk=6230&Pos=3&ColRank=2&Rank=272

The German Greens, as with other European Green parties, draws its strength disproportionately from young, public sector middle-class workers. One explanation that is often advanced for the rise of the Green movement is the emergence of 'post-materialist values': quality of life issues are more important than increasing income and enhanced career status. Such a view presupposes that a society has achieved a certain level of material comfort, and so the Green phenomenon may rest on a contradiction: the possibility of a Green politics depends on the generation of surplus goods and, therefore, the consumer society of which Greens are so critical.

## Aldo Leopold and the 'Land Ethic'

It is argued that ecologism only emerged as a distinct ideology in the 1960s: prior to that there was no conscious movement around a distinct set of ideas (Dobson, 2000: 14–15). Aldo Leopold died in 1948, and so clearly insofar as he was an ecologist, his ecologism was of a non-ideological kind. However, Leopold is important as a precursor of ideological ecologism. The essence of his 'land ethic' was that 'land' was an interdependent system, and not a commodity; human beings were part of the 'land community' and not masters of it; for human beings to understand themselves they must grasp the 'whole' of which they are a 'part'; and 'a thing is right when it tends to preserve the integrity, stability, and beauty of the biotic community . . . it is wrong when it tends otherwise' (Leopold, 1994: 150). What Leopold called 'land' was what later ecologists would call the eco-system, biosphere, Gaia, 'earth' ('Spaceship Earth'), and by 'community' Leopold meant an interdependent whole, the members of which were not simply human beings, or even all sentient beings, but all the life-forms.

## Biography     Aldo Leopold (1887–1948)

American conservationist, scientist and ecological activist and theorist, Leopold was born in Burlington (Iowa).

In 1909 he received the degree of Master of Forestry from Yale University, and then for the following 19 years worked for the US Forest Service. He was first posted in New Mexico and Arizona, and then in 1924 transferred to the Forest Products Laboratory in Madison (Wisconsin).

In 1928 Leopold left the Forest Service to conduct game surveys of Midwestern states, funded by the Sporting Arms and Ammunition Manufacturers' Institute (the findings were published in 1931). Appointed a Professor of Game Management in 1933, the remaining 15 years of his life were divided between academic research, including field studies, and employment by the state on Conservation Commissions. Leopold's work of the 1930s was undertaken against the profound ecological crisis of the 'dust bowl' (1931–9), illustrated in John Steinbeck's novel *The Grapes of Wrath*, and graphically portrayed in the photographs of Dorothea Lange.

Underlying the land ethic was a controversial philosophical claim: from observation of the empirical world human beings can derive reasons for action. This violates Hume's 'naturalistic fallacy': claims about how people should behave cannot be generated from observational facts – the moral 'ought' cannot be derived from an observation of what 'is'. This is a recurrent problem with ecologism and we discuss it in more detail in Summary and Criticisms of Ecologism. Another philosophical, or ethical, claim is that the history of morality is characterised by an 'expanding circle' of concern, whereby we now consider the ownership of other human beings – slavery – wrong, but we have not yet expanded the circle of concern to include the 'land'. The land ethic enlarges the boundaries of the community to include soils, waters, plants and animals. In fact Leopold links these two philosophical claims by arguing that morality has undergone an ecological evolution, suggesting that the moral 'ought' emerges over time from a growing realisation of what 'is'. Such evolution has its origins in:

> the tendency of interdependent individuals or groups to evolve modes of co-operation. The ecologist calls these symbioses. Politics and economics are advanced symbioses in which the original free-for-all competition has been replaced, in part, by co-operative mechanisms with an ethical content. (143)

The extension of ethics to land is an 'evolutionary possibility and an ecological necessity'. Certainly, Leopold argues, individual thinkers have condemned the abuse of the land, but 'society' has yet to embrace the land ethic. The conservation movement is the embryo of such social affirmation. Another important and influential claim was that human beings think they understand the mechanisms that underlie nature, whereas in fact they do not, with the implication that we should adopt a precautionary attitude to nature. In fact, in contemporary ecological thought this claim sits alongside the quite contradictory claim that science can 'prove' there is an ecological crisis.

Biography,
p. 224

Leopold's land ethic was shaped by his experiences of state-sponsored conservation of the 1930s and 1940s in the United States, and this led him to a salutary conclusion: respect for the land cannot be achieved if the state assumes sole moral responsibility for the environment. Rather, *individuals* must change their motivations, and this is a powerful and central claim of the ecological movement. Leopold noted that farmers accepted free public advice and technical assistance, and consequently progress was made with practices such as strip-cropping, pasture renovation and soil liming, but no progress was achieved against fencing woodland off against grazing, and none in preventing the ploughing and grazing of steep slopes. In short, the farmers accepted those remedial practices that were profitable, and ignored those that were beneficial to the 'community' as a whole – community in Leopold's wide sense – but damaged the farmers' profit margins. And increasing the level of environmental education is pointless without a change in attitudes and motivations – that is, without a recognition of obligations to the land. He observes that the existence of obligations is taken for granted when what is at issue are better roads or schools but 'their existence is not taken for granted, nor as yet seriously discussed, in bettering the behaviour of the water that falls on the land, or in the preserving of the beauty or diversity of the farm landscape' (145).

A difficulty which Leopold observes in moving from dominion over the land, driven by the desire for profit, to stewardship of the land, is that many members of the land community have no economic value: 'of the 22,000 higher plants and animals native to Wisconsin, it is doubtful whether more than 5 per cent can be sold, fed, eaten, or otherwise put to economic use' (145). But such plants and animals have, Leopold claims, 'biotic rights'. This would seem to entail a rejection of a human-centred attitude to the environment, but it is unclear whether this is really the case, with Leopold suggesting that if a private landowner were ecologically minded he would be proud to be the custodian of an eco-system that adds 'diversity and beauty' to his farm and community (146). And, furthermore, the assumed lack of profit in 'waste' areas has proved to be wrong, but only after the destruction of most of it.

To express the interdependence of nature Leopold uses the image of a pyramid, with a plant layer resting on the soil, an insect layer on the plants, a bird and rodent layer on the insects, and so on up through various animal groups to the apex layer, which consists of the larger carnivores. There exist lines of dependency between these layers, largely determined by the need for food and energy. Industrialisation has changed the pyramid in a number of ways. First, by reversing evolution: evolutionary change lengthened the food-chain through the emergence of more complex life forms; industrialisation shortens the chain by the elimination of both predators and of seemingly useless organisms. Second, by exploitation, which puts geological and other formations to new uses, such as the generation of energy, and removes them from the 'natural chain'. Third, transportation disconnects the chain and introduces forms from one environment to a new, quite different one, and with sometimes unintended consequences. Leopold summarises the idea of the pyramid as an energy circuit in three basic ideas:

1. Land is not merely soil.

2. Native plants and animals keep the energy circuit open; others may or may not.

3. Man-made changes are of a different order than evolutionary changes, and have effects more comprehensive than is intended or foreseen (148).

But Leopold does not dogmatically assert that human-made changes necessarily threaten the continuation of life. He concedes that Europe has been transformed over the last two millennia, but that the 'new structure seems to function and to persist'; Europe, he concludes, has a 'resistant biota . . . its inner processes are tough, elastic, resistant to strain' (148). However, the correct perspective for an ecologist to adopt is global, and the earth as a whole, he maintains, is like a diseased body, where some parts seem to function well, but the whole is threatened with death. And, as with many ecologists, he identified population growth as a major cause of this 'disease':

> The combined evidence of history and ecology seems to support one deduction: the less violent the man-made changes, the greater the probability of successful readjustment in the pyramid. Violence, in turn, varies with human population density; a dense population requires a more violent conversion. (Leopold, 1994: 149)

Conservationists fall into two groups, labelled by Leopold A and B: group A regards the land as soil and its function as a commodity, whereas group B regards the land as a biota, and its function as 'something broader', but 'how much broader is admittedly in a state of doubt and confusion' (1994: 149). While he may not have been aware of it, this distinction is an early statement of a divide which becomes clear after the 1960s – that between environmentalists and ecologists. Crucial to the coherence of ecologism is an explanation of that 'broader' function or value which troubled Leopold.

## Arne Næss and 'Deep Ecology'

Arne Næss is credited with coining the contrasting phrases 'deep ecology' (more precisely: 'long-range deep ecology movement') and 'shallow ecology', with the spatial language intended to denote the depth of questioning of human values and reasons for action. Deep ecology offers a comprehensive conception of the good for society and individuals, whereas shallow ecology offers a less-than-comprehensive, possibly merely political understanding of environmental values. Næss presents the idea of depth and comprehensiveness in the form of a table with four levels, with Level 1 being the most comprehensive, or 'deepest'.

| Level 4 | Actions | Individual behaviour. |
|---------|---------|-----------------------|
| Level 3 | Policies | Particular policies carried out by governmental and non-governmental agencies. |
| Level 2 | Platform principles | Packages of policies derived from an ideological standpoint or movement. |
| Level 1 | Ultimate values | Grounded in, for example, a comprehensive philosophical or religious position. |

**Biography**   **Arne Næss (1912–)**

A Norwegian, Næss was appointed to a university chair in philosophy at the age of 27, and continued as Professor of Philosophy at Oslo University until 1969.

Although his personal interests always included a love of the natural world – he is famous as a mountaineer, making the first ascent of Tirich Mir (7,690 metres) in the Hindu Kush in 1950 – his philosophical work on ecological theory, or what he called 'ecosophy', only really started after he resigned his professorship. But there are continuities with his pre-1969 work; that earlier work focused on semantics – a branch of linguistics – and Næss argued that the meaning of words must be recovered from their context. There is a parallel here with the interdependence of human beings in nature.

Næss argues that we do not have to agree on ultimate values in order to engage in deep ecological action; there is a process of moving up and down the stages, such that action can be guided by a plurality of different sets of ultimate values. We will explore the coherence of this idea shortly, but the point to make here is that the criticism that deep ecology is intolerant because it fails to respect the pluralism that exists in a modern society is not necessarily valid. Næss's emphasis on the plurality of ultimate values was, in part, born out of his experience in creating cross-cultural peace and ecological activist movements. As Næss argues:

> ecologically responsible policies are concerned only in part with pollution and resource depletion. There are deeper concerns which touch upon principles of diversity, complexity, autonomy, decentralization, symbiosis, egalitarianism, and classlessness. (Næss, 1973: 95)

What Næss sought to do was develop a set of 'platform principles' (Level 2) – in other words, a 'manifesto', albeit a non-dogmatic one – around which people with diverse ultimate values can unite. Below are eight principles formulated by Næss and his friend and fellow deep ecologist George Sessions while out on a hiking trip in Death Valley, California:

1. The well-being and flourishing of human and non-human Life on Earth have value in themselves (synonyms: intrinsic value, inherent value). These values are independent of the usefulness of the non-human world for human purposes.

2. Richness and diversity of life forms contribute to the realisation of these values and are also values in themselves.

3. Humans have no right to reduce this richness and diversity except to satisfy vital human needs.

4. The flourishing of human life and cultures is compatible with a substantial decrease of human population. The flourishing of non-human life requires such a decrease.

5. Present human interference with the non-human world is excessive, and the situation is rapidly worsening.

6. Policies must therefore be changed. These policies affect basic economic, technological and ideological structures. The resulting state of affairs will be deeply different from the present.

7. The ideological change is mainly that of appreciating life quality (dwelling in situations of inherent value) rather than adhering to an increasingly higher standard of living. There will be a profound awareness of the difference between big and great.

8. Those who subscribe to the foregoing points have an obligation to directly or indirectly try to implement the necessary changes (Næss and Sessions: www.deepecology.org/deepplatform).

Biography, p. 227

Unlike Leopold, Næss was a trained philosopher, and so shows a greater awareness of the need for a credible philosophical basis for ecologism. Deep ecology requires an explanation of how particulars, such as individual animals, fit into the whole; Næss argues that part of the definition of an organism, such as a human being, is that it exists only in relation to something else. He uses the metaphor of the knot – a knot exists only as part of a net, and human beings are knots in the biospherical net (95). Human beings are intrinsically valuable, but any statement of that value must make reference to the 'whole'.

Næss accepts that any realistic form of social organisation requires some 'killing, exploitation, and suppression' (95). However, in principle, we should be biospherical egalitarians, meaning we should have deep respect for all forms of life – to restrict that respect to human beings is to mis-recognise humans, for the value we attach to each other must depend on a full understanding of who we are – 'knots in the biospherical net'. On this point, ecologists and Marxists may find common ground, although Marxists are anthropocentric. Diversity enhances the potential for survival, and the chance of new modes of life; ecological diversity should translate into respect for cultural diversity. But diversity must be of the right kind – diversity due to class hierarchy is incompatible with the 'symbiosis' inherent in the biospherical net. This is important, because it is possible to read into nature hierarchy rather than equality; what Næss must show is that mutual dependence really does imply equality. After all, there is a sense in which a master is dependent on his slave.

Deep ecologists, Næss argues, must fight pollution and resource depletion, and in this struggle they have found common cause with shallow ecologists, or environmentalists. But such an alliance can be dangerous because it distracts attention from the comprehensive concerns which ecologists should have. For example, if prices or taxes are increased in order to reduce pollution, then we need to know who will bear the cost – if it is the poor, then the egalitarianism implicit in the biospherical net is not being respected. Deep ecology favours 'soft' scientific research that limits disturbances to the environment, respects traditions, and is aware of our state of ignorance. Leopold also made reference to human ignorance and, as many writers on the ecological movement have noted, this suggests affinities between ecologism and conservatism.

Ch 2: Conservatism, pp. 36–8

Autonomy and decentralisation are central to Næss's understanding of the forms of political organisation appropriate to deep ecology: 'the vulnerability of a form of life is roughly proportional to the weight of influences from afar, from outside the local region in which that form has obtained an ecological equilibrium' (Næss, 1973: 98). A self-sufficient community produces less pollution, and depletes fewer resources, than the existing interdependent world. But such a community is more democratic because the chain of decision making is much shorter – if decisions are made through a chain of authorities, such as local, national and supra-national, then if those decisions are made by majority vote the chances of local interests being ignored increase with the addition of every link in the chain.

## Garrett Hardin and the Ethics of the Lifeboat

Garrett Hardin was a highly influential environmentalist. Although his arguments were neither original, nor profound, there are good reasons for discussing his work. First, he was concerned with a major issue for environmentalists: population growth (a secondary, but related, issue that concerned him was immigration to the developed world from the developing world). Second, he is sometimes, and quite erroneously, labelled an ecologist, as distinct from an environmentalist, and his arguments are quoted in political debates against ecologists. Third, he challenged one of the fundamental human rights – the right to procreate – and, more generally, his work raises important questions about global justice.

Hardin's most famous essay was 'The Tragedy of the Commons', which was based on a presidential address delivered at a meeting of the Pacific Division of the American Association for the Advancement of Science at Utah State University in June 1968. In the following 30 years it was reprinted in many collections, and Hardin himself revised it several times. The central problem is, by Hardin's own admission, not original: we are to imagine common lands on which herdsmen graze their cattle. So long as the numbers of herdsmen and cattle are low the commons will recover from the effects of grazing, new grass will grow, the cattle will be fed, and the herdsmen will make a living and so not starve. However, if the number of herdsmen and cattle grow – perhaps because population growth is no longer kept in check by war and disease – there will

| Biography | Garrett Hardin (1915–2003) |
|---|---|

An American, Hardin graduated in Zoology from Chicago University in 1936, and received a doctorate in Microbiology from Stanford University in 1941.

Most of his academic career was spent in the Department of Biological Sciences at the University of California, Santa Barbara, from where he retired as professor in 1978.

In his many works he sought to foster an interdisciplinary approach to environmental challenges, and was very much a 'public intellectual', debating issues such as abortion, population growth, food aid, nuclear power and immigration.

come a point at which the commons will not recover, and will indeed deteriorate to the point where even the original low level of grazing would not be supported. Even if an individual herdsman recognises the consequences of his actions – that is, can see clearly the 'tragedy' before him – it is in his interests to continue grazing and, in fact, to increase the number of cattle in order to compensate for the poorer yield.

Hardin makes a point that appears to echo those of deep ecologists: the harm from an individual action cannot be 'pictured' – the effects may not be discernible for years, and effects are, in any case, cumulative. Such is the case with the tragedy of the commons. Morality must take into account the full effects of an action; in Hardin's words, it must be 'system sensitive'. Without questioning the validity of Hardin's argument, it is important to distinguish his 'system' from that of Leopold or Næss – the long-term effects which concern Hardin are the effects on *humanity*. Hardin's argument, while concerned with environmental degradation, is thoroughly anthropocentric.

Almost all moral and political theorists have accepted that actions have to be assessed against their full consequences, so Hardin's argument is directed much more at popular moral beliefs, rather than at previous thinkers – it is doubtful that he is aware of the heritage of the arguments he propounds. Hardin argues that a popular morality focused simply on the rights of individuals, without regard to the 'system', will have catastrophic consequences; in particular, he objects to the United Nations declaration, as restated in the Declaration on Social Progress and Development (1969) (http://www.unhcr.ch/htm/menu3/b/m_progre.htm) that 'parents have the exclusive right to determine freely and responsibly the number and spacing of their children' (Article 4):

> If each human family were dependent only on its own resources; if the children of improvident parents starved to death; if, thus, overbreeding brought its own 'punishment' to the germ line – then there would be no public interest in controlling the breeding of families. But our society is deeply committed to the welfare state, and hence is confronted with another aspect of the tragedy of the commons. (Hardin, 1994: 334–5)

Hardin's comment makes reference to 'our society' – meaning the United States – and its commitment to the welfare state. The tragedy of the commons is, of course, a metaphor for the world's resources, and not every society has a welfare state. However, Hardin's audience is his own people, and the question of population growth is, for Hardin, closely linked to that of immigration. Since population growth is much higher in the developing world than in the developed world, migration from the former to the latter is a consequence of population growth. And Hardin has three fairly straightforward policy proposals: end the despoliation of the 'commons' insofar as this is within the power of the United States and other developed countries to do; stop food aid to the developing world; and severely restrict migration to the developed world.

We will say something about these proposals shortly, but we need to consider Hardin's underlying philosophical position. Hardin is not a philosopher, and so we have to engage in some speculation to capture his basic position, but it seems to amount to this: human beings are naturally selfish, or, at least, they are overwhelmingly concerned with their own survival. That some people are lucky to live in relatively wealthy societies and others in poor societies may be cause for a bad conscience, but it does not change the ethical situation. That most Americans are descended from people who 'stole' from Native Americans does not mean that they have an obligation to help the less fortunate:

> We are all the descendents of thieves, and the world's resources are inequitably distributed. But we must begin the journey to tomorrow from the point where we are today. We cannot remake the past. We cannot safely divide the wealth equitably among all peoples so long as people reproduce at different rates. To do so would guarantee that our grandchildren and everyone else's grandchildren, would have only a ruined world to inhabit. (Hardin, 1974: 567)

Hardin employs the analogy of a lifeboat to illustrate his argument. Two-thirds of the world is desperately poor, while a third is relatively wealthy. Each of those wealthy nations can be likened to a lifeboat; in the ocean outside the lifeboat swim the poor of the world, who would like to clamber on board. If there are 50 people on a boat designed for 60, and 100 swimming in the water around the boat, what are we – where 'we' means those in the boat – to do? We could respond to the Christian call to be 'our brother's keeper' or the Marxist injunction to give to each 'according to his needs', but since all 100 are our brothers (and sisters) and all are equally in need, we have to choose: we could choose 10, which would leave us with no emergency capacity and would require us to explain why we did not admit the other 90, or we could take all 100, with the consequence that the boat will sink. Alternatively, each of the 50 could choose to sacrifice his or her life, but that altruistic act will not solve the global crisis.

The 'harsh ethics' of the lifeboat become harsher when population growth is taken into account. The people in the boat are doubling their numbers every 87 years; those swimming on the outside are doubling their numbers every 35 years. Hardin argues that it is misleading to talk about satisfying human needs, as if needs were minimal conditions, such as basic food and healthcare, which once met left a surplus to be distributed. Rather, because the satisfaction of needs has the effect of increasing the population, there is no end to the satisfaction of needs. The only 'ethical' response is to refuse to satisfy the needs by restricting immigration – stopping people getting on the lifeboat – and not giving food aid to those 'outside the boat'. A consequence of this harsh policy would be that countries, once solely responsible for their own well-being, would learn to manage, albeit after a great deal of suffering.

## Summary and Criticisms of Ecologism

### Summary of Ecologism

From our discussion of Leopold and Næss, and drawing on other ecological writings, we can summarise the key components of ecologism as follows:

1. The belief that there is something which can be called 'ecology' or the 'biosphere'; this is an interconnected whole on which all life depends.

2. The natural world, which includes all forms of life, has intrinsic value, and should not be used as an instrument to satisfy human wants; there is much debate within the ecological movement about the nature of this value, and we discuss this below. However, there is an intuitive sense that ecologism requires being 'in touch' with nature.

3. The quality of human life will be enhanced once human beings recognise 1 and 2: ecologism is not concerned to devalue human beings, but rather to get us to think about who we really are.

4. The structure of the natural world should be mirrored in the social and political world; the interdependence – but diversity – of the former translates into a commitment to a more equal society, respectful of difference.

5. To achieve ecological and social justice requires not simply a change in the social, economic and political organisation of society, but a fundamental change in human motivation.

6. Ecologism is a distinct ideology, which sees in both liberalism (capitalism) and socialism a common 'enemy': industrialism. Industrialism *by definition* cannot be compatible with an ecological consciousness. For ecologists the earth is a physical object, with natural physical limits; industrialism, which is committed to economic growth, cannot respect the integrity and finitude of the earth.

7. Ecologists seek a 'sustainable society' – that is, one which is in tune with nature. In practical terms, this requires a reduction in consumption.

8. Although there is a division within deep ecology, a strong theme in ecological thought is distrust of 'technological fixes' – that is, a belief that advances in technology will overcome environmental problems.

## Criticisms of Ecologism

To conclude the chapter we discuss the main alleged tensions, contradictions and incoherences in ecologism.

### Ecologism has an Incoherent Value Theory

The central claim of ecologism is that there is value in the natural world that cannot be explained simply by reference to human wants, needs or consciousness: nature, or the environment, or the ecosystem has *intrinsic value*. The difficulty with this claim is that to say something has value is to make an evaluation, and such evaluation presupposes a capacity to evaluate, and only human beings possess such a capacity, therefore values are human centred.

An ecologist might respond by asking us to imagine a beautiful valley that no human being has ever seen – would something be lost if that valley ceased to exist? And if we conclude that something would be lost, then does that not show that value is independent of human consciousness? The difficulty is that the question asks us to *imagine* such a valley; while it is possible that a valley exists which no human eyes have ever seen, we nonetheless have the *concept* of a valley, and criteria for evaluating its beauty – after all, the artistic imagination entails the creation of something that does not 'really' exist. Perhaps, however, the ecologist is making a different claim: value does indeed depend on the human capacity to evaluate, but it does not follow that values are human centred. A distinction must be made between conative and cognitive explanations of value: if you think a mountain range is beautiful it may be because something in your emotional machinery triggers a positive reaction to it, or, alternatively, it may be because you think that the mountain range has features that any rational being can appreciate. The first explanation is conative, while the second is cognitive. The test of the difference is whether you can persuade another person that the mountains are beautiful – if you can then this suggests that the appreciation of such beauty is not reducible to your particular emotions. Lovelock makes an interesting comment in his article on nuclear power that we discussed at the beginning of the chapter: 'as individual animals we are not so special, and in some ways are like a planetary disease, but through civilisation we redeem ourselves and become a precious asset for the Earth; not least because through our eyes the Earth has seen herself in all her glory' (*Independent*, 24 May 2004).

If by 'intrinsic value' ecologists mean that the value of nature is not reducible to the emotions of individual human beings, then there are certain implications for ecologism. First, while it does provide a ground for environmental respect and protection, it still places human beings in a privileged position – although we cannot disprove the possibility, we have no reason to believe that non-human animals, let alone non-animal members of the 'biotic community', are capable of such appreciation of the natural environment. Second, if the 'natural world' has intrinsic – or cognitive – value, then the possibility exists that the created world also possesses intrinsic value, and where there exists a conflict between the two worlds it is not clear which should have the greater claim to protection.

An alternative strategy for placing value on the environment is to deny that a distinction exists between human beings and nature, such that it is meaningless to talk about *your* emotions or subjectivity, as distinct from that which is 'outside' you. If we collapse the difference between 'self' and 'other', where the other includes, for example, the mountain range that you are looking at, then it is unnecessary to talk about intrinsic value. However, it is difficult to understand what this extended self would be like, but, more significantly, the *political* effect of accepting that such a self exists would be to internalise all the conflicts which presently exist between selves, understood in the narrow, everyday sense of individual self-conscious beings.

## Ecologism cannot Bridge the Gap between Facts and Values (is and ought)

As we have seen, ecologists tend not to respect the distinction between facts and values, or 'is' and 'ought'. Of course, we should not accept uncritically the claim that the distinction cannot be bridged, and elsewhere we have addressed this challenge, but here we are concerned with ecologists' arguments. The approach adopted by many ecologists is to draw *analogies* between the natural world and the social world. Andrew Dobson offers the following (Dobson, 2000: 22):

| Nature | | Society and politics |
|---|---|---|
| Diversity | → | Toleration, stability and democracy |
| Interdependence | → | Equality |
| Longevity | → | Tradition |
| Nature as 'female' | → | A particular conception of feminism |

We discuss below whether ecologism is, for example, tolerant, but the concern here is with the nature of the ecological argument; in effect, we are being asked to look at nature, consider its intrinsic value, and draw conclusions about how we should behave towards it, and to each other. The problem, which Dobson acknowledges, is that people can draw quite different conclusions from nature: interdependence can imply hierarchy rather than equality, and the supposed femininity of nature may imply 'natural roles' that restrict human autonomy. Dobson talks about the 'lessons from nature', but it is not simply that we disagree about the social implications of our observation of the natural world, but rather that there are no lessons – or, in more philosophical language, reasons for action – to be derived from such observation. This leads to the next objection, which also connects the first two objections together: the ecologists' conception of human reason.

## Ecologism has an Incoherent Attitude to Human Rationality

It was argued that ecologists have to make some concession to human centredness: for nature to have intrinsic value there must exist beings capable of evaluation. But there is, arguably, a further concession to be made to anthropocentrism: the capacity to evaluate depends upon complex rational machinery that seeks to connect together different values, experiences and actions. Rationality depends on language and not simply a non-linguistic 'observation' of nature; when you, or Arne Næss, stand on the mountaintop and view the mountain range, your appreciation involves complex *and abstract* processes. Human beings' capacity to abstract from what confronts their senses is essential to their ability to believe on the basis of reasons, and to act from reasons. The idea of interconnectedness, which is a core doctrine of ecologists, is made possible by human reason; arguably, there is no interconnectedness in the world, except what the human mind connects together. This is not to say that there is no physical world external to the mind, nor that its value depends on the subjective attitudes of individual human beings, but rather that the 'human mind', defined as a set of capacities shared by individual human beings, and made possible through language, is the means through which the world is viewed as interconnected.

More specifically, ecologists have an incoherent attitude to natural science. Without wishing to get too deeply into the philosophy of science, a major aspect of natural science is the acquisition of knowledge through repeatable experiments – experiments that must take place in a controlled environment (there are other understandings of natural science, and certainly natural science does not equate to the entire sphere of human reason). Science, so defined, necessarily abstracts from the 'particular', and seeks to acquire knowledge by finding something which is not unique to a particular thing – the individual rat in the laboratory is only of scientific interest insofar as its physiological or psychological behaviour is generalisable, that is, its behaviour must not be peculiar to that particular rat. This observation is not about the ethics of vivisection, but rather about how we acquire knowledge of the world: natural science is advanced through distance from nature, and not by being 'in touch' with nature. Yet at the centre of ecologism as a political movement is continual appeal to the 'scientific evidence' of environmental degradation – evidence acquired through a fundamentally anti-ecological rationality.

In part, the ambivalent attitude to natural science has its roots in the ecologists' conflation of science and technology, and, relatedly, of human rationality in general with a particular variant of it: instrumental rationality. Science developed in the early modern period as the result of changes in humans' understanding of their place in the world – only once the material world is seen as lacking in intrinsic spiritual qualities is it possible to treat it in an experimental way (Kuhn, 1962: 111–35). Technology, on the other hand, dates back to the earliest human activity – it is simply the marshalling of natural processes to serve human ends. Of course, advances in scientific understanding have aided technological advance, and many ecologists will argue that neither science nor technology are in themselves to be rejected, but rather it is the degree of intervention in, and alteration of, natural processes which is at issue. The danger with ecologism is that it fails to distinguish between human enquiry – the drive to understand the world – from human wants, that is, the desire to use the natural world for human ends. Human centredness is narrowly defined by ecologists as instrumental reason; nature is used as a means, or instrument, for human ends. But you do not need to be an ecologist in order to challenge instrumental reason; you can move completely within a human-centred view of the world and still raise *rational* objections to the idea that because we have the scientific knowledge to do something, such as clone human beings, then we should do it.

## Ecologism Rests on a Naive Distinction between 'Nature' and 'Society'

Throughout this chapter we have operated with the distinction between 'nature' and 'society', or the natural world and the human world. This accords with an everyday sense that there is a distinction: imagine looking out of the window at a tree-lined street of apartment blocks. Human beings have constructed the apartments and planted the trees, but because the apartments function according to human design, whereas the trees, despite being planted in neat lines, develop according to processes understood, but not 'set in motion', by human beings, we reasonably enough say the trees are part of nature, and the apartments are part of the artificial, human world.

That distinction is valid, but difficulties arise for ecologists when they make further claims: (a) that the natural world forms an interconnected whole *set apart from* the human world, and on which the human world is dependent; (b) that the natural world has intrinsic value, whereas the human world does not. The interconnectedness–separateness thesis can be challenged in the following way: there is no part of the globe untouched by human activity, and therefore insofar as there are connections, these are between the two worlds. Of course, the ecological critique rests precisely on accepting as a fact that human beings have transformed the world, and for the worse! Their point is that we depend on the natural world, understood as a whole connected together through complex processes, such that the human world is secondary. This claim could be accepted by *environmentalists*: certainly, if we do not allow, say, fish stocks to be replenished because of over-fishing or marine pollution, there will be no fish in the supermarket, and no profits to be made from fish.

An *ecological* argument would require accepting not simply (a), but also (b): the natural world is separate and valuable in a way the human world is not. This is open to challenge. Venice is clearly one of the great human creations – a 'world heritage site' – built on a lagoon, and requiring considerable human intervention in the natural environment. That city, or at least the part of it most people understand as Venice, is under threat of sinking due to the combined effects of subsidence and rising sea levels; in addition, the lagoon is polluted through heavy industrial activity in the region. That there are natural processes at work, which are in part the result of a global environmental crisis, can be accepted by *environmentalists*, but that Venice itself has less value than naturally occurring phenomena is surely open to challenge. That, however, is the conclusion that an *ecologist* must draw.

The priority given to the natural world by ecologists rests in part on a 'hierarchy of needs', with physical reproductive needs at the base, and other needs, or 'wants', of lesser importance. In the aftermath of the 2001 outbreak of 'foot-and-mouth' disease in Britain there was a debate about whether the relatively generous compensation paid to farmers should be extended to hoteliers and other parts of the tourist industry that had been badly affected by the outbreak. A Green Party spokesperson argued that food production was 'more fundamental' to human beings than tourism. Behind this comment lay an image of British society as a self-subsistent food economy, where other human activities were somehow frivolous in comparison. Yet people working in the tourist industry were dependent on that income to satisfy *their* basic needs.

Ecologists sometimes suggest that we can have the benefits of the modern human world even if we remove the material conditions – industrialism – for modernity. Kirkpatrick Sale argues for a self-sufficient community which does not engage in significant trade with other communities; such a community would ensure 'a wide range of food, some choices in necessities and some sophistication in luxuries, [and] the population to sustain a university and large hospital and a symphony orchestra' (Sale in Dobson, 2000: 118). But setting aside economic considerations about whether a low-trade world could sustain a high level of medical care, the social world that gives rise to relatively cosmopolitan institutions such as universities or orchestras has been one in which there is interaction between communities and cultures. Perhaps the argument is that we should preserve the cultural achievements of a modern industrial society, but without the costs; if that were Sale's point, then it would amount to a much more generous compliment to an industrial society than most ecologists are prepared to pay.

## Ecologism either (a) Assumes a Naively Optimistic View of Human Nature, or (b) Requires an Unrealistic Transformation of Human Nature

If there is an environmental crisis, then what kind of response is required to overcome it? Presumably something has to change in terms of the relationship between human beings and nature. There are three possibilities: (a) changes in technology that conserve resources, slow down depletion or allow for economic growth without serious environmental consequences; (b) changes in the way we organise society, providing incentives or sanctions so as to alter behaviour; (c) changes in human motivation, which alter behaviour without requiring external incentives or sanctions. Ecologists are sceptical about (a), and prefer that (b), social and political changes, follow from (c), changes in motivation. It is significant that Hardin rejects (a) and (c), but endorses (b), arguing that only coercive measures will avert a global disaster.

A thread that runs through ecologism is that human behaviour in an industrialised society is bad for the environment, but also bad for human beings. This suggests that there is a 'real' human nature, which is fundamentally good, but it is distorted by human acquisitiveness, which is fed by, for example, advertising. Since the achievement of a sustainable society depends on a change in motivation, a great deal depends on the plausibility of this view of human nature. But, furthermore, ecologists must show that it is impossible to create and maintain a sustainable society without a change in motivation: technology will not fix environmental problems, and **coercion** is unacceptable and will lead to authoritarian regimes. Ecologists must argue either that the real human nature will emerge fairly quickly as we move towards sustainability, perhaps because the human benefits of such a society will soon be apparent, or that changing human beings will be a major task. That task would be made easier if it could be shown that ecologism is a reasonable political doctrine – that is, one which people with diverse beliefs could accept.

### Ecologism is a Religion, and as such Incompatible with the Value Pluralism of the Modern World

The last point brings us to a major objection raised, in particular, by liberals: ecologism, unlike environmentalism, is not simply a political programme, but requires individuals to endorse religious or spiritual beliefs that they might reasonably reject. Despite Arne Næss's insistence that ecologists can come together from a variety of different religious and philosophical perspectives, the ecological critique of industrialism identifies human motivation as the source of acquisitive attitudes, demands very significant changes in the way society is organised, and holds out the prospect of a reconciliation between human beings and nature that extends beyond political ideas. Most orthodox monotheists – Jews, Christians, Muslims – would interpret ecological ideas as a form of pantheism (earth as God) or panantheism (earth as part of God), standing against the metaphysical separation of God as creator from his creation. Many atheists would treat ecologism with the same suspicion that they treat other religions.

### Summary

Ecologism's distinctiveness can be found in its emphasis on the interconnectedness of life on earth, and the demand for a fundamental change in human relations to nature – where nature, of course, is part of humanity, and humanity part of nature.

It offers a critique of both liberalism and socialism, and while recognising the important differences between those ideologies it finds commonalities: a commitment to economic growth that is incompatible with the finite nature of the earth. Humanity's ambitions exceed the resources of its home.

## Questions

1. Are there major philosophical differences between environmentalists and ecologists?
2. Is ecologism compatible with democracy?
3. Is ecologism compatible with socialism?
4. Should an ecologist be concerned with animal rights?

## References

Declaration on Social Progress and Development: http://www.unhchr.ch/html/menu3/b/m progre.htm

Dobson, A. (2000) *Green Political Thought* London: Routledge.

Hardin, G. (1994) 'The Tragedy of the Commons' in Christine Pierce and Donald Van de Veer (eds), *People, Penguins and Plastic Trees: Basic Issues in Environmental Ethics* London: Wadsworth.

Hardin, G. (1974) 'Living on a Lifeboat', *Bioscience* 24(10), 561–68.

Kuhn, T. (1962) *The Structure of Scientific Revolutions* Chicago, Ill. and London: University of Chicago Press.

Leopold, A. (1994) 'The Land Ethic' in Christine Pierce and Donald Van de Veer (eds), *People, Penguins and Plastic Trees: Basic Issues in Environmental Ethics* London: Wadsworth.

Næss, A. (1973) 'The Shallow and the Deep, Long Range Ecology Movements' *Inquiry* 16, 95–100.

Næss, A. and Sessions, G. 'Deep Ecology Platform', at www.deepecology.org/deepplatform

## Further Reading

Dobson (2000) is the clearest introduction to Green political thought. Other useful discussions of ecological thought and practice include: John Barry, *Rethinking Green Politics: Nature, Virtue, and Progress* (London: Sage, 1999); Alan Carter, *A Radical Green Political Theory* (London & New York: Routledge, 1999); John Dryzek, *The Politics of the Earth: Environmental Discourses* (New York: Oxford University Press, 2005); Robyn Eckersley, *The Green State: Rethinking Democracy and Sovereignty* (Cambridge, Mass. and London: MIT Press, 2004); David Pepper, *Eco-socialism: From Deep Ecology to Social Justice* (London: Routledge, 1993). A good collection of the most important writings on ecologism is Andrew Dobson (ed.), *The Green Reader* (London: Deutsch, 1991). More philosophical are the following: John Benson, *Environmental Ethics: An Introduction with Readings* (London: Routledge, 2000); Robert Elliot (ed.), *Environmental Ethics* (Oxford: Oxford University Press, 1995); Robert Elliot and Arran

Gare (eds), *Environmental Philosophy: a Collection of Readings* (Milton Keynes: Open University Press, 1983); Dale Jamieson (ed.), *A Companion to Environmental Philosophy* (Malden, Mass. and Oxford: Blackwell, 2003); Robin Attfield, *Environmental Philosophy: Principles and Prospects* (Aldershot: Avebury, 1994).

## Weblinks

The following sites are 'theoretical' in orientation:

- A very extensive list of links: http://www.erraticimpact.com/~ecologic/
- A couple of websites (largely) hostile to ecologism and environmentalism: http://www.lomborg.com/ (Lomborg is author of *The Skeptical Environmentalist,* a book in which he questions the global warming thesis); http://www.environmentalism.com/

These sites are activist in nature:

- http://www.foe.co.uk/
- http://www.earthwatch.org/
- http://www.greenpeace.org/international/

On nuclear power:

- Environmentalists for Nuclear Energy (Lovelock is a member of this organisation, and the article discussed above can be found here): http://www.ecolo.org/
- World Nuclear Associaton (another pro-nuclear power body) is: http://www.world-nuclear.org/
- Union of Concerned Scientists (US organisation opposed to nuclear energy): http://www.ucsusa.org/clean_energy/nuclear_safety/index.cfm
- Swedish Anti-nuclear Movement: http://www.folkkampanjen.se/engfront.html

# Chapter 10

# Fundamentalism

## Introduction

Politicians and the media speak more and more about the threat of 'fundamentalism' and how fundamentalism stands at odds with liberalism and democracy. But what is fundamentalism? How and why does it arise? Is it solely an Islamic phenomenon, or can other religions also have their fundamentalist proponents? Indeed, we will argue that all ideologies can be expressed in a fundamentalist fashion. What is the relationship between fundamentalism and the contemporary world?

## Chapter Map

In this chapter we will explore:

- Fundamentalism as a relatively new concept and more than a label.

- Fundamentalism as an ideology that can be either secular or religious.

- Fundamentalism and 'fundamentals'. The contradictory relationship to modernity.

- The rejection of democracy and the propensity to violence.

- The relationship between Islam and fundamentalism. The link between fundamentalism and the Christian right in the United States. Fundamentalism in Israel.

- Huntington's 'clash of civilisations' and fundamentalism.

# The Diversity of Fundamentalisms

A Palestinian boy runs in front of the controversial security barrier in Jerusalem, 5 January 2004

You are poring over the newspaper one day and note the bewildering array of references to fundamentalism. There are chilling quotations from Osama Bin Laden. There is also a piece on the election campaign of the American president with emphasis on his concern to placate, and yet somehow distance himself from, Christian fundamentalists. Meanwhile the Israeli president is under fire for seeking to move any settlers out of (a few) Palestinian areas, and there is speculation as to whether he is doing this in order to maintain the other settlements that the international community deems illegal. His critics within Israel are labelled 'Jewish fundamentalists'. In the Business section of the paper there is a lively debate about globalisation with one of the contenders referring to 'market fundamentalism'. The paper seems to assume that the term 'fundamentalist' is self-explanatory, although it is clear that very different movements are being given the same label. Most are religious, but not all, and each is strongly opposed to the other.

- Is the concept of fundamentalism coherent? Consider whether the term applies to all religions, or to one religion in particular.

- It is often noted that in Enver Hoxha's (communist) Albania, religion was actually banned while portraits of the 'leader' peered out from every tree. Can someone committed to atheism, such as a Marxist, or a secularist, also be fundamentalist in character?

- Fundamentalists claim that they are seeking to restore the purity of their particular creed. Yet fundamentalism seems to be a reaction to change and modernity. Just what is the relationship between fundamentalism and contemporary life?

- We are continually being told that the world is becoming a global village. Has globalisation something to do with the rise of fundamentalism?

## Label or Concept?

Fundamentalism is a relatively recent idea (although an old phenomenon). It relates to the interpretation of a creed that is intolerant of argument and debate, so that those who oppose a particular variety of fundamentalism are deemed 'enemies' and 'traitors'. Giddens, a sociologist who writes extensively on fundamentalism, comments that the term has only come into currency quite recently. As late as 1950 there was no entry for the word in the *Oxford English Dictionary* (Giddens, 1994: 6). This gives us an important clue as to its meaning, since although fundamentalists see themselves as looking to some kind of 'original' blueprint, the concept, as we will define it, is quite new and cannot be understood without analysing the pressures of the modern world.

see
Introduction,
pp. 3–9

Sidahmed and Ehteshami argue that fundamentalism is a label rather than a concept (1996: 14), and it is true that the term can be used in a dogmatic manner without thought being given as to what it might mean. But it will be argued here that the term can be a concept (i.e. something with a proper theoretical basis) and, therefore, it is not merely a descriptive but an evaluative term. Fundamentalism tells us what a creed looks like in such a way that it is unattractive to those who are open-minded. As with all political concepts, fundamentalism is both descriptive and evaluative, and the fact that the concept will be used negatively (as something to avoid), does not mean that we are not describing it as accurately as we can.

Fundamentalism (as are liberalism and secularism) is a contested category (i.e. it arouses controversy) but this does not make it so ambiguous that coherent exposition is impossible. We are not simply using the concept as a term of abuse: we are trying to expound it in as fair a way as we can.

## Fundamentalism and Religion

The term fundamentalism was first applied in a religious context at about the turn of the last century, and referred to a defence of Protestant orthodoxy against the encroachments of modern thought. In the first decade of the twentieth century a series of 12 volumes entitled *The Fundamentals* was produced in the United States, containing 90 articles written by Protestant theologians. Three million copies were printed and distributed free of charge. But, as the *New Oxford Dictionary* points out, although one of the meanings of fundamentalism does relate to a strict and literal interpretation of the Bible by Protestants, the term, says the dictionary, can also be linked to any religion or ideology, 'notably Islam'.

Certainly, within religion, 'restorationist' movements in Christianity and Judaism show striking similarities to fundamentalist Islamic movements. Recent developments in Hinduism and Shinto also reveal commonalities with what is happening elsewhere (Kepel, 1994: 2–3). Moreover, fundamentalism can refer not only to any religion, but to any ideology; for example, reference is often made to 'market fundamentalism'. Any ideology, no matter how potentially tolerant, can be presented in fundamentalist terms, and therefore we cannot agree with the argument that the term relates essentially to understanding religion.

It is true that one fundamentalism feeds off another, and the construction of globalisation in fundamentalist terms has provoked a defensive religious fundamentalism as a response. The idea that the world has to conform to a view of liberty and democracy that stems from the White House in the United States – a fundamentalist kind of liberalism – has encouraged groups to espouse, for example, an Islamic fundamentalism in opposition.

Giddens comments that fundamentalism protects a *principle* as much as a set of doctrines, and hence can arise in religions such as Hinduism and Buddhism that had hitherto been ecumenical and tolerant. Fundamentalism, he adds, not only develops in religion but can arise in any domain of life subject to forces undermining traditional forms – whether this concerns the idea of nation, relations between people of different cultures, the structure of the family or relations between men and women. People feel threatened by these changes and look for ideas that attack the European Union, feminism, anti-racism, or whatever. This reaction need not (as our examples suggest) take a purely religious form. Secular ideologies may also be expressed in fundamentalist fashion. Think of the interpretation of French republicanism used to justify banning the headscarf among Muslim schoolgirls. The neo-conservatives in the United States could be described as fundamentalists even though they do not subscribe to Islam, and militantly atheist regimes such as Stalin's Russia could be seen as treating Marxism in a fundamentalist fashion.

It is wrong, therefore, to assume that fundamentalism has to be religious in character, let alone Islamic, although veiled Muslim women and bearded Muslim men, book burners and suicide bombers have emerged, as Sayyid points out, as fundamentalist icons in Hollywood films, including, for example, *Not Without My Daughter* and *True Lies* (Sayyid, 1997: 8).

## Exercise

You live in a cosmopolitan city that has a large Muslim population. One day you pass a stall where people are handing out literature and you are surprised to see that freedom is regarded as a pernicious Western concept. When you suggest that the answer to the world's problems is 'more democracy', it is clear that those handing out the literature vigorously disagree and argue that only a return to 'true Islam' can save the world.

- Is this an accurate picture of the Islamic tradition? You have Muslim neighbours who seem quite liberal minded.

- Strong opposition by Islamic fundamentalists to Darwinism is expressed. Where else have you heard opposition to Darwin's theory of evolution?

- Your friend, who hears this debate, says that all religion is wrong, and this is why she is a convinced secularist. Can secularism be as intolerant and 'judgemental' as religious fundamentalism?

## Fundamentals and Fundamentalism

Some writers suggest that fundamentalism merely involves a concern with the 'fundamentals' of a creed. This is far too broad a view of fundamentalism, and it is also somewhat naive. It leads writers to describe as fundamentalist mainstream groups that are pluralistic, democratic and inclusivist (Moussalli, 1998: 14).

A useful definition and observation is the following. Fundamentalism is a tendency that 'manifests itself, as a strategy or set of strategies, by which beleaguered believers attempt to preserve their distinct identity as a people or group'. This identity is felt to be at risk in the contemporary era, and these believers fortify it 'by a selective retrieval of doctrines, beliefs and practices from a sacred past'. These retrieved fundamentals are refined, modified and sanctioned in a spirit of shrewd pragmatism, as a bulwark against the encroachment of outsiders. The fundamentals are accompanied by 'unprecedented claims and doctrinal innovations'. These retrieved and updated fundamentals are meant to regain the same charismatic intensity today that (it is believed) was in evidence when the 'original' identity was forged from formative revelatory experiences long ago (Sidahmed and Ehteshami, 1996: 5).

Although fundamentalists hark back to a past that they seek to re-enact, this past is heavily doctored with mythology. The retrieval by fundamentalists (as was pointed out above) is 'selective' and 'innovatory'. Tariq Ali comments that fundamentalist Islamists chart a route to the past that, mercifully for the people of the seventh century, never existed (2002: 304). This is why it cannot be said that all Muslims are 'fundamentalists'. The leaders of fundamentalist movements are not theologians, but social thinkers and political activists.

It is often assumed that fundamentalists are genuinely concerned with resurrecting the fundamentals of a religious system. Hiro speaks of Islamic fundamentalists as releasing Islam from scholastic cobwebs and ideas imbibed from the West (1988: 1–2). But this, in our view, is not so. Fundamentalists are not conservatives trying to recover old truths. They want to remould the world in the light of doctrines that are quite new. Take the view that the regime in Saudi Arabia has of the Islamic religion. It can certainly be described as extremely conservative, but it is not fundamentalist. On the contrary, the gap between the wealthy few and the majority of salaried Saudis has been exploited by fundamentalist forces. It would be more accurate to say that conservative governments such as the regime in Saudi Arabia has provoked fundamentalism, rather than being fundamentalist itself. The fact that the royal family is pragmatic in its domestic and foreign policy and adopts a Western outlook and behaviour instigates the growth of fundamentalist tendencies as a reaction to it (Nehme, 1998: 277; 284).

Of course, terminology differs. Roy makes a distinction between an Islamism that is willing to get involved in social and political action in revolutionary fashion and a 'neo-fundamentalism' that is concerned simply with religious teaching (1999: 36). What Roy calls Islamists we call fundamentalists, and it is for this reason that we identify Islamic fundamentalism, for example, as a militant and anti-modernist movement that exploits Islam rather than seeking to defend its basic tenets. Muslims in general oppose violence and militancy: the Islamic University of Gaza may want people to return 'to our basics' (Jensen, 1998: 203), but it is not fundamentalist. Fundamentalists, as we define them, may claim a respect for fundamentals, but we should not overlook the cynicism, demagoguism (i.e. liberties taken with logic and reason) and 'selective retrieval' involved in their activity.

## Modernity and Tradition

Ali describes religious fundamentalism as a product of modernity (2002: ix) and yet, as will become evident later, it is hostile to modernity. This is true of all fundamentalism, whether religious or secular. As Kepel points out, Christian fundamentalists seek not to modernise Christianity but to Christianise modernity, just as Islamic fundamentalists seek, he says, to 'Islamize modernity' (1994; 66; 2).

Fundamentalism is best described (forgive the apparent paradox) as a modern movement opposed to modernity. Fundamentalism is a product of modernisation – urban and intellectual in character. Fundamentalists use modern methods of propagating their ideas and recruiting adherents: what they attack are the emancipatory traditions, the belief in freedom, equality and self-government, that have characterised modern ideas since the Enlightenment. It is important to emphasise here the tension between form and content. Armstrong argues that fundamentalisms are 'essentially modern movements' that could take root in no other time than our own. They have absorbed, she says, the pragmatic rationalism of modernity that enables them to create an ideology which provides a plan of action (2001: viii; xiii).

But how can fundamentalism be *both* traditionalist and anti-traditionalist, modern and anti-modern? It is traditionalist in the sense that fundamentalists *claim* to be resurrecting traditions (although, as has been argued, such claims need to be taken with a healthy pinch of salt). But, as Giddens notes, the point about traditions is that you do not have to justify them – they normally contain their own truth, a ritual truth, asserted as correct by the believer (1994: 6). Fundamentalism arises in the novel circumstances of global communication (1994: 48), where traditions are being challenged, and these traditions cannot, it seems, be effectively defended in the old way. Hence the context is one of profound anti-traditionalism. We rather like Roy's description of Islamism (or what we call Islamic fundamentalism) as the *shariah* (the holy book dealing with law) plus electricity (1999: 52), while Armstrong speaks of fundamentalist movements having a 'symbiotic relationship' with modernity (2001: xiii).

The backdrop of fundamentalism is a globalised world in which cross-cultural communication has not only become possible but also obligatory. Fundamentalism accentuates the purity of a given set of doctrines, not simply because it wishes to set them off against other doctrines, but because it rejects the idea of debate and discussion with people who have different points of view. It is opposed to what Giddens calls a dialogic engagement of ideas in a public space (1994: 6). While fundamentalists reject the notion of a 'changing of places' essential to dialogue, the audience is nevertheless global. An imaginary tradition is championed in an aggressive, dogmatic and polarising way.

There is a curious love/hate relationship to the market. On the one hand, Osama Bin Laden T-shirts can be seen for sale in shops in Mozambique next to T-shirts with adverts for Coca-Cola emblazoned on them. Suya Mura is a traditional village in Japan that is publicised for its tourist potential (Giddens, 1994: 86–7). At the same time, fundamentalism Bin Laden-style rages against the wickedness and corruption of international capitalism. Modern technology, the internet and the Wall Street stock exchange are utilised in order to advance fundamentalist opposition to modernity – i.e. to liberal values.

Not surprisingly, many of those who challenge modernity are themselves products par excellence of this modernity. They have been through a secular education often with a bias towards technical disciplines, and they handle sacred texts in a way that challenges the conservatism of rabbis, (Muslim) ulemas or priests (Kepel, 1994: 4). Armstrong makes the point that whereas Westerners tended to see the Ayatollah Khomeini – the first ruler of Islamic Iran – as a throwback to the Middle Ages, much of his message and ideology was modern. He described Islam as 'the religion of those who desire freedom and independence. It is the school of those who struggle against imperialism' (Armstrong, 2001: 250; 256; see also Sayyid, 1997: 90). A very modernist formulation! Gray notes that radical Islamist views resemble European anarchism far more than they do Islamic orthodoxy (2003: 24; 79).

Indeed some writers even see a kind of postmodernism in fundamentalism. Brown speaks of it as a 'foundationalism without a grand narrative' (1995: 35). In other words, fundamentalism combines cosmopolitan relativism (Muslims are different) – hence there are no 'grand narratives' that many postmodernists say they dislike – with a dogmatic belief in rightness and wrongness – hence 'foundationalism'. Falk argues, for example, that politicised religion is a form of postmodern protest against the mechanisation, atomisation and alienation of the modern world (cited by Wolff, 1998: 50). But we would see postmodernism as a critique of modernism that goes beyond it, rather than an anti-liberalism which rejects democracy, the Enlightenment and universal promise. It is, therefore, better to speak of fundamentalism as an anti-modernism, rather than a postmodernism.

It is the deficiencies of modernity that produce fundamentalism. It has been said that the question of fundamentalism cannot be dissociated from the process of nation and state building and its failures. A fundamentalist is someone who has become conscious of the acute inequalities within and between countries, but who is also convinced that the current strategies of development will not succeed in alleviating them. Fundamentalism has developed in a situation where the **state** failed to provide the newly urbanised citizens with structures to replace the old communal ones. The alienated individual projects his frustrations on a world scale, seeking to create a community of believers who share a similar *Weltanschauung* (world outlook) (Zoubir, 1998: 127; 131–2).

It does not follow that, because fundamentalism is a kind of modernist reaction against modernity, we defend modernity. On the contrary, it is (as noted above) the failures of modernity that have created such an extreme and negative reaction. We are certainly not implying that liberalism or modernity itself is a desirable and natural 'norm'.

## Fundamentalism, Democracy and Violence

The refusal of dialogue makes fundamentalism dangerous, for increasingly the use of violence is counter-productive and the only way of advancing humanity's interests is through argument and debate. By rejecting democracy, fundamentalism necessarily leads to violence.

(Abstract) ethics, not democracy, is the watchword, and the value expected in the political domain is not liberty, but justice (Roy, 1999: 10–11). Choueiri, in his analysis of Islamic fundamentalism, comments that democracy is seen as a violation of God's sovereignty – the desires and opinions of secular majorities represent an outright usurpation of God's laws. Choueiri notes that, in fundamentalist eyes, humanity has reverted to an age of ignorance. Some movements support democracy simply as a means to a non-democratic end (1996: 20–1). As Ali Belhaj, star preacher for the Islamic Salvation Front in Algeria, has put it, democracy is no more than a corruption or ignorance that robs God of his power and seeks to bestow this power upon his creatures (Kepel, 1994: 46).

Is it true that all forms of fundamentalism reject democracy? Kepel argues that the various movements of re-Christianisation cannot reject democracy as an alien graft on their own system: they have to speak the language of democracy and this 'democratic constraint' influences what these movements actually say (1994: 197). Yet Armstrong cites a US fundamentalist who praises the early puritans for *opposing* democracy, and she refers to US fundamentalists who see democracy as a modern heresy to be abolished, and look towards the reorganisation of society along biblical lines (2001: 273; 361). Moreover, as will be seen in Wilcox's (1996) analysis of the religious right, fundamentalist Christianity can also be militantly exclusivist and extol violence. Naturally, different fundamentalist movements are affected by their particular environment (the degree of poverty, unemployment and authoritarianism), and this accounts for their differential severity and harshness.

Nevertheless, the link between fundamentalism and the dislike for democracy applies generally, and explains the propensity by fundamentalists for violence. Thus the public and private violence of men against women – a gender fundamentalism – involves a refusal to communicate in situations in which patriarchal conditions are under challenge. There is no question of men imagining what it is like to be a woman, for differences are absolutised, and used to justify the domination over the 'other'. Similarly, with the violence of what Giddens calls exclusionary ethnic groups (1994: 48): fundamentalisms of various kinds can act to sharpen up pre-existing ethnic or cultural differences. Whenever fundamentalism takes hold degenerate spirals of communication threaten where one antipathy feeds on another antipathy, hate is heaped upon hate (Giddens, 1994: 243; 245).

Violence, as we have argued elsewhere, involves a radical absence of common interest, so that the target of violence is seen as an enemy rather than a fellow human being. Active trust established through an acceptance of difference is the enemy of fundamentalism. By difference, Giddens means the opposite of what we have called 'division'. Dialogic democracy involves a recognition that everyone is different and this difference is a positive and unifying attribute (1994: 129). In a post-traditional age, he argues, nationalism stands close to aggressive fundamen-talisms, embraced by neo-fascist groups as well as by other sorts of movements or collectivities (1994: 132). The point about fundamentalism, as it is conceptualised here, is that it is *new* so that, as Giddens points out, neo-fascism is not fascism in its original form – it is a species of fundamentalism steeped with the potential for violence (1994: 251).

## What is Islamic Fundamentalism?

It is widely held that fundamentalism is a 'green threat' in the post-cold war world. The Islamic religion is seen as the new enemy to democracy, the US and the West – a cancer destroying 'Western' values. But to conflate the Islamic religion with fundamentalism is itself a fundamentalist distortion of reality, intended to project all conflicts as a war either by or against Islam, some kind of resurrection of the crusades. It is a view held by the Christian right and extreme Zionists, and it involves a dramatic and unwarranted homogenising of Islam.

As Ali points out in his revealingly entitled *The Clash of Fundamentalisms*, the world of Islam has not been monolithic for thousands of years. The social and cultural differences between Senegalese, Chinese, Indonesian, Arab and South Asian Muslims are far greater than similarities they share with non-Muslim members of the same nationality (2002: 274). Roy even argues that Islamism has 'social-democratised' itself (1999: xi). A comparison between Zoubir's (1998) analysis of Islamic fundamentalism in Algeria and Robinson's (1998) assessment of the Muslim Brotherhood in Jordan demonstrates not only the diversity within Islam, but the necessary features that make up an Islamic *fundamentalism*.

Following the successful liberation war with France the state in Algeria, Zoubir points out, lost its legitimacy and its *raison d'être* in the eyes of a youthful and disenchanted population (1998: 132). Little was done to provide employment or housing for the young people who deserted the countryside for the shanty towns. The Algerian regime offered modernisation without secularisation, with a demagogic and equivocal position on religious and cultural issues. It was, and still is, corrupt and inefficient, and this has led to an identity crisis with disastrous consequences – an identity crisis that has been intensified by the defeat of Arab nationalism and the humiliations suffered by Arab regimes against Israel (1998: 133). Many mosques were built in Algeria and, were it not for their totalitarian conception, the fundamentalists could have provided the basis of a credible counter-hegemony programme along classic Gramscian lines. But whereas the Italian Marxist Gramsci urged the construction of a working-class hegemony or intellectual and moral supremacy based upon socialist values, fundamentalists in Algeria have sought an illiberal and anti-democratic domination. Many of the individuals who followed Nasser or Marx in the 1960s are fundamentalists today. Chaotic liberalisation of trade, and a cut in food subsidies and unemployment have all fed fundamentalism. Large segments of society have been marginalised, leading to widespread anger, despair, banditry and utter hatred towards the state and its clienteles (Zoubir, 1998: 139).

Robinson's study of Muslim brethren in Jordan and their party, the Islamic Action Front (formed in 1992 when parties were legalised) is a study of Islamists who are not fundamentalists since, as Robinson points out, these organisations express their opposition to secularism in democratically permissible ways (1998: 173). A leader of the Muslim Brethren says: 'we have never believed in violence or intellectual terrorism' (Robinson, 1998: 182). But as it becomes more working class in composition and Palestinian influence increases, the Islamic Action Front has become increasingly divided (1998: 189). If inequalities continue to grow and the crisis in Israel/Palestine worsens, then this Islamic movement may turn to fundamentalism, not because it is Islamic, but because it will react negatively to a failing modernity.

Algeria not only offers a classic case study of the conditions that give rise to (Islamic) fundamentalism, but it also provides a model of how not to deal with the problem. Zoubir notes that the FIS (Islamic Salvation Front) emerged as the most mobilised and best-structured party in the country – it was legalised in 1989 despite its avowed opposition to republican principles (1998: 143–4). It looked certain to win the elections in 1992 when the army stepped in, cancelled the elections and banned the organisation. Since 1992 terrorism and banditry have plagued the country and successive governments have failed to regain a minimum level of trust and legitimacy (Zoubir, 1998: 154).

Ali argues that had the FIS been allowed to become the government then divisions beneath the surface would have come to the fore. The army could then have warned that any attempt to tamper with rights guaranteed by the constitution, would not be tolerated (2002: 306). This would, at least, have put the argument squarely in favour of the concept of democracy that the FIS explicitly rejected. In fact, since the army's counter-productive action and the mutual escalation of terrorism it has engendered, faith in the FIS has also been eroded, as Zoubir points out, and the only concern by Algerians is civil peace, physical and economic security (1998: 157).

The comparison between the FIS in Algeria and the Islamic Action Front in Jordan is revealing. It not only shows that there is significant diversity between Islamic movements even in the Middle East, but reveals the kinds of conditions which need to be present before a fundamentalist movement can take root. Islamic ideology differs considerably from country to country or movement to movement. It delineates a wide spectrum of thought, from the transparently ultra-conservative to a convolution of eclectic liberal ideas. It is thus inappropriate to categorise, as Bina puts it, all these movements as 'fundamentalist'. If applied indiscriminately the yardstick of fundamentalism runs counter to the very act of reconciliation of Islam with existing social formations that are, by necessity, transitory and historical (1994: 17–18). Adherence to Islam, as with other religious movements and movements in general, necessarily reflects the particular conditions in which fundamentalism takes root.

Nasser's Egypt had been a beacon of Arab progressivism. Nasser sought to destroy the Muslim Brotherhood and his government tried to turn the clerical graduates of the Islamic University of Al Azhar into mere transmission belts for his ideology. Nasser treated the Muslim Brotherhood with 'unexampled brutality' and those leaders who had not been hanged took refuge in oil sheikdoms in the Arabian Peninsular (Kepel, 1994: 18). In 1966 Sayyid Qutb, a member of the Brotherhood, was executed: his message, hugely influential, was that true Muslims should break with the existing world and build a real Islamic state (Kepel, 1994: 20). Armstrong quotes his comment that 'Humanity today is living in one large brothel! One only has to glance at its press, films, fashion shows, beauty contests, ballrooms, wine-bars, and broadcasting stations' (2001: 240). After the traumatic military defeat by Israel in 1967, Islamic orthodoxy began to gain increasing numbers of adherents. The sharp increase in the price of oil that followed the Arab–Israeli war of 1973 accelerated the flight from the countryside.

| Biography | Sayyid Qutb (1906–66) |
|---|---|

Born in a small town in Upper Egypt, Qutb moved to Cairo as an adolescent in order to further his education. He obtained his first job as an inspector in the Ministry of Education.

Qutb began to write in the late 1920s as a poet and literary critic, presenting social and political matters from a secular standpoint. By 1948, however, he adopted a more Islamic perspective, according to the limited knowledge of Islam that he had. *Social Justice*, his first Islamic book, was published in 1949.

After his return from a two-year study tour in the United States that ended in 1950, Qutb joined al-Ikhwan al-Muslimun (the Muslim Brotherhood), becoming one of their leading spokespeople. He sought to understand Islam in a new way, writing a *tafsir* (explanation) of the Qu'rān called *Fi Thilalil-Qu'rān* (In the Shade of the Qu'rān). Qutb was not interested in following the traditional approach of explaining the Qu'rān. He used his own opinions to expound the Qu'rān in a way that was over and above traditional sources. He treated the Qu'rān in ultramodernist fashion – as a work of art, not a repository of literal truth.

Qutb came up with a set of statements collected from all of the various Islamic sects that have sprung up since the earliest years of Islamic civilisation. He was influenced by the *Mu'tazili*/Sufi philosophical school of thought – a system of belief that runs completely contrary to the so-called 'Wahhabi' creed. His revolutionary ideology of *takfir* (excommunication) appealed to the youth who were increasingly critical of the Muslim Brotherhood. This accounts for Qutb's appeal to insurrectionary groups.

Qutb condemned the separation of the sacred from the secular in Christianity and warned that Islamic reformers threatened to create the same divide in Islam, preventing it from ordering all aspects of life according to the precepts of the Qu'rān. After his movement openly opposed the government of Jamal Abdul Nasser, Qutb spent the rest of his life in prison after 1954, except for a brief period in 1964–5. After being temporarily released Qutb was reapprehended, tried and executed for treason in 1966.

Yet in Egypt, as elsewhere, it is possible to be an Islamist without being a fundamentalist. Abul Fotouh, who is head of the Egyptian Medical Association and a leader of the Muslim Brotherhood, does not find the Western way of life at odds with Islam. 'At the end of the day', he comments, 'we have a set of common humanist values; justice, freedom, human rights and democracy' (*Economist*, 2003: 6). However, Hammoud indicates that in Egypt it is the particular circumstances rather than the particular religion that have given rise to a fundamentalist opposition. The economic situation has led to increased inequality, productivity has decreased and unemployment has rocketed (Zoubir, 1998: 306). Fundamentalists in

## Myths about Fundamentalism

- Fundamentalism is necessarily about religion.
- Fundamentalists seek to return to 'fundamentals'.
- Fundamentalists are hostile to all things modern.
- All Muslims are fundamentalists.

Egypt, as elsewhere, have begun to offer social and relief services that the modern state has signally failed to provide. The use of repression and emergency against opponents has helped to create a revolutionary opposition, and devastated confidence in notions of dialogue and consensus that are crucial to a democratic culture (1998: 329–31).

## US Fundamentalism and the Religious Right

Anyone who thinks that fundamentalism is a purely Islamic phenomenon should pay some attention to the ideas and impact of Christianity in Italy (and France) or on the religious right in the United States. When US Christian fundamentalists Jerry Falwell and Pat Robertson declared that the attacks on 11 September were a judgement of God for the sins of secular humanists, they were expressing a viewpoint not far removed from that of the Muslim hijackers (Armstrong, 2001: viii). In Italy, an organisation called the 'People's Movement' provided a valuable back-up resource for the Christian Democrats, although it reserved the right to campaign against any Christian Democrat suspected of harbouring secularist sympathies. Its weekly journal stigmatised secularised Christians as 'Catho-communists' (Kepel, 1994: 72–3). In France, an estimated 200,000 people have been involved with a charismatic revival, with supporters making common cause with those Islamic fundamentalists outraged by the 'Islamic veil' affair, where the state insisted that Muslim schoolgirls must dress in a secular fashion.

Fundamentalism (strictly defined) in the United States was rooted historically in the American South, and the depression of 1929 was seen 'as a sign of God's vindictive punishment on an apostate America as well as a sign of Christ's imminent return' (Kepel, 1994: 107). A poll in 1969 revealed that there were some 1,300 evangelical Christian radio and television stations, with an audience of about 130 million. Between 1965 and 1983 enrolment in evangelical schools increased sixfold, and about 100,000 fundamentalist children were taught at home. The enemy were 'secular humanists' who, fundamentalists alleged, sought to reduce the world to slavery (Armstrong, 2001: 267; 269; 272).

In Kepel's view, Reagan was elected in 1980 largely because he captured the votes of most of the evangelical and fundamentalist (using the term somewhat narrowly) electors who followed the advice of politico-religious bodies such as the Moral Majority. Just as the Islamic militants, the young US fundamentalists have had higher education (usually studying the applied sciences), and they have come from the large cities in the northern and southern states (Kepel, 1994: 8, 137).

Boston argues in his critique of Pat Robertson that Robertson's political unit, the Christian Coalition (launched in 1989) has a budget of $25 million with 1.7 million members and 1,600 local affiliates in all 50 states (1996: 16). Robertson owns the Christian Broadcasting Network (CBN) and, in his view, only Christians and Jews are qualified to run government. Not surprisingly, he and his movement deny the separation of Church and state. His support for Israel is premised on the assumption that he believes that Zionism in Israel will unwittingly contribute to the conversion of Jews to Christianity. In the 1980s he was a champion of South Africa's system of apartheid. The wealth of CBN can be seen from the fact that the

Network can clear between $75 and $97 million tax-free profit, and the political impact of Robertson's Christian Coalition is evident in Boston's contention that it holds the country's majority party, i.e. the Republicans, in a headlock (Boston, 1996: 132; 166; 183; 238).

Predictably the Christian Coalition, as with the Moral Majority before it, is also virulently anti-feminist in character (Wilcox, 1996: 9), and Coalition supporters follow the historic pattern of religious fundamentalists of keeping themselves apart from an impure world and (in their case) doctrinally impure Christians. Wilcox estimates that about 10–15 per cent of the public support the religious right, and there may be as many as 4 million members of the Christian Right and possibly 200,000 activists in politics (1996: 36; 71). The movement has always used the best technology available. In general, the Christian Right opposes any notion of compromise, and they tend to be intolerant of those with whom they disagree. They do not accept the civil liberties of liberals, although it is true that the more members of the religious right participate in conventional politics, the more reconciled to democracy they become (1996: 107–8; 111). For many, imposing Christianity on non-believers increases the odds that the souls of these hapless infidels will spend eternity in heaven. Fringe elements (in an interesting counterpart to Muslims who believe in a punitive version of the shariah) favour Mosiac law that would involve stoning sinners (1996: 125).

Some fundamentalists showed their contempt for US law by blockading abortion clinics and, in the words of Randall Terry, saw themselves as working for a nation 'not floating in an uncertain sea of humanism, but a country whose unmoving bedrock is Higher laws' (Armstrong, 2001: 360). As with fundamentalism elsewhere, there is a reaction against modernism that Christian fundamentalists fear will inevitably erode traditional values. As Wilcox points out, there is a small but significant trend to liberalism in the US public, and young Americans are far more liberal than the older cohorts they are replacing (1996: 144). Falk has analysed the increasing convergence of religion and politics as a growing adherence to postmodernism (1988), but although postmodernism challenges the separations and dualisms of the liberal tradition, fundamentalism does not.

For this reason, liberation theology is not fundamentalist at all, but seeks to challenge religious conservatism in exciting and innovative ways. It stands in contrast to what Falk himself calls a few islands of fundamentalist success that disclose the religious revision of modernism in an oppressive direction (1988: 380). It is not the rise of postmodern religion that is fundamentalist or cultist in character. It is rather movements that reject or merely negate modernism. The West, as Falk puts it graphically, has 'killed' God with its consumerist spirit (1988: 381) so that there has been a remarkable surge of fundamentalist religion in the last few decades (1988: 385). This is why it is problematic to speak of US fundamentalism as exhibiting, in Armstrong's words, postmodern tendencies, although she is right to note that it has 'a hard-line totalitarian vision' of the future (2001: 362).

Even in the 1980s it was clear that the 'coming out' of US fundamentalists in the form of the 'moral majority' and evangelical Christianity represented a determined assault on the modern lifestyle of 'secular' Christianity. The AIDS epidemic has been seen as a kind of objective confirmation of the fundamentalist

How to read:

**Armstrong's *The Battle for God***

This is a very useful history of fundamentalism. The new preface should be carefully read and so should the introduction. Part One takes the story up to 1870, and can be skipped. Concentrate on Part Two. Chapter 5 'Battle Lines (1870–1900)' should be skim read, and so should Chapter 6 on 'Fundamentals'. Chapter 7 looks at developments between 1925 and 1960 and deserves a more careful read, while Chapters 8, 9 and 10 are important to an understanding of contemporary fundamentalism and require close attention. Although the book focuses on fundamentalism as a religious phenomenon, it does deal with Jewish, Christian and Muslim attitudes, and the after-word provides important insights into the role of religion in the modern world.

critique of modernism, and fundamentalists express their hostility to the preoccupation with means rather than ends associated with modernist solutions (Falk, 1988: 387). When Falk argues that a religion with postmodern strivings links emotion to reason and sees connections and relatedness as primary categories of knowledge (1988: 388), he demonstrates (however unwittingly) why the fundamentalism of the religious right in the United States cannot be seen in postmodernist terms. Indeed, what makes the religious right fundamentalist is the violence of its language and some of its practice (think of bombings against abortion clinics, for example), and the stark chasms it poses between the purists 'saved' and those whose lifestyle and values commit them to eternal damnation.

## Jewish Fundamentalism and the Israeli State

A tiny minority of orthodox Jews in the 1920s began to see in Zionism – a belief that Israel represents a natural homeland for the Jews – a more holistic vision after the trauma and constrictions of exile, as Armstrong notes, and they were strongly opposed to secular Zionists. In the 1940s they established their own schools (2001: 259). Rabbi Yehuda, who led the Gahlet, an elite group within religious Zionist circles, declared that every Jew 'who comes to Eretz Israel [biblical Israel] constitutes . . . another stage in the process of redemption'. The war of 1967, in which Israel conquered the Golan Heights, the West Bank and the Gaza Strip was deemed proof that redemption was under way (Armstrong, 2001: 261, 263).

Kepel sees 1977 as a signpost year in which the dominant Zionist tradition was critically re-examined as Labour lost its first election in the history of Israel. Judaism was redefined in terms of observance and ritual (1994: 6). The war of 1973 ended in 'a psychological defeat for the Jewish state', and in the confusion and questioning of certainties there emerged the Gush Emunim (Bloc of the Faithful) that became the self-proclaimed herald for the re-Judaisation of Israel.

## Four Facts about Fundamentalism

1. Fundamentalism is a concept rather than a label and it relates not simply to religion but to any ideology.
2. Although fundamentalism takes the form of a return to fundamentals, in fact fundamentalists are highly selective and innovative with regard to sacred texts.
3. Fundamentalism is a product of modernity and makes use of modern technology although it also rails against modernist ideas.
4. Fundamentalism espouses the use of violence to settle conflicts of interest, and is profoundly anti-democratic.

Gush Emunim was formed by a bloc of hawkish secularists and religious Zionists. It replaced the legal concept of the state of Israel with the biblical concept of the Land of Israel, and sought to plant more and more settlements in the occupied territories (1994: 140–1). The Zionist ideal needed to be renewed and fully realised. Israel was seen as a unique state that was not bound by international law (Armstrong, 2001: 280; 282).

After Rabbi Kook's death Gush Emunim split: a few identified the Palestinians as Amalekites, a people so cruel that God had commanded the ancient Israelites to slay them without mercy (Armstrong, 2001: 346). Terrorism was resorted to: Gush Emunim extremists were suspected of murdering students at the Islamic University of Hebron and making attempts on the lives of Palestinian mayors, and the organisation encouraged other groups to embrace the cause of re-Judaisation as well. Ultra-orthodox groups began to recruit among university students and among Sephardic Jews, who were often immigrants from the Arab countries in which groups such as Gush Emunim had been quite unknown.

Religious parties represent such groups in parliament and they exercise real leverage on coalition governments. These groups argue for a sharp break between

## Differentiating Religious Fundamentalisms

1. *Islamic fundamentalism* is not the same as devotion to Islam. Fundamentalism arises in situations of severe social, political and economic dislocation, and as the portrait of the Egyptian Muslim Brotherhood reveals, Muslims can espouse liberal and democratic values.

2. *US fundamentalism* expresses itself as a bigoted and intolerant Christianity. Its proponents have substantial resources, owning radio stations and targeting the Republican Party. US fundamentalism is anti-feminist, anti-Semitic and anti-Islam and it rejects modernity. Hence it is anti-modernist rather than postmodernist in character.

3. *Jewish fundamentalism* takes the form of a religious orthodoxy that opposes secular Zionism and seeks an Israel that is not bound by international law and expands to its biblically ordained frontiers.

## Biography — Osama Bin Laden (1957–)

Born in Saudi Arabia to a Yemeni family. His father had made his fortune in the construction business and had close ties with the Saudi royal family. At school and university Bin Laden was a member of the Muslim Brotherhood.

When the Soviet Union invaded Afghanistan in 1979 Bin Laden went to Pakistan and met Afghan rebel leaders who were resisting the occupation. He returned to Saudi Arabia to collect money and supplies for the Afghan resistance and eventually joined the fight himself. He opened a guest house in Peshawar as a stopping-off point for Arab mujahidin fighters. Eventually their numbers became so large that he built camps for them inside Afghanistan.

Bin Laden gave the umbrella group for his guest house and camps the name al-Qaeda, Arabic for 'the base'. The jihad against the USSR and the Afghan government was supported by Saudi Arabia, Pakistan and the United States, and Bin Laden is alleged to have received training from the CIA. While in Afghanistan he founded the Maktab al-Khidimat (MAK), which recruited fighters from around the world.

After the Soviet withdrawal the 'Arab Afghans', as Bin Laden's faction came to be called, failed to receive the recognition that he felt they deserved, and an offer to create an army of mujahidin to defend the Saudi kingdom after the Iraqi invasion of Kuwait was turned down.

Bin Laden was particularly incensed by the stationing of US troops on Saudi soil. He returned to Saudi Arabia to work in the family construction business, but was expelled in 1991 because of his anti-government activities there. He spent the next five years in Sudan until US pressure prompted the Sudanese government to expel him, whereupon Bin Laden returned to Afghanistan. By the mid-1990s he was calling for a global war against Americans and Jews, and in 1998 he issued a fatwa that amounted to a declaration of war against the United States.

Two simultaneous bomb attacks against US embassies in Kenya and Tanzania followed a few months later. Although Bin Laden never acknowledged responsibility, those arrested named him as their backer. Experts say that Bin Laden is part of an international Islamic front, bringing together Saudi, Egyptian and other groups. It seeks the 'liberation' of Islam's three holiest places – Mecca, Medina and Jerusalem.

Bin Laden's organisation is believed not to be a tightly knit group with a clear command structure, but a loose coalition of groups operating across continents.

US officials say that his associates may operate in more than 40 countries across Europe and North America, as well as in the Middle East and Asia. According to the US State Department, his organisation was responsible for the bombing of the World Trade Center in 1973 as well as the atrocities of 11 September, and he is regarded as 'one of the most significant sponsors of Islamic extremist activities in the world today'. A video of him was released shortly before the US presidential election in 2004.

---

Jews and gentiles, with a demand for the strict observance of prohibitions and obligations. As with Protestant fundamentalists, devout Islamists or Catholic organisations such as Communion and Liberation, secularism is seen as suffocating by 'reborn' Jews, with the Enlightenment blamed for plunging humanity into 'a hostile sea of doubt' and cutting it adrift from 'firm moorings in a theocentric universe' (Kepel, 1994: 140–3). Some, such as the Russian émigré, Herman Branover who went to Israel in 1972, found Zionism and Israeli society intolerably secular. Nevertheless, even secular Zionists were held to be the unwitting bearers of a messianic redemption (1994: 147; 155).

Ideas and Perspectives:

## Fundamentalism and the State

Some fundamentalists see the nation-state as an alien Western invention and look towards some kind of revolutionary international to cleanse the world of its imperfections. Yet the emphasis on violence and polarisation show that whether or not fundamentalists consciously support the need for a state, their arguments are statist through and through. The view of opponents as enemies to be crushed by an organisation that monopolises truth and legitimacy projects in extreme form attitudes which exist even in the liberal state. Hence the ease with which the US president after '9/11' began to invert the sentiments of al-Qaeda, declaring that 'those who are not with us, are against us'.

While we are not suggesting that the state per se is a fundamentalist organisation, there is a continuity between the extolling of violence against enemies by fundamentalists and the use of force by the state. The same cynical, instrumental and ambiguous attitude towards modernity is evident in both, so that although they are different, fundamentalism – particularly if it can be blamed on a rogue state – is grist to the mill of the state's own contradictory identity. The cover of Tariq Ali's *The Clash of Fundamentalisms* shows a juxtaposition of Bush and Bin Laden that is both amusing and insightful.

An institution that links conflict with violence and seeks to justify monopolistic practices must operate in terms of divisions and dualisms which under pressure can easily become fundamentalist in character. The state, while not fundamentalist in itself, harbours fundamentalist leanings in its bureaucratic soul.

Stern religious observance is regarded by fundamentalists here, as elsewhere, as compatible with making use of the technology and apparel of the modern world. Gush Emunim received some support from the Israeli party Likud, but subsequently resorted to a terrorism that was officially denounced (Kepel, 1994: 161; 163). A plan to dynamite the mosques on the Temple Mount in Jerusalem was foiled by the Israeli secret service. Kepel finds striking similarities between these Jewish conspirators and the Islamic fundamentalist group which assassinated Sadat in 1981 – a process of re-Judaisation or re-Islamisation taken to extremes. Gush Emunim has a membership of some 50,000, most of them resident in the occupied territories (1994: 169–70). From the mid-1980s the ultra-orthodox Jews (the haredim) became the most highly visible advocates of re-Judaisation, drawing support particularly from Sephardic Jews (1994: 178). The orthodox parties are able to wield substantial power. Although they receive only 15 per cent of the vote, they control several ministries and obtain large subsidies to strengthen their network of practising Jewish communities (Kepel, 1994: 180; 190). The Lubavitch believe that Israel should be cleansed of its Zionist accretions in order to become a 'Torahcracy' over the Land of Israel (i.e. Israel as projected in the Bible) (Kepel, 1994: 189). Hence they should, in our view, be regarded as extreme Zionists rather than anti-Zionists.

The assassination of Rabin, as did the assassination of Sadat, showed, as Armstrong points out, that two wars are being fought out in the Middle East. One is the war against Israel; the other is the war between the secularists and the religious (2001: 353).

## The 'Clash of Civilisations': a Fundamentalist Thesis?

The link between fundamentalism and the state is well exemplified by Huntington's contention that globalisation is leading to a clash of civilisations. He explicitly identifies his position with the realist theory of international relations (1996: 185), and argues that the tools of realism – a state-centric view of the world which remains basically changeless – leads to an understanding of (violent) conflict in terms of cultural and what he calls 'civilisational' difference.

While he concedes that minorities in other cultures may espouse Western values – by which Huntington means the values of what he calls democratic liberalism – dominant attitudes in non-Western cultures range from widespread scepticism to intense opposition to Western values (1996: 184). Although almost all non-Western civilisations are resistant to pressure from the West – including Hindu, Orthodox, African and even Latin American countries – the greatest resistance to Western power has come from Islam and Asia (1996: 193).

Civilisations, Huntington argues, are the ultimate human tribes, and the clash of civilisations is tribal conflict on a global scale. Trust and friendship between the civilisations will be rare (1996: 206). He sees a deeply conflictual relationship (Huntington takes it for granted that conflict is always violent), not simply between Islamic fundamentalists and Christianity but between Islam itself and Christianity. Conflict is a product of difference. In civilisational conflicts, unlike ideological ones, kin stand by their kin (1996: 209–10; 217). Thus, the Gulf War is interpreted as a war between civilisations (1996: 251), and religion, in Huntington's view, is the principal defining characteristic of civilisation, so that what he calls 'fault-line wars' are almost always between people of different religions (1996: 253). At the global level, the clash is between the West and the rest. At the micro or local level, it is between Islam and others (1996: 255). The longer a fault-line war continues, the more kin countries are likely to become involved (1996: 272).

Huntington takes the view that it is futile and counter-productive for countries to integrate their peoples. A multicivilisational United States, he argues, will not be the United States: it will be the United Nations. We must reject the divisive siren calls of multiculturalism (1996: 306–7; 310). Cultural identities inevitably collide in an antagonistic manner. 'We know who we are only when we know who we are not and often only when we know whom we are against' (1996: 21). Here is realism with a cultural twist! Nation states are and will remain the most important actors in world affairs, but their interests, associations and conflicts are increasingly shaped by cultural and civilisational factors. Huntington has recently argued that the United States is now threatened by immigrants from Latin America who are altering the national identity of traditional America.

*The Clash of Civilizations*, it could be argued, is itself a kind of fundamentalism. But not only does it not arise from, it is staunchly opposed to the Islamic tradition. Huntington believes that human history is the history of civilisations (1996: 40).

Islamic civilisation in particular and non-Western culture in general are on the ascendant, and it is wrong to assume that with 'modernisation' the world becomes more amenable to Western values. In fact, he argues, the world is becoming more modern and less Western (1996: 78). Of course people are different, but for Huntington these differences can only lead to exclusion and antagonism. Thus he insists that religion posits a basic distinction between a superior in-group and a different and inferior out-group, and cultural questions (such as the mosque at Ayodhya or the status of Jerusalem) tend to involve a yes–no, zero sum choice. For self-definition and motivation, people need enemies (1996: 97; 130). Here is the core of a quasi-fundamentalism.

Of course civilisational differences are real and important, but Huntington is wrong to see them as a necessary source of antagonism. Abou El Fadl has rightly stressed the mixed lineage of civilisations (2003: 82). It is true that many Muslims are not convinced when the US attempts to present its demonisation of political figures such as the deposed Iraqi leader Saddam Hussein as something other than raw hostility to Islam per se. But it needs to be remembered that it was a US-led NATO that intervened in Kosovo to defend the human rights of people of Muslim faith against their Serbian (and Christian Orthodox) oppressors. This hardly fits the clash of civilisations thesis.

Huntington himself links what he calls 'Muslim assertiveness' to social mobilisation, population growth, and a flood of people from the countryside into the towns (1996: 102; 98). This is surely a social rather than a purely cultural explanation for antagonism. Moreover, only a realist schooled in state-centric analysis and rooted in US triumphalism could ignore the adverse effect of the insensitivity and arrogance of US policy makers upon others. It is not that the differences he speaks of are unimportant. Rather it is that he fossilises them, fails to see the contradiction between the 'culturalist' and sociological dimensions of his analysis and ignores the tensions within the so-called Western tradition between neo-liberal and social democratic strategies and values. His work is a good example of the way in which an extreme **statism** (with its conservative and superficial assumptions) can lead in the direction of fundamentalism. Divisions are taken for granted, so that it could be argued that there is a danger that the fundamentalism of the 'other side' is merely inverted rather than transcended.

## Criticisms of Fundamentalism

- Fundamentalism differs from the state, but it is important to note the continuities. Fundamentalism seeks to monopolise the truth and use violence against enemies. So does the state. Of course fundamentalism is much more extreme than, say, the liberal state, but it takes to an extreme what are statist tendencies.

- Huntington's 'clash of civilisations' thesis is an example of a kind of academic quasi-fundamentalism that absolutises differences, and sees violent conflict in terms of cultural and 'civilisational' values. Instead of seeking to distinguish between, for example, liberal and fundamentalist Islamic doctrines, he treats Islam as a homogenous culture that is staunchly opposed to 'Western values'.

## Summary

Fundamentalism is sometimes seen as a mere label. In our view it is more than this. It is a concept despite the fact that it is a relatively new idea. Although fundamentalism is often identified with religions, any ideology, no matter how secular, can take a fundamentalist form. Fundamentalism is not about the 'fundamentals' of a creed. Fundamentalists exploit the creeds they espouse in order to make them dogmatic, militant and violent in character.

Fundamentalists have an ambivalent attitude towards modernity. On the one hand they oppose it; on the other they not only make use of it, but fundamentalism can only be understood as part of the modern world. Fundamentalism sees deep divisions between the 'pure' and the 'contaminated'. It rejects dialogue and debate, and regards violence as the only way of tackling conflict.

It is wrong to assume that Islam is necessarily (or has a particular tendency to be) fundamentalist in character. Where Islamists turn to fundamentalism this is not because of their religion, but because of the particular circumstances in which they find themselves. Fundamentalism can take a Christian form. If we look at the Christian right in the United States we see that not only are they wealthy, but they are politically influential and reject democratic values. In Israel Jewish fundamentalism has a love/hate relationship with Zionism. On the one hand, Jewish fundamentalists are concerned at the way in which some Zionists treat religion purely as a national identity rather than a sacred creed. On the other hand, they see the state of Israel as a first step towards building an Israel of biblical proportions.

The 'realism' of Huntington can be viewed as a kind of academic quasi-fundamentalism as a result of the author's contention that differences between civilisations necessarily lead to violence and antagonism.

## Questions

1.  Is fundamentalism simply about religion?
2.  Is fundamentalism inherent in Islam?
3.  Is the media treatment of fundamentalism fair?
4.  Is fundamentalism a modern phenomenon?
5.  How should democrats handle fundamentalists?

## References

Abou El Fadl, K. (2003) '9/11 and the Muslim Transformation' in M. Dudziak (ed.), *September 11 in History* Durham, N. Caro. and London: Duke University Press, 69–111.

Ali, T. (2002) *The Clash of Fundamentalisms* London: Verso.

Armstrong, K. (2001) *The Battle for God* New York: Ballantine Books.

Bina, C. (1994) 'Towards a New World Order: US Hegemony, Client-States and Islamic Alternative' in H. Mutalib and H. Taj ul-Islam (eds), *Islam, Muslims and the Modern State* Basingstoke: Macmillan, 3–30.

Boston, R. (1996) *The Most Dangerous Man in America* New York: Prometheus Books.

Brown, W. (1995) *States of Injury* Princeton, New Jersey: Princeton University Press.

Choueiri, Y. (1996) 'The Political Discourse of Contemporary Islamist Movements' in A. Sidahmed and A. Ehteshami (eds), *Islamic Fundamentalism* Boulder, Col.: Westview Press, 19–33.

*Economist, The* (2003) 'In the Name of God', 13 September.

Falk, R. (1988) 'Religion and Politics: Verging on the Postmodern' *Alternatives* XIII 379–94.

Giddens, A. (1994) *Beyond Left and Right* Cambridge: Polity Press.

Gray, J. (2003) *Al Qaeda and What It Means to be Modern* London: Faber & Faber.

Hammoud, M. (1998) 'Causes for Fundamentalist Popularity in Egypt' in A. Moussalli (ed.), *Islamic Fundamentalism* Reading: Ithaca, 303–36.

Hiro, D. (1988) *Islamic Fundamentalism* London: Palladin.

Huntington, S. (1996) *The Clash of Civilizations* New York: Simon & Schuster.

Jensen, M. (1998) 'Islamism and Civil Society in the Gaza Strip' in A. Moussalli (ed.), *Islamic Fundamentalism* Reading: Ithaca, 197–219.

Kepel, G. (1994) *The Revenge of God* Cambridge: Polity Press.

Moussalli, A. (1998) 'Introduction to Islamic Fundamentalism: Realities, Ideologies and International Politics' in A. Moussalli (ed.), *Islamic Fundamentalism* Reading: Ithaca, 3–39.

Nehme, M. (1998) 'The Islamic-Capitalist State of Saudi-Arabia: The Surfacing of Fundamentalism' in A. Moussalli (ed.), *Islamic Fundamentalism* Reading: Ithaca, 275–302.

Robinson, G. (1998) 'Islamists under Liberalization in Jordan' in A. Moussalli (ed.), *Islamic Fundamentalism* Reading: Ithaca, 169–96.

Roy, O. (1999) *The Failure of Political Islam* London and New York: I.B. Tauris.

Sayyid, B. (1997) *A Fundamental Fear* London: Zed Books.

Sidahmed, A. and Ehteshami, A. (1996) 'Introduction' in A. Sidahmed and A. Ehteshami (eds), *Islamic Fundamentalism* Boulder, Col.: Westview Press, 1–15.

Wilcox, C. (1996) *Onward Christian Soldiers* Boulder, Col.: Westview Press.

Wolff, K. (1998) '*New* New Orientalism: Political Islam and Social Movement Theory' in A. Moussalli (ed.), *Islamic Fundamentalism* Reading: Ithaca, 41–73.

Zoubir, Y. (1998) 'State, Civil Society and the Question of Radical Fundamentalism in Algeria' in A. Moussalli (ed.), *Islamic Fundamentalism* Reading: Ithaca, 123–67.

## Further Reading

- Giddens's *Beyond Left and Right* (referenced above) contains a very useful chapter on fundamentalism.

- Kepel's *The Revenge of God* (referenced above) contains invaluable material about religious fundamentalism.

- Moussalli's edited volume *Islamic Fundamentalism* (referenced above) is very useful and comprehensive.

- Wilcox's *Onward Christian Soldiers* (referenced above) provides a survey of the religious right in the United States.

- Huntington's *The Clash of Civilizations* (referenced above) is a real, if contentious, classic.

## Weblinks

Quite good on the link between religion and fundamentalism:
http://www.vexen.co.uk/religion/fundamentalism.html

For the question of the market and fundamentalism, see:
http://www.opendemocracy.net/debates/article-2-95-1248.jsp

For a piece on fundamentalism as a concept, see:
http://www.shellier.co.uk/fundamentalism.htm

# Conclusion

One of the questions that interests students of **politics** is the relationship between studying politics as an academic discipline and the practice of politics in the world outside. We thought that it might be useful to tackle this question by way of concluding this volume.

## Academic Political Theory and Politics

What makes concepts political is that they respond to conflicts that arise in the world of practice. Academic political theory should address itself to the kind of issues that politicians themselves raise, and which are part and parcel of public debate.

We have already noted, in the discussion about ideologies, the problem of trying to treat politics in a purely neutral manner as though it was a study of mere behaviour or an analysis of words. But it does not follow from a critique of what came to be called 'apolitical politics' that academic political theory has no differences from the kind of political theory which appears in party manifestos and in the speeches of politicians.

The fact that academic political theory has something in common with the theory of the publicist and propagandist does not mean that it does not also have something which is different from everyday discourse. Academic political theorists write for individuals who are either academically trained or who are anxious to educate themselves in a systematic and coherent way. Academic political theory is not primarily geared towards convincing an audience of the ideological correctness of its position. Its task is to stimulate rather than persuade, so that rhetoric is curtailed in favour of logic, and sober evidence is offered in place of extravagant emotion. It is not the task of the academic political theorist to exhort people to undertake a particular course of action at a particular time and particular place. Although thinking about a problem is crucial to solving it, this is not the same as actually organising people to implement a solution.

Academic political theory can and should seek to raise the tone of public political debate. Good causes can be strengthened by good arguments, while party positions and publicist writing provide challenging points of reference to make academic political theory more relevant and useful. There is nothing wrong in Thatcher making use of Hayek's work on the free market, even if, as many political theorists would argue, both were mistaken! Academic political theory differs from the theory of the public political world, but it is still *political* in character because, despite these differences, it has common features.

We hope that the mix of classical and new political ideologies has shown the relevance of theory to political practice, and that when you read the newspaper, see a TV programme or follow the arguments of a text, you will be better placed to make up your own mind as to the wider significance of the positions reported or championed.

# Glossary

**Abstraction**   A conceptual and practical process that mystifies and conceals underlying social relationships.

**Anarchism**   A theory that seeks to abolish the state, but adopts statist tools of analysis and hence enjoys no success.

**Atomistic**   An approach that treats individuals and entities in purely discrete terms and ignores the relationships between them.

**Capitalism**   A system of production that divides society into those who can hire the services of others, and those who are compelled to work for an employer.

**Citizen**   A person able to govern their own life. Citizenship is an emancipatory situation towards which we move, but can never actually reach.

**Civic nationalism**   The view that nations can be held together by civic ties, such as willingness to participate in legal and political institutions. The alternative view is **ethnic nationalism**.

**Class**   An identity that divides people based upon economic, social, regional, religious, gender, ethnic and other differences.

**Coercion**   A concept and practice that is close to, but not the same as, force. Coercion involves a threat to use force where this force is credible.

**Communitarianism**   A theory that stresses that all people belong to communities and can only identify themselves in relations with others.

**Conflict**   A clash of interests that can be tackled through violence, but only resolved through non-statist pressures. Conflicts of the latter kind are inevitable and arise from the fact that we are all different from one another.

**Consent**   Uncoerced acceptance of something, such as state authority.

**Conservatism**   Conservatism is an ideology that is sceptical about reason: because human beings have limited rational capacities they must rely on tradition to guide them.

**Constraint**   A natural or social pressure that ensures we do something that we had not intended to do.

**Contractarianism**   A stream of liberal thought that imagines the state to be the product of a decision between individuals to agree to submit to it. Contractarianism implies individuals consent to the state.

**Culture**   The often taken-for-granted web of social relations that encompasses many domains of experience, shapes a person's character, and may provide him or her with a set of values by which to live.

**Deep ecology**   A form of ecologism, stressing both the interdependence of nature and the need for fundamental human change; it is contrasted with 'shallow ecology', which is essentially environmentalism.

**Difference**   Identifications that separate people and inevitably cause conflict to arise.

**Division**   Differences that undermine common interests and necessitate the use of force.

**Dualism**   A gulf between two entities, conceptual or real, that is impossible to cross. It points to a divide rather than a difference.

**Ecologism**   An ideology centred around 'ecology', stressing the interdependence of all forms of life.

**Egalitarianism**   A type of political theory that makes equality a fundamental concept.

**Emancipation**   The capacity of people to act freely, and thus govern their own lives.

**Environmentalism**   A movement which highlights the importance of preserving the earth's natural resources and guaranteeing a fair share of those resources for future generations. Unlike ecologism it can be combined with many different ideologies.

**Essentialism**   An attitude that stresses the importance of one determining attribute and ignores all others.

**Ethnic nationalism**   The view that nations are held together by ethnic ties (*see* ethnicity). The competing view is civic nationalism.

**Ethnicity**   The identification with tangible, visual symbols and signs such as dress, food or religious observance.

**Fascism**   A movement or political and social system that rejects parliamentary democracy, bans other political parties and movements, is hostile to the ideas of the Enlightenment and liberalism, and is particularly opposed to socialism and Marxism.

**Feminism**   A theory that works for the emancipation of women.

**Force**   A pressure that undermines the agency of individuals by physically harming them.

**Freedom** (or **liberty**)   The absence of constraint, or, alternatively, the existence of choice.

**Free-riding**   Gaining the benefits of cooperation without paying the price. This problem is central to the resolution of the prisoner's dilemma.

**Fundamentalism**   A belief in an ideology that is dogmatic, allows no debate, and holds to the absolute truth of the doctrine espoused.

**Genocide**   The attempt to destroy an entire ethnic or racial group; genocide can take place without mass murder – mass sterilisation is a form of genocide.

**Globalisation**   A linkage between peoples of the globe that enables them to understand and empathise with one another.

**Goodness** (or **goods, the good**)   That which is worth pursuing – 'goods' need not be moral goods: a sharp knife is 'good' for killing people. The 'good' (singular) denotes a view of the world, such as a religion. (*See also* **rightness**).

**Government**   The resolution of conflicts of interest. It can occur at every level in society; it is inherent in social relationships, and needs to be contrasted with the state.

**Green movement**   The organised political expression of either ecologism or environmentalism.

**Hierarchy**   An asymmetrical linkage that is inherent in relationships. It is normally assumed to be repressive, but it need not be.

**Human rights**   Entitlements to treatment which it is claimed individuals have simply by virtue of being human.

**Identity**   The sense of belonging to something or of sharing an attribute, such as religious belief, gender or ethnicity, with other people.

**Ideology**   A set of beliefs that are tied to either defending, placing demands upon or bringing about a state.

**Individual**   A person who is separate from others but who finds their identity through relating to these others.

**Justice**   Distributive justice is concerned with the fair distribution of the 'benefits' and 'burdens' of cooperation (retributive justice is a quite separate concept – it is the idea that a punishment should 'fit' a crime).

**Legitimacy**   Power that has been authorised through an appeal to a wider constituency.

**Liberalism**   An ideology that takes freedom (or liberty) to be a fundamental value; it also regards individuals as naturally equal, although natural equality is, for many liberals, compatible with significant material inequality.

**Libertarianism**   A form of liberalism that takes private property rights to be of fundamental importance.

**Liberty**   *See* 'freedom'.

**Market**   A mechanism that enables exchanges to occur, but in a way which conceals the real power that people possess.

**Marxism**   A theory whose potential for emancipation is undermined by notions of class war, revolution and dictatorship.

**Modernism** (or **modernity**)   A term that denotes the onset of the liberal period so that modernism is used as a synonym for liberalism.

**Multiculturalism**   The existence of a number of cultures in a single political system; alternatively, an ideology which recognises as important that fact or values such diversity.

**Nation**   A collective, normally territorial, entity which commands allegiance. Some theorists argue that nations are the product of modernity, others claim they are 'primordial' or perennial.

**Nationalism**   An ideology that takes the nation to be of fundamental value.

**Natural**   A process that is developmental. What is natural is therefore susceptible to historical change.

**Neo-conservatism**   An American stream of conservatism that stresses natural rights and the importance of resisting what it sees as tyranny.

**Order**   A stability in the possession of things; security against violence and a trust in others that promises will be kept.

**Patriarchal**   A static concept and practice that enshrines male domination. Patriarchy need not be pursued by biological men.

**Perennialism**   A body of theory concerned to explain the rise of the nation. Perennialists claim that nations pre-date modernity, although nationalism – consciousness of nationhood – is modern.

**Political obligation**   The moral obligation to obey the state. Many political theorists, especially anarchists, question whether political obligation is possible.

**Politics**   A public process that involves resolving conflicts of interest. Politics is undermined by force, and is inherent at every level in all societies.

**Post-liberalism**   A theory that accepts liberalism but goes beyond it, by extending liberal values to all individuals and thus challenging the need for a state.

**Postmodernism**   A theory that goes beyond modernism and therefore challenges the dualisms and one-sidedness expressed in the modernist tradition.

**Power**   The capacity to exert pressure on a person or group so that they do something they otherwise would not have done.

**Prejudice**   Used in a specific sense by conservatives to mean judging the right action by appealing to habit and experience rather than rational analysis.

**Pre-modern**   A theory and practice that has yet to obtain the institutions and to support the values of liberalism (or modernism).

**Private**   The sphere of life in which conflict is imperceptible or embryonic.

**Private property**   The division of material goods according to which individuals have an entitlement to a certain good, and can exclude other people from its use.

**Public**   The sphere of life in which conflict is manifest and has to be resolved.

**Race**   A concept used to categorise people according to how they look (phenotypical similarity).

**Radicalism** An approach that stresses that individuals and collectivities only find their identity in relationships with one another.

**Reconstruction** The reworking of concepts so that an alternative to the status quo is charted.

**Relational** An approach that stresses that individuals and collectivities only find their identity in relationships with one another.

**Relationship** A linkage that is vitiated by force but whose mutuality is necessarily hierarchical in character and sustained by coercion and constraint.

**Relativism** The rejection of universalism: moral norms are dependent on a cultural context.

**Religion** An organised system of belief and practice centred around an idea of 'holiness' – that is, something outside historical experience.

**Revolution** A fundamental transformation of something: revolutions can be social, economic, intellectual and political.

**Rightness** That which is obligatory: for example, you should keep your promises. A person can do the right thing for bad reasons, so rightness must be distinguished from goodness.

**Rights** Individual entitlements to something.

**Socialism** An ideology that asserts society is of equal importance to the individual, and it can therefore be regulated publicly in the interests of the individual.

**Sovereignty** The ability to govern one's own life: sovereignty is an absolute concept that can only express itself in particular historical circumstances.

**State** An institution that claims a monopoly of legitimate force for a particular territory. This claim makes it contradictory and paradoxical.

**Statism** An approach that creates or accepts divisions and thus the need for force to tackle them.

**Terrorism** The use of political violence in situations in which people have reasonable avenues of peaceful protest.

**Toleration** The willingness to allow other people to behave in ways of which we disapprove. The first major historical form of political toleration was religious toleration.

**Totalitarianism** A movement or system that aspires to control every aspect of society in an authoritarian manner. It therefore rejects liberalism and democracy.

**Universalism** The belief that there are moral codes or values binding on all people, irrespective of culture. The alternative position is cultural or ethical relativism.

**Utilitarianism** A stream of liberal thought that maintains political institutions should maximise the overall level of utility in society (utilitarians disagree about the definition of 'utility', but possibilities include pleasure, happiness and preference satisfaction).

**Violence** A synonym for force.

# Index